Politics in the USA

Praise for previous editions:

> A sound, comprehensive and clearly written exposition of American politics.
>
> *Times Literary Supplement*

M.J.C. Vile's classic introductory text, *Politics in the USA,* has now been thoroughly revised and updated to take account of the considerable developments in American politics over the last ten years.

The book provides students with an essential background to the history and development of the American political system as well as an explanation of its key structures, processes and institutions. The book establishes a framework within which to understand the intricacies of politics in the world's most powerful nation.

This new edition provides students with:

* a chapter on US foreign policy including the significant developments under Clinton and George W. Bush, including the Iraq War;
* an analysis of Bush's presidency and the rise of neoconservatism;
* the discussion of controversial issues such as abortion, immigration, the death penalty, Hurricane Katrina, and Guantánamo Bay and civil rights;
* suggestions for further reading and relevant websites for each chapter.

This is the most up-to-date and readable textbook on American politics. As such, it will be of interest to all students of politics and international relations.

M.J.C. Vile is Professor Emeritus of Political Science at the University of Kent.

Politics in the USA

Sixth edition

M.J.C. Vile

LONDON AND NEW YORK

First published 1970
by Routledge
2 Park Square, Milton Park, Abingdon, Oxon OX14 4RN

Simultaneously published in the USA and Canada
by Routledge
270 Madison Ave, New York, NY 10016

Routledge is an imprint of the Taylor & Francis Group, an informa business
© 2007 M.J.C. Vile

Typeset in Baskerville by
Prepress Projects Ltd, Perth, UK
Printed and bound in Great Britain by
Antony Rowe Ltd, Chippenham, Wiltshire

British Library Cataloguing in Publication Data
A catalogue record for this book is available from the British Library

Library of Congress Cataloging in Publication Data
Vile, M.J.C.
Politics in the USA / by M.J.C. Vile – 6th ed.
p. cm.
Includes bibliographical references and index.
1. United States – Politics and government. I. Title.
JK271.V55 2007
320.973–dc22
2006025475

ISBN 10: 0-415-41419-9 (hbk)
ISBN 10: 0-415-41418-0 (pbk)
ISBN 10: 0-203-43704-7 (ebk)

ISBN 13: 978-0-415-41419-7 (hbk)
ISBN 13: 978-0-415-41418-0 (pbk)
ISBN 13: 978-0-203-43704-9 (ebk)

Contents

List of illustrations

Figures

Maps

Tables

1   A government of limited powers

The Constitution of the United States is little more than two hundred years old. It has survived civil war and the territorial expansion from thirteen largely agricultural former colonies on the eastern seaboard to an industrial nation of fifty states that stretch across the continent to Alaska and to Hawaii. It has overseen the emergence of the most powerful democracy in the world. The American political system was subjected to severe strains in the twentieth century: the need to mobilise for two world wars, the depression of the 1930s, the changing role of government since the Second World War, the challenge of the civil rights movement, the impact of the Vietnam War and the shock of the Watergate affair which resulted in the resignation of President Richard Nixon. In the first years of the twenty-first century the challenges seemed to multiply rapidly: the terrorist attack on the World Trade Center in New York and on the Pentagon, the wars in Afghanistan and Iraq, Hurricane Katrina and its aftermath. The major challenge to American society, however, has been developing since the end of the war in Vietnam. That war jolted the faith of Americans in the inevitability of progress, and in the superiority of their system of government. It also brought to an end the era of the 'melting pot', the assumption that all Americans, whatever their origin, would assimilate to American values, adopt English as their first language, and necessarily revere the institutions embodied in the Constitution of the United States. In other words, America has had to face the fact that it is a multicultural society.

In spite of these challenges, superficially the most striking characteristic of the American Constitution is its continuity and stability, the unchanging shape of its major structures. Within this apparently stable framework, however, deep and significant changes in the nature and working of the American political system have taken place: the changing character of the system of federalism; the continuously fluctuating relationship between Congress and the presidency; the transformation of the system of political parties; the rise of the mass media and their impact upon the political system; the changing role of the Supreme Court; these and many other factors affect the working of politics in the United States at the beginning of the twenty-first century.

It will be our task to explore the building blocks that go to make up this complex pattern, to try to bring out the rich variety of American political life, and to assess the direction in which it is moving.

The challenge of American history

The history of what was to become the United States of America illustrates the diversity of the origins of the country, and also explains the structure of its institutions. In the sixteenth century the European powers, Spain, France and England, began to settle on the mainland of North America. Spain made repeated efforts to colonise Florida, establishing the city of St Augustine in 1565, then pushing northwards and establishing missions. Florida became British in 1763, reverting to Spain after the War of Independence. Spain also settled California, but not until the eighteenth century, establishing a mission at San Diego in 1769. California became part of the newly independent Mexico in 1821, and was ceded to the United States in 1848 along with New Mexico, Texas having been annexed in 1844. France, in addition to its colonisation of Canada, expanded into the Mississippi Valley and founded the city of New Orleans in 1718. By the middle of the eighteenth century France laid claim to a huge tract of land stretching from the Gulf of Mexico to Hudson's Bay. The defeat of the French by the British in Canada in 1759 and the purchase of Louisiana by the United States in 1803 ended French colonial power in North America. The Dutch established New Amsterdam, renamed New York when captured by the British in 1664. Alaska was part of the Russian Empire until purchased by the United States in 1867. The Kingdom of Hawaii was annexed by the United States in 1898 and became the fiftieth state in 1959.

The English, in contrast to the Spaniards and the French, developed their American colonies largely through commercial expansion, the Crown granting huge tracts of land to companies to develop trade. Starting with the Royal Charter of the Virginia Company in 1606 a series of expeditions were mounted which by the 1770s had resulted in the establishment of thirteen colonies poised on the east coast of the continent. Each colony had its distinct social composition and religious affiliations, and its own economic interests. Each colony had its own constitutional structure; attempts were made to establish a system of government reaching across the colonies, but they did not succeed, and therefore until the Revolution the colonies' political links were with London. Thus when independence came in 1776 the colonies transformed themselves into independent states, each state establishing its own constitution, and only loosely affiliating with other states through the Articles of Confederation in order to conduct the war against Britain.

When the Convention of the representatives of the states met in Philadelphia in 1787 to recommend a new form of government for the United States of America they had two main concerns. First, they wished to create a system of government that would be strong enough to defend their territory against attack, and which would have the basic unity through a common currency to provide the opportunity for economic development. But they did not wish to destroy the states, or to strip them of their role as the main sources of civil and criminal law for their citizens. They therefore invented a modern system of federalism, in which the functions of government were divided between the newly created government of the United States and the governments of the states. Their second concern was to create a government which was strong enough to provide stability for an emerging nation but which would not be dominated either by a single person or by the elected representatives of the people. They were equally afraid of autocracy and of mob rule. They adopted a system of separation of powers, setting up barriers between the legislative, executive and judicial branches of government, giving them the ability to check each other's actions. It is this combination of federalism and the separation of powers that gives to the United States its particular characteristic as a system of limited government, in which no single part of the system has the power to dictate to the others. The result is the complex process of policy-making that we will explore in later chapters. Having created the *structures* of government in the Constitution they then turned to the setting up of the Bill of Rights of 1791, reflecting their fear that the new government might abuse its power and oppress its citizens. The Bill of Rights set further restrictions on the power of governments, initially limiting the power of the federal government and later the powers of state governments, in ways which are of considerable importance today, particularly in the field of civil rights.

Federalism

The United States is a federal system of government, in which fifty individual states each have their own position of legal autonomy and political significance, sharing authority and functions with the central government, which, rather confusingly, is called 'the federal government'. When the thirteen original states came together in 1787 to draft a constitution they wished to unite in order to be able to provide for their common defence and to ensure that certain essential activities were performed by the future 'Government of the United States'. They did not wish to lose their individual identities, or to give up their power to control those matters which directly affected their own citizens. Virginia and New York, Massachusetts and South Carolina were proud of their separate communities, and of the considerable degree of autonomy that they had enjoyed under the distant rule of the British Parliament. They therefore rejected the particular form of the unitary nation-state that had been established in Britain and France in which all legal power, 'sovereignty', was concentrated in the hands of the central government. They placed sovereignty in the Constitution, and distributed the powers of government between the states and the federal government, so that neither level of government was all-powerful, neither could simply control the other.

This modern form of federalism, which was adapted from the model of ancient Greece, has been copied, with variations, all over the world, in Switzerland, Canada, Australia, India, Germany and other countries, and is now being laboriously evolved in Europe. The states are not sovereign bodies, but they do exercise powers and carry out functions that in unitary states, such as the United Kingdom, are normally allocated to the central authority. The Constitution set up a division of power between the federal and state governments, which initially limited the former principally to the fields of defence, foreign affairs, the control of the currency and the control over commerce among the states. All other powers, the residual powers, were left to the states. This division of power has been eroded with time, so that today the functions of the federal government have been extended beyond all recognition, touching most of the important concerns of the citizens of the United States. The federal government remains limited in its powers by the Constitution. However, the greatest protection for the continued power of the states lies in the decentralised nature of American politics. The United States Congress could, if it wished, considerably diminish the powers of the states, but the pressures exerted upon Senators and Members of the House of Representatives, by their constituents and by interest groups, ensure that the powers of the states are respected. Thus although the power of the states relative to the federal government has been considerably reduced, they continue to be extremely important and politically powerful centres of government activity.

The importance of the American states as legal entities is still considerable. At the time of the ratification of the Constitution almost every important government function was exercised by the states. Even today most of the civil and criminal law that governs Americans' lives is state law. Family law, traffic law, commercial law, even the question of whether a murderer should face the death penalty or not, are, in the first instance, a matter for the state legislature to decide. For example, in 1996 a referendum was held in California that allowed the use of marijuana for medical purposes and other states followed suit; in 1997 the state of Oregon passed its Death with Dignity Act, which authorised doctors to employ euthanasia in certain circumstances. The Attorney General of the United States attempted to prevent the state legislation from being implemented, but the US Supreme Court held his actions unlawful. The states have important regulatory functions, laying down many of the rules that business, agriculture and the trade unions must observe. Take a very modern activity – the energy industry. There is a federal regulatory body for the energy industry, the Federal Energy Regulatory Commission, but its jurisdiction is limited to the regulation of wholesale trade in energy and the transmission of natural gas, oil and electricity across state lines. State agencies regulate the sale and transmission of energy within the state, setting retail prices and enforcing service and quality standards

The states have extensive powers of taxation, and together with their local governments spend very large sums on social welfare, education, health and hospitals, and other services. For more than a century after independence the combined expenditures of the states, together with the cities and counties under their control, exceeded those of the federal government. However, as the role of government in economic and social policy changed, particularly after the Great Depression of the 1930s, the importance of the federal government increased and federal expenditures surpassed those of the states.

The powers and functions of the American states far exceed, therefore, the role of local governments in unitary countries, and they enjoy considerable constitutional and legal autonomy in the way they fulfil this role. They are subject to two major limitations: first, they must observe the Constitution of the United States and obey valid laws of the federal legislature made under that Constitution. If state laws offend against the Constitution or conflict with valid federal laws, then the Supreme Court will declare the state laws to be unconstitutional. In the same way, if an Act passed by Congress is found to be an improper exercise of power over state governments, then the Supreme Court will invalidate the federal law. The Court invalidates federal statutes in this way from time to time, but it invalidates far more laws of the states. Over the past two centuries the Court has gradually expanded the constitutional power of the federal government, and consequently restricted the power of the states, but federalism in America is still very much alive and it draws its vigour from the diffusion and decentralisation of political power as well as from the precepts of constitutional law.

The second limitation on the power of the states is their relative lack of financial resources compared with those of the federal government. The latter's ability to tax effectively is greater than that of any individual state, or of all the states combined, and this financial power enables the federal government to obtain the compliance of the states by offering them grants-in-aid to which conditions are attached. Since the 1930s the federal government has chosen to administer many of its programmes through state and local governments, and has therefore put them in the position of acting as its agents. In 2003 state and local governments received $387 billion from the federal government in grants-in-aid, but most of the social welfare programmes that are set up in this way require the states to match the money provided by the federal government with their own funds from state taxation. The level of provision of social welfare benefits varies considerably from state to state; rich states can provide better benefits than poorer states. In 2004 the average monthly payment to the disabled varied from $960 in Nevada to $819 in Maine; the average weekly payment for unemployment benefit ranged from $351 in Massachusetts to $172 in Mississippi. To some extent these differences reflect differing levels of income in the states; to some extent they reflect differing social philosophies from state to state. It makes a real difference which state you live in.

There have been powerful centralising forces at work, particularly in the twentieth century. It can be argued that the states have lost so much of their autonomy that the United States is no longer truly federal in character, but is now simply a highly decentralised unitary state. Attempts have been made to reverse this process, particularly by Presidents Nixon and Reagan. They proposed the introduction of 'revenue-sharing', which would return functions to the states and finance their activities through unconditional block grants. The attempt to return to an earlier era did not have much success at the time, but recent changes in federal legislation, particularly in the field of welfare, have moved power back to the state governments.

The separation of powers

The Founding Fathers of the American Constitution were determined to prevent any section of the new government from abusing its power. They had experienced what they considered to be the despotism of George III, the King of Great Britain, and of the royal governors of the colonies, but the democratic excesses of the state legislatures after the revolution had also frightened them. Like most of the men of wealth and property in the eighteenth century, the framers of the Federal Constitution did not believe that government should exercise considerable power. They were frightened by two spectres: despotism and democracy. They wished to avoid the tyranny of one man, or of many. They therefore constructed a constitution that would avoid both evils, by separating the parts of government, and by balancing them against each other.

The twin doctrines of the separation of powers and checks and balances characterise the American Constitution. The president was to be elected indirectly by means of an Electoral College that would remove the choice of this official from the hurly-burly of mob politics. The Congress was to be divided into a House of Representatives, which represented the people in proportion to population, and a Senate, which gave equal representation to the states. The judicial power was to be vested in a Supreme Court. No member of the legislature was allowed to be a member of the executive branch (with the exception of the vice-president), thus ruling out cabinet government on the English model, which at that time was seen as a monarchical or aristocratic device to control the representatives of the people. The personnel of the three branches of government – legislature, executive and judiciary – were strictly separated, except for the vice-president, who was named as the presiding officer of the Senate. But the Founders were not satisfied that this alone was a sufficient check to the abuse of power, in particular the abuse of power by the legislature. They had witnessed the experience of the American states during and after the Revolution, when the state legislatures had interfered in executive and judicial affairs, and there had been nothing to prevent them from doing so, except, as Jefferson put it, 'parchment barriers', that is written constitutional provisions. They therefore instituted a number of checks to the exercise of power. The president was given a limited power to veto legislation, and the Supreme Court would interpret the laws and the Constitution, although the latter power was implicit rather than explicit in the

Constitution. The Americans had moved back somewhat, therefore, towards the ideas behind the eighteenth-century constitution of England, but they did not go all the way. They were not prepared to give to their president the prerogatives that had been exercised by the British monarch. They gave to Congress the power to declare war, they subjected the making of treaties and of the appointment of senior officials and judges to the approval of the Senate, and they provided that the president's legislative veto could be overridden by a two-thirds majority of both Houses of Congress. Thus they erected the structure of government in such a way that no single part could of itself exercise supreme power. To obtain effective action there had to be agreement between the differing parts of the system of government. To ensure the stability of this system they provided that the Constitution could be amended only by a long and difficult process, which required the agreement of three-quarters of the legislatures of the states. Thus the major *political* problem in the United States has been the working of this Constitution, particularly in moments of crisis, in order to get the necessary decisions taken.

The Bill of Rights

The Constitution came into effect in 1789 and set up the institutions of the new government, but only after a heated debate that brought about a compromise between the supporters and the opponents of the proposed new regime. The Convention which produced the constitutional framework was dominated by the Federalists, the proponents of a central authority with sufficient powers to establish and maintain an effective system of government to serve the needs of the 'United States' as a whole. In order to come into force, however, the constitution had to be ratified by at least nine of the twelve states that had been represented at the convention. There was great opposition to the new system from the Anti-Federalists, those who feared that the federal government would become dominant over the states and would be able to oppress their citizens. In state after state there were demands for amendments to be made to the draft constitution to meet these fears. The formal requirement of ratification by nine of the states was achieved on 21 June 1788, but two of the largest states, Virginia and New York, had still not agreed to implement the constitution. Without them the new government would hardly be able to survive. The leaders of the Federalists pledged themselves to make changes in the Constitution, and as soon as the first Congress was assembled, a resolution was introduced to add ten amendments to the Constitution, which were ratified in 1791 and became the Bill of Rights. It set out in detail the protection that was felt to be necessary to guard American citizens against possible oppression by the new federal government. The freedom of religion, of speech, of the press, the freedom to bear arms, freedom from arbitrary arrest, and the right not be deprived of life, liberty or property without due process of law were set out in the Bill of Rights.

Federalism and the separation of powers fragmented the constitutional system, ensuring that no section of the government could exercise supreme power. To these limitations on the power of government the Bill of Rights added another set of checks to the exercise of power, but it did not guarantee that all Americans were free from oppression. The Bill of Rights was directed against the federal government, and its framers intended that each state should be left to safeguard the rights of its citizens. However, two groups of people who lived in America, most of whom had been born there, were not citizens: the first group were slaves, the second American Indians (Native Americans). The Constitution did not abolish slavery, although it did give Congress the power to abolish the *slave trade*, but not before 1808. Slavery was eventually abolished in 1865 by the Thirteenth Amendment to the Constitution, but the rights of the former slaves, and of their descendants, were not secured by the constitutions of the states, certainly not in the South. In the Southern states laws were passed setting up racial segregation in education, in transport, and in public and private facilities such as libraries and restaurants. Blacks were excluded from the exercise of the vote, and often subjected to 'mob justice', the rule of the lynch mob. It was not until the mid-twentieth century that the Supreme Court of the United States extended the protection of the Bill of Rights to the areas covered by state law, and racial discrimination, political manipulation and the improper use of police powers came under judicial scrutiny. The American Indians, later to be confined to reservations, were not citizens. Chief Justice Marshall summed up their legal status in the case of *Cherokee Nation* v. *Georgia* in 1831. Indians, he said were 'in a state of pupilage. Their relation to the United States resembles that of a ward to his guardian.' At the end of the nineteenth century and the beginning of the twentieth citizenship was extended on a piecemeal basis to Indians, for example to those who had served in the armed forces in the First World War, but it was not until 1924 that all Indians were made citizens of the United States.

Unity and diversity

The settlement of the area that now forms the United States involved a long, continuous process of expansion from the original colonies established on the eastern seaboard, a process that has not ended even at the present time. The vast influx of population into Colorado, Arizona and New Mexico in recent years and the development of Alaska represent, in differing ways, the last stages of the passing of that phenomenon that dominated the history of America throughout the eighteenth and nineteenth centuries – the moving frontier.

The moving frontier of settlers, with its saga of pioneering feats, of cowboys, of Indian fighters and of the life of its frontier towns, has been proposed by some historians as the prime explanation of the nature of American society, American politics and even the American national character. Whatever the exact importance of the frontier, the broad outlines of its significance for

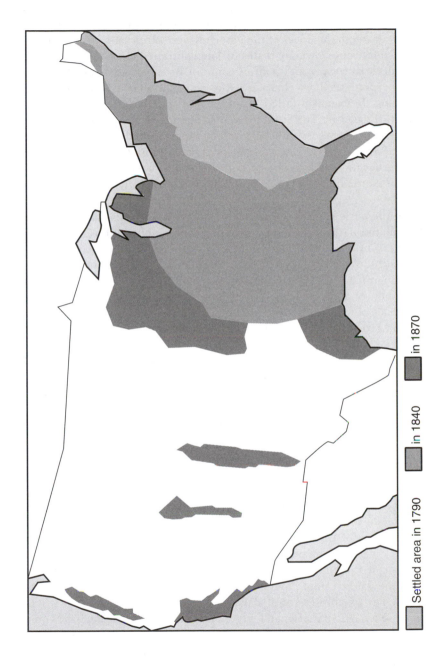

Settled area in 1790 ▦ in 1840 ▦ in 1870

Map 1.1 The progress of settlement

America can hardly be in dispute. The frontier was a continuous recreation of the story of American society. It was a reminder of the 'open', democratic character of America, in which a man might carve out his own fortune from the wilderness. It was a constant portrayal of the opportunities that America offered, for although the hopes of the pioneers were often sadly disappointed, they were sometimes glowingly realised. The continued westward expansion gave to American society and politics some of its most persistent traits. It helped to perpetuate those characteristics that had marked America from the beginning. If socialism failed to find a root in America because feudal class structures had never existed, it was certainly excluded from later development by the open conditions created by the frontier. It was not until the 1920s and 1930s, when the era of expansion was over and America began to resemble rather more closely the economic systems of 'closed' European nations, that American politics took on something of the attitudes of Western Europe.

Even in the early stages of American history the regional differences in climate, soil and natural resources gave rise to distinctive interests and differing ways of life in the colonies. New England, the Middle Atlantic states and the South differed in the crops they produced, in the role of commerce in their economic life and, particularly because of the existence of slavery, in the very structure of their society. As settlement progressed inland, there began that series of tensions between the more highly developed areas and the farmers and settlers on the frontier that provided some of the most persistent themes of American politics. Farmers resented the eastern commercial and financial interests that provided the material resources and the capital necessary to subdue the wilderness – at a price. The concentration of industry and commerce near the eastern seaports, and the consequent growth of urban centres in the northeast region, exacerbated all the traditional differences between city and rural dwellers. Furthermore, as each new area of the United States was settled it acquired a character of its own, partly because of the nature of its economic structure, partly because of the people who settled it. The moving frontier became the unrolling of that map of regional and sectional differences that formed the basis of American politics in the nineteenth and twentieth centuries, and which even today plays a muted but essential role in the working of American politics.

The existence of the frontier provided the mechanism by which some of the most divisive elements in American politics were introduced. As the development of the South progressed, the value of African slave labour in producing the South's staple commodities, first tobacco and later cotton, was recognised. The establishment of slavery, together with the fact that it was best suited to a particular area and largely restricted to that area, has been a cardinal influence upon American politics to this day. The place of blacks in American society, their historic sense of resentment at their former status, and their struggle to achieve social and economic equality with white Americans are still a major factor in American politics, not merely in the South, but across the nation. The improvement in the economic and social status of the descendants of the former slaves, particularly since the 1950s, can be counted as a considerable achievement, but inequality between the white and black population is still embedded in American society. In 2004 28 per cent of the white population had had a college education, but only 17 per cent of the black population had a university degree. The median family income for whites was $55,938, for blacks $34,608.

As westward expansion continued in the first half of the nineteenth century, with the continuous creation of new states, the balance of power between North and South that had been established by the Constitution was endangered. The problem of whether the new states would be slave or free dominated the politics of the era. If slave, they could be expected to side with the South; if free, to align themselves with the North. The holocaust of the Civil War, the effects of which have not been fully eradicated even today, was the result of the inability to find an acceptable formula to deal with this problem.

Westward expansion, the filling of the vacuum beyond the frontier, provided that seemingly endless supply of cheap land which was, particularly in the period after the Civil War, the engine that made possible mass immigration into the United States. Between 1865 and 1920 over 28 million immigrants entered the United States, and in six separate years between 1905 and 1914 the yearly migration exceeded 1 million people. The changing composition of the immigrant population over the years meant that concentrations of particular national groups built up in particular areas, and in particular cities. The choice of the motto of the United States, *E Pluribus Unum* (Out of Many, One), which applied to the union of the states, could hardly have been more fitting, although those early Americans could not have conceived of the extent of the diversity that was to characterise the American population. It has been variously estimated that in 1790 between 60 and 80 per cent of the population of the United States was of English or Welsh stock, with up to 14 per cent of Scottish and Irish stock. Germans at that date accounted for the only sizeable group of non-British or -Irish origin, and they were concentrated in Pennsylvania. In the early nineteenth century there was an influx of Irish and Germans; but after the Civil War, when the really heavy immigration began, the emphasis changed to immigrants from southern and eastern Europe. In the peak year of 1914 over 73 per cent of the 1,218,000 immigrants were from these parts of Europe. In 1790 82 per cent of the population of the state of Massachusetts was of English stock. By 1920 two-thirds of the population of the state were immigrants or the children of immigrants, and the Irish, Italians, Poles and Jews, together with a number of minor groups such as Lithuanians, Greeks, Armenians and Syrians, far outweighed the 'old-stock' inhabitants.

At the end of the nineteenth century the expansive movement within the United States overflowed into a relatively mild episode of imperialism, as a result of which Puerto Rico, Hawaii and the Philippines were acquired.

Alaska 1959   Hawaii 1959

Washington 1889
Oregon 1859
Idaho 1890
Montana 1889
N. Dakota 1889
Minnesota 1858
Vermont 1791
Maine 1820
New Hampshire
Massachusetts
Rhode Island
Connecticut
New Jersey
Delaware
Maryland
Nevada 1864
Utah 1896
Wyoming 1890
S. Dakota 1889
Wisconsin 1848
Michigan 1837
New York
Pennsylvania
W. Virginia 1863
Ohio 1803
Indiana 1816
Virginia
N. Carolina
S. Carolina
California 1850
Arizona 1912
Colorado 1876
Nebraska 1867
Iowa 1846
Illinois 1818
Missouri 1821
Kentucky 1792
Tennessee 1796
Georgia
Florida 1845
New Mexico 1912
Kansas 1861
Oklahoma 1907
Arkansas 1836
Mississippi 1817
Alabama 1819
Texas 1845
Louisiana 1812

Map 1.2 The establishment of the American states
Note: The states without dates of entry were the original thirteen states.

The Philippines have since gained full independence, but Hawaii followed a different course and in 1959 it became the fiftieth state of the Union and the first state to have Asians as the largest racial group in its population. In the 1970s and 1980s there was an influx of Vietnamese and Koreans into the United States. The most important change in the balance of the composition of the population, however, has been the rapid growth in the population of Hispanics, Spanish-speakers, mostly from Puerto Rico, Mexico and Cuba. As we shall see, this development, in the view of some observers, signals a fundamental change in the nature of the American polity. The problems that face a political system and a society in attempting to assimilate different nationalities and races on this scale are daunting to say the least. The influx of immigrants brought with it the elements of diversity – in language, in religion, in social customs and in attitudes towards social and political problems that provide the warp and woof of American life today. That the United States has largely achieved the creation of a single nation from such varied peoples is little short of a modern miracle. In an age when racial problems are in the news from all parts of the world, it is as well to bear in mind the American achievement, even though its success is by no means total.

Politics and the Constitution

The relationship of the political life of a country to the formal and informal structures of its constitution is a matter of great complexity. For centuries constitutions have been considered to be important for the maintenance of freedom and the rights of the individual, as well as ensuring order and stability in society. However, the view has been increasingly expressed that constitutional provisions, and particularly the more formal, legalistic aspects of the Constitution, have little or no importance in determining the outcome of political struggles. It is argued that it is to 'social forces' that we must direct our attention if we are to understand the working of politics. It is perhaps surprising that this point of view has been expressed more forcibly in modern America than in most other countries of the world, in spite of the fact that constitutions and constitutionalism would seem to have played such a significant part in American history. In this work we shall attempt to give full weight to 'social forces' in our description of the working of American politics, but it would be pointless to attempt to describe American political processes other than within the framework of the American constitutional system. Social groups and movements are the raw material and the driving force of the political process, but the exact form in which they operate, and the precise results that they achieve, must depend to a considerable extent upon the nature of the channels through which they have to work. More precisely, the channels through which the social forces must operate are part of the whole complex of influences that have made these social forces of America just what they are.

It will become apparent during the course of the discussion that the

American Constitution has indeed had an important impact upon the way in which politics is carried on, but it must be made somewhat clearer what we mean by 'the Constitution'. The formal Constitution, the document that emerged from the Philadelphia Convention in 1787, has been hardly changed to this day. It remains fundamentally the same, in spite of the mere twenty-seven amendments that have been made in the course of the last two centuries. Thus, to the problems of meeting the challenges set by American society and history there is added the difficulty of working a Constitution that was devised by the men of the eighteenth century to meet eighteenth-century needs, and in accordance with eighteenth-century ideas about a desirable system of government. The Founding Fathers had not heard of atomic power, Keynesian economics, radio and television, the railway or the aeroplane; yet the American system of government has to deal with these aspects of modern life and many others unknown to the founders of the American polity. Much of this burden is carried by the Supreme Court of the United States, which has the task of interpreting an eighteenth-century Constitution in a way which will make sense in the twenty-first century. But it is the working political system that has to translate this Constitution into action, and to produce results that will be satisfactory in the modern American context.

Of course, the above description relates only to the formal, written Constitution, but many aspects of it have been profoundly altered in practice, and certain modes of behaviour, although not written in the Constitution, have become just as fixed as if they were rigid constitutional rules. We shall see this in particular in the working of the system of electing the president, which operates in strict law as laid down in the Constitution, but in fact produces a result very different from that which the Founders intended. Then there is a whole range of political institutions, such as the congressional committee system and the White House Office, which have grown up as a means of ensuring a much greater degree of contact between the legislative and executive branches than the Founding Fathers intended. Furthermore, the working of the party system, and the existence of pressure groups, provide extra-legal links between the parts of government, and thus articulate them in practice.

The United States political system is the conscious creation of the human mind, an artificial creation, fashioned out of the wilderness within the past 400 years. Although short by European or Asian standards, its history is packed with incident, for the United States has had in that period to pass through those stages of political development that elsewhere have taken 1,000 or 2,000 years. When the original colonists sailed for America they went for two main reasons: either to escape from religious oppression or to make their fortune in the New World. When they arrived they had to govern themselves as well as to combat the wilderness and the indigenous peoples. The ideas they held about government were inevitably largely drawn from the society that they had left behind. The people of Massachusetts, Rhode Island and Virginia established their own forms of government but, throughout most of the period up until the Revolution, colonial political ideas followed closely upon those of the mother country. There was, however, from the beginning, a basic incompatibility between these European ideas about politics and the actual circumstances of American life, an incompatibility that became more and more evident as the eighteenth century progressed, and which burst into the open with the outbreak of the Revolution. For the society that established itself in America was not composed of a cross-section of the then existing European society; neither were the circumstances in which it found itself those of Europe. As Louis Hartz has explained, the most important factor of American history is that it lacked altogether an *ancien régime*. Feudalism never existed in America in spite of the existence of the great landowners and planters of colonial times, or of the bond-slaves who arrived from Europe to serve out their time under their American masters. America is not, and never has been, a classless society, but there is a very real sense in which it has always been a middle-class society, without the extremes, except in relation to black slavery, of European class attitudes. In an age when Europe was dominated by kings and nobles, America represented an ideal of a more egalitarian society in which, with ability and industry, a man might easily rise to the highest positions. The absence of a socialist tradition in America is in large part the result of the fact that there was not the same class structure for the socialist to react against as in Europe. This is what is often referred to as 'American exceptionalism'.

There was always an underlying conviction among Americans that they had broken away from the corruption of old Europe to create a new and clean society. They were influenced, it is true, by European institutions and European ideas, for they had no other source upon which to draw, but they felt able, by the exercise of human reason, to select those things that were good and to reject those that were bad. Thus when they came to write the Constitution of the United States they were deeply influenced by the balanced constitution of eighteenth-century England, but they did not copy it slavishly. They created something new, something unique, and they were aware that they were doing so. *The Federalist Papers*, written in 1787–8 by Alexander Hamilton, James Madison and John Jay, urging the acceptance of the proposed Constitution, provide perhaps the greatest example of human reason attempting to combine the wisdom of tradition with the rational solution of new and unprecedented problems. There is, therefore, a sense of uniqueness in the American experience that ensures the autonomy of the American political tradition.

The fact that the American polity is a conscious creation is an explanation of its 'Americanness', but it is also the explanation, in part at least, of other aspects of American life that it is harder for the outsider to understand. Isolationism, the sense that America should not become embroiled with the problems and rivalries of Europe or the rest of the world, became associated in the 1930s and 1940s with groups who had a particular reason, usually their ethnic origins, for not wanting to become involved in Europe's quarrels. But isolationism went deeper than this, and its reappearance in different guises at different times in America must be seen in the context of an antipathy towards becoming tainted by that corrupting influence of Europe that Thomas Jefferson feared in the eighteenth century. In other nations that have a highly developed national consciousness, the process of the evolution of that consciousness has been slow and gradual. Because, however, America is a conscious, artificial creation from diverse peoples, at no time in its history has it been able to enjoy the luxury of allowing feelings of nationality and community to grow naturally. There has been, throughout most of American history, a conscious social policy of Americanisation, one might almost say of indoctrination in the values and ideals of American society. A society that had to cope with a continuous influx of immigrants of varying nationalities and creeds could not allow itself to be indifferent to their mode of assimilation into the American way of life, or to allow them to give full rein to the ideas and customs that they brought from their homelands. America is a free society, in which the freedom of speech and the press are jealously guarded; yet the limits of what is socially or politically acceptable are more clearly drawn, more consciously maintained, than in older, more self-confident societies. In such a society it was felt that political freedom could be safeguarded only if the minimum degree of conformity deemed necessary for its survival was actively maintained. The American political system had to encompass great diversity within certain boundaries of accepted actions and beliefs. The fear was that to open the gates too far was to invite the waters of diversity to overflow the banks of an orderly society. The tensions that this situation created can be seen at every level of American political life, for one of the major functions of the American political system was seen to be its task of ensuring a minimum uniformity in a situation of potentially explosive diversity.

In the 1960s the Vietnam War disrupted this sense of the need for a single cultural entity which was 'America'. The extent of the dissent against the war, and the blossoming of alternative lifestyles which this dissent fostered, first in San Francisco and then in other cities in the United States, and finally the disastrous end to the war, saw the spread of non-conformity on an unprecedented scale. The attempt to impose a single cultural conformity on America was no longer possible. The United States had always been composed of people of many different origins, but it had not been recognised as 'multicultural'. The impact of the Vietnam War and subsequent extensive Hispanic immigration made multiculturalism a real issue in the United States. However, the attack on America in September 2001 and the war in Iraq has complicated the picture. Loyalty to 'American values' has once again become an important political issue. We shall look at legislation such as the Patriot Act and other security measures and their impact on American society.

The United States was a consciously created entity with a revolutionary tradition. The mere act of travelling to the New World to settle was, for many of the early Americans, itself an act of rebellion against the rulers and religions of Europe. The breaking of the ties with Great Britain in a violent and glorious act of defiance set the seal upon the American self-image as the propagator of revolutionary ideals of freedom and democracy. America became to the downtrodden peoples of Europe the symbol of the ability of man to break the shackles of tradition and to triumph through reason and determination. No American could declare allegiance to the principles of true conservatism, that is, of utter resistance to all change, and remain an American. Yet the American revolutionary tradition is of a very special variety. Those 'aristocratic' leaders of the American Revolution who took their places at the head of the movement for independence were not firebrand revolutionaries with extreme ideas of democracy and equality. They were not the Jacobins of revolutionary France. They achieved the remarkable feat of leading a revolutionary war to a successful conclusion while maintaining the existing structure of American society. They enshrined in their Constitution a respect for the slow processes of the law, for the sanctity of property and contract, and for the leadership of the solid men who had a stake in the community. The counter-revolutionaries of 1787 who wrote the American Constitution were the same men who had led the Revolution itself in 1775–6. Thus there is in America an equivocal reaction to the idea of democratic revolutionary movements in the rest of the world. Americans are democrats, but conservative democrats; revolutionaries who oppose revolution. Thus the soil was prepared for the flowering of 'neoconservatism' at the end of the twentieth century, one element of which is to seek to foster democracy in countries such as Afghanistan and Iraq, if necessary by force.

Further reading

Dahl, R. (1956) *A Preface to Democratic Theory*, Chicago: University of Chicago Press.
Esler, G. (1997) *The United States of Anger*, London: Penguin.
Hamilton, A., Madison, J. and Jay, J. (2000) *The Federalist, or The New Constitution*, edited by William R. Brock, London: Phoenix Press.
Hartz, L. (1955) *The Liberal Tradition in America*, New York: Harcourt, Brace.
Huntington, S.P. (1981) *American Politics: The Promise of Disharmony*, London: Harvard University Press.
Kelly, A.H., Harbison, W.A. and Belz, H. (1991) *The American Constitution: Its Origins and Development*, 2 vols, 7th edn, New York: W.W. Norton.
Lipset, S.M. (1964) *The First New Nation*, London: Heinemann.

Websites

US Constitution online: www.usconstitution.net
There are many thousands of websites giving information on the American political system and they are being added to all the time. Fortunately, the *New York Times* provides a Politics Navigator for websites covering the whole field of American politics. It can be accessed at www.nytimes.com/ref/politics/POLI_NAVI.html

2 The nature of American politics

In attempting to describe and explain the operation of a political system, it is necessary to arrange a vast amount of detailed information into a recognisable pattern that will give meaning and shape to the activities of those who live in it and make it work. In the case of the United States, the problem of identifying the major determinants of political behaviour is complicated by the enormous diversity of American life, and by the way in which constitutional structures and the patterns of political action are continually acting and reacting upon each other. Before we plunge into the detail of American politics, therefore, it is necessary to reflect for a moment upon the theories that have been proposed to explain the motive forces behind political systems, and the implications of these differing explanations for our understanding of the American system. These 'models' of political life will help us through the complexities of American politics at all levels of activity, in the electorate at large, in the structures of party and pressure groups, and in the workings of congressional and presidential politics.

Models of politics

One of the most powerful sources of political loyalty and action has always been the sense of attachment to a region or community. When this identification becomes so closely interwoven with the interests of a particular area or a particular group of people to the point where life ceases to have any real importance other than within that context, then people may be prepared if necessary to die to defend those interests. In countries with a very highly developed national consciousness it is the nation itself that becomes the *sole* focus for this sort of loyalty, but on the way to the realisation of such national solidarity there are many stages. Local and regional loyalties can be as important as the attachment to the country as a whole. The United States grew out of distinct colonial communities, extending gradually across the continent, in a way that tended to emphasise local loyalties. The constitutional structure of federalism that was evolved in 1787 gave opportunities for the continued expression of regional loyalties through the governments of the states. Thus American political history has been strongly characterised by *sectional* patterns of behaviour, in which the inhabitants of a particular geographical region, at all levels of society, have felt themselves united against the conflicting interests of other sections. The most dramatic confrontation of this sort was, of course, the Civil War in which North and South became for a time distinct warring nations. But at a less dramatic level, sectionalism has been a moving force in American politics throughout its history. The unity of the section was dependent upon some common interest which set it off from the rest of the country and which was of sufficient importance to unite its inhabitants in spite of class or other internal divisions. Frequently this common interest was economic, a crop or product upon which the whole livelihood of the region depended, such as the importance of grain for the states of the Mid-West, and of cotton and tobacco in the South. Thus throughout the nineteenth century agricultural sectionalism deeply affected American political behaviour. The historian Frederick Jackson Turner described the sections of the country as faint reflections of European nations. The extreme example of sectional loyalty was provided by the presidential election of 1860, in which in the whole of ten Southern states not a single vote was cast for the candidate of the Republican Party, Abraham Lincoln.

In the last quarter of the twentieth century such extremes of sectionalism no longer exist, and indeed the United States has developed a sense of national identity and unity that in its own way is more cohesive than that of older nations in Europe. Yet sectional and regional factors continue to play a vital role in the working of American politics, a role that can be observed in the stubborn decentralisation of the party system, in the machinery of elections and in the working of congressional politics. It is in the interrelationship between this unique brand of nationalism and the reality of the decentralisation of political power that the special quality of the American system is to be found.

The second model of political motivation is that which looks to the *class structure* of society as the major determinant of political behaviour. Although a number of political thinkers, such as Locke and Montesquieu, have emphasised this aspect of political behaviour, it was Karl Marx who saw class as the ultimate explanation of people's actions. Taken to extremes this is, of course, quite incompatible with sectionalism as a force in politics. If political loyalty is really a matter of social class, then regional loyalties will have no part to play in the political system, and, to the extent that these regional loyalties continue to exist, then class solidarity across the nation will be diminished. In fact, recent American political history is, in large part, the story of the complex interaction of these two political motivations, with sectionalism declining as class-consciousness waxed. Each of these styles of political behaviour has, of course, very different implications for the type of party system one would expect to find. Indeed, if either sectional or class politics is taken to the extreme, then party politics as we understand it would be ruled out. There would simply be civil war, either between geographical regions or between classes. The working of the democratic system depends upon the fact that these extremes are never realised, and that political parties must appeal both to different sections of the country and to different classes of the population.

Our third approach to the political system we may describe as the *pluralistic* approach. This views the political system as a large number of groups each with a different interest, so that politics is a continually changing pattern of group activities and interactions. Economic, class and geographic factors are important parts of the pattern, but many other kinds of groups are also important: religious groups, ethnic groups and other social groupings. Furthermore, although economic groups play an important part in the political system, they do not coalesce into two or three big classes for purposes of political action. They are divided among themselves, union opposing union, one type of producer battling with his competitors, agriculture ranged against industry, small businessman against big businessman, the retailer against the manufacturer, and so on without end. Class and regional loyalties are fragmented, each group seeking for support to win its battles wherever that support is to be found. Thus we have a picture of the political system as a collection of a very large number of groups, of varying size and importance, battling for their interests in a society where no single group dominates. Since the membership of these groups overlaps considerably, there are Catholic businessmen and Protestant businessmen, Irish-American labour leaders and Italian-American labour leaders – there is a continual set of cross-pressures upon the leaders of these groups which helps the processes of compromise between them and moderates their demands. At the extreme, the role of government in such a society is simply to hold the ring, to act as referee between the groups to enable the necessary bargaining and compromise to take place. The political machinery becomes simply the mechanism through which equilibrium is achieved between the contending interests. As the government's main autonomous interest becomes that of maintaining law and order there is little scope for active leadership to give direction to national policy, and political parties have little coherence or discipline, being merely organisational devices devoid of policy content. Pluralism is very much an American view of the political process and many accounts of the working of the system of government, and in particular the role of interest groups in it, are couched in these terms. It is essential to approach American politics from a pluralistic viewpoint but, as with the other models so far discussed, the temptation to push it to an extreme as the *sole* explanation must be resisted.

A rather different approach to the nature of the American system, but one closely related to both class and pluralistic theories of politics, is the belief that the United States is governed by a series of *elites*, or indeed by a single power elite. The latter view, associated with the name of C. Wright to place great emphasis upon the power and wealth of those e population that control crucial areas of the economy. President himself a great general, warned against the influence of the military-industrial complex when he came to the end of his term of office. Thus, certain relatively small groups of men cease to be just part of an internal bargaining process and become, behind the scenes, the real rulers of the country. The formal political machinery becomes less and less significant in the taking of the really important decisions, so that the electorate, and even the Congress, is bypassed. This interpretation of American politics, even though it can degenerate into a conspiracy theory that attempts to explain every important decision as the results of the secret manipulations of the power elite, must be given serious consideration. There *are* elite groups in the United States, as in any large industrial society, and they exercise great influence in certain circumstances, a fact that will become clear when we examine the way in which specific policy decisions are arrived at.

The final model of political behaviour we must employ in the analysis of American politics is *individualism*. In the other accounts of the political system to which we have referred, a class, a section or a group swallows up the individual. Political behaviour is 'determined' by class ideology, regional loyalty or group interest, and the individual has little or no significance in affecting the outcome of political situations. Such interpretations of political life seem to bear little relation to the mainstream of traditional democratic thought. For theorists such as John Stuart Mill the individual citizen was the central concern of writers on politics, and personality and individual choice were crucial elements in the way in which political decisions are taken. It is ironic that it is in America, the land of individualism *par excellence*, that students of political behaviour have demolished the classical description of the democratic political system as composed of rational, informed individuals making up their own minds. They have suggested that, in twentieth-century Western democracies at any rate, the influence of family, class, local community or other relevant social grouping is far more important in determining voting behaviour than knowledge of the issues that face the electorate. In reality, however, individualism plays a role of greater importance in America than in the political system of any other modern democratic state. To attempt to describe the working of the American political system without paying great attention to the importance of personal factors in the choice of candidates, or to the influence of personality on voting behaviour, would be to miss the very essence of American political life.

Each of these 'models' of political behaviour and motivation has, of course, very different implications for the type of party organisation that we would expect to find in systems of government in which they play a dominant role. They suggest very different opportunities for the exercise of leadership in the political system, very different attitudes towards ideology and 'issues' in the political process, and very different results in terms of party cohesion and discipline, particularly in the legislature. Taken to extremes, these models of the political system are mutually exclusive, each giving rise to a very different style of political life. The fascination of the American political system lies in the fact that it represents a complex amalgam of all these different patterns of politics, in a constantly changing kaleidoscope of sectional, class, pluralistic and individualistic styles of politics. None of these 'explanations' of political behaviour can be written off as insignificant, and, equally, none of them can be considered to be the dominant pattern of American political life. The significance of each of these elements differs from time to time, from issue to issue. At one point, because of economic circumstances, the class factor may become relatively more important in the understanding of the political situation. At another, as the result for example of an external threat, the 'military-industrial complex' may exercise considerable influence. When economic and external crises recede, personal and pluralistic factors may dominate the political scene. American politics are conducted at several levels and in many different arenas. The significance of one or other political style may alter at the level of presidential politics from that of congressional politics, or differ at state level from that of the federal government, or in the party system as compared with the structure of pressure groups.

It is in this spirit that we must approach the study of American politics, seeking out the elements of class, sectional, pluralistic and individualistic politics, putting them in perspective at the different levels of political life, and exploring their implications for political organisation. Only in this way can we hope to make sense of the complexity and diversity of American political patterns and to see the political system as a whole.

Sectionalism and nationalism

Sectionalism is the tendency of people in a particular geographical area, such as the South, New England or the Mid-West, to give their primary political allegiance to that region and its interests. Sectionalism has been a factor in American politics ever since the differing characteristics of the seventeenth-century settlements in Virginia and Massachusetts began to interact with the differing climatic and economic conditions to be found on the southeastern and northeastern seaboards. The Constitution adopted in 1789 represented a bargain between the Northern and Southern states that provided the uneasy basis for American political life until the outbreak of the Civil War. The Republican Party, the party of Abraham Lincoln, was the party that led the Northern states to victory in that war; the Democratic Party was associated with the defeated South. This gave a twist to the distribution of political power in America that persists to the present day. It was the election of 1896, however, that set the high-water mark of sectionalism as a political force in modern politics. The populist supporters of William Jennings Bryan gained control of the Democratic Party's Convention in that year, and secured his nomination as the party's presidential candidate. Populism represented an attack upon privilege and upon the power of financiers and industrialists; it was a movement of the 'common man', and as such it would seem to mean an injection of a strong class element into the American political scene. But although the Democratic Party platform of 1896 pledged the party to support the interests of the farmer and the labourer, it was only able to capture the votes of the agrarians of the South and West. The industrial workers of the East voted strongly for the Republicans and the extreme sectional pattern of politics in that election can be gauged from Map 2.1.

At the end of the nineteenth century there was a reaction against the populists and what they represented. Conservatives in North and South alike set about the creation of political machines in which they could maintain their ascendancy, working through the medium of the Republican Party in the North and through the Democratic Party in the South. Before 1896 the two parties had been relatively well balanced throughout the country, but by 1904 there remained only six states in which the parties were evenly matched. The Republican Party almost ceased to exist in the South, while the Democrats were almost as powerless in the North.

As the twentieth century progressed, however, the forces that had produced and maintained this sectional alignment were gradually eroded. The nationalising influences of the growth of communications and of America's involvement in world affairs tended to diminish local patriotism, but perhaps the most important factor was the problem of an economy that was no longer 'open' in the sense in which it had been in the expansive years of the nineteenth century. The years of economic depression were the background to the Democratic victories of Franklin D. Roosevelt in 1932, when the old sectional alignment was shattered, and in 1936, when he won every state in the Union with the exception of Maine and Vermont. Genuine competition between the two parties gradually spread into more and more of the states and even in the deep South a new kind of politics began to emerge.

Yet important as sectionalism undoubtedly was at the beginning of the

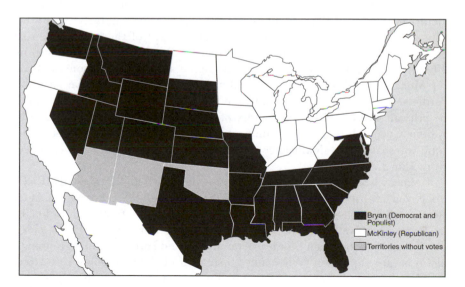

Map 2.1 The election of 1896

century, we must not overstate its importance. Although one party might consistently win elections in a particular state or region over a long period of time, this fact might mask the existence of a strong minority for the opposing party. As the century progressed the minority gradually began to achieve some sort of parity with the previously dominant group. V.O. Key has shown that even in the Deep South, that most distinctive of regions, it was only in matters concerning racial problems that the South differed profoundly from other regions in the make-up of public opinion. Much of the impression of Southern conservatism in economic and social matters is largely due to the way in which the one-party politics of the Southern variety distorted the operation of the machinery of representative government. However, even if public opinion does not differ radically in different parts of the country, the fact that the political system produces significant regional differences in the attitudes of Senators and Congressmen is of the greatest importance. It is in Congress that the effects of regional differences in political behaviour still have their greatest impact on the decisions of government.

Sectionalism declines in importance as nationalising forces develop, but the regional differences still remain as the bedrock of political behaviour. Thus since the 1930s there have been two kinds of presidential election. When, for one reason or another, tides of support for one candidate sweep across the country there are 'landslides' which may completely swamp any regional or sectional differences. But when the election is more closely contested, and popular support for the candidates is more evenly divided, then the regional differences re-emerge and can become decisive in determining the outcome of the election. Roosevelt's landslide victory of 1936 was an example of an election in which regional differences were completely irrelevant to the outcome. Similarly in 1964 Lyndon Johnson achieved an overwhelming victory over Senator Barry Goldwater, winning majorities in forty-two of the fifty states. In 1972 Richard Nixon, with 61 per cent of the votes cast, won every state except Massachusetts, and in 1984 Ronald Reagan also won in 49 states, losing only in Minnesota, the home state of his opponent, Walter Mondale. Such sweeping electoral victories represent decisive national verdicts, but in more closely contested elections sectional differences may be critical. Thus, in 1960 the victory of the Democratic candidate, John F. Kennedy, was achieved by the slimmest possible margin of 0.1 per cent of the total votes cast. The significance of sectionalism in the result can be judged from Map 2.2.

Kennedy won a majority of the states of the South and East, whilst Richard Nixon almost swept the board in the West and Mid-West. For a number of reasons, particularly his support of civil rights and his Catholicism, Kennedy performed less well in some parts of the country than others. In the close election of 1976, between Jimmy Carter and Gerald Ford, sectional groupings again became apparent. With only 51 per cent of the vote going to Carter, his victory depended on his greater pulling power in the South and the industrial North, while Ford won every state in the West as well as a number

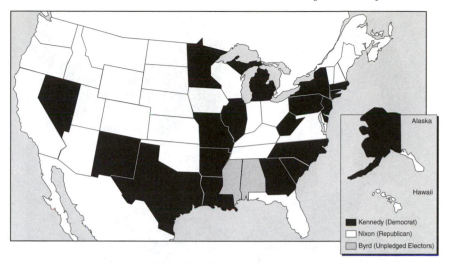

Map 2.2 The election of 1960

of Mid-Western states. The election of Bill Clinton in 1992 also illustrates the underlying sectional nature of American politics. Clinton gained only 43% of the total vote as opposed to 38% for George Bush and 19% for Ross Perot. Clinton won every West Coast State, all the northeastern states except Maine (the home state of George Bush), and a strip of Mid-West states. Bush won most of the states in the South and a number of Mid-West and mountain states. In 1996 the sectional pattern was even clearer. Clinton won every northern state except Indiana, and the states of the Far West; Robert Dole won seven states of the old Confederacy plus a block of ten western states.

Sectionalism was particularly evident in the very close election of 2000. In the words of Gerald M. Pomper, 'Not only two candidates, but virtually two nations confronted each other'. The Democratic candidate, Al Gore, won 20 states in the North and East and on the Pacific coast; George W. Bush won all the states in the South, the Border states, the Mid-West and the West, with the exception of New Mexico (see Map 2.3).

The evidence suggests, therefore, that the United States has become progressively more of a nation in the political sense since the Second World War. Increasingly, the tides of opinion sweep across the country, swamping the regional differences that were once so dominant in American politics. Nevertheless, the extent of this 'nationalisation' of American politics should not be exaggerated. When election results are close and the nation is uncertain about its choice of a leader, it tends still to divide along regional lines, the old differences re-emerging. Furthermore, the nationalisation of politics is apparent at the presidential level, but it does not extend down to the congressional level. Popular Republican presidential candidates like Eisenhower and Reagan found that their popularity did not translate into victories for their party in Congress. Thus in 1980 the great landslide for Ronald Reagan

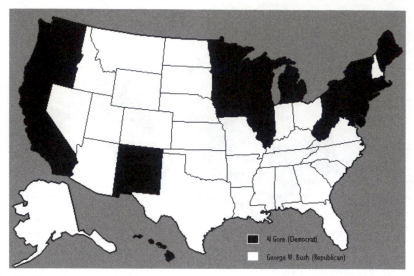

Map 2.3 The election of 2000

nevertheless left him facing a House of Representatives dominated by a majority of 242 Democrats over 193 Republicans, and again in 1984 his popularity and his sweeping presidential victory could not secure a majority in the House of Representatives for the Republican Party. In 1996 President Clinton, the candidate of the Democratic Party, won the election for the presidency, but the Republicans secured majorities in both the House of Representatives and the Senate. However, the increasing polarisation of American politics in recent decades, which we will examine in Chapter 3, resulted in Republican majorities in the Senate and the House of Representatives in 2004, alongside the Republican President, George W. Bush.

Urban–rural–suburban politics

The relatively straightforward categories with which we began this chapter soon begin to look somewhat inadequate when we delve into the rich detail of the American political scene, for sectional, class and other aspects of the political pattern overlap and intermingle. The first major overlap is represented by the blending of geographical sectionalism and class politics owing to the uneven distribution of industry across the country, and to the consequent divisions between the urban and rural populations. During the nineteenth century sectionalism was largely the consequence of the differing crops and products resulting from different climatic and soil conditions. With the growth of industrial power, and the rapid concentration of population in urban centres, however, the clash of interest between city and country became a vital factor in the political scene. The greatest impact of the flood of poor immigrants at the turn of the twentieth century was felt in the cities, and at the same time there was an internal migration from the farms to the cities. The result was the concentration of the underprivileged, the poor and the less well educated in the great cities of the North and East. The proportion of the population of the United States living in cities of over 100,000 people rose from 12.4 per cent in 1880 to nearly 30 per cent in 1930, during which time the total number of people living in such cities shot up from 6 million to 36 million. Here was the raw material for the transformation of the political system of the United States into something very different from that of the sectional alignment of 1896, but one in which geography continued to play a part.

The Great Depression of the 1930s was the catalytic agent that transformed this vast mass of human beings into what came to be called the 'normal' Democratic majority. Samuel Lubell has shown that it was Alfred E. Smith, the unsuccessful Democratic candidate for the presidency in 1928, before the Depression actually began, who first drew the political battle lines between the cities and the rural areas. It was the New Deal policies of Franklin D. Roosevelt, however, that fixed the urban masses of the North and East in the Democratic column. In 1924, in the twelve largest cities in the United States, the Republicans had an overall majority over the Democrats of 1,252,000 votes. Twenty years later, in the same twelve cities the Democratic majority over the Republicans was 2,296,000 votes. This enormous change of allegiance represented, in Lubell's phrase, the revolt of the underdog. Economic, ethnic and religious factors combined to create a body of support for the Democratic Party that broke the hold that the Republicans had had upon the presidency, with short breaks, since the Civil War. The urban masses of the North became one prop of the Democratic Party, in uneasy alliance with the southern whites who used the Democratic Party to maintain white supremacy in the southern states. This remarkable coalition, the New Deal coalition, papered over the deep ideological cleavages between Northern and Southern Democrats. They came together because historical accident, and the already existing organisational structures, provided both wings of the Party with an unprecedented opportunity to exercise power. This was the basis of the Roosevelt system that set the pattern for American politics after 1932 for thirty years. The northern wing of the Party dominated the presidency, while the southern wing gained a strategically vital position in Congress, in particular by its control of committee chairmanships. The president and the Congress came to have different 'constituencies' because of the methods of their election. To gain election to the presidency a candidate had to woo California and the great populous urban states of the North and East, while Congress was more representative of, and more responsive to, suburban and rural interests. The resulting tension between president and Congress on a wide range of policies became, because of the coalition nature of both great political parties, a great source of internal strife *within* the parties as well as between them.

The years since the end of the Second World War have, however, brought a new complication to this pattern of urban–rural politics. The rapid development of suburbia has transformed America both visually and politically. These suburbs, spreading out many miles into the country around urban areas, represent a whole new way of life, and their impact upon politics is as great as was that of the Roosevelt revolution. They represent a new type of community, in which the old guidelines to political behaviour are no longer so reliable. The population of the suburbs is ethnically diverse while its economic composition is relatively homogeneous. Neither the old pattern of city politics based upon ethnic differences nor the urban–rural alignment is so relevant. As Robert C. Wood has pointed out, the suburbs fit neither into the class patterns of the early twentieth century nor into the sectional patterns of the nineteenth. Yet old political loyalties die hard, and the persistence of party allegiance is one of the facts of political behaviour, even when the original reasons for choosing one side rather than another have long become irrelevant. Perhaps the greatest significance of the rise of suburbia is to provide an overlap with another of our patterns of political behaviour, individualism. Suburbanites tend to think of themselves as independents in politics, discriminating between candidates rather than parties, paying attention to different issues at the various levels of government, and making use of all the opportunities for ticket-splitting that the American electoral system provides.

Pluralism in American politics

The group basis of politics became the subject of intensive study only in the twentieth century, and significantly it is two American works, *The Process of Government* by Arthur F. Bentley, published in 1908, and David B. Truman's *The Governmental Process* of 1951, that most typify this approach. We shall look closely at this view of the political system in a later chapter when discussing interest group politics, but here we shall concentrate upon three aspects of group politics of particular significance at the level of electoral behaviour, the politics of class and of ethnic and religious groups.

The overlapping group nature of the American political system can be gauged from the results of the 2004 presidential election (see Table 2.1).

Class

That class is a factor in the voting behaviour of the American electorate is clear. The further up the income scale the more likely people are to vote Republican. At the end of the nineteenth century the triumph of sectionalism had as its corollary a relative lack of emphasis upon class in American voting behaviour; but as sectionalism declined in importance, the class alignments of American voters became more significant. The growth of an underprivileged urban working class during the first two decades of the twentieth century formed the basis of a transformation from the sectional politics of the earlier age. The economic depression of the late 1920s and the

Table 2.1 The 2004 presidential election

	Per cent of votes cast	
	Bush	Kerry
All	50.73	48.27
Family income		
Less than $15,000	36	63
$15–30,000	42	57
$30–50,000	49	50
$50–75,000	56	43
$75–100,000	57	42
Over $100,000	58	41
Ethnicity		
Blacks	11	88
Hispanics	44	53
Asians	44	56
Whites	58	41
Race and gender		
Black females	10	90
Black males	13	86
White females	55	44
White males	62	37
Religion		
Jewish	25	74
Catholic	52	47
Evangelical	78	21
Church attendance		
Never attend	36	62
Attend occasionally	47	53
Attend weekly	61	39

Note
Figures do not necessarily add to 100 because of votes cast for other candidates including Ralph Nader.

Source: NBC/National Election Pool.

1930s established a distinct relationship between class and party allegiance, though one that was subject to considerable variation from election to election. Franklin Roosevelt's New Deal policies turned the Democratic Party into the champion of the working man. A majority of manual workers voted for the Democrats throughout this period and, with the exception of the election of 1936, a majority of non-manual workers voted for the Republicans. Lipset has pointed out that, if these crude occupational categories are broken down, we find that, the further down the social scale a group is placed, the greater the percentage preference for the Democratic Party. In 1948 nearly 80 per cent of American manual workers voted for the Democrats, a higher percentage than most left-wing parties in European countries could achieve. In the 2004 election, the Democratic candidate, John Kerry, received 63 per cent of the votes of those electors with a family income of less than $15,000 per annum, but only 41 per cent of the votes of those with a family income of over $100,000 per annum. Thus a connection between social class, income and voting behaviour clearly exists, but it is by no means a simple one, and there is a considerable variation from one election to another in the extent of 'class voting'. In 1948, for example, the issues before the electorate were largely of an economic kind, and the voting patterns reflected class interests to a high degree. The elections of 1956 and 1972, however, present a different picture. In 1956 almost as many manual workers voted for the Republican, Dwight Eisenhower, as for the Democratic candidate, and in 1972 the Republican candidate, Richard Nixon, received the support of 57 per cent of the manual workers, as against only 43 per cent voting for his Democratic rival, George McGovern. In 2004 61 per cent of members of trades unions voted for John Kerry, the Democrat, while only 38 per cent voted for his Republican rival, George W. Bush.

There are therefore wide variations from election to election in the extent to which voters are influenced by their perceptions of their class interests in their voting behaviour. Of course, the attribution of sectional or class motivations on the basis of the sort of statistics quoted above is a very difficult exercise. What is apparently class voting may be motivated in quite different ways, because religious, ethnic and regional groupings all overlap with class to a very considerable extent. Exactly why a low-paid Irish Catholic industrial worker in the North-East votes Democratic rather than Republican can hardly be explained by any simple formula. Angus Campbell and his co-authors in their study *The American Voter* found that a third of the American population was 'unaware' of its class position, and that social class played a significant role at a conscious level in the political behaviour of only a fairly restricted and sophisticated portion of the population. The relative volatility of the American electorate, the readiness to switch votes from one party's candidate to another at successive elections, is also a measure of the limitations upon appeals to class orientation as a source of voting behaviour. American elections can produce 'landslide' results that would be unthinkable in a system where stable class voting is the norm. The figures in Table 2.2 give the percentage of the total votes cast that have gone to the Democratic and Republican Party candidates in presidential elections since 1936.

These figures reveal that, from 1936 to 1984 at any rate, there was a startling propensity for large sections of the electorate to switch their allegiance from

Table 2.2 Percentage of votes cast for the Democratic and Republican presidential candidates, 1936–2004

	Democrat	Republican
1936	60.8	36.6
1940	54.8	44.8
1944	53.4	45.9
1948	49.4	45.0
1952	44.4	54.9
1956	43.1	57.4
1960	49.7	49.5
1964	61.1	38.7
1968	42.4	43.4
1972	37.2	60.2
1976	50.0	48.0
1980	41.0	50.5
1984	40.4	58.5
1988	45.5	53.1
1992	42.9	37.1
1996	49.2	40.7
2000	48.3	47.8
2004	48.1	50.6

Note
Percentages do not total to 100 because of the intervention of third parties.

the candidate of one party at a presidential election to the candidate of the other party at the next election, or at least to abstain from voting for the party that they previously supported. The tendency to switch votes from one election to the next reflected the declining significance of sectional influences, the increasing 'nationalisation' of American politics. The era of the 'post-industrial society' ushered in a political system in which the electorate was more independent, less committed to a particular party allegiance. Landslide victories by Roosevelt in 1936, Johnson in 1964, Nixon in 1972 and Reagan in 1984 showed how waves of sentiment could sweep through the whole country, carrying all before them.

However, the above figures show a greater degree of balance between the two major parties in the period since 1988. This reflects the swing of many white voters in the South from their traditional allegiance to the Democrats, giving their support to the Republicans, at any rate in voting for the presidency. The change in the voting behaviour of Southern whites is the most significant change in the American political system in recent decades, making the South the pivotal section in presidential politics.

Ethnic politics and multiculturalism

From the early 1930s, minority groups such as Italian-Americans, Irish-Americans, the Jewish community and blacks tended to vote for the Democratic Party. The tendency was particularly noticeable in the large cities, but in 1948 in the small city of Elmira, New York, Berelson and his collaborators found that, while 81 per cent of the white native-born Protestants voted Republican, only 33 per cent of the Jews, 19 per cent of blacks and 18 per cent of the Italian-American voters followed suit. Here again, there is an overlapping of our simple categories. Minority groups, particularly blacks and foreign-born immigrants, generally belong also to the lower-income groups. Nevertheless, Berelson found that the tendency of these groups to vote for the Democrats was not particularly affected by their socio-economic position. The significance of such group voting can be very great. In the nineteenth and early twentieth centuries blacks had traditionally been loyal to the Republicans, the party of Lincoln; but Roosevelt's economic policies, and the commitment of the Democratic Party at the national level to civil rights, led blacks to support the Democratic presidential candidates in ever-growing numbers. Civil rights legislation made it possible for more and more blacks to get their names on the voting rolls, and as a consequence their electoral importance, particularly in Southern states, increased dramatically. Thus in two of the most closely fought elections since the Second World War – the victory of John F. Kennedy over Nixon in 1960 and of Jimmy Carter over Ford in 1976 – the allegiance of black voters to the Democratic Party's candidates was a vital factor in delivering victory to them. In 2004 88 per cent of black voters cast their votes for the candidate of the Democratic Party, John Kerry. Other ethnic groups play less dramatic, but no less significant roles in electoral behaviour.

In the 1950s and 1960s Republican Senator Joseph McCarthy led a crusade against communists in government. Samuel Lubell, in his *Revolt of the Moderates*, found that McCarthy's power base could be traced to those ethnic groups who were deeply affected by the cross-pressures they experienced as a result of America's involvement in two world wars. Lubell showed that in McCarthy's home state of Wisconsin there had been a considerable shift away from the Democratic Party by German-Americans, because that party was associated with the policy of war against Germany. In 1932 eight largely German Catholic counties in Wisconsin voted 74 per cent Democratic, but by 1952 the Democratic vote had dropped to 32 per cent. This change was reflected in German-American communities throughout the country. Lubell emphasised that, as the, then, second most numerous 'foreign stock', the German-Americans held the balance of power in many states, especially in the Mid-West. Such support provided a formidable reservoir of emotion upon which a man like McCarthy could draw, for these people wished to emphasise their American patriotism, and at the same time to give expression to attitudes towards communism that were related to their religious beliefs. In the same way the complex interrelationship between Catholic doctrine and the need to assert their Americanness led the Irish Catholics of New York to give overwhelming support to McCarthy.

At the lower levels of the political system ethnic divisions play a crucial role. The politics of New York City or Los Angeles present the extreme picture of ethnic diversity and its effects. In New York City in 2000, the total population was more than 8 million; over a quarter of the population were of Hispanic or Latino origin and a quarter were black or African-American, although there is some overlapping of these categories. Nearly 10 per cent were of Asian origin. In 2005 Michael R. Bloomberg, a liberal Republican, was re-elected as Mayor of New York, winning the support of 50 per cent of black voters and a third of the Latino voters. In the City of Los Angeles in 2000, 46.5 per cent of the population of nearly 4 million were of Hispanic or Latino origin, 10 per cent were of Asian origin and 11.2 per cent were black. 57.8 per cent of Angelinos reported that a language other than English was spoken in the home.

This complex of ethnic and class divisions not only has implications for local or city elections, but also may be a decisive factor in congressional politics, or even in the complicated processes by which the president of the United States is chosen. It is possible that differing attitudes towards such concepts as 'the public interest' may be affected by ethnic origins, although it is very difficult to demonstrate direct relationships between particular ethnic groups and specific attitudes towards governmental structure or policy. James Wilson and Edward Banfield have suggested that 'Anglo-Saxon' and Jewish voters in certain Ohio communities were more favourably disposed to increasing public expenditure than were Polish or Czech voters enjoying the same level of income. Some of the ethnic divisions within American society cut very deep, as is evidenced by the position of blacks, yet one might expect that, as groups of 'hyphenated Americans' become assimilated both culturally and economically, they would become indistinguishable in their political behaviour from the rest of the population. This 'assimilation theory' may well be correct *in the long run*, but it is important to remember that great waves of European immigrants were still flowing into the United States until well into the first half of the twentieth century, and the second half was characterised by a massive influx of Puerto Ricans, Mexicans, Vietnamese, Koreans and other Asians. It is one of the most frequently observed facts of political life that political loyalties tend to outlive the factors that created them. Local conditions and local leadership can give a quite remarkable persistence and coherence to ethnic political behaviour.

America has always been ethnically diverse, and as we have seen, in the last half of the nineteenth century and in the twentieth century, immigrants flooded into the United States on an unprecedented scale. But, although the origins of Americans were to be traced to countries all over the world, American *culture* was amazingly uniform. English was the language used in schools and public institutions. Immigrants were under pressure to learn English, and in many cases 'foreign-sounding' names were anglicised. Furthermore, the educational system was an overt instrument of Americanisation, to instil values and beliefs, in particular the tenets of the Constitution, into the children of immigrants. The pressures were all on the need for homogeneity, and for a very good reason. The fear of subversion, not necessarily in the sense of treasonable actions, but in the sense of undermining the consensus on which the political system depended, was ever present. The Vietnam War, and more recent immigration, legal and illegal, have brought about a change in these attitudes. The Vietnam experience and the way in which dissent was legitimised damaged the confidence of Americans in their cultural identity. The effects of this experience coincided with a large-scale immigration of a group of people – Latinos – who did not wish to be assimilated in the way in which earlier immigrant groups had been. By 2004 there were over 41 million people of Latino or Hispanic origin in the United States, and their numbers continue to increase. Federal government programmes of bilingual education began in 1968 to provide education for Spanish-speakers, but the question then arose whether this kind of programme was intended to help Latinos to assimilate to the English language culture of America or to be able to survive in that culture whilst retaining Spanish as their first language. In 1974 the Supreme Court ruled in *Lau* v. *Nichols* that teaching students in a language they did not understand was a violation of their civil rights, thus giving an impetus to bilingual programmes. Legislation was passed requiring that election registration forms, ballots and election materials should be made available in languages other than English in districts where a significant minority spoke a language other than English as their first language. The language problem took a new turn in 2006 with the launching of a Spanish version of the American National Anthem, entitled 'Nuestro Himno', bringing about a chorus of condemnation from conservative groups.

Predictably there was a backlash against this 'Latinisation' of America. Moves began to establish English as the 'official language' of the United States, and to try to limit immigration from Latin America. By 2005 twenty-seven states had legislated to make English the official language of the state, and a Bill making English the official language of the federal government was passed by the House of Representatives in 1996, but did not reach the statute book. The nature of the Latino challenge to the established 'Anglo' culture of America has great political implications. The Spanish-speaking section of the American electorate is growing, and will continue to grow. Their influence at local level, such as in cities like Los Angeles, is already considerable and their voting power at state and eventually federal level will continue to increase. The long-run effect of Latino immigration on the American political system is difficult to predict, although it will certainly be profound. The Latino population is not as coherent as the African-American population; it is drawn from a number of different countries, with differing ethnic origins, white, black, American Indian. However, in 2006 the Latino community found a new basis for solidarity against the 'Anglos' with the development of an immigrants' rights movement. Concern about the extent of illegal immigration led to attempts by the government to control the border with Mexico more effectively and to find a solution to the problem raised by approximately 11 million illegal immigrants in the United States. The possibility of large-scale deportations led to demonstrations by hundreds of thousands of Latinos in a number of cities, threats of strikes, boycotts and other action. This issue will be considered further in Chapter 11. The problems of establishing a multicultural society in America may mirror those of other societies faced with similar challenges in other parts of the world.

Religion and religiosity

Religion has been a factor in American politics ever since the Pilgrim Fathers made landfall on Cape Cod. Furthermore, the regional distribution of religious belief has served to complicate the sectional differences of American politics. In colonial times Quaker-dominated Pennsylvania, the Roman Catholics of Maryland and the Dutch Reformed Church in New York separated Puritan New England and Anglican Virginia. The mass immigration of the nineteenth and twentieth centuries transformed the pattern of religious affiliation, for a very high proportion of the immigrants were Catholic. There are 50 million Catholics in the United States today, more than in Italy. Because the waves of immigrants headed for the cities of the North and East, the pattern of sectional attitudes became further complicated, and because they were poor, Catholic immigrants contributed a further dimension to the pattern of sectional, class and religious influences that today form the fabric of American politics. Thus the electorate of the Southern states remains almost completely Protestant in composition, whereas the concentration of Catholics in Northern states such as Massachusetts gives to those states a quite distinctive political style. The *Statistical Abstract of the United States* lists thirty-five different Christian denominations and twenty-one 'other religions' to which Americans declared their adherence in 2001, in addition to the nearly 30 million Americans who stated they had no religion.

Like the other factors in American politics, religion plays a significant but varying role at the national level. In state and local politics its impact varies greatly from area to area and from issue to issue; but of its importance there can be little doubt. Religious factors have played an important role in presidential politics, in helping to influence the voting behaviour of Senators and Congressmen, or in the determination of political battles over contraception laws in Massachusetts or the closed shop in Ohio. The comparison between the candidacy of two Catholics for the presidency in the twentieth century with that of John Kerry in 2004 illustrates the way in which attitudes to Catholicism have changed. The candidacy of Al Smith in 1928 evidenced the extent of the bitterness that then existed against Catholics, although his defeat cannot be attributed primarily to religious motivations among the electorate. In 1956, when Eisenhower's personal appeal was so great, Catholics split almost fifty–fifty between the parties, but four years later roughly 80 per cent of Catholics voted for the Catholic candidate, John F. Kennedy, and only 20 per cent for his Protestant opponent. In the election of 1960 Kennedy increased the percentage of the Democratic vote by nearly 20 per cent in states with high proportions of Catholic voters compared with only 2 per cent in states where the number of Catholics was low. The following example, given by John H. Fenton, of the effect of religious divisions within a community, although it may not be typical, shows how religious affiliation can affect politics. In Nelson County, Kentucky, which was half Baptist and half Catholic, Kennedy received only 35 per cent of the vote in four predominantly Baptist precincts, but in five largely Catholic precincts he received 88 per cent of the total vote. Nationally, however, the tendency of Catholics to vote for a member of their own church was more than offset by those Protestant voters who switched to the support of Nixon on religious grounds. By contrast, the candidacy of John Kerry in 2004 seemed to provoke relatively little religious controversy. Although Kerry is a practising Catholic, in the campaign he adopted 'liberal' attitudes towards issues such as abortion. In fact he came under attack more strongly from some Catholic bishops who condemned his advocacy of a woman's 'right to privacy'. In the event a majority of Catholics voted for George W. Bush, in a slightly greater proportion than the electorate as a whole, perhaps because of their perception of his views on moral issues.

The most important recent manifestation of the significance of religion in American politics lies in the revival of fundamentalist Protestant ideas and the involvement of their proponents in elections and in attempts to influence government policy at all levels. The 'born-again' movement and the 'Moral Majority' demanded that fundamentalist religious values should be adopted as the guiding lines for action in all fields of government policy. In the election of 1976 the Democratic candidate, Jimmy Carter, received the support of many southern fundamentalists who desired a more conservative and 'Christian' approach to government. Carter was, however, a great disappointment to them, and in the run-up to the election of 1980 the Republican candidate, Ronald Reagan, assiduously courted this group. Political divisions along religious lines were particularly evident in the 1984 elections. While Catholic voters split relatively evenly between Reagan and Mondale, 73 per cent of white Protestants voted for Reagan and 80 per cent of those whites who described themselves as 'born-again Christians' voted for him. The leaders of the Moral Majority also conducted campaigns against 'liberal' Senators and Congressmen, and many of the latter were beaten in the election. In state and local politics fundamentalist groups battled to further their views on subjects such as abortion, women's rights and the teaching of evolution in the schools.

By the time of the election of George W. Bush in 2000 the connection between the religious right and the Republican Party was firmly established. Bush, himself a Southern Methodist, received the support of fundamentalist

Christians, particularly in the South, where 73 per cent of white evangelicals voted for him. But Bush also targeted Catholics, a majority of whom voted for him. In fact, since 1996, as Everett Carl Ladd has shown, it is 'religiosity', the extent of regular church attendance, rather than religious affiliation which is important in affecting voting behaviour. Voters who were not active church attenders voted overwhelmingly for Clinton, whilst a majority of regular church attenders voted for the Republican candidate, Bob Dole. In 2000 white Protestants who identified themselves as very highly committed to religion voted 87 per cent for Bush as opposed to 13 per cent for Al Gore, the Democratic candidate.

The role of individualism and personality

The patterns of sectional, class, ethnic and religious politics that we have looked at so far would seem to leave little room for the emergence of truly individualistic behaviour on the part of the electors or their representatives. Yet if we look at the trends of political behaviour in America we find that individualism in politics became increasingly important in the twentieth century. At the end of the nineteenth century, American political attitudes were strongly party-oriented; that is to say, voters identified themselves very strongly with a particular political party. It was in the nature of politics at that time that party identification was founded largely upon historical and regional loyalties rather than upon class but, as the twentieth century progressed and class voting increased in importance, the ties between the voter and his party progressively declined. That these two things happened at the same time was a reflection both of the extreme nature of the sectional alignment of 1896 and of the fact that, as the century progressed, much of the electorate became increasingly alienated from political life. Walter D. Burnham has pointed out that an increasingly large proportion of the electorate are peripheral voters, who are not closely tied to one party or another, and who participate in elections only when they feel strongly moved to do so by the impact of a personality or an issue sufficiently strong to make them re-enter the political universe. The following figures of voting turnout (Table 2.3) illustrate this decline in political activity in the electorate.

Voter turnout declined during the 1970s, and in 1976 only 54.4 per cent of the potential electorate turned out to vote in the contest between Ford and Carter; in 1980 the Reagan–Carter battle tempted only 53.9 per cent of the electorate into the polling booths. In 1996 a low point was reached when only 49 per cent of the electorate turned out to vote for the presidential candidates, Clinton, Dole and Perot. In 2004, however, turnout rose to 60.7 per cent, largely as a result of the public interest roused by the circumstances of the attack upon the World Trade Center and the war in Iraq.

Turnout for congressional elections in years when a president is not being elected is even lower, and voting for state and local elections is lower still. However, we should not be too hasty in our judgement of the American

Table 2.3 Voter turnout: presidential elections

1848–72	75.1%
1876–96	78.5%
1900–16	64.8%
1920–28	51.7%
1932–44	59.1%
1948–60	60.3%
1964–76	58.2%
1980–92	52.7%
1996–2004	53.6%

electorate in this respect. The number and frequency of elections is greater in America than in any comparable country, and ordinary people cannot be expected to be in a continuous political ferment. When they do feel strongly about any issue or candidate they have more opportunity than anywhere in the world to make their views known.

In recent decades voters have been increasingly ready to change sides from one party to another, and it has been estimated that as many as 40 per cent of the electorate consider themselves to be independents rather than firm supporters of either of the parties. One of the most important manifestations of this decline in close party identification is to be found in the phenomenon of 'split-ticket' voting. At each election the electorate is confronted by a ballot paper, or a voting machine, which allows the voter to cast ballots for a number of candidates for different offices at federal, state and local level. Each of the major parties, and some minor ones, will have candidates for all or some of these offices on the ballot. The voter may simply vote for all the Republican candidates, or all the Democrats; this is voting 'the straight ticket', and usually it is much simpler to do, requiring only a single mark on the ballot paper or the operation of a single lever on the machine. The voter is also free to 'split the ticket'; that is, to vote for one or more Republicans for some offices, and for Democrats for the others – or indeed, where three or more parties appear on the ballot, to spread votes across all of them, voting for individual candidates, regardless of party. At the federal level voters can discriminate between candidates for the presidency, the Senate and the House of Representatives, voting Republican for two of these offices and Democrat for the third, or any combination they wish.

The complexity of the ballot paper and the trouble involved in making the necessary discrimination between candidates might suggest that split-ticket voting would be relatively rare. Not so! Campbell and Miller found that in 1952 as many as one-third of the voters split the ticket, and in 1956 two-fifths of the electorate did so. The potential importance of this practice at the federal level was illustrated by the vote in 1952, when nearly 40 million Americans voted for the Republican candidate for the presidency, Dwight

Eisenhower, but only 28 million voted for Republican candidates for the House of Representatives.

During the 1960s this pattern of voting Republican for the presidency and Democrat for Senate and House candidates – 'presidential republicanism' – became extremely important, particularly in the Southern states. As the ties of party loyalty weakened in the United States, and the behaviour of the electorate became more volatile and independent, the tendency towards split-ticket voting increased. In 1996, 65 per cent of voters reported that they had split the ticket at some time. One of the best ways to measure the propensity of the electorate to split its votes between the candidates of different parties is to compare the vote for the presidential candidates in a particular state with the votes for the senatorial candidates. Both offices, the presidency and membership of the Senate, are 'national' offices, and the vote for each is a state-wide vote for one office. In other words, as far as possible, the 'constituencies' are comparable. In the election of 1960, 82.7 per cent of the voters in Virginia supported the Democratic candidate for the Senate, but only 47.0 per cent voted for the Democratic presidential candidate, John F. Kennedy. Although partisanship has increased in recent years split-ticket voting is still an important factor in the outcome of elections. In the election of 2004 there were thirty-four Senate seats up for election, and the elections took place on the same day, and on the same ballot paper, as the election for president. In seven states the voters chose the candidate of one party for the presidency and the candidate of the opposing party for the Senate. In five states the Republican, George W. Bush, received a majority of the votes but a Democratic senator was elected. In two states John Kerry was successful at the presidential level, but a Republican won the Senate race. In some of these states the number of voters that split the ticket was relatively small, but in two states the extent of ticket splitting was remarkable: North Dakota and Indiana. In North Dakota, George W. Bush had a majority of 85,599 votes over the Democratic challenger, John Kerry, but in the election for the Senate the Democratic candidate, Byron L. Dorgan, who had been Senator from North Dakota since 1992, had a majority of 113,590 over the Republican candidate. In Indiana, Bush won by 510,427 over Kerry, but the Senate race went to the incumbent Democratic Senator Evan Bayh, who had a majority over his Republican opponent of 593,066.

One of the aspects of the phenomenon of split-ticket voting is that voters may be inclined to vote for incumbent candidates, those who are already in office, whom they judge to have been doing a reasonably good job, irrespective of the voter's party identification – presumably on the basis of choosing the devil you know rather than the devil you don't. The importance of being an incumbent is illustrated by the re-election to the Senate of Arlen Specter from Pennsylvania in 2004. In 1980 the Republicans won Pennsylvania for Ronald Reagan and Arlen Specter, Republican, was elected to the Senate for the first time. In 1992 Bill Clinton won the presidency for the Democrats and carried Pennsylvania by a large majority, but on the same ballot Specter was re-elected and, although the Democrats have carried Pennsylvania for the presidency in every succeeding election (although with diminishing majorities), Arlen Specter won the Senate seat for the Republicans for five successive terms. Specter's success depended in part on having rather different views on policy compared with many of his Republican Party colleagues; he is pro-choice on abortion and has supported stem-cell research and family planning programmes.

Such examples could be multiplied by examining the votes for members of the House of Representatives, by looking at state offices such as the governorship, and so on. Much of this split ticket voting is to be attributed to sectional differences in attitudes within the party, so that the national presidential candidate may have policy views that differ considerably from those of the local party. Clearly there is, however, a very considerable personal element in these split-ticket voting situations, where a senatorial candidate may have a local reputation that brings in a much larger vote than the more remote presidential candidate can hope to generate. It is always difficult to assess the importance of the personality of a candidate upon voting decisions, and it may well be that personality alone is not enough, and will not sway the voters unless there is some other latent factor which the personal appeal of the candidate serves to bring into operation. The importance of personality will also vary according to circumstances. Thus, in areas where party organisation is minimal, personality may be decisive in some state and local elections. Even at the presidential level, the fact that Eisenhower could attract the votes of a quarter of those who normally voted Democratic was startling evidence of what personal appeal can achieve if the circumstances are favourable. Eisenhower would have won the election for whichever party he stood, and at one time or another he was considered as a potential candidate by both parties. Similarly, when he was active in Californian politics, the future Chief Justice of the US Supreme Court, Earl Warren, was able to win the nomination of both parties at the same election for the post of governor. Senator Wayne Morse of Oregon was able to change his party allegiance during his term of office and still gain re-election to the Senate. These are extreme examples, but they indicate that we ignore the importance of personality in American politics only at the risk of altogether failing to understand it.

The most recent expression of the role of personality in American politics, and perhaps the most questionable, is the part played by celebrities. Ronald Reagan, an actor who appeared in innumerable B movies, was elected governor of California in 1966 and again in 1970. He won the presidency in 1980 with a landslide vote, and was re-elected in 1984. Another 'celebrity', but not from the entertainment industry, to take up a political carer was John Glenn, the first American astronaut to orbit the Earth, who was elected Senator from Ohio in 1974 and served in the Senate until 1999. Perhaps the most extraordinary example is the election of a wrestler turned actor, Jesse 'The Body' Ventura, as Governor of Minnesota in 1998 representing the Reform Party. Ventura appeared in three films with Arnold Schwarzenegger, body-

builder and star of the 'Terminator' film series, who was elected Governor of
California in 2003. It is expected that future elections for the governorship
of the state will be contested by film stars. This development is perhaps not
surprising in an era when television is so important in elections, but it has
to be said that another profession still remains more important in providing
recruits for elective office – lawyers.

Politics in California

The local sub-divisions of the states – the cities, counties, towns and myriad
different elective bodies at local level – also exercise varying degrees of political power. The decentralisation of American political power can best be
seen by examining the autonomy and the political role of a state such as
California and the relationship between towns and counties and the state
government that is their legal master. It becomes clear immediately that local *government* has significance in America that it has long lost in Europe. To
understand the politics of the presidency, or the workings of the Congress of
the United States, it is necessary to start by looking at the roots of American politics, at the characteristics of the electorate, at regional variations in
political style and behaviour, at the way in which politics is conducted at the
state and local level. Only then can we understand the nature of the presidency, its strengths and its weaknesses; only then can we understand the contradictions of a Congress that can be at one and the same time a parochial
assembly and a body of national legislators. The study of American politics
must build up from its local components in a way that is no longer so true of
the study of most European countries, for the diversity that remains at the
base of American life prohibits either the easy generalisation or the simple
explanation of political behaviour. It is this pattern that we shall follow, con-
structing a picture of the American scene that will help to make explicable
what happens at the more glamorous level of President and Congress, and
without which the events that make the headlines in the newspapers of the
world are often quite incomprehensible. Let us look, therefore, at the politics
of an important state, California.

California, the 'Golden State', was admitted to the Union in 1850, as the
thirty-first state. The indigenous home of a large number of Native American
tribes, it was settled by Spain in the eighteenth century, becoming part of
newly independent Mexico in 1821. American settlers started to arrive in
the 1840s and began to agitate for independence from Mexico. In 1846 the
United States declared war on Mexico and in 1848, following the end of the
Mexican War, Mexico ceded California to the United States. Gold was discovered in the same year and the resulting gold rush brought many different
nationalities to California to find their fortune.

California is often presented as a microcosm of the United States, but
also as an extreme version of American society. It is a very diverse state in
many ways. From the Mexican border, the southern desert changes to agri-

cultural land, to the vineyards and forests of the north, up to the border with Oregon 800 miles away. The state has varied industries, including oil and gas production, mining, the computer powerhouse of Silicon Valley, tourism and of course Hollywood. There are great cities, Los Angeles and San Francisco, and innumerable smaller cities and towns. California has a population of over 36 million of which 15 million are white, 13 million are Hispanic, 4 million are of Asian origin, and 2 million are black. If it were a separate sovereign country it would be the world's sixth largest economy, surpassing most of the world's most populous countries.

The state constitution reflects the Constitution of the United States in embodying the separation of powers between the legislative, executive and judicial branches. The legislature is bicameral with a Senate and an Assembly. The governor has a veto over legislation, but as in the federal government the veto can be overridden by a two-thirds majority of both houses of the legislature. In addition to the elected governor and legislature a number of state officials are also directly elected: the lieutenant governor, the attorney general, the secretary of state, the treasurer, the controller, the insurance commissioner and the school superintendent. In the nature of the Californian political system these officials can be drawn from different political parties, but are still required to work together. The justices of the state Supreme Court and the appellate courts are nominated by the governor, but then must be confirmed in office by the voters at the next election; the lower levels of the judiciary are also elected. The state constitution comes close to establishing federalism *within* the state by giving considerable autonomy to counties, cities and other local governments.

The governor has an important role, if an impossible one to carry out effectively. The governor must propose legislation to the legislature and prepare a state budget, which totalled $85 billion in 2005. The problem of persuading the legislature to accept these proposals is a daunting one. Political parties in California are weak, internally divided parties; to quote David G. Lawrence: 'In the Democratic Party, liberals, moderates, and various caucus groups fight among themselves. In the Republican Party, fiscal conservatives, social issue conservatives, and more pragmatic moderates vie for influence over education, abortion, gun control, gender issues, and gay rights.' In such circumstances party discipline is difficult to achieve and the situation is made even more difficult by the fact that the governor may be facing a legislature dominated by a majority of the opposing party. When Republican Arnold Schwarzenegger was elected governor in 2003 he faced a Senate and Assembly both with Democratic majorities. These difficulties are compounded by the fact that in 1990 the voters of California passed Proposition 140 which introduced 'term limits' restricting state legislators to a maximum of six years in the Assembly and to eight in the Senate.

To add to the complexity of the institutional structure there are three instruments of participatory democracy – the initiative, the referendum and the recall. The initiative allows citizens to propose legislation, which is then submitted to the voters and if approved becomes law, without the legislature even considering it and without the governor's signature. The state constitution requires the collection of signatures totalling 5 per cent of the vote cast in the last previous election for a proposition to be placed on the ballot for consideration by the electorate. Two of the very many initiatives to have become law in this way are Proposition 13 in 1978, which slashed the property tax level in half, with very serious consequences for local services, and Proposition 22, passed in 2000, which outlawed gay marriages in the state.

The referendum enables voters to prevent the implementation of state constitutional amendments, or laws intending to raise money through the issue of state bonds. Compared with the initiative, the referendum has been relatively unimportant, but recently the third of the participatory instruments, the recall, has acquired new significance. The recall is a procedure which allows voters to remove from office state and local elected officials, including judges, in the period *between* elections. In 2003 a movement began to remove the Democratic state governor, Gray Davis, who had gained re-election only in 2002 and still had three years of his term of office to run. In the ensuing election the recall was approved and Davis was replaced by Republican Arnold Schwarzenegger. The problem of these participatory procedures, particularly the initiative, is that they become yet another instrument for the manipulation of the policy process by pressure groups.

This diversity and complexity results in California's particular brand of politics, the politics of 'hyperpluralism'; the idea of majority rule in the state has given way to rule by minorities. To quote David Lawrence again, 'The exercise of political power has become a highly competitive tug-of-war between institutions, policymakers, political parties, numerous interest groups, and voters.' Because the role of the American states is still so important and the decisions that they take make a considerable impact on the lives of their citizens, this tortuous policy process has a real impact on the quality of government in California. The problem of coordinating the activities of government becomes almost insoluble; state finances are in a continuing crisis; what are intended as instruments of majoritarian democracy instead give to relatively small groups the opportunity to exercise undue influence to achieve their own self-interested ends. Thus vitally important policy areas, such as the supply of water and the generation of electricity, which are essentially matters for the state government, are not being adequately addressed.

The nature of politics within the state has considerable consequences also for the government of the United States. California has fifty-three members in the House of Representatives, 12 per cent of the total membership, as well as its two Senators. A number of the chairmen of congressional standing committees come from California. As the largest state in the Union, with fifty-five members in the Electoral College, its potential impact on the outcome of presidential elections is enormous. The disorganised politics of the state feed into the behaviour of its delegations in Congress and into the conduct of presidential elections.

We have tried to isolate four main strands of political behaviour in the electorate, and we shall see in later chapters how these strands continue right through the political system. Of course the patterns of political behaviour are more complicated than this, for in reality sectional, class, pluralistic and individualistic influences overlap and interact. Each election, each political situation, becomes a unique combination of these elements, and we are faced with an ever-changing panorama of political life, responding to changing social, economic and strategic forces, internal and external. However, though in constant change, and although the patterns never repeat themselves exactly, there are certain restraints and certain persistent structures that give continuity and shape to the political system. Constitutional forces, the electoral system, the party system: these provide the framework within which more transient political forces work themselves out, and it is to these that we must now turn our attention.

Further reading

Dahl, R.A. (1967) *Pluralist Democracy in the United States: Conflict and Consent*, Chicago: Rand McNally.

Kaufmann, E.P. (2004) *The Rise and Fall of Anglo-America*, London: Harvard University Press.

Lawrence, D.G. (2004) *California: The Politics of Diversity*, Belmont, CA: Wadsworth.

Schlesinger, A.M. Jr (1992) *The Disuniting of America: Reflections on a Multicultural Society*, New York: Norton.

Wright Mills, C. (2000) *The Power Elite*, Oxford: Oxford University Press.

Websites

One of the glories of the internet is to be able to access the web editions of newspapers as they are published. The following are fascinating for students of American politics:

The New York Times: www.nytimes.com

The Washington Post: www.washingtonpost.com

The Los Angeles Times: www.latimes.com

The Chicago Tribune: www.chicagotribune.com

3 The two-party system

The patterns of sectional, class, pluralistic and individualistic political behaviour in the American electorate suggest, at first sight, that the most likely shape for the party system would be a number of different parties, each giving expression to the interest of an important section of the political universe. Surely only a multi-party system could give expression to such diversity. Yet a second look at the evidence of the previous chapter throws some doubt on this suggestion. Are the numerous cross-pressures of American politics, the overlapping patterns of group behaviour, consistent with the existence of a number of relatively stable political parties of the kind to be found in continental European countries? In fact, two political parties, the Democrats and the Republicans, dominate the scene without any serious rivals on the horizon. There have been important third-party movements in American history, and even today there are many minor parties. In 1968 George Wallace, the candidate of the American Independent Party, polled 13.5 per cent of the total vote, and in 1924 Robert La Follette, the Progressive candidate for the presidency, attracted the vote of one-sixth of those who went to the polls. In 1992 Ross Perot, running as an Independent, polled 19 per cent of the total vote, and may have been responsible for the defeat of George Bush. Perot ran again in 1996 but attracted a very much smaller proportion of the vote. Ralph Nader, the candidate of the Green Party, attracted only 2.7 per cent of the presidential vote in 2000, but his intervention meant that George W. Bush rather than Al Gore carried the state of Florida, which ensured the election of Bush. Another type of third-party movement, the breakaway States Rights Party of 1948, won five of the Southern states that normally went to the Democratic Party. In 1964 there were six minor candidates for the presidency, including the first black ever to run for the office, and in 1980 an independent candidate, John Anderson, polled over 5.5 million votes, 7 per cent of the total. However, when there is no stimulus for a protest vote to draw electors away from the two major parties they may between them poll over 99 per cent of the votes cast, as they have done in most of the elections since 1952.

Thus the diversities of political life suggest that we might expect to find a multi-party system of the most thoroughgoing and unstable variety, and yet in fact there is in operation an established two-party system of the most inclusive sort. How is it that, from the morass of groups and interests, two parties emerge with a seemingly unchallengeable grip on political power? The answer lies in the complex relationships between the constitutional framework of government, the organisational structure of the political parties, and the ideological bases of political behaviour. For the American party system is a two-party system only in a very special sense. We must not look at the American party system simply in a two-dimensional way, for it has many dimensions, and becomes a 'two-party system' only if viewed from a particular standpoint. From another point of view it is an agglomeration of many parties centred on the governments of the fifty states and their subdivisions, and yet from another point of view it is a loosely articulated four-party system based upon Congress and the presidency. The names 'Democrat' and 'Republican' are *not* meaningless labels, as Lord Bryce suggested they were at the end of the nineteenth century; nevertheless, they do tend to obscure the fact that for most purposes America operates under a multi-party system which coalesces into two great coalitions for strictly limited purposes.

Fifty party systems

The major function of American political parties is to provide candidates for office and to secure their election. The effective offices for which candidates have to be nominated are very numerous, particularly at state and local levels. The rewards of office – the spoils, as they are sometimes referred to – are to be found at all levels of government, and there are important policy decisions to be taken, involving the expenditure of billions of dollars by federal, state and local officials. The fact that the Constitution diffuses authority among these levels of government has had a strong disintegrating effect upon party structure. The constitutional division of authority between the federal government and the states is reflected in the realities of the distribution of effective political power. Conceivably, the effects of the constitutional fragmentation of authority might have been offset by a strongly centralised party system binding the parts of the government together, but the conditions that might have led to such a centralisation of power have not been present in the system. As a result, national party organisations have had a very restricted function to perform in the political system, concerning themselves mainly with the nomination and election of presidential candidates. The national parties have tended to be coalitions of state and local parties, forming and re-forming every four years for this purpose. Thus, rather than a single party system, we have fifty state party systems with the national political parties related to them in a complex pattern of alliances.

It is by no means fanciful to think of politics in the United States operating within a framework of fifty party systems rather than one. A great centralisation of government power undeniably took place during the twentieth century, giving to the federal government in Washington an interest, and an influence, in a large number of fields of action that in earlier times were almost exclusively the concern of the states, and yet these states are by no means political dodos. They continue to exercise important governmental functions. Perhaps the most important single fact about American politics today is that the centralisation of decision-taking power in the hands of the federal government has *not* been accompanied by a corresponding increase in the power of the national political parties over the state and local organisations. Governmental power has been centralised, but political power has remained diffuse. This is one of the crucial facts about American politics, which helps to explain why the most powerful government in the world may, at certain times, be directed by political forces originating from remote parts of the country with seemingly little relevance to the problems under consideration. Organisationally, the national parties are weak and sporadic in operation. The continuously operative and powerful political organisations are at the state and local level, although their degree of coherence and effectiveness varies considerably from place to place. The constitutional basis of this diffusion of power is reinforced by historical events, such as the Civil War, which have tended to entrench a particular political pattern in a region; by the regional differences of interest that characterise the subcontinent; by a general resistance to the idea of 'big government'; and by the vested interests of those groups, particularly local politicians, who benefit from the status quo. Thus there exists a whole network of disintegrating factors that reinforce each other and prevent the emergence of powerful national parties that could coerce state and local parties.

There are good reasons for describing politics in, say, Mississippi as constituting a different and distinct political system from that of New York or Michigan. The very quality and nature of political life differs greatly from state to state. In a number of states one party maintains a position of dominance such that the opposing party can only fitfully win certain state and local offices. In the states of the Deep South the Democratic Party was for a long period the only effective political organisation, establishing one-party systems in those states, which enabled them to maintain white supremacy by excluding blacks from the political process. The progressive disillusionment of Southern whites with the civil rights policies of the national Democratic Party since the 1960s enabled the Republicans gradually to gain support with white voters in the South. In 1994 for the first time since the reconstruction period following the Civil War the Republicans held a majority of governorships in Southern states, and a majority of the Senators and Congressmen from those states were Republicans. Since then the Republicans have tightened their grip further on the Southern states. In 2004 all the Senate seats up for election in the southern states were won by Republicans and of the twenty-two Southern Senators eighteen were Republican after the election. We will examine the pivotal role of the South in the political system in a later chapter.

The presidential and congressional parties

The structure of American federalism provides one of the most important disintegrating influences on American politics, but the Constitution struck a further blow at the basis of any attempt to centralise political power. The Founding Fathers, in their determination to limit the power of government, also established a strict separation of personnel between Congress and the president's administration, and gave to president and Congress a different electoral basis and different constituencies. The president cannot dissolve Congress if it displeases him, nor does he resign if his proposals are rejected by it. Thus, although both president and Congress are concerned with the passage of legislation and with the way that it is put into effect, there are very few formal links between them. A major function of the political parties throughout their history has been to provide such links between the separated branches of government; but their success in coordinating these activities has been only partial. Indeed, as a result of this institutional division of governmental power, each of the political parties has been divided into a *presidential* wing and a *congressional* wing.

The distinctive quality of these two wings of each of the major political parties led James McGregor Burns to describe the American party system as a four-party system. The presidential Democrats, the presidential Republicans, the congressional Democrats and the congressional Republicans are, he argued, 'separate though overlapping parties'. Each has its own institutional patterns and ideology, representing a different style of politics. The presidential Democrats differ from the congressional Democrats in their electoral base, appealing, in part at least, to different sections of the population. The presidential party seeks its major support in the urban areas of the large industrialised states, while many Democratic senators and congressmen are much more responsive to rural and suburban influences. The presidential wings of both parties tend to be closer together doctrinally than they are to the respective congressional wings of their own parties. Indeed, the conflict between the two wings of a party may be more bitter and intense than the conflict between the parties themselves.

It is, of course, difficult to draw precise lines between the presidential and congressional wings of the party. Some members of Congress must be numbered among the supporters of the presidential wing, although usually they are relatively few in number, and each of the two wings will make attempts to influence or even control the other. The nomination of Senator Barry Goldwater by the Republicans in 1964 represented the success of the congressional Republicans over the presidential Republicans, and his ensuing defeat at the hands of the electorate illustrated the differing bases of support upon which the two wings of the party must depend. Goldwater was out of his element in presidential politics, and never seemed able to come to terms with the new context in which he found himself. Although both John F. Kennedy and Richard Nixon had served in the Senate before election to the White House, few senators have been able to make the transition to the presidency, experience as the governor of a state being considered a better apprenticeship. President Lyndon Johnson had been Democratic leader of the Senate, but he succeeded to the presidency as a result of the assassination of John F. Kennedy and was subsequently elected in his own right.

The ideological content of American politics

The constitutional and structural aspects of the party system that we have surveyed are understandable as far as they go, but something more is needed to comprehend fully why America has a 'two-party' system. What is politics about in America, and what role do ideas play in the working of the system? What are the issues that give life to the political system?

The relation between ideas and political structures is always very complex and nowhere more so than in the United States. Political ideas take different forms and exist at different levels of consciousness. The term 'ideology' is usually applied to a system of thought in which a number of ideas about the nature of the political system and the role of government are logically related to each other, and developed as a consciously held guide to political action. Socialism, communism and fascism are the prime examples of such ideologies. In this sense ideology plays a very small, indeed an almost negligible role in American politics. These ideologies have never been held by any more than a tiny proportion of the American population and although there are a number of political parties based upon these ideas, among them the Communist Party USA, the Socialist Labor Party of America and even the American Nazi Party, these organisations have never had a significant effect on American politics, at any rate at the national level. This is often referred to as 'American exceptionalism', the fact that American politics has always been different from the politics of old Europe. Yet there is an important role for ideas in American politics, and an understanding of the American ideology, 'Americanism', is essential for a full understanding of the two-party system.

The American ideology is fundamentally the ideology of Western liberal democracy but, whereas in the nineteenth and twentieth centuries in Britain this set of ideas could almost be taken for granted, in the United States it had to be continuously and consciously asserted. The apparent contradictions in American life stemmed very largely from this felt need to *impose* an ideology that has as its main tenets freedom of speech and freedom of political action. The diverse characteristics of American society are such that many Americans felt that the toleration of unusual behaviour or unusual ideas might lead to the break-up of their society; there had to be a minimum conformity enforced by society. Ideas that introduced the germ of a divisive force into the community could not be tolerated.

Thus all tendencies towards a sharp polarisation of ideas were consciously resisted. Both major parties shied away from ideological commitments, and those issues that cut deepest into American society usually also cut across the parties. When important problems of a potentially divisive nature arose, such as the Vietnam War, or civil rights, the tendency of the national leaders of both parties was to move towards a middle course, avoiding extremes. There arose what has been described as a *consensus* of ideas, a broad agreement upon the basic attitudes towards the political system and political problems, which was shared by the vast majority of the American people.

This consensual basis of American politics had a number of important results. First, it allowed particular issues to be discussed as isolated problems, to be solved empirically without reference to any set of fundamental principles, so that within the accepted limits of what was considered an 'American' solution, compromises could be found both within and between the parties. Second, as a corollary to this, it made possible the cross-party voting that was, and to a degree still is, so characteristic of the American legislature. Here constitutional and ideological factors reinforced each other. Congressmen when casting their votes do not have to worry about governmental instability of the sort that would result from cross-voting in a parliamentary system. Legislators can make up their minds on the merits of the proposals in front of them, or they can respond to constituency or other pressures. American senators and congressmen therefore have voted against their party leadership with a frequency and a regularity that would be intolerable in a more ideological context. Party loyalty is a factor in the legislator's behaviour, but it is valued for its results rather than as an end in itself. Furthermore, consensus politics leaves much more room for the play of personalities in politics than when there is a strong ideological background to the division between the parties. Third, it created, in the American context, a positive need for outlets for extremist views, *outside* the party system, on the part of those minorities, either of the left or of the right, who felt that American society needed fundamental change, but could see no hope of obtaining it through the established parties. The moderating effect of the two-party system, appealing as it does to the vast majority of Americans, can drive dissident groups into extremism and violence to achieve their ends. Most important of all, however, the ideological consensus provided an umbrella that made possible a two-party system of the American kind. The parties have important electoral and organisational roles to play, but they are not in any sense tied to nicely wrapped-up packages of political policies. They can divide on organisational and electoral matters without their organisation being disrupted by differences on questions of policy. On policy questions, as we shall see, the divisions within the parties have often been as great as the divisions between them, but this was tolerable in the American context in a way that would be inconceivable in Europe. The ideological framework allowed the two-party system to evolve and to operate.

Liberalism and conservatism

In recent decades, however, this apparent absence of ideology has receded. To many Europeans, America has come to be a bulwark of conservatism in the world, a powerful force against revolutionary change. And yet America of all countries in the world has been the most liberal, if by that word we mean a readiness to accept change. As Daniel Bell has put it, America was perhaps the first large-scale society in the world to have change and innovation 'built into' its culture. American thought has always been dominated by the desire to *create* a new society, to *develop* its economy, to *move* to higher standards of living and a better life. It is this commitment to the very idea of change that has made American society so distinct from that of Europe, because there were no real conservatives in America to react against. For about 150 years it was even considered undesirable to be labelled as a conservative. However, after the Second World War the climate began to change. The word 'liberal' came to be used by those on the right as indicating anyone who was 'soft on communism', or was too concerned with asserting civil rights for blacks and other disadvantaged groups. The label 'conservative' came to be sought after. Clinton Rossiter in his *Conservatism in America*, published in 1955, wrote that 'After generations of exile from respectability, the word itself has been welcomed home with cheers by men who, a few short years ago, would sooner have been called arsonists than conservatives.' Rossiter argued for a 'New Conservatism' which 'would steer a middle course between ultra-conservatism and liberalism.' However, conservatism came to be claimed by a number of differing groups, sometimes with little in common.

There was the development of what we might label as 'traditional conservatism', which in the American context means an antipathy to 'big government', a desire to balance the budget, to lower taxes and to reduce the role of the federal government, in particular in relation to the welfare state; in foreign affairs traditional conservatives tended towards isolationism, the desire to withdraw from involvement in foreign entanglements, leading at the extreme to a policy of 'Fortress America'. Senator Barry Goldwater ran for the presidency on the Republican ticket in 1964 on the assumption that 'America is fundamentally a conservative nation', although some of his views sounded so radical that he won the support of the John Birch Society and the super-patriots. Yet when it came to a vote it seems that Goldwater's brand of conservatism was not popular, even in traditionally Republican areas. In rock-ribbed Maine, in 'conservative' New England, only 31.2 per cent of the voters chose Goldwater, and many of these voted out of loyalty to the Republican Party rather than positively for Goldwater's more ideological brand of politics.

However, Goldwater's defeat was not the end of the growth of conservative ideology in America, although it might have seemed so in 1964. Lyndon Johnson's overwhelming victory re-established for a time the Democratic Party's New Deal philosophy in the shape of Johnson's Great Society programmes, but the election of Richard Nixon four years later ushered in a new era of conservatism, which continued under Ford and Carter, and which was extended and deepened by President Reagan. Carter was a Democrat, but from the South and certainly not fully in the tradition of Roosevelt and Kennedy. In Reagan's 1980 campaign for the presidency the open avowal of conservative values became an electoral asset. The emphasis was placed upon cutting back government expenditure and bureaucracy, maintaining the social fabric through greater efforts at crime control, decentralising government by returning functions to the states, and encouraging individualism and self-help. As James Reichley has noted, 'American conservatism, as it was practised under Nixon and Ford, and as it continues to be practised today, surely qualifies as an expression of a distinct social ideology.' Newt Gingrich, the Republican Speaker of the House of Representatives, who took office in 1994, saw himself as the spearhead of the conservatives in opposition to President Clinton. Gingrich developed his 'Contract with America' which set out a programme of ten aims including tax cuts, a constitutional amendment requiring the budget to be in balance, and welfare reform.

Another strain of conservatism is 'libertarianism' – the belief that all government action is evil and should be kept to an absolute minimum. Thus groups on the extreme right of American politics, who are really not conservative at all, have appropriated the title of 'conservative'. A group such as the John Birch Society really consists of right-wing *radicals*, who wish to change society fundamentally, not maintain its present form, or wish to use methods in politics that are so far outside the American tradition as to be anything but conservative of American values. These groups have been described as the 'pseudo-conservatives' of the present age, falling outside the consensual framework of the American ideology, although claiming loudly to be the only true Americans. The John Birch Society defines its role as:

> Identifying the overall enemy as unrestrained government power in any of its forms, whether communism in Beijing or socialism in Washington, DC. In order to succeed in its goal of world merger under socialism, the conspiratorial apparatus must deceive us into accepting totalitarian controls here at home, such as national service, national industrial policy, a national police force, national health care, national curriculum and teacher certification, national food and vitamin labeling, even national control of parking lots (to force us into mass transit), to name a few new government power grabs on the horizon.

Militia groups, the extreme form of libertarianism, prepared to use armed force to fight the federal government, sprang up, particularly in the West.

The newest, and in some ways the most successful proponents of 'conservatism' are the neoconservatives, or neocons, who have come to play a significant role in the administration of President George W. Bush. They have developed a 'Neocon Persuasion' differing from both the traditional conservatives and the libertarians. Drawing on the inspiration of Leo Strauss, a philosopher at the University of Chicago, a group of academics and intellectuals, many of them Jewish, had become disillusioned with the direction being taken by America in both domestic and foreign policy. The 'godfather' of this persuasion was Irving Kristol, a former Trotskyite, who described how he saw the role of neoconservatives:

> The historical task and political purpose of neoconservatism would seem to be this: to convert the Republican Party, and American conservatism in general, against their respective wills, into a new kind of conservative politics suitable to governing a modern democracy.

For Kristol some of the tenets of the traditional conservatives and the libertarians were mistaken. Neocons should accept the reality of a strong state 'seeing it as natural, indeed inevitable', because 'people have always preferred strong government to weak government, although they certainly have no liking for anything that smacks of overly intrusive government.' Although sharing the traditional conservative preference for lower taxes, the neocons are quite happy to accept large budget deficits in order to stimulate the economy and to finance necessary government expenditure, particularly on the military. They are even prepared to acknowledge some debt to the ideas of Franklin D. Roosevelt, who was anathema to traditional conservatives. In the field of foreign affairs, Kristol asserts that there is no set of neoconservative beliefs concerning foreign policy, 'only a set of attitudes derived from historical experience.' Patriotism and antipathy to world government are at the heart of these attitudes, as is a rejection of isolationism. The overwhelming military superiority of the United States must be used to further the national interest and its 'ideological interests' as well as more material interests. 'The United States will always feel obliged to defend . . . a democratic nation under attack from non-democratic forces, external or internal . . . That is why we feel it necessary to defend Israel today, when its survival is threatened.' Their commitment to the spread of democracy throughout the world, by the use of military force if necessary, was one of the ideological underpinnings of the invasion of Iraq.

The neocons might have remained simply a small group of intellectuals, but they formed alliances with two other groups which transformed them into a formidable force in American politics. They gained the support of a number of prominent figures who had held office in previous Republican administrations and were destined to hold office in the administration of George W. Bush, the most important being the future Vice-President, Richard Cheney, Bush's Secretary of Defense, Donald Rumsfeld, and the Deputy Secretary of Defense, Paul Wolfowitz. In 1997, during the administration of President Clinton, all three of these signed a Statement of Principles issued by a pressure group, the Project for a New American Century, which completely embraced the neoconservative foreign and defence policies and foreshadowed the invasion of Iraq.

The other, perhaps rather unlikely, allies of the neoconservatives were the fundamentalist Christians, who were becoming increasingly aware of their potential political influence. Irving Kristol has described the reason for this as the neocons' sense of 'The steady decline in our democratic culture, sinking to new levels of vulgarity,' which laid the basis of a political alliance with religious conservatives. On their side many fundamentalist Christians saw a deeper reason to ally with the neocons. In the words of Pat Robertson, a fundamentalist minister and former contender for the Republican presidential nomination:

> Why is America in favor of Israel? Because we have a great history of biblical belief – Judeo-Christian – and we believe God gave the land to the descendents of Israel. It was not given to Palestine, it wasn't given to so-called Palestinians. It wasn't given to Saudis or the Syrians. It was given to the descendents of Abraham, Isaac and Jacob through Joshua. God said, 'You step on it and conquer it and I will give it to you.' We are looking at a time dating back 3,000 years. This has been the land of Israel. And it belongs to them. And God is not going to let anybody take it away from them.

This statement reflects the Christian fundamentalist reading of the Bible, that the establishment of a Jewish state is a fulfilment of prophecy and a step toward the second coming of Jesus Christ and the apocalypse. This alliance between fundamentalist Christians, neoconservatives, Bush Republicans and supporters of Israel was to provide the basis for American foreign policy at the beginning of the twenty-first century, and it was also to give American politics, for a time at least, a new and more intense ideological and partisan character.

Why two parties?

So far we have described American politics as four national parties or wings floating upon a potentially disruptive multi-party system at the state and local level. The disintegrating factors are very evident, but how then do we account for the fact that there are still essentially only two parties, Republicans and Democrats? Why is it still meaningful to talk in some sense of an American two-party system? Part of the answer to this question lies in the role of ideology in the American political system, but undoubtedly institutional considerations are also very important. From a historical and constitutional point of view, the greatest force towards the creation and maintenance of the two-party system would seem to be the existence of the office of the presidency, and the mode of election to it. This is the only truly 'national' office to be fought for; it is the focal point of all national political life. The simple, obvious fact about the office of president is that only one person can fill it. The Senate or the House of Representatives could dissolve into a multitude of factional groups, but only one person can occupy the president's chair in the White House.

This simple fact immediately tends to polarise the political spectrum. The method of election prescribed by the Constitution, and the conventions that have grown up around it, powerfully reinforce this polarising influence of the presidency. As we shall see later, the campaign manager of a presidential aspirant has to think in terms of gaining an *absolute* majority of votes in the Electoral College, which in law chooses the president; a simple majority of Electoral College votes will not do. The only successful strategy for the capture of the presidency is to create a great coalition behind one candidate, and the only potentially successful riposte is the creation of a second similar coalition. To create or encourage splinter groups is to lose all hope of controlling this vital position. The ability of a party to master the technique of coalition-building is the measure of its ability to command the presidency. Once in that position, the advantage that it has gained is to a considerable extent self-perpetuating. Thus, much of American political history is the history of long periods of domination of the presidency by one party, with lasting changes of control occurring only in circumstances that bring about a revolutionary change in the assumptions upon which the coalition was built. The 'swing of the pendulum' in American presidential politics is, therefore, generally a long, slow, ponderous swing.

This is an explanation of two-party politics at the presidential level, but not at the congressional level. In a sense, as we shall see when we come to look at congressional politics, the two-party system in Congress is often more apparent than real. Congress tends to dissolve into voting blocs in which party allegiance is a factor, but only one among many. Nevertheless, Congressmen and Senators do divide into Democrats and Republicans. One contributory factor, no doubt, is the well-known tendency of single-member simple majority electoral systems of the Anglo-American variety to discourage the election of third-party candidates. However, although this system discourages minor parties in each separate constituency, it does not necessarily discourage the emergence of three or more parties at the national level, particularly where there are strong regional forces at work, as there are in the United States. The electoral system would not of itself prevent the emergence of a Southern States' Rights party, a party representing Western farmers, an urban workers' party of the North and East, and so on. Because America does not have a system of responsible parliamentary government on the English model, the impulse to vote only for a candidate of a party that seems likely to be able to form a majority in Congress does not have the same force as it does in parliamentary systems.

Within Congress, however, there are organisational reasons for the maintenance of two parties: in particular, the organisation of the committees of Congress, and the desire to control the chairmanships of committees and the office of Speaker. Perhaps the most important factor tending to maintain two and only two parties in Congress is the very existence of the presidency, and the consequent relationships that have developed between presidential and congressional politics. We shall look later at the ways in which both president

and Congress attempt to influence the behaviour of the other; these links between the two institutional structures are promoted by the two-party system
and help in turn to prevent the submerged multi-party system from becoming an open one.

The explanation of the persistence of the two-party system at state and
local level is rather more difficult. For a large part of American history, in
many parts of the country the two-party system did not really exist at all at
this level. In those states where there was no real two-party competition,
the battle between the parties was replaced by intra-party factionalism. The
labels 'Democrat' and 'Republican' were adopted for historical or purely expedient reasons rather than as a true commitment to a particular political
party. In so far as two-party politics did operate in the states, however, the
prevalence of the Republican–Democratic division would seem to be the result of a projection downwards of the presidential and congressional battles.
The distribution of patronage – the spoils of office – from the presidency
downward was, in the past at least, a powerful force for maintaining the links
between party organisations at the various levels. Thus the most powerful institutional mechanism for the purposes of maintaining the coherence of the
American 'two-party' system is the way in which politics revolves around the
presidency, permeating the whole structure to provide the integrating forces
that alone prevent the disruption of the parties into many fragments. This
is not to suggest that political power simply flows downwards in the United
States – far from it! Rather, it is to point to the *interdependence* of the various
levels of political activity. And this is a true interdependence, for the politics
of the presidency are affected by developments in state and local politics just
as much as they are affected by what happens in Washington. Indeed, the interrelationships between federal, state and local politics in the United States
are much more genuine and alive than the connection between national
and local politics in a more highly centralised country like Great Britain. In
Britain national politics has an autonomy of its own, operating seemingly
in a sphere almost unconnected with what happens at the lower levels. It
would be a foolish Senator or Congressman, or indeed a foolish president,
who acted upon such an assumption in America.

Grass roots democracy

It is difficult to generalise about the politics of the states, cities and counties of America because they vary so much, both in formal structure and in
political practice; but, given their importance for the way in which decisions
are taken at higher levels, it is necessary to explore this diversity. It is often
assumed that 'democracy' is more characteristic of small, well-integrated societies than of large complex ones. As society develops, the argument goes,
the division of labour and the increasing technicality of the decisions to be
made lead inevitably to elitist rule, or at the very least to a modern group
pluralism that may be far removed from the ideals of majority rule and direct
participation associated with the Greek origins of democracy. It may be true,

from the point of view of the machinery of government, that direct participation is conceivable in small societies, but not in large ones. It does not necessarily follow, however, either that a small society will be democratic or that, if the wishes of the majority prevail, *social* equality and *social* democracy will follow on from political equality. Sometimes small communities are much more intolerant of deviant or eccentric behaviour than large ones. Thus we have to tread warily when relating generalisations about the nature and extent of 'democracy' to the size of a community, or even simply to the degree of majority rule in a community.

However, the closeness of local government to the people provides the *opportunity*, at least, of greater participation, and from this point of view the most democratic political institutions in America are the New England towns. When the first settlers landed in New England they divided up their new territory into 'towns'. A map of 1755 shows a projected line of these towns to be established in the Province of New Hampshire as a frontier against the native Americans. However, the towns were not urban areas. They were large tracts of virgin territory, at the centre of which a village or hamlet would be built. The whole area of New England was eventually divided up in this way, and the towns still exist as the basic unit of government in the New England states and in the state of New York. The system of government adopted for these towns was extremely democratic in form, all the major business being conducted in a town meeting at which all the citizens attended and voted. They might have voted in the seventeenth century for measures that we to-day would consider harsh and unjust, but that was the spirit of the age.

A few New England towns in rural areas still operate this system of direct democracy. In western Massachusetts, for example, one may find towns with a population of less than a thousand people still running their local affairs at an annual town meeting that fixes tax rates, sets the budget for the coming year, and elects the town officers – the selectmen, the constable, the fire chief and others. The town meeting may be an all-day affair, with the citizens coming and going, listening to the discussion, casting their votes and enjoying the New England dishes prepared by the townsfolk. The views of the selectmen who carry out the town's decisions and prepare the budget are listened to with respect, but they are not always accepted. The arguments about whether or not to construct a new bridge, or about the amount of salt and grit to be used on the roads in winter, end in a vote that the citizens may well soon regret, but at least they will have decided it themselves. However, direct democracy has its disadvantages and limitations. Decisions on technical matters may be swayed by the eloquence of the ill-informed, and the town's votes may leave the programme presented by the selectmen in disarray. Such direct democracy is possible, however, only in the small rural towns. With growth, and with the increasing complexity of government business, many towns have been forced to adopt a representative town meeting, and to supplement the activities of part-time selectmen with the services of a professional town manager.

The New England town is an interesting institution, but throughout the United States it is the counties and the cities that are the major providers of local government services and the focus of local political organisation. Townships exist in some areas, but they have few functions and little power. There are over 3,000 counties in the United States. The county provides local services, such as the construction and maintenance of highways and bridges, and administers welfare services which are financed by the federal, state and local governments. A county board of supervisors or commissioners is elected to oversee the county's affairs, but there may be quite a large number of other elected officials or boards concerned with one or other of the county's services, in particular the sheriff and the district, or county, attorney. This pattern of counties covers the whole of the United States with the exception of Alaska, Connecticut and Rhode Island, but the counties vary enormously in size and importance. Loving County in west Texas has a population of 71; other counties include large urban areas, or great cities, or parts of cities. Thus Cook County, Illinois, contains the city of Chicago, and Los Angeles County, California, has a population of over 10 million people.

Superimposed upon this pattern of counties, towns and townships is the vast fabric of cities spreading across the continent. Municipal corporations with their charters were established in the colonies along English lines from the beginning. The enormous growth of urbanisation means that over 80 per cent of the total population now live in the cities. The status and power of the governments that serve these urban areas are so varied that it is very difficult to formulate generalisations about them. At one extreme is the small city of a few thousands, and at the other the City of New York with a population of over 8 million. Most cities have a city council of up to thirty or so members, and a directly elected mayor. Senior officials of the city may also be directly elected, and the relative power of council and mayor varies greatly.

The fragmentation of political organisations and of decision-making is most evident in the government of the great metropolitan areas, which have emerged as the dominant pattern of life in modern America. These great conglomerations of urban development, with populations running into several millions, may extend across state boundaries and encompass a number of cities as well as numerous other semi-autonomous local government units. The New York metropolitan area bridges three states – New York, New Jersey and Connecticut – engulfing the cities of New York, Jersey City and Newark and many hundreds of other governmental units. Whereas the economic and social problems of the metropolis are closely interrelated throughout the whole area, political organisation is decentralised along historical boundaries that seem to have little relevance to modern problems.

The structure of the parties

The different patterns of political behaviour that we found in the American electorate, if they are truly reflective of deeply significant attitudes, must be reflected in, and work through, the political structures that alone can reconcile these potentially conflicting forces. The political structures of the United States are likely therefore to be as complex as the diversity of American political attitudes suggests. We find in fact that the party system, the electoral system and the complex of interest groups – the three basic structures through which political attitudes are transmitted to the decision-making institutions of government – reflect these different styles of political thought and behaviour. Thus the party system is expressive of the sectional, regional characteristics of the American polity to a very high degree. At the same time, the parties can reflect class and pluralistic interests because of the way in which the electoral system enables strongly marked regional groupings, such as the urban areas of the East or the farmers of the Mid-West, to gain representation. The electoral system, through the complex machinery of American elections, allows the individualistic elements in American politics full expression, particularly through the system of primary elections. Finally, the interest group structure is the vehicle par excellence for the articulation of group demands, including those with a marked sectional or class bias.

American government is divided government, and the fragmented structure of the political parties reflects this fact, but the parties must also transcend these divisions for certain purposes, and above all for the purpose of electing the president. The electoral machinery and party organisation differ from state to state, from county to county and from city to city. In some areas political organisations have been highly developed and efficient. Thus in Michigan the political activity of the automobile workers' union (the United Auto Workers) resulted in what John H. Fenton has described as 'issue-oriented' politics. As a consequence, politics became more ideological, and voting behaviour in the legislature was more disciplined than in other states. The statement of political principles made by Michigan's Democratic Governor Jennifer Granholm in 2006 could *almost* be the manifesto of New Labour in Britain:

> I'm a proud Democrat because our party has the right economic plan and the right priorities for Michigan. We fight for jobs, because a good job is the foundation of a good life. We fight for education, because we believe every child should have the opportunity to succeed. We fight for health care, because we know there are too many people in our state who don't have it and can't afford it. We fight to preserve our middle class way of life, because it's a way of life our families have worked so hard to build. We're a party with a plan and we're putting it to work for our families.

At the other extreme, party organisation may be almost non-existent as a continuing factor in the political process. At each election the candidates in such areas create their own organisations, gathering around them friends and supporters to conduct their campaigns. Indeed, this creation of campaign organisations on an ad hoc basis to fight elections is by no means confined to the local level. Presidential candidates do not depend entirely on the formal party machinery to conduct their campaigns. They gather round themselves groups of men and women dedicated to their support who will organise the fight from the primary stage to the general election. The nature of the primary system necessitates this strategy. In 2004 initially there were ten candidates vying for the Democratic presidential nomination. Each of these had to create a team of helpers and advisers to plan and prosecute their primary campaigns, often composed to a considerable extent of supporters from their home states. Inevitably the candidate who secures the nomination will take some of these supporters on to the general election campaign. The personnel are different because a candidate wants his own supporters to run his campaign, and the style of the campaign is different because it reflects the personality of the candidate and of those who advise him.

American political battles cannot simply be viewed as contests between two rival organisations representing the views of fairly cohesive sections of the electorate. The 'official' party machinery is often involved in bitter disputes with rival factions in the party, and it is by no means a foregone conclusion that the official party organisation will be successful in promoting its own candidates for office. More and more, the practice of 'unofficial' groups taking part in elections has grown up. 'Spontaneous' citizens' groups, or groups of doctors or lawyers, or ethnic interest groups, may set up campaign headquarters and work, with a greater or lesser degree of coordination with the official party, in support of the candidate they favour.

Thus much of the real stuff of American politics is not the battle *between* party organisations, but the battle over who shall take control of the party. This is true from the presidency downwards. The early stages of a presidential election are occupied with the conflict between rival candidates for their party's nomination. Every contender for the office of president has first to build a power base in state politics, either as senator or governor, and then to make a bid to take over the national party organisation in one way or another. Each candidate will start off with a group of dedicated workers, usually drawn largely from their home state. If successful in gaining the nomination as the party's presidential candidate, these people will probably be among the leading organisers of the campaign at the national level and, if successful in getting their candidate elected as president, they may end up as part of the new administration in the White House.

National politics and state politics are inextricably interwoven, but the fragmentation of party organisation and power goes much further down the line. It is difficult to build a cohesive party organisation even at state level. The diffusion of authority that the Founding Fathers sought in the United States Constitution is taken to almost ridiculous lengths in the states. Not only do state constitutions enshrine the separation of powers and checks and balances, with an elected governor faced with two legislative assemblies. The electorate may intervene in the policy-making process through the medium of the initiative, the referendum or the recall. Major state officials, such as secretary of state, attorney general, treasurer, auditor and others, are usually subject to election. These officials may exercise statutory powers weakening the position of the governor. Furthermore, they may not be members of the same political party. Thus a Democratic governor may be faced with a Republican lieutenant governor and secretary of state, a Democratic treasurer and auditor, and a Republican attorney general. In many states officials such as the secretary of agriculture or the superintendent of public instruction may also be elected. A wide variety of offices at county and other levels of government are elective – sheriff, superintendent of schools, county surveyor, coroner, constable or fire chief – although in the larger cities these posts may be appointive offices. All these elected offices are, of course, in addition to the elected positions of state Senator or Representative, mayor, councilman, or county commissioner. Even the judiciary is elective, in whole or in part, in thirty-four states.

There is, therefore, a plethora of elective offices, legislative, administrative and judicial, many of them with their own special powers, and able to resist direction or domination from above. This combination of direct election and checks and balances provides a political system of such complexity that few of those involved in it, either as electors or officials, can hope fully to grasp its implications, or to know how to work it. It is this complexity that gave rise to the 'politocrats' or political 'bosses' whose ability to work the machinery of government, usually by erecting a system of corruption and influence, made them enormously powerful. The boss could create a political 'machine' based upon the provision of rewards to supporters and party workers in return for their unquestioning allegiance. The enormous numbers of poor and illiterate immigrants at the beginning of the twentieth century provided a clientele that needed services in the form of help with finding jobs, relief when sick or unemployed, or help with legal problems, and who were prepared to give their support in the form of votes to whoever provided these services. This unquestioning electoral support gave the political machine the ability to dominate the government of a county or city, and to use its financial resources to its own ends. Inevitably, such an operation involved corruption and intimidation, and often also connections between the machine and organised crime. The bosses themselves might not even hold elective office but directed affairs from behind the scenes through their control over the party machine. Thus a system that was intended to ensure the responsibility of government to the people actually resulted in the exercise of power in a quite irresponsible way. Although county and city bosses at the beginning of the twentieth century could be all-powerful in their own bailiwick, it was a political system that was very difficult to extend to encompass the politics of a whole state. A few, notably Huey Long of Louisiana, became state bosses, but generally the system added to, rather than detracted from, the decentralised character of American politics. Really cohesive power and organisation was to be found at the county level, but rarely above that level.

The circumstances that gave rise to the machines and their bosses have altered, and the mainstay of their power has vanished. Many of the former immigrants, their children and their grandchildren are citizens who understand their rights. More important, the social security programmes of the federal government have removed much of the demand for relief services upon which machine politics was based. The machines have lost their power, and the great bosses of the past no longer dominate. But the decline of the boss and of the machine has not been paralleled by the rise of any other political organisation that could give cohesion to politics. The remnants of the machines, often locked in battle with pressure groups, still provide the political structure of many cities and counties. The philosophy of the machine, which was to treat politics as a business – the business of getting votes and winning elections, as Banfield and Wilson put it – still persists. The old machine was really non-partisan, although it might have been nominally Republican or Democratic, and this non-partisan, non-ideological approach is still typical of some city governments. The spoils of office are still considerable and attractive. Patronage is important, with many jobs to be distributed and contracts worth millions to be awarded for highway construction, parking facilities and public buildings. The line between 'honest graft' and 'dishonest graft' is often difficult to draw. Thus, although the problems facing American governments are quite staggering in their complexity and difficulty, and day-to-day decisions are taken that deeply affect the lives and conditions of their citizens, there is often a strange hiatus between the working of politics and the people most closely affected by it.

Party organisation

The 'informal' elements of the American party structure may well be, in practice, the most important, but there is a formal structure of organisations rising up from the local level to the national. This formal party organisation consists of a pyramid of committees starting at the base with ward, precinct, town and township committees, and going up through city and county committees, to state committees, and then to the National Party Committee. Within each state there is great variation in the way in which these committees are constituted. Broadly speaking, the practice is for the lowest level of committees to be elected by the party's supporters, and for the higher levels to be selected from the membership of these lower levels, although direct election may also be used for selection further up the scale. The National Committee is responsible for conducting the party's presidential election campaign and for organising the national convention of the party, but there are also congressional and senatorial campaign committees, emphasising the fact that presidential and congressional politics are distinct.

The National Committees are federal in composition. The Republican National Committee consists of one national committeeman and one national committeewoman from each state together with each state Republican party chairman and representatives of the District of Columbia and a number of

American possessions such as Puerto Rico and the Virgin Islands. This results in a large gathering but the Democratic National Committee is much larger still, reflecting the fact that in the 1970s the Democrats decided to ensure that the various groups that made up the party, particularly women, young people and ethnic minorities, should be represented both in the National Committee and in the National Convention. The Constitution of the Democratic Party provides that, in addition to 'the chairperson and the highest ranking officer of the opposite sex of each recognized State Democratic Party', a further 200 members are elected by state parties, apportioned according to a formula taking into account each state's population. Representatives of Democratic congressional leaders, state governors, mayors and other Democratic local and state officials, the National Federation of Democratic Women and Young Democrats are also included. The size of the National Committees makes them ineffective for conducting electoral campaigns, the real responsibility falling upon the party's National Chairman and the staff. The National Chairman is formally elected by the National Committee, but is in practice the nominee of the party's presidential candidate.

Thus the really important part of the national party machinery, except for the nominating conventions, is the National Chairman and the staff, which is strongly augmented in an election year. The National Chairman is there to promote the election of the party's presidential candidate, but after the election is over the chairman of the defeated party may remain in office until the next convention four years later, although the person to whom he or she was committed is no longer even the titular head of the party. A defeated presidential candidate has no automatic claim to the leadership of the party, and usually the defeated party goes virtually leaderless through the lean years between elections. Once the election is over, the staff of the National Committees is cut back to a minimum and the national party has little to do until the next presidential election. Even in the mid-term election years, when congressional elections are taking place, the National Committee is largely dormant. Senators and Congressmen have separate campaign committees and resent attempts by the National Chairman to dictate policy or to interfere in congressional affairs.

Party organisation consists, therefore, of a 'pyramid' of committees, but this does not in any way imply that the lower levels of the pyramid are subject to control or direction by the levels above them. In a highly organised city party, the city leaders may be in a position to appoint and replace ward leaders at will, and some county chairmen still exercise a power reminiscent of the old-time bosses. But the state chairman is not in a position to issue orders to city and county leaders. Still less can the National Committee give directions to state chairmen or committees; it can only work towards gaining their cooperation. The sanctions that are available to central party committees in more highly centralised countries have no place in American national politics. The ideological links between party members are weaker than in European political parties, so that mere appeals to party allegiance will have little impact. The selection of party candidates at state and local level is completely outside the control of national party leaders. Even President Franklin D. Roosevelt at the height of his popularity with the electorate could not influence his party to the point of obtaining the removal or defeat of candidates of whom he disapproved. The patronage power is perhaps the only real weapon left to national leaders to try to obtain the cooperation of local political leaders. However, the growth of civil service requirements at the federal level has greatly reduced the number of jobs to be distributed, and most of these are handed out at the beginning of the president's term of office.

Thus the power of national party leaders, including the power of the president over his own party, is indeed limited. The separation of powers and the structure of the federal system destroy the basis of any attempt by party leaders to centralise authority in a few hands. The president cannot discipline Congress by dissolving it if it displeases him, nor can he use his position as leader of the party to undermine the power of Congressmen or Senators in their constituencies. The powers and influence of the president will vary according to a number of different factors, to be discussed in Chapter 7, but these must be used in ways very different from that of a British prime minister. Presidential politics is a very special game with rules all of its own. National party organisation 'floats' upon the shifting sands of state and local politics. The national parties are great coalitions of state and local organisations, and as such they tend to change with the tides of events rather than attempting to direct them.

Extremism and violence

The diversity of the origins and interests of Americans has, over the whole course of their history, given rise to severe tensions within their society. The insistence upon conformity to the norms of the American ideology was one means of controlling the potential conflicts in such a society, but it has also had the result of driving those with more intense feelings into using extra-constitutional channels to achieve their aims. Given the nature of the American experience, it is not surprising that many of the more extreme movements have been generated by the concern of certain groups to assert an equality of status with other Americans or to insist upon their patriotism or 'Americanness'. Other extremist movements have represented an inability to cope with the complexity of the modern world: a desire to opt out of foreign involvement or to find simple, direct solutions for the enormously complex problems which face the United States. Ethnic politics provides endless possibilities for waves of extremism to sweep over certain elements in the population. Catholics, Jews and blacks have all been the subject of attack by extremists who have been ready to make use of violence to give expression to their hatred and fear of what they considered to be alien elements in the community. Yet the groups that have themselves been the subject of violent attack may turn to this very same political weapon as a means of asserting themselves in the community. Thus in the 1850s Catholics and immigrants came under attack by the Know Nothing, or American, Party, which was able to achieve 25 per cent of the vote in the presidential election of 1856. The Ku Klux Klan, although notorious for its efforts on behalf of white supremacy, was also actively anti-Catholic. By the 1930s, however, many Catholics in their turn were giving strong support to the anti-Semitic movement led by Father Charles Coughlin, which ended up with the expression of outright support for Hitler. By the 1950s the emphasis had changed again and, although the attacks upon communism by Senator Joseph McCarthy drew strong support from Irish and Italian Catholics, McCarthy avoided attacking Jews and other ethnic minorities.

The greatest source of ethnic conflict in the 1960s was of course the battle for equality by blacks, and the resultant explosions of violence in Northern cities as well as in the Southern states. The problem of the status of the black community is one that the normal political machinery failed to solve. It represents a classic example of the way in which the American political machinery can be used to prevent a solution from emerging, so that the problem becomes progressively more and more difficult, until only a violent resolution seems open to the group that feels its demands are not being registered through the normal channels. The movement for 'black power' represented a demand for action to short-circuit the ponderous and complicated constitutional system with all its built-in checks and balances. In the Southern states the Ku Klux Klan were blamed for murders, beatings, bombings and church burnings, and Klan members were put on trial for the murder of blacks and civil rights workers. As a natural reaction blacks in Southern states formed themselves into armed organisations to defend themselves. The Deacons for Defence and Justice was formed in Louisiana and spread into Mississippi and other Southern states to give blacks the protection that they felt they could not depend upon from the normal law enforcement agencies. More recently the extensive Latino immigration, particularly in California, has exacerbated racial tensions between blacks and Latinos. Los Angeles County has an estimated one thousand gangs, mostly Mexican, and gang warfare makes the area one of the most dangerous in the United States.

Race riots have long been a feature of the fringes of the American political process. In the early years of the twentieth century these were mainly attacks by whites on the black community, as in 1906 in Atlanta and in Chicago in 1919. However, after the Second World War the increasing frustration of blacks with their depressed economic and social position led to a series of riots. In 1964 there were outbreaks in Harlem, Chicago and Philadelphia. In 1965 five days of violence in Watts, a district of Los Angeles, followed allegations of police brutality against blacks. During the course of the riots, there were thirty-four deaths, 1,000 injuries and 4,000 arrests. They were brought to an end only when the governor of California brought in 20,000 soldiers of the National Guard to restore order. 1967 saw extensive violence in many cities throughout the United States. In 1992 the beating of a black man, Rodney King, by the Los Angeles police, and the subsequent acquittal of the officers charged with the assault, led to widespread rioting in which thirty-eight people were killed. Again the National Guard was called out and the federal government intervened, calling in marine units to maintain order.

Other manifestations of extremism have little to do with ethnic problems, on the surface at least. The John Birch Society, the Minutemen and the fundamentalist movements of the Reverend Dr Schwartz and the Reverend Billy Hargis found their targets in the communist influences that they saw everywhere in American public life. The Minutemen were a group formed to train for armed guerrilla warfare against communism; right-wing militia movements are deeply opposed to the federal government, and are prepared to use armed force against it. The bombing in 1995 of the Federal Building in Oklahoma City, killing 168 people, was attributed to members of the militia.

The John Birch Society advocated the use of communist tactics to fight the agents of communism whom they believed to have taken over government, churches, schools, universities and business corporations alike. Robert Welch, the founder of the John Birch Society, described President Eisenhower as 'a dedicated, conscious agent of the communist conspiracy', and named the President's brother Milton as his superior in the Party, from whom he took his orders. The Society also believed that John F. Kennedy fed the communist point of view to the American public. In 2005, the President of the John Birch Society, John F. McManus, identified the attempts of the Bush administration to establish the Free Trade Area of the Americas (FTAA) as part of a conspiracy to undermine American national sovereignty dating back to the eighteenth century.

However, extremism is not a right-wing monopoly. The later years of the Vietnam War saw the rise of militant left-wing movements, particularly among students. The New Left sprouted its crop of organisations demanding radical changes in the structure of American society, and in the political system, geared as it is to producing compromise solutions, or to shelving difficult problems for which no easy compromise solution is possible. The Black Liberation Front, the Young Socialist Alliance, the W.E.B. Dubois Clubs and the Progressive Labor Movement were some of the movements that focused discontent over racial discrimination, and anger over the American involvement in Vietnam, into a general attack on the values of American society. The ending of the Vietnam War seemed for a time at least, to take the steam out of the protest movement and to have returned the United States to a more 'normal' political atmosphere.

Violence as a political weapon is no newcomer or stranger to the American scene. Whether in the hands of the white supremacist, the advocate of black power, the anti-Castro guerrilla or the right-wing libertarian, it seems a simple direct solution to intolerably complex problems, in an intolerably complex system of government. America, with its traditions of frontier life, with its insistence upon the right of the individual to bear arms in his own defence, is a society in which violence has always simmered below the surface, ready to break out when a particularly difficult problem resisted solution through the normal channels. Four American presidents have been assassinated, and a number of unsuccessful attempts have been made. The assassinations of President Kennedy and of his brother Bobby, the killing of Martin Luther King and the attempted assassination of President Reagan are examples of a long series of political acts of violence in the United States. There have been examples also of 'official violence', such as the assault in 1993 by the FBI on the compound near Waco, Texas, occupied by a religious sect, the Branch Davidians, in which over 70 men, women and children died, although there is controversy about how many were killed by government action and how many committed suicide. Nevertheless, too much emphasis should not be placed upon these aspects of the political situation, although of course it is these that hit the newspaper headlines. In a sense it is the extraordinary success of the American political system in solving the vast majority of its problems that highlights the extremism generated by its failures. The fact that the system has worked, and continues to work, is a matter for wonder when the magnitude of the problems it has faced is appreciated.

The clash on issues

The major American political parties, Republicans and Democrats, are more ideologically differentiated at the congressional and presidential levels than at the level of the electorate. As we have seen, ideology is important in American politics, but during most of their history it was not the distinguishing factor between the major parties; rather, it distinguished them from the more peripheral political organisations. Nevertheless, this does not mean that Democrats and Republicans were as indistinguishable as Tweedledum and Tweedledee, or that American politics has been devoid of vital and significant issues. The popular images of the two parties differ quite considerably. The Democratic Party is often described as the party of the working man, whereas the Republicans are seen as the party of big business, more favourable to the rich than to the poor. This characterisation of the parties is largely fashioned by their policies since 1932, by the New Deal/Fair Deal/Great Society complex of ideas which the Democrats fostered and which Republicans have been lukewarm about, or have strongly opposed. In particular, the Republicans have in general been opposed to expanding the role of government, especially the federal government, in economic and social matters, whereas the Democrats have been in favour of more positive government action to promote social welfare and to regulate business activity. Nevertheless, in all occupational groups large numbers of Americans see no real differences between the two major parties.

Thus, although the parties tend to take different stances on different issues, there is no real ideological coherence in the bundle of issues that one party supports and the other opposes. Furthermore, neither party is ever wholly united against the other. Always there are members of one party who, on a particular issue, feel more in sympathy with the majority view in the opposing party. The intra-party divisions can be just as deep and just as bitter as the inter-party divisions. And there are issues enough to be bitter about, for the problems facing the United States, in domestic and in foreign affairs, are real enough. Civil rights for ethnic minorities, racial integration, the war on poverty, the provision of health care, the role of the federal government in education, the problems of urban renewal, the attitude of the United States towards Latin America, the 'War on Terror', the invasion of Iraq; these are just a few of the tortuously complex problems that have faced policy-makers in recent years. So the content of American politics is by no means dull or uneventful. The politics of consensus does not result in a shortage of issues. Furthermore, the role of government in American life is much greater than many people outside the United States imagine. The view of the United States as an extreme laissez-faire capitalist society is very far from the truth. Regulation of labour and industry, and government intervention in economic life, have in many respects gone much further than in European countries. Federal government expenditure on social welfare constitutes approximately 10 per cent of the national income; the demand for government action to solve social problems has been a characteristic of American society through-out its history. America is a much-governed country, for regulatory activities and welfare services are the active concern of three levels of government, in part competing with each other, in part cooperating.

The explanation of the two-party system lies therefore in the complex interrelationships between the constitutional structure, party organisa-tion, ideology and the issues that face American politicians. The Constitu-tion provides a stable framework within which political forces can form and re-form over individual issues and create coalitions, some relatively stable, others quite transient. The Constitution does not demand of president and Congress a degree of unified, coherent action that they probably could not sustain in view of the latent multi-party tendencies in the political system. The presidency does, however, provide an institutional focus for politics that tends to polarise the political system around two great party organisations. The basic ideological consensus allows this organisational tendency towards two parties to evolve without its being disrupted by strong commitments to particular principles or programmes. It enables the two major parties to de-velop a different emphasis towards the role of government in society without coming into a head-on collision, and it makes it possible for each issue to be considered almost in isolation and a judgement to be made in pragmatic terms. The advantages of this system in a diverse society like the United States are obvious, for it damps down potentially serious divisive tendencies; but there are, of course, disadvantages as well. It makes it virtually impos-sible to achieve a planned, coherent set of policies to deal with related prob-lems, for the criteria applied to the solution of each problem are as diverse as American society itself. The structure of federalism makes for an added complication, in that effective collaboration between federal, state and local governments is difficult to achieve, as the failure to cope with Hurricane Katrina demonstrates. This makes for the application of governmental power in a spasmodic and uncoordinated fashion. In one sense this is what the Founding Fathers wished to achieve in 1787, but they could hardly have foreseen the sort of problems that would face America in the twenty-first century.

Faced with this situation, many observers have proposed reforms that, they hope, would lead to a political party system more like that to be found in Britain. Such proposals are, however, filled with danger for the American political system. How far would a realignment of the parties into a more 'European' left–right division help the situation? The assumption behind this argument is that the Republican Party could absorb the right-wing elements across the nation, that the Democratic Party would offer a more attractive haven for the dissident left, and that a more 'responsible' political system would emerge, oriented towards the solution of particular issues by advocating and carrying through clear policy mandates. The major objections to this line of argument are: first, that it would require a considerable change of public opinion and of congressional attitudes to bring it about; and, second, that it might result not so much in healthy competition between the parties as in a desperate and potentially disastrous fight for existence. The moderating influence of the traditional parties would be lost, and the attempt to define two political camps more clearly could lead to intense political bitterness and frustration.

The pivotal role of the South

The Southern states, particularly the eleven states that seceded and formed the Confederacy during the Civil War, have always had a distinctive political style and culture that set them off from the rest of the United States. In recent decades, however, they have come to play a vitally important role in the outcome of presidential elections, and have transformed the working of the political system by the influence they exercise in the Republican Party in Congress.

The economy of the South was, until 1865, built upon the 'peculiar institution' – slavery – and this penetrated the whole society and its politics. The abolition of slavery in 1865 was followed by the passage of the Fourteenth Amendment in 1868, which guaranteed citizenship to the emancipated slaves, and by the Fifteenth Amendment in 1870, which asserted that the right to vote 'shall not be denied or abridged by the United States or by any State on account of race, color, or previous condition of servitude'. The former slaveholders, and indeed the whole of the white population of the Southern states, faced a political dilemma; would the newly freed slaves, who formed a large part of the population in a number of states, be allowed to exercise political power through the franchise and therefore be able to change the whole structure of Southern society? The reaction of the white community was to create a political system that would deny the exercise of political power to the black population of the South. This was achieved through the establishment of the Democratic Party as the only effective political organisation in these states, an organisation that would dominate the governments of those states, and which would ensure the election of Senators and Representatives to the federal government in Washington who would defend the South from attack.

Before the Civil War the Democratic Party had had both a southern wing and a northern wing, but during the war the North, eventually to be victorious, was led by Abraham Lincoln, the Republican President. After the end of the war, therefore, in the defeated South no Republican would be acceptable to the white population, although in the 'reconstruction' period after the Civil War Republicans were elected as a result of the regime that was imposed on the South by the North. The Republicans became the dominant party in the North, and inevitably the white South turned to the Democrats to oppose the regime in Washington, which was seen as oppressive and determined to destroy all that Southern whites held dear. Thus a sectional party system was established; the Republicans dominated the North, but in the states of the Old Confederacy the Democratic Party effectively established one-party systems, where Republicans had little chance of election and consequently rarely attempted to contest elections. Elective offices at local, state and federal levels were filled by the nominees of the Democratic Party bosses, and the elections became merely a rubber stamp, confirming these choices. Politics became an inter-factional battle within the Democratic Party, rather than a battle *between* political parties. Take the representation of the South in the Senate of the United States; from the 1870s in seven states of the Deep South only Democrats were elected to the Senate until the 1950s and 1960s, and in Arkansas no Republican has been elected to the Senate since 1877. The first post-reconstruction Republican to be elected from Georgia was in 1993. The Democrat-dominated legislatures in the Southern states passed laws enforcing racial segregation in education, transport and other areas of society, and also limited the participation of black citizens in the political process through laws imposing literacy requirements and other restrictions on registering for the vote.

The grip of the Democratic Party on Southern politics began to change after the Second World War. The role of black soldiers during the war and the sense that the United States was operating a social system which was indefensible in the second half of the twentieth century led to the growth of a civil rights movement with the aim of removing the discrimination against black Americans. In 1948, campaigning for election, President Harry Truman ran on a civil rights platform, which was anathema to Southern whites. When John F. Kennedy ran for the presidency in 1960 on a civil rights platform and his successor Lyndon Johnson presided over the passage of the Civil Rights Act and the Voting Rights Act, the traditional, automatic support for the

Democrats in the South began to erode. It had become clear that the Democratic Party at the national level had aims very different from its Southern wing. However, the problem that faced Southern whites, and still does, is that if politics in a state, such as Mississippi, where blacks make up over 36 per cent of the population, moves from the dominance of one party to a competitive two-party system, the black population will hold the balance of power and be able to demand concessions in exchange for throwing its support to one party or the other.

The strategy adopted by Southern whites in this situation was 'presidential Republicanism'. The American electoral system allows voters to 'split the ticket', that is to vote for the candidate of one party for one office, such as president, and to vote for candidates of other parties for other offices, such as Senator, Representative, Governor and so forth. Southerners could continue to vote solidly for Democrats for Senator and Representative, and at the same time vote for the Republican candidate for the presidency, and they did so in increasing numbers. The phenomenon grew of Democratic presidents whose most determined opponents were Democratic Senators and Representatives from the Southern states. In Congress the 'Conservative Coalition' became the most powerful bloc; it consisted of conservative Republicans and Southern Democrats who would oppose liberal measures sponsored by Democratic presidents and supported by liberal Republicans and Democrats. This was a recipe for legislative deadlock.

As presidential Republicanism became more widespread it resulted in the election of Republican presidents, faced often by nominal Democratic majorities in the Senate or House, but enabling the president to govern successfully with the support of the Conservative Coalition. Republican Presidents Nixon, Ford, Reagan and George Herbert Bush were all faced throughout their terms of office by a House of Representatives with Democratic majorities and for much of the time by Democratic majorities in the Senate as well. This phenomenon of 'divided government', the presidency held by one political party and one or both houses of Congress by the opposing party, became the distinguishing factor of the second half of the twentieth century in American politics. However, although this strategy enabled Southern politicians to block policies of which they disapproved, it had disadvantages for the South. When the South had formed a solid wing of the Democratic Party and a Democrat was in the White House the South had enjoyed a lot of benefits, even though Southern Democrats might dislike the holder of the presidential office: jobs in the administration, ambassadorial posts, judicial appointments, participation in the 'pork barrel' process of allocating federal funds. But when, largely as a result of split-ticket voting in the South, a Republican president was in office, Southerners were cut off from the spoils of office.

A further problem arose from the increased registration of black voters and their greater participation in elections. Since the presidency of Franklin Roosevelt blacks have voted overwhelmingly for the Democrats. The South began to see more and more black Democrats as mayors of important cities, such as Atlanta and New Orleans, and the election of black Democrats as members of the House of Representatives from congressional districts with large black populations. At the national level, blacks were becoming more and more important in the Democratic Party; the Democratic Party in the South was becoming more and more schizophrenic.

The reaction of Southern whites, in increasing numbers, was to switch their allegiance to the Republicans, not simply at the presidential level, but for other state-wide posts as well. Thus by 2006 seven of the eleven states of the Deep South had Republican governors and of the twenty-two Senators from these states eighteen were Republican – a situation inconceivable even twenty years earlier. At the presidential level the devotion of the South to the Republicans is even more marked. In the election of 1980 Reagan won all the Southern states with the exception of Georgia, and in the elections of 1984, 1988, 2000 and 2004 the Republican candidate swept the South gaining majorities in every one of the states of the Deep South. Only Clinton, himself a Southerner, was able to make inroads into the South, winning four of the eleven states in 1992 and 1996. The South has therefore become pivotal in presidential elections, and was critically important in the election of George W. Bush in 2000, when the outcome of the election depended on the result in Florida. George W. Bush also benefited from the support of Christian fundamentalist groups, which are very strongly represented in the Southern states. The danger of this developing situation is that the Democratic Party in the South becomes increasingly the representative of the black population and the Republicans the party of the whites.

The reforms that have been proposed in order to try to bring about a more responsible policy-oriented political system have been intended to strengthen the position of the president in relation to Congress, and to give to national party leaders a greater ability to discipline and control the lower echelons of the party. The centralisation of party finances, the creation of stronger national party organisations and the subjection of members of Congress to party discipline are major aims of such reforms. In order to increase the stature of the president, reformers have proposed that presidential candidates should be selected by a nation-wide direct primary, while others would like to see closer links between president and Congress, providing for the election of the president by Congress, or by a more radical movement towards a Cabinet system of government. The danger of most of the proposals for reform of the party system is that they might tend to cause a disintegration of that system rather than a solidification of it, making the parties *less* responsible, and less responsive, than at present. There is always the danger that the latent multi-party system that lies beneath the deceptively straightforward two-party system might emerge and take over American politics.

Further reading

Bibby, J.F. (2002) *Politics, Parties and Elections in America*, Belmont, CA: Wadsworth.

Black, E. and Black, M. (1992) *The Vital South: How Presidents are Elected*, London: Harvard University Press.

Black, E. and Black, M. (2002) *The Rise of Southern Republicans*, London: Harvard University Press.

Epstein, L. (1989) *Political Parties in the American Mold*, Madison, WI: The University of Wisconsin Press.

Fukuyama, F. (2006) *America at the Crossroads: Democracy, Power, and the Neoconservative Legacy*, New Haven, CT: Yale University Press.

Mickelthwait, J. and Wooldridge, A. (2005) *The Right Nation: Conservative Power in America*, London: Penguin Books.

Milkis, S.M. (1993) *The President and the Parties: The Transformation of the American Party System since the New Deal*, Oxford: Oxford University Press.

Stelzer, I. (ed.) (2004) *The Neocon Reader*, New York: Grove Press.

Websites

Democratic Party: www.democrats.org
Republican Party: www.gop.com
Guide to US Politics and Elections: www.politics1.com

4 Politics and elections

The structure of the American party system reflects the decentralisation of authority under the Constitution and the sectional diversity of American society; it reflects also the problems of political organisation in the most election-conscious nation in the world. There are approximately one million elective offices to be filled in the United States, and in any one year there may be 120,000 or 130,000 elections held, most of them for local school boards. Inevitably, the electoral system that regulates the filling of these offices is one of the structures that most faithfully reflects the geographical factors in American political life, because constituencies are based upon geographical areas, but it has other important dimensions as well. The complex election machinery makes full allowance for the expression of the individualistic and personal elements in the American electorate. It gives to the individual voters almost embarrassingly rich opportunities to express their views on the personalities of the candidates, and to enter fully into the processes of choosing those who will govern. Party organisation, already fragmented by the effects of federalism and the separation of powers, is subjected to further disintegrating forces by the introduction of primary elections, by the use of the long ballot and by the opportunities for split-ticket voting.

The complexity of the electoral system is due in large part to the fact that the electoral law, whether it relates to federal, state or local elections, is almost wholly a matter of state law, with wide variations in practice among the fifty states. The fact that American elections take place at fixed intervals structures the whole programme of political life. The exact dates of future elections are known, so that there is a long process of electioneering, building up over a two-year period to the climax of the presidential campaign every four years. Indeed, in a sense, the jockeying for position in the next presidential election takes place almost as soon as the polls close. The fact that the elections take place upon the appointed day, regardless of the movement of world events or the complexities of domestic issues, means that elections are determined by the circumstances of the time, rather than as in a parliamentary system, where they are part of the machinery available to the government to try to influence the course of events. Elections to the Senate and the House of Representatives take place every two years, one-third of the Senate and the whole of the House standing for election. Thus we have the phenomenon of 'mid-term' elections, that is the election of all 435 Representatives and perhaps thirty-two or more Senators half-way through the term of office of the incumbent president, an arrangement that can result in some strange political situations, and that provides considerable difficulties for political strategists. The fact that the president cannot dissolve Congress, no matter how intransigent it becomes, and remains in office for four years, whether or not the administration's policies receive the support of Congress, gives to each branch of the government a degree of mutual independence that is clearly reflected in the behaviour of presidential and congressional candidates at election time. There are four major steps in an American presidential election: the caucuses and primaries, the conventions, the campaign culminating in the election, and the vote in the Electoral College. Let us trace the process through each of these stages.

Caucuses and primary elections

At the end of the nineteenth century America saw the development, at county and city level, of some of the most formidable and cohesive political organisations that have ever evolved in a democratic system of government. Yet for the most part American elections are not fought between rival, highly organised parties. Much of the vital stuff of American politics consists of battles between different groups *within* a particular party, often between the official party organisation and other groups or factions that oppose it. The official party organisation can be attacked, and at times defeated, by other groups within the party, bitterly divided from it on grounds of personalities or policies. Fratricidal strife is the hallmark of American political life, with the bitterest battles being fought within as well as between the parties. This strife has been institutionalised by the adoption of the device of the primary election. The electoral process must begin with the selection of candidates for office and their nomination. It is at this first stage, rather than in the election proper, that the really decisive choices may be made, for it is the selection of the people who will at a later stage be the representatives and leaders of the party that determines its true character. The selection of party candidates may be achieved in a number of ways: by a group of party leaders meeting in caucus; by delegates at a party meeting or convention; by party supporters; or by a combination of these methods. Elections in which party supporters choose their candidates prior to the general election are called *primary elections*.

The caucus system was the earliest method adopted for choosing candidates for elective office; a caucus is a meeting of party leaders or activists to decide on policy or to select candidates for office. In the nineteenth century, party leaders in the secrecy of 'smoke-filled rooms' selected candidates for the United States Senate, the House of Representatives, and state and local

Figure 4.1 The electoral process

offices in this way. As political bosses then dominated the American parties, this method of selection entrenched the power of party leaders and perpetuated their control over the party. In the early years of the Republic, caucuses of members of Congress selected candidates for the presidency. After 1840, however, delegates from the several states selected presidential candidates in national nominating conventions. Political bosses still played an important role in the bargaining that went on between state delegations in order to find a candidate acceptable to the various factions, and wheeling and dealing still characterised the selection of presidential candidates well into the twentieth century. Nominating conventions were intended to make the selection of candidates more open and democratic, but the belief in the democratic character of the convention system proved illusory. Party leaders could manage conventions so that they became a mere facade for oligarchic control by professional politicians. As part of the revulsion against 'bossism' and all that it entailed, primary elections were introduced in order to break up the oligarchies of city and county machines. Caucus meetings are still held in a number of states – fifteen in 2004 – to select delegates to the national conventions.

Primary elections give party members a *direct* voice in the choice of party representatives through the medium of a public, state-controlled election, in which any member of the party can stand as a candidate and all members can vote. Primaries are intended to bring the instruments of mass democracy, the political parties, under democratic control. The primary elections used in the United States are in principle extremely democratic, for the definition of 'party member' that qualifies the elector to vote in a primary is extremely widely drawn. Party membership does not entail fee-paying or card-holding membership in an organisation. It usually means nothing more than the declaration by the ordinary member of the electorate, when he or she registers as a voter, of having voted for a particular party in the past, or intending to do so in the future, without of course in any way committing him or her to the support of a particular party at the forthcoming election. Thus a registered Democrat may vote in the Democratic primary to choose the candidates for that party in the general election, but when election day comes he or she is quite free to vote for the Republican candidate. In a few states democratic principles are taken to the ultimate extreme, for in the so-called 'open primaries' voters are allowed to vote in whichever primary they choose, without being restricted by their party choice at the time of registration. Such a system is totally disruptive of party organisation, and for a time both parties abandoned the open primary, but a number of states have now returned to it.

In 2004 presidential primaries were held in thirty-five states. In most of these elections delegates are chosen for the national conventions, committed to the support of particular candidates, at least on the first ballot in the convention. In some cases the primary vote merely expresses the preference of the voters for a particular prospective nominee for the presidency, without binding the delegates, who will nevertheless feel inclined to support the winner of the primary in their state, particularly if that candidate looks likely to win the nomination. The fact that the primary season stretches over months, moving from state to state, tends to make the earlier ones more significant, because they may start a trend in favour of one of the candidates. This has in the past caused a certain amount of manoeuvring by states wishing to have an influence in the early stages of the primary battles. In 1988 a number of Southern and Western states decided to hold their primaries on the same day, and in 1996 seven states held their primaries on 'Super Tuesday', 5 March. The result was to boost the candidacy of Bob Dole in the Republican primaries, turning them into a kind of Southern declaration in his favour.

In response five of the New England states held 'Yankee primaries' on the same day in early May, in order to register their collective view. The pressure to hold primaries earlier and earlier in the year continued in 2004. New Hampshire held its place as the leader in late January, but by mid-March the Democrats had already held primaries in twenty-four states, ten of them on 'Super Tuesday', 2 March. There are demands, from time to time, to simplify the process of candidate selection by holding a single nation-wide primary, but there is little likelihood that such a reform will be implemented.

Primaries are, therefore, in a sense a party matter, but they are by no means discreetly conducted internal affairs. They are usually fought with as much publicity, effort and bitterness as the elections proper for which they are in theory only the preliminary rounds. Rival candidates for the party's nomination conduct public campaigns and engage in every electoral tactic, including extreme attempts to discredit their opponents. Primaries are often a battle between the chosen candidates of the established party organisation and challengers to their authority, who create their own organisations to contest the primary. In Massachusetts this internecine strife is even further institutionalised by the holding of a 'pre-primary convention', at which the party delegates endorse a list of the contenders for nomination for various offices as the official candidates in the primary. Yet the 'official' candidates may subsequently be defeated in the primary and replaced by their successful opponents as the party's official representatives at the general election. In those areas where only one party has any hope of winning at the general election the primaries become the true battleground for office, where factions within the party fight out the contest for power, and where success in the primary is tantamount to election.

The bitterness of the primary contests extends to the highest level of the political system, the nominations for the presidency of the United States, for here the most is to be gained and the most to be lost. The presidential primaries may become the forum for bitter personal battles between the foremost leaders of the same political party, carried on in the full glare of publicity before the eyes of the whole country, indeed of the world. The 1964 Republican primaries in which Senator Goldwater and Governor Rockefeller contended for the party's presidential nomination were savage battles. When the battles were over, Theodore H. White remarked, 'the Republican Party was so wounded that its leaders were fitter candidates for political hospitalisation than for governmental responsibility.'

Equally important may be the internal political divisions in the state where a presidential primary is being held. Candidates for the presidential nomination inevitably become involved in the factional fights at state and local level, for each aspiring president will have supporters in the state, who will hope to gain in their local political struggles by the success of their champion at the national level. However, the result of these cross-currents of national and state politics may be very serious for contenders for the presidential office.

If the dominant leadership of the state party is opposed strongly to a leading contender in the presidential primary in the state, the state party might be torn apart in the ensuing campaign, deepening personal animosities within the party and weakening its organisation and morale. The resulting divisions within the party may have a considerable impact upon the presidential election itself, and indeed upon the politics of the presidency for many years. The danger of such a situation arising may decide contenders for the nomination not to enter for the primary in a particular state.

Whether or not to enter for the primaries used to be a difficult decision for the presidential aspirant, although nowadays it has become an indispensable route to the nomination. The primary trail to the national convention, taking up the spring months of a presidential election year, is an expensive and exhausting process. Primary elections follow hard upon each other across the country: New Hampshire, Virginia, Wisconsin, California, Connecticut. Few candidates would wish to fight them all, and it becomes a matter of tactics to decide which to contest. In 1960 John F. Kennedy chose the primaries as his route to the nomination, unlike the candidates who were more favoured by the professional politicians in the party, and who chose to remain in the background. Kennedy had to demonstrate his popular appeal, and in particular to prove that a Catholic could win votes in Protestant areas. His victory over Hubert Humphrey in West Virginia, a state with an overwhelmingly Protestant population, was a major factor in his successful bid for the nomination. In the election of 1968 the profound impact of the early primary victories of Senator Eugene McCarthy upon the political fortunes of President Johnson indicated the importance which the primaries could attain in the era of televised politics. The Democratic National Convention went on to accept Hubert Humphrey as its candidate, in spite of the fact that he had fought few primaries and that 80 per cent of the delegates elected through primaries were supporters of Eugene McCarthy or of Robert Kennedy, who had been assassinated. However, at that time only one-third of the delegates to the convention were chosen by primary elections, and the party machine, dominated by President Johnson, could still deliver the nomination to the president's candidate. By 1980 the situation had changed dramatically. Seventy per cent of the delegates to the Democratic Convention were elected via the primary route, and the possibility of manipulating the convention was correspondingly reduced. In subsequent elections the proportion of delegates chosen through primary elections fluctuated, but in 1996 over 85 per cent of the delegates to both the Democratic and Republican Conventions were selected through the primary route, emphasising that nowadays entering the primaries, and fighting almost all of them, is no longer a matter of choice for the aspiring presidential candidate; it is essential.

The primary election campaign of 1992 illustrates very well the process of presidential candidate selection in an age of weak political parties and the power of television. There were five major candidates for the Democratic nomination: Senator Paul Tsongas from Massachusetts, Governor Bill Clinton from Arkansas, Senator Tom Harkin of Iowa, former Governor Jerry Brown of California, and Senator Bob Kerrey of Nebraska. A number of other prominent Democrats hovered on the sidelines, but for one reason or another decided not to declare themselves as candidates for the nomination. The first primary was held on 18 February in New Hampshire. Senator Tsongas won, as was to be expected as he himself was from New England, but Bill Clinton came a good second. A week later the South Dakota primary was won by Senator Kerrey, and Clinton achieved only 19 per cent of the votes. In early March Clinton, the Governor of Arkansas, won a convincing victory in the southern state of Georgia, came second to Tsongas in Maryland and Utah, and came second to Brown in Colorado. At this point no candidate had established a position of dominance, but Clinton was doing better than anyone else. He had only 198 delegates committed to him – he needed 2,145 to secure the nomination – but he had more delegates than any other candidate. At this point Kerrey and Harkin withdrew from the race.

The stage was set for Super Tuesday, 10 March. When the Democratic Party decided in 1988 to stage a group of primaries in the South early on the same day in the campaign it was in order to give a clear indication that one candidate had strong support in that section. It worked well for Clinton in 1992. He won by large margins in Louisiana, Mississippi, Oklahoma, Tennessee and Texas. Only in the New England states of Massachusetts and Rhode Island, where the primaries were held on the same day, did he lose to Tsongas. Clinton went on to win in Illinois and Michigan later in the month, and Senator Tsongas decided that he would not actively contest any further primaries. Only Jerry Brown remained a threat to Clinton. In early April Clinton won the primaries in New York and Wisconsin; although his majorities over Brown were not convincing, particularly in Wisconsin where Clinton managed only 37.9 per cent to Brown's 35 per cent, it had become clear that Clinton was the front-runner, and could not be caught. Although many voters distrusted him, he went on to win in state after state, eventually winning thirty of the thirty-six primaries that he contested. By the end of the primary season in June he had the support of more than enough of the delegates to the forthcoming convention to secure the nomination.

In 2004 a similarly open situation existed for the nomination of the presidential candidate of the Democratic Party. The incumbent President, George W. Bush, was running for re-election, so there was no real interest in the Republican primaries; the outcome was a foregone conclusion. For the Democrats the situation was very different; the defeated candidate in the 2000 election, Al Gore, had decided not to run for the nomination in 2004, and the field was wide open. Ten candidates put themselves forward. Initially the front runner was Howard Dean, a former Governor of the state of Vermont; seven other candidates were, or had been, US Senators, including John Kerry of Massachusetts, John Edwards of North Carolina and Joseph Lieberman of Connecticut. The other two hopefuls were Richard Gephardt, a Member of the

House of Representatives for Missouri and Wesley Clark, a former General in the US Army, who had served as Supreme Allied Commander of NATO.

In 2003, before the caucuses and primaries for the presidential election of 2004 got under way, Howard Dean had been very successful in gathering support. He had raised considerable sums of money and had developed the use of the internet to communicate with potential supporters to an extent never before attempted by presidential aspirants. Towards the end of the year he was clearly well ahead in the public opinion polls, suggesting that he was likely to get the nomination. However, in the Iowa caucuses held in mid-January 2004, Dean came third after Kerry and Edwards and in the first primary, held in New Hampshire on 27 January he was in second place behind Kerry. Kerry continued to win primary elections in a number of states, although Clark beat him in Oklahoma and Edwards won first place in South Carolina. Other candidates for the nomination who had done poorly gradually withdrew; after Kerry won the primaries in Virginia and Tennessee, Clark withdrew, leaving only Dean, Edwards and Kerry in the race. Dean withdrew after coming third in the Wisconsin primary on 17 February and when Kerry won eight of the nine primaries held on Super Tuesday, including the Southern state of Georgia, Edwards withdrew, leaving John Kerry as the victor.

The primaries exhibit some of the most individualistic elements in American politics. It is possible for an almost unknown candidate to win a victory over the established party organisation, and primaries also provide opportunities for the voters to express their views and preferences, even for candidates who are not technically up for election. Many primary laws allow the voter to write in the name of a candidate, and so to cast a vote for a candidate whose name does not appear on the ballot. The likelihood of such write-in votes constituting a majority of the votes cast is small, and yet strange things do happen in American politics. In the 1964 New Hampshire presidential primary, Goldwater and Rockefeller were the names on the Republican ballot, yet the winner of the primary was Henry Cabot Lodge, Ambassador to Vietnam, who had not even campaigned, and who at the time of the election was many thousands of miles away. A small group of enthusiastic supporters urged the New Hampshire voters to write in Lodge's name.

Thus primary elections introduce many complications into the rich complexity of the American political scene. Introduced as a challenge to the power of the professional politicians, they have made life more difficult for that hardy breed and they have aided the tendency towards weaker party organisation that has been under way for several decades. Primaries have not, of course, completely democratised the political parties. To the extent that they have done so, they highlight the dilemma of the reformer in this field. How does one break the power of an oligarchy without destroying altogether the basis of strong leadership? If the parties were strongly ideologically oriented, then party allegiance might be a substitute for organisational power as a basis for the exercise of leadership, but they are not. Another alternative might be the cohesive force of spoils and corruption but, although American politics are not free from these things, they have declined considerably in importance. The power of the professional politicians has not evaporated, but they have had to adapt themselves to new techniques and learn how to live with the primaries.

The national conventions

American political parties are great coalitions of sectional, class and pluralistic interests that come together for certain purposes, the most important being to contest the election of the president of the United States. It is in the national conventions of the parties that their most difficult task is performed: the choice of candidates for the presidency. The peculiarities of the national conventions can be understood only if they are seen as arenas in which political parties, composed of very diverse economic and social interests, and embracing groups with very different views on domestic and foreign policy, are forced to choose *one* person as their representative, to lead them in the forthcoming election, and thereafter perhaps to wield the power of the presidency. Thus the Democratic Party is composed of Southern whites and Northern blacks, of automobile workers from Detroit and small businessmen from California, of Irish-American truck drivers from Massachusetts and Spanish-speaking Puerto Ricans, together with millions of other Americans across the continent. Yet only one person can be the standard-bearer of the party and what it will stand for in the following years, at the presidential level at least.

It is hardly surprising, then, that outwardly the national conventions present a picture of bombast and ballyhoo, in which brass bands raucously punctuate the proceedings, processions of banner-waving supporters and attractive drum majorettes take over the floor of the convention hall in a well-organised chaos, and speakers make vague appeals for party unity based upon historical and emotional considerations rather than upon future policy. Clearly, the problem that they are there to resolve is not one that can be dealt with simply by calm reasoning and persuasive argument from the rostrum; it is the much more emotional problem of settling upon a leader whom the vast majority of the party are prepared to follow. Behind the ballyhoo, however, lies a long period of careful preparation for the convention, the effort by candidates to gain the support of important figures, the making of bargains and concessions to waverers, the hard-headed political bargaining which alone can bring order out of chaos.

National conventions are enormous affairs. There can be as many as 5,500 delegates at a national convention, as well as a host of reporters, television crews and spectators. The delegates are chosen in a variety of ways. Some are chosen in the presidential primaries and are committed in some degree to the winners of the primary in their state. Others are chosen in state and district conventions across the country by a variety of different methods. The delegates to this lower level of conventions may be elected in primaries, or selected by conventions at county level or by ad hoc meetings of party members.

In earlier times the convention was the arena in which presidential candidates were really chosen. To gain the nomination a candidate must win an *absolute* majority of the votes in the convention, and balloting will continue until a candidate gets more than 50 per cent of delegate votes. Thus, in the months before the convention, candidates must try to get as many of the delegates as possible committed to their support, in the hope that when the convention opens they will have either sufficient support to win outright on the first ballot or at least enough committed votes to convince waverers that they are in a position eventually to win the nomination. Before primary elections became an important part of the process of selecting delegates the conventions were the battleground in which party factions fought out their differences. This could result in numerous ballots being necessary before agreement could be reached on a candidate who was acceptable to a majority of the delegates. In 1924 it took 103 ballots for the Democratic convention to nominate John W. Davis. It was also possible for a compromise candidate to secure the nomination while not being one of the leaders on the first ballot. In 1940 Wendell Willkie won the Republican nomination on the sixth ballot, although on the first he had received only 105 votes compared with 360 for Thomas Dewey and 189 for Senator Taft. The extension of the primaries to cover three-quarters of the states, together with the way that television helps to crown the emerging favourite candidate before the end of the primary season, now make extended balloting unlikely, and candidates are much more likely to be nominated on the first ballot. The convention then becomes little more than a coronation ceremony to honour the new chief.

The reasons for this can be seen in the developments that have taken place since the 1970s in the methods of choosing presidential candidates. Presidential primary elections have increased in both number and significance, and, combined with the enhanced role of television in electoral politics, have transformed the nature of the presidential race. At the 1968 Democratic Convention in Chicago, held under the aegis of Mayor Richard J. Daley in an atmosphere of violence and tension, the representative of the liberal activist elements of the party, Eugene McCarthy, was beaten by the candidate of the party establishment, Hubert Humphrey, who then lost the general election to Republican Richard Nixon. In the following year the McGovern–Fraser Commission on Party Structure recommended a number of changes in the method of delegate selection to the Democratic National Convention in order to democratise its proceedings. These and later changes were intended to ensure the quota representation of women and minority groups, and to assure a truer reflection of the voting in the composition of the delegation from each state. These reforms certainly achieved their aim of taking the decisions about candidate selection away from the political bosses in the Democratic Party. At the Democratic Convention in New York City in 1980, 50 per cent of the delegates were women, 14 per cent were blacks and 6 per cent were from other minority groups. But the reforms had unforeseen effects. The number of states operating presidential primaries rose dramatically from seventeen in 1968 to thirty-eight in 1988, when over 80 per cent of the delegates to the convention were selected by primary elections, compared with only one-third twenty years earlier. Although the number of states holding primary elections declined to thirty-five in 2004, winning the nomination is no longer a question of appealing to the members of the convention but of winning the primary elections. Winning the primaries is now a matter of convincing millions of voters, through the channels of the mass media, that you are the worthiest candidate to represent the party. The changes in the rules for delegate selection contributed very powerfully to the further disintegration of party organisation, and the lessening of the influence of professional politicians.

As a reaction to the disintegrative effects of the new rules the Hunt Commission was established to make recommendations for the selection of delegates to the Democratic Party's national convention in 1984. The Hunt Commission did not change the basic thrust of the principles underlying the McGovern–Fraser reforms, but it moderated their effects, and changed the balance of the 1984 convention back towards a greater reliance on the professionals in the party. A greater role in the convention was given to 'superdelegates' – party officials, Senators, and Congressmen not formally committed to a candidate before the meeting of the convention. In addition a threshold was introduced to prevent candidates with only a very small percentage of the primary vote from securing delegates. As a result of the changes made by the Hunt Commission, fewer presidential primary elections were held in 1984, and the number of delegates committed to a candidate before the opening of the convention fell back to just over 50 per cent. The successful candidate for the Democratic nomination, Walter Mondale, was more of an old-line politician, not a candidate created by the media. His defeat in the 1984 presidential election led yet again to the appointment of a commission, 'the Fairness Commission', to review the rules for delegate selection. However, the only significant change that they recommended for the national convention to be held in 1988 was an increase in the proportion of superdelegates, thus leaving the Democratic Party, in the words of the *New Republic*, with a 'caucus mentality – Democrats as gays, women, blacks, Hispanics, Jews, unionists, anything but just Democrats – (that) still holds the party in thrall'. This perception of the party as simply a conglomeration of pressure groups remains one of its greatest problems in the battle for political office.

When an incumbent president is seeking the nomination he is usually in a very powerful position, for to replace him would be to repudiate the party's leader while he was still president of the United States, and to condemn the party's record over the previous years. But it is possible for a challenge to be made to an incumbent president, forcing the convention to hold a ballot. Contested ballots were held when President Truman sought the nomination in 1948 and when President Roosevelt asked for his fourth term in 1944. But even in 1948, when the President's prestige was at a very low ebb, the challenge was weak and had little hope of success, and in 1944 it was trivial. In the nineteenth century a number of incumbent presidents were unsuccessful in seeking a nomination for a further term of office, but all but one of them (Franklin Pierce) were former vice-presidents who had succeeded to the presidency on the death of their predecessors. No incumbent president who sought the nomination has been rejected since 1884. As President Truman said, 'a President in the White House always controlled the National Convention'. President Johnson's withdrawal from the contest for the nomination in 1968 represents a rather special case, for he preferred not to wait for the convention and a possible trial of strength with his opponents. In 1980 the strong challenge made by Senator Edward Kennedy to the re-nomination of President Carter faded away.

When a decision has been reached, the nominee makes an acceptance speech to the convention and receives its homage as the party's leader in the forthcoming battle. The man who a few hours before was just another politician wooing the delegates has suddenly become the man who might be the next president of the United States. Once the nomination has been made, the intra-party battle, which has largely dominated the political scene for months, must give way to the contest between the parties, and self-inflicted wounds must be sewn up in order to present, as far as possible, a united front to the enemy. This switch from the bitterness of internal conflict to the competition between parties for office, whether at the level of the presidency or for state and local office, is one of the perennial wonders of the American political scene. The transition from defeated candidates for the nomination to loyal supporters of the party's chosen leader is often made to seem as complete and as beautiful as the transformation from caterpillar to butterfly. In 1960 Lyndon Johnson was the strongest opponent of John F. Kennedy for the Democratic nomination for the presidency, yet overnight he became Kennedy's 'running-mate' as vice-presidential candidate, working hard to bring the Southern states solidly behind the Kennedy–Johnson ticket. However, the battles for the nomination in primaries and conventions, reflecting as they do real divisions within the parties, may have a lasting effect on party unity. Sometimes even a pretence of papering over differences of policy or personality is not made. Defeated chieftains may refuse to make their peace with the candidate, and state and local leaders may campaign vigorously under the party banner in their own bailiwicks, pointedly ignoring the party's national leader, as many Southern Democrats ignored John F. Kennedy in 1960, or indeed openly opposed him. At the extreme, a defeated faction may openly dissociate itself from the party's candidate and nominate its own. In 1948 the Southern wing of the Democratic Party, disgusted with the nomination of President Truman on a civil rights programme, bolted the party and campaigned for Governor Strom Thurmond of South Carolina under the banner of the States' Rights Party. The decentralisation of the American party system allows dissatisfied local politicians to make the best of a bad job. As the 1964 campaign drew to its close and it became increasingly clear to Republican politicians that Goldwater's bid for the presidency was lost, many of them withdrew into their local political battles, and left the national candidate to fight on virtually alone.

The national convention has two other major functions to perform: to formulate the party platform, and to nominate the vice-presidential candidate. Before the convention meets, a Resolutions Committee or Platform Committee is appointed to consider the content of the party's programme and to report to the convention. Often party platforms are dull documents phrased in vague and general terms in order not to offend important sections of the party, yet this is not always the case. It was the strong civil rights proposals contained in the 1948 Democratic programme that provoked the defection of the Dixiecrats. In 1960 the content of the Republican platform became a major point of dispute between Richard Nixon and Governor Rockefeller when the latter, finding the draft programme vague and inadequate, threatened to fight it on the floor of the convention if alterations were not made. In general, however, given the nature of American party politics, it is impossible for the party programme to be a bold, exciting document, and as it is drawn up before the presidential candidate has been nominated he cannot be closely bound by what it contains.

The nomination of the vice-presidential candidate follows the balloting for the presidential nomination. Throughout much of its history the office of vice-president has been insignificant, and as a consequence the nomination of a vice-presidential candidate was not considered a matter of great consequence, particularly as it comes at the end of the convention when delegates are tired and wish to get away. The position came to be used as a sop to the unsuccessful faction at the convention, so giving balance to the ticket, by drawing the vice-presidential nominee from a region of the country different from that of the presidential candidate. In recent years, however, the stature of the vice-presidency has been growing, and consequently a rather different attitude towards the nomination of vice-presidential candidates has been perceptible. In 1940 President Roosevelt threatened that he would not run for a third term if Henry Wallace was not nominated for the vice-presidency. Wallace, and later Richard Nixon, were both active and important vice-presidents. The assassination of President Kennedy dramatised, as no other event could, the potential importance of the man holding the vice-presidential office. In 1964, partly because there was no contest for the presidential nomination in the Democratic Party, there developed a distinct campaign on behalf of Hubert Humphrey for the vice-presidential nomination. In an unprecedented move President Johnson appeared on the rostrum at the convention and put Humphrey's name before the delegates. The selection of Spiro Agnew by Mr Nixon as his vice-presidential running-mate suggested a return to the earlier view of the insignificance of the office, but the quality of more recent nominees has reflected the desire for a more weighty role for the vice-president, and perhaps a recognition of the importance of the succession in the case of the death or resignation of the president. The selection of Geraldine Ferraro in 1984 as the first woman candidate for the vice-presidency clearly represented an attempt, unsuccessful as it proved, by the Democrats to attract a larger proportion of female voters. As we shall see, Vice-President Cheney has played a more important role in the administrations of President George W. Bush than was the case with any previous vice-president.

The campaign and the Electoral College

The dispersal of the national conventions brings to an end the long and exhausting process of selection for which the candidates have been planning, working and campaigning for months, even for years. After a short pause the general election begins, with its even more intensive and exhausting campaign, building up over eight or nine weeks to the climax of election day itself, on the day after the first Monday in November. The American people will then give their final verdict upon those who aspire to the presidency; yet the way in which the campaign is conducted, and the very nature of the institution of the presidency itself, depend upon the electoral machinery devised by the Founding Fathers in 1787. For, just as the strategy of presidential nominating politics is determined by the need to obtain an absolute majority of the votes at the convention, so the strategy of the presidential campaign is determined by the need to obtain an absolute majority of votes in the Electoral College. Although Americans vote for their president early in November, and usually a few hours after the polls close the result of the election is common knowledge, it is not until a month has passed that the election of the president actually takes place, when the members of the Electoral College cast *their* votes. Although in itself this procedure is usually a formality, hardly noticed by the world, it is, nevertheless, a procedure that has a profound effect upon the way in which presidential elections are conducted, upon the strategy of the candidates' campaign managers, and upon the type of candidate who is chosen for the presidency.

At the end of the eighteenth century the Fathers of the Constitution wished to isolate the election of the president from the turbulence of 'mob politics'. They were creating an elective head of state at a time when democratic government was virtually untried – in France Louis XVI was still on the throne, Hohenzollern and Habsburg dominated Europe, and even in England a hereditary aristocracy ruled in collaboration with a still influential king and a corrupt and unrepresentative House of Commons. The Americans were embarking upon a great adventurous experiment, but they wished to be cautious also, and not to give this potentially powerful office over to demagogues. They provided, therefore, for a system of *indirect* election for the presidency. They created an Electoral College, in which each state was to have a number of votes equal to the number of Senators and Representatives to which it was entitled in Congress. The state legislatures would determine how the Electors were to be chosen, and the Electors would then choose a president from among the men most suited for the position, remote from the white heat of a popular election. Today the Electors are chosen by popular vote in November, but in law it is still the Electoral College that makes the final decision in December. Strictly speaking, when Americans cast their vote for president they are really choosing between competing lists, or slates, of Electoral College candidates, although today it is the names of the candidates for the presidential office which appear on the ballot papers, rather than the names of the candidates for the Electoral College. The continuing importance of this eighteenth-century institution was dramatically demonstrated in the election of 2000 when the outcome of the election was determined by the votes of the Electoral College, not the votes of the American electorate.

Of course, the idea that the members of the Electoral College could quietly and calmly choose a president according to their best judgement was a delusion. The mechanisms of organised politics soon entered into the process, and the candidates for the Electoral College soon became pledged to cast their votes for one of the contenders for the presidency. The members of the Electoral College thus ceased to exercise any individual judgement and merely registered the decision of the voters in their state. The Electoral College does not even meet to deliberate as a body – the members meet in the state capitals and their votes are carried to Washington.

It is true that the operation of the Electoral College is not yet quite a formality. Occasionally individual Electors have changed their minds after the November election and refused to cast their votes for the candidate to whom they were pledged. In 1948 a Tennessee Elector refused to cast his vote for President Truman, although the latter had carried the state, and cast his vote instead for the States' Rights candidate. In 1956 an Alabama Elector refused to vote for Stevenson, to whom he had been committed, and in 1960 an Elector in Oklahoma pledged to support Richard Nixon cast his vote for Senator Byrd. In 1968 a North Carolina Elector switched his vote from Nixon to George Wallace. In 2000 one Elector committed to Al Gore abstained from voting and in 2004, one Elector from Minnesota who was pledged to support John Kerry in fact voted for John Edwards for president

These minor deviations from the normal practice have made no difference to the working of the Electoral College, but the strategy adopted in certain Southern states in the past had potentially a more important effect. In 1960, as an alternative to setting up a dissident third party, Democrats in Alabama and Mississippi who were opposed to the official candidate, John F. Kennedy, put up an unpledged slate of candidates for the Electoral College. This was in a sense a reversion to the earlier ideas of the Founding Fathers, for it was intended that these Electors should not be committed to one candidate or another, but should be free to choose according to the outcome of the election in other states. If it was a very close election in terms of Electoral votes, these uncommitted Electors could tip the balance in favour of one candidate or another in return for concessions to the Southern point of view, or they could throw the election into the House of Representatives (see below). Although it was a close election in terms of the popular vote, Kennedy had a good margin of Electoral votes, and the unpledged slate that won in Mississippi cast their votes for Senator Harry F. Byrd along with some of the unpledged Electors from Alabama.

The Electoral College, therefore, would seem at first sight to be merely a rather complicated mechanism for the indirect registration of the people's will. Yet that is not the case at all. To understand why the structure of the Electoral College is so important, it is necessary to examine the way in which, purely by convention, the states have come to operate the machinery of the College. The Constitution simply laid down that 'The Electors shall meet in their respective States, and vote by ballot for President and Vice-President', but it did not stipulate the manner in which balloting should take place. The most obvious way to conduct the balloting might be to allocate the Electoral College votes among the candidates proportionately to the number of votes they received in the popular election. Thus in 2004 John Kerry won 54.3 per cent of the popular vote in California, and George W. Bush won 44.4 per cent, other candidates received the remaining 1.3 per cent. California, with the highest population in the country, had fifty-five votes in the Electoral College, so it would seem that the obvious way to distribute these votes would be to give thirty to Kerry and twenty-five to Bush. This would seem surely to be the fairest way to express the views of the 12 million Californians who voted in the election. In fact, most of the States do not allocate Electoral College votes in this way. By convention, all the Electoral College votes of a state are given to the candidate who attains a plurality, that is a simple majority, of the popular vote in the state. This is called the 'unit rule' and it operates in all the states other than Maine and Nebraska, both states with small populations unlikely to affect the outcome of the election. Thus, in the example given above, all of California's 55 Electoral College votes went to Kerry.

The effect of this method of casting the Electoral College votes is to increase enormously the effects of sectional and geographical factors on the selection and election of presidential candidates. The significance of the more populous states becomes disproportionately great. To succeed in an election a candidate must get an absolute majority in the Electoral College, and the votes of a relatively small number of large states will put him or her well on the way to achieving this aim.

There is a total of 538 Electoral College Votes to be won, so that a candidate needs 270 to win. When aiming at this figure the big votes of California (fifty-five votes), Texas (thirty-four votes), New York (thirty-one votes), Florida (twenty-seven votes), Pennsylvania (twenty-one votes), Illinois (twenty-one votes) and Ohio (twenty votes), become critically important. Each candidate hopes to capture some of these large states with enough of the middle group, like Massachusetts, New Jersey or Virginia, and some of the smaller states to reach the magic figure. Thus the states with large populations play a disproportionate part in electing the president, in influencing presidential politics, and consequently in widening the gap between congressional and presidential politics. In this way the Electoral College usually exaggerates the margin of victory gained by the successful candidate. In 1960 John Kennedy had a popular vote majority of only 0.1 per cent over Nixon, but he finished up with 62 per cent of the Electoral College vote to Nixon's 36 per cent. In 1964 President Johnson's 61 per cent of the popular vote turned into 90 per cent of the Electoral vote. On the other hand, it is possible for a candidate to be elected with fewer popular votes than his rival, as happened in 1876, 1888 and, of course, in 2000.

After each decennial census the allocation of seats in the House of Representatives is revised to take account of shifts of population, and this leads to the reallocation of Electoral College votes among the states. The population trends of the second half of the twentieth century reflected the fact that, as a result of technological changes, the heavy industry that characterised the North and East of the United States was in decline, whilst the new information technology based on the development of computers and other electronic devices was able to be undertaken much more widely across the country. The attractions of living and working in the warmer climate of the South and West drew many people to move to those areas. California's Silicon Valley became the iconic home of the software industry, and Florida attracted retired citizens in droves. Immigration also affected different areas to differing degrees; the Cubans concentrated in Florida, other Latinos in California and other Southwestern states. The consequence of these population changes was a shift of political power to the South and West, making California, Texas and Florida much more significant in presidential elections, and reducing the importance of New York, Illinois or Pennsylvania.

The most dramatic result of this eighteenth-century method of electing the president occurs if no candidate succeeds in obtaining an overall majority of the vote in the Electoral College. In this case the House of Representatives decides the election, by a rather extraordinary procedure. The House chooses a president from the three top names in the Electoral College ballot, *each state delegation exercising one vote*, irrespective of the number of members in the delegation, or of the population of the state. Thus the state of California would have the same voting power as Nevada or New Mexico. Each state delegation determines how to cast its vote by a majority vote within the delegation. As the delegation would usually be divided between the two parties, voting within delegations might go along party lines, but in some situations, the members of the House might vote across party lines to choose a compromise candidate, or even in order to reject a candidate of their own party to whom they objected. The outcome of such a vote in the House could be a most extraordinary choice, in which the expression of the popular will might be ignored. Other even more bizarre possibilities exist. The Constitution provides that to be elected a candidate must receive an absolute majority of votes in the House, as in the Electoral College, but the former can go on, ballot after ballot, until a result is reached, whereas there is only a single ballot in the College. However, suppose that a deadlock ensues, and no president is elected. The Constitution provides that in such a situation, if no president has been elected by the date on which the new president should take office, then the vice-president-elect shall act as president. Of course if the Electoral College failed to elect a president they might also fail to provide an absolute majority for any vice-presidential candidate. In such a case the Senate chooses the vice-president from the two top candidates, and one glimpses the extraordinary, though fortunately extremely unlikely, possibility that the vice-presidential candidate of a party with a minority of the popular vote might become vice-president, and then act for a time as president.

Such an extreme situation has not occurred, but on two occasions the election has been thrown into the House of Representatives – the presidential elections of 1800 and 1824. In the former case Thomas Jefferson was elected, but only after thirty-six ballots in the House. On the second occasion the election of John Quincy Adams turned upon the vote of one member of the New York delegation, General Stephen Van Renssalaer, whose decision to vote for Adams seems to have been arrived at in a rather strange fashion. As Van Renssalaer sat in the House deliberating upon how to cast his vote he bowed his head in prayer, only to see on the floor a piece of paper with Adams' name written on it. He picked it up and cast the vote that decided the issue. In the election of 1968 the possibility of a deadlock occurring seemed very real. The intervention of a third-party candidate with wide support, Governor George Wallace of the American Independent Party, might have prevented either of the major party candidates from achieving an overall majority in the Electoral College. Wallace hoped that if this were to happen he could use his position to bargain for policy concessions on civil rights from the other two candidates. If the election had been thrown into the House the Southern states might have been able to cause a deadlock there, possibly with disastrous consequences for the political system. In 1992 and 1996 Ross Perot could have had a similar role, but he failed to gain a single Electoral College vote in either election. During the extraordinarily protracted election of 2000 the real possibility arose of the failure of either candidate to achieve an absolute majority in the Electoral College, which would have had unforeseeable consequences.

These complications in the Electoral College system have led to many proposals for its reform or abolition, but perhaps the greatest criticism of the system is that it turns the only really national event in the American political calendar into a process of sectional coalition-building. It is within this context that the presidential campaign is conducted. Some students of voting behaviour have suggested that election campaigns are little more than ritualistic performances through which the candidates must go, although their influence on the result of the election is usually very small, and nowhere near as significant as the amount of time, energy and money that is spent on them would suggest. Yet no politician dare make such an assumption; certainly in a close race like that of 1960 almost any aspect of the campaign might have been 'decisive' – Kennedy's telegram of support to the jailed black leader Martin Luther King, or even the fact that Nixon perspired freely on television. Equally in the cliff-hanger of 2000 the switch of a few thousand votes from one candidate to the other in one or more states could have changed the outcome. Yet, although the campaign allows the electorate to see and choose between rival candidates, it also fulfils a deeper function in the political system. It is the first step by which the future president is recognised as the leader of the nation and seeks to establish a basis for the exercise of the presidential authority. Every president has in some degree to establish a charismatic authority over this diverse and individualistic nation; for, as we shall see later, it is in the ability to claim the status of national leader that the main strength of the president lies. The powers of the presidency are great, but the constitutional machinery is so complex, with so many barriers to the effective exercise of power, that a president has to try to impose his policies on the machine by sheer force of will, and to do this successfully must have popular support. With the exception of someone like General Eisenhower, few of those who enter the presidential race have a truly national reputation when they first make a bid for the office.

With the coming of television and the aeroplane, the means are at hand with which the candidates can attempt to impress their personality upon a nation of 280 million people spread over thousands of miles. The discussion of policies *may* be important in the campaign, according to the circumstances of the time, but essentially the campaign is a battle of personalities. It is perhaps in the very nature of this democratic system that, in attempting to create a position of authority, the candidates must submit to a process that is almost lethal in the demands it makes upon them, and that will almost certainly involve them in embarrassing, even humiliating, situations. In the course of the campaign a candidate may travel 50,000 miles, making speeches on both sides of the continent in a single day. The candidate will address great rallies and speak to a handful of voters at a street corner, shaking as many hands as is humanly possible, being photographed wearing the comic headgear of this or that association or, like the president of the United States campaigning for re-election in 1964, give cowboy whoops from the saddle of a horse while his audience laughed and clapped in appreciation. The person who wishes to be president has to convince the electors that he or she is an ordinary citizen who understands the problems of everyday living and, at one and the same time, is capable of dealing with complex questions involving war and peace, and of making decisions daily that deeply affect the welfare of all Americans.

The election of 2000

The presidential election of the year 2000 was an extraordinary affair. It was the closest election since 1960; it was the most extended in modern history, the result not being declared for five weeks after the election; it was extremely controversial, culminating in a decision of the United States Supreme Court. The Democratic candidate, Al Gore, won the popular vote, with a majority of more than half a million votes over his opponent, the Republican George W. Bush; 48.4 per cent of the total vote for Gore, 47.9 per cent for Bush. Nevertheless, because of the working of the Electoral College, Bush was eventually declared the winner with 271 Electoral votes to 266 for Gore (one member of the Electoral College, committed to Gore, abstained from voting).

To win the presidency it is necessary to gain an *absolute* majority (270) of the votes in the Electoral College. If no candidate achieves this the election is thrown into the House of Representatives, a very strange way of electing a president. On election night it seemed likely that Gore had won 267 Electoral College votes, three short of the total needed, and Bush had won 246. The remaining 25 Electoral College votes, which would decide the election, would depend on the result in the State of Florida, where George W. Bush's brother, Jeb Bush, was Governor. Initially it seemed that Bush had won Florida by a margin of 1,784 votes out of a total of almost 6 million, and on election night Gore conceded defeat, only to withdraw his concession later. Florida state law requires a recount in such a close race, and it was this that produced the extraordinary scenes that fascinated the nation, and indeed the world, for five weeks.

In a number of counties in Florida the electorate cast their votes on punch card machines. This involved the voters recording their votes by using a stylus to punch holes in a rather complicated ballot paper, which would then be read by a machine. Initially the Florida authorities ordered a recount by running the machines again, but the Gore camp asked for a *manual* recount in a number of counties, which would mean that each ballot would be checked visually. This was no simple task. The system was extremely inefficient, in that the small pieces of paper – known as chads – which were punched out of the ballot cards by the voters were sometimes only partially perforated, and the manual recount made it necessary to make judgements about the intentions of individual voters. Furthermore in one county, Palm Beach County, the design of the ballot paper was so confusing that many voters were misled into voting for a different candidate from the one they really intended to vote for. Manual recounts were carried out in a number of counties, against the background of legal disputes in state and federal courts about the validity and continuation of the recounts. As the recounts continued Bush's majority in the state fluctuated, at one point falling to a mere 154 votes, with the possibility that if the recounts continued his majority would disappear altogether. However, there was a deadline for the reporting of the election results which would inevitably bring the process to an end.

The election took place on 7 November; by law the members of the Electoral College would meet in the state capitals on 18 December to cast their votes for president and vice-president. If the Florida result could not be certified by then the consequences were unforeseeable. Federal law provided for the results of the election to be certified by the state authorities at least six days before the vote in the Electoral College, if the results were not to be challenged. Katherine Harris, the Florida Secretary of State, a Bush supporter, twice certified results declaring Bush the winner in Florida, but the state courts continued to sanction recounts in county after county. On 8 December the Florida Supreme Court ordered recounts to continue in a number of counties. The Bush camp appealed this ruling to the Supreme Court of the United States, which handed down its decision in *Bush* v. *Gore* on 12 December, hours before the deadline. The decision, by a majority of 5–4 of the Justices, ordered all recounts to cease. Thus, in an opinion which critics have characterised as 'deeply flawed', the judiciary determined the result of the election in favour of George Bush. The final majority for Bush in Florida was certified as 537 votes. On 18 December, George W. Bush was confirmed as the next president of the United States

House and Senate elections

The election of the president takes place every four years, but elections for one-third of the Senate and the whole of the House of Representatives take place every two years. Thus when the president is in the middle of his term of office, just beginning the climb up to the next test of strength at the presidential election two years hence, a large proportion of the legislators come up for re-election. These mid-term elections differ in many respects from elections in presidential years, and their results can be of critical importance to the incumbent president. At the extreme, mid-term elections can result in a change of control, so that one party controls the presidency and the other party controls either the House or the Senate, or both Houses, as happened in 1994, when the Republicans won majorities in both House and Senate and President Clinton still had two years of his first term to complete. For the remaining two years a Democratic president may have to cope with a Republican Congress, or vice versa.

The constitutional gulf between Congress and presidency can result in situations where a president can be faced with majorities of the opposing party in the legislature for the whole of his four-year term. In the election of 1956 the American people returned Republican President Eisenhower to power with a huge popular majority, but elected Democratic majorities to the Senate and the House of Representatives. However, the system of government did not crumble, for enough Democrats were prepared to go along with the Republican president to make the system workable. In the elections of 1968 and 1972 Republican presidents were elected, but both Houses of Congress remained in the hands of Democratic majorities throughout their terms of office. In 1996 Democratic President Clinton was re-elected with a large majority on the same day that the Republicans won majorities in both the Senate and the House of Representatives.

If the president's party also has majorities in one or both Houses of Congress, at the mid-term elections the president's party usually loses support, and sometimes the shift of party strength may be considerable. In 1994, in the middle of President Clinton's term of office, the Democrats lost fifty-six seats in the House of Representatives to the Republicans. The loss of support at mid-term is partly a reflection of the normal disillusionment with the party in power, and partly because local issues tend to be more important at mid-term than in presidential election years. At mid-term, therefore, the president is faced with a difficult tactical problem; to what extent should the president and members of the administration campaign in support of their party in the congressional elections? There are dangers both in giving only lukewarm support and in wholehearted involvement. If the president is actively committed to ensuring a victory for the party, then an ensuing defeat for them is a defeat for the president as well. The president's prestige will suffer a serious blow and the result will be doubly damaging to hopes of legislative support for the administration's policies in the last two years of the administration. Furthermore, if the president conducts a hard-hitting campaign on behalf of the congressional party it will to some extent antagonise those members of the other party in Congress who have been sympathetic to the president's aims and on whose support it may be necessary to depend in the future. On the other hand, if the president remains aloof from the battles in which the members of the party are engaged, it may endanger morale in the party and antagonise members of Congress who feel that they have a claim to be supported. The dilemma is compounded by the fact that some of the bitterest enemies of the president's policies will be found among the ranks of Senators and Congressmen of the same party, and the president will not be keen to see them back again in the next Congress. A possible solution to the problem is for the president to give selective support at mid-term to those members of the party in Congress who have supported the administration's policies. However, this is a tricky strategy, which will embitter the president's opponents within the party and may well not be particularly successful in the morass of state and local politics at mid-term. To try to eliminate this problem and to bring Congress into closer harmony with the presidency, President Lyndon Johnson proposed an amendment to the Constitution that would give Congressmen a four-year term to coincide with that of the president, but there seems little likelihood of such a change being made.

The exact nature of the relationship between the forces affecting the election of the president and those influencing congressional elections is not very clear, even in presidential election years. The fortunes of a political party may show a close relationship between the outcomes of presidential and congressional elections, but how far do the character and popularity of a presidential candidate affect the results of House and Senate elections? Does the successful presidential candidate carry the members of the party into office riding upon the presidential coat-tails? And what about the relatively uninspiring candidate for the presidency; are the chances of election of party colleagues damaged? In 1952 the Republicans won control of both Senate and House together for the first time since 1928. Was this not the 'coat-tails effect' in operation, in which the Republicans were swept into power by the magic of Eisenhower's name? And yet four years later Eisenhower was re-elected with an even greater percentage of the poll, but the Democrats retained the control of House and Senate that they had won in the mid-term elections of 1954. The lustre of Eisenhower's name seemed to do Republican candidates little good on that occasion. Because John F. Kennedy performed less well as a vote-getter than his party as a whole in 1960, does this mean that *he* rode into office on the coat-tails of his party, or perhaps that congressional Democrats did less well because of his candidacy than they might otherwise have done? In 1994 Democratic candidates for the Senate and the House of Representatives seemed to gain little advantage from the popularity of President Clinton. The so-called 'coat-tails effect' provides one of the enigmas of American politics. The evidence suggests that a popular presidential candidate may have a considerable effect upon the turnout of voters at the elections, but probably does not have much effect upon the way in which the electorate cast their votes in congressional contests. Voters' reactions to congressional candidates seem to depend much more upon local factors than upon the influence of the national leader of the party. If this is the case, it is of the greatest importance for the working of American politics, for it is the Congressman's or Senator's perception of constituents' attitudes that will determine the extent to which he or she supports presidential policies in Congress. If re-election depends more upon local issues and attitudes than upon the appeal of the presidential candidate to the voters, then Members of Congress will react accordingly in the legislature, giving the president support when, and only when, they feel that this is what their constituents want.

Thus the gulf between presidential and congressional politics that was created by the makers of the Constitution in 1787 has been widened in a number of ways.

There is one other important way in which the tensions in the American political system between Congress and president were aggravated: the impact of gerrymandering and the mal-apportionment of congressional constituencies. Gerrymandering is the practice of drawing constituency boundaries in such a way that one political party gains an unfair advantage over the other. Congressional district boundaries are drawn up by the state legislatures, and they could be drawn in an irregular way so that pockets of strength can be linked together in one constituency. Alternatively, boundaries can be drawn so that the concentration of the supporters of one party in a few constituencies where it will receive large majorities will enable the other party to take a relatively large number of constituencies with small majorities. Another way of giving one party an unfair advantage over the other is to provide for constituencies of very different sizes, so that congressional districts are mal-apportioned among the population. This can be done by deliberately drawing boundaries in such a way that one constituency may have two or three times as many voters as another, or it may be done simply by ignoring movements of population. The mal-apportionment of state legislatures and of congressional districts was historically one of the major reasons for the difference in emphasis between congressional and presidential politics. The fact that the election of the president depended so greatly on the large urbanised states contrasted strangely with the electoral base of Congress. Rural interests dominated many state legislatures, a domination often maintained by mal-apportionment. In their turn, the state legislatures created congressional districts that over-represented rural interests. In Texas in 1962 the largest congressional district contained 951,527 people while the smallest had only 216,371. Thus the different constituencies of president and Congress emphasised strongly differing interests.

In 1962, however, the Supreme Court of the United States handed down a judicial decision with endless political ramifications. In the case of *Baker* v. *Carr* the Court decided that it was unconstitutional for a state to retain a mal-apportioned legislature, and the American courts set about re-shaping the American legislatures. In 1964 the Supreme Court applied the same principle to congressional districts, stating that 'as nearly as is practicable, one man's vote in a Congressional election is to be worth as much as another's.' The effect of this ruling was to reduce the over-representation of rural areas, and to give greater importance to the role of suburbia in modern America. The increase in the number of Representatives from suburban districts increased the number of independent-minded members of Congress, and also the incidence of ticket-splitting, for the affluent suburban electorate is generally better educated and independent minded. President Clinton drew a good deal of support from these areas in 1996, in spite of the fact that many of the districts that voted for him elected Republicans to the House of Representatives.

Elections and the states

Each of the fifty states elects its governor, state legislators, and state and local officials, often on the same day and on the same ballot as presidential and congressional elections, although many cities, townships, school districts and other elective bodies have elections at other times of the year. It is difficult to generalise about this enormous array of elections and the way in which they are conducted. The governorship of a great state, like New York or California, Pennsylvania or Texas, is an office to be coveted, both for its own sake and because it may form that essential basis of state political power that is needed in order to make a bid for the presidency itself. At the other end of the political spectrum, it may be the height of political ambition to become one of the selectmen of a New England town of a few hundred people. The movement of the great tides of national politics may affect the outcome of some of the state and local contests, and equally the politics of the presidency itself may be dependent upon the outcome of local political battles. State politics is not wholly autonomous and distinct from national politics, but neither is it dependent upon, or subservient to, national trends. Indeed, the candidacy of a well-known and popular figure for a state governorship may well have a considerable effect upon voter turnout for congressional elections, as was the case when Nelson Rockefeller ran for Governor of New York in 1958.

Political campaigns at state and local level differ widely – in some areas the 'lone wolf' campaign is the norm, in which each candidate runs for office on their own, creating their own organisation as they go along. Elsewhere the parties are highly organised and in control of local politics. Similarly, the finance for campaigns may be run on a shoestring, or involve millions of dollars in a state-wide campaign for the governorship. Electoral tactics are as varied and ingenious as the American imagination. In 1958 Senator Kuchel, campaigning for the governorship of California, staged a 'telethon' in which he appeared before the television cameras in Los Angeles in a programme lasting for over twenty hours. Constituents were able to telephone the Senator and ask him questions; he discussed campaign issues and had voters in to meet him before the cameras. Vice-President Nixon used a carefully staged telethon in the 1960 presidential campaign. In 2004 Howard Dean in campaigning for the nomination of the Democratic Party made extensive use of the internet to organise support.

Perhaps the most important aspect of the variety of political styles in the states is the fact that it is the states themselves that control the machinery of election for all elective offices, including federal offices. This control of the election machinery has been used as a weapon in the political battle rather than as a piece of neutral machinery of representative government. Electoral law has been used to prevent blacks, poor whites or immigrants from exercising the vote. Poll taxes, literacy tests, residence requirements and making primary elections open only to white voters have all been used in the past to discriminate against 'undesirable elements'. This form of electoral discrimination has been attacked by the courts and by Congress. The Supreme Court declared the 'white primary' unconstitutional in 1944. In 1957 and 1960 Congress passed Civil Rights Acts providing federal machinery to aid blacks who had been improperly deprived of the right to register as voters. In 1964 a further Civil Rights Act strengthened the power of the US Attorney General to supervise voting registration, and regulated the administration of literacy tests by the states. In the same year the Twenty-Fourth Amendment to the Constitution was ratified, outlawing the use of the poll tax as a prerequisite for voting in federal elections. As a result of these measures, and of the registration drives by civil rights workers on behalf of black voters, black registrations in the Southern states had risen by 1964 to over 2 million, giving rise to the situation, long feared by Southern whites, where in a number of states the outcome of elections could depend upon the black vote, so providing the basis for the transformation of Southern politics. By the end of the twentieth century the registration of blacks was proportionately almost as high as that of whites, and their importance in the outcome of elections, particularly at the presidential level, became considerable because of the tendency of a large majority of black voters to support the Democratic Party.

The form of the ballot is also a matter of state law, and it is difficult to assess the importance of differing practices in the states on the working of the electoral system. The 'long ballot' results from the great number of state and local offices to be filled. Ballot papers reached ludicrous proportions – at the extreme they could be six feet long and contain a thousand names. Voting machines have now replaced the ballot paper nearly everywhere, and have cut down corrupt practices at election time, but even these machines can be rigged if election officials are corrupt. County election officials can make important decisions regarding the procedures to be used, including the design of ballots. A variety of differing voting machines are in use, each with different characteristics. The presidential election of 2000 hung upon the outcome of the vote in Florida and the inefficiency of the punch card machines used in that state, which together with alleged dubious practices by some election officials, caused turmoil.

The introduction of machines has greatly speeded up the counting of the votes, and, together with the introduction of computers, has created an election problem possibly unique to the United States. The polls close at 7 p.m. in Connecticut, on America's eastern seaboard, but because of the time difference it is then only 4 p.m. in California. Within a short time of the end of voting in the East the television sets across the nation are giving out the computer's predictions of the election result, and yet there are millions of people still to vote in the Western states. How does this affect their behaviour? Do the supporters of the candidates whose defeat has just been predicted lose heart and ensure defeat, or are their party workers spurred to new efforts, while the supporters of the apparent victor become overconfident and lethargic as they have presumably already won?

Campaign finances

The American political system involves more electioneering than any other in the world; so many different offices to fill, at so many different levels – primary elections, run-off elections, congressional elections, presidential elections, state and local elections. These electoral battles involve the expenditure of huge sums of money. It has been estimated that election expenditures by candidates for the presidency, the Senate and the House of Representatives totalled over $4 billion in 2004. To gain re-election President George W. Bush spent $359 million, and his opponent, John Kerry, spent $285 million. The total expenditures on the presidential campaign and the national conventions were more than $1 billion, 56 per cent greater than four years earlier. Candidates in the primaries raised $673.9 million seeking nomination. In addition to the spending by candidates and on the conventions, individuals, parties and other groups spent $192.4 million advocating the election or defeat of presidential candidates in the campaign of 2004.

The vital importance of the media, especially television, and coast-to-coast campaigning by the candidates, each with a large retinue of advisers, speech writers, organisers, and press officers, means that it is impossible to fight a presidential election without considerable financial resources, and at each election the costs rise. Raising money becomes an essential and arduous task for the candidates' supporters. In 2004 the Republican National Committee spent $45.8 million on generic media advertising; the Democratic National Committee spent $24 million. Money cannot guarantee success in an election, but it surely helps, and increasingly candidates for office are drawn from individuals who can make a significant contribution to their campaign from their own resources. Clearly, if one candidate has access to a great deal of money and another is starved of finance, the outcome of the election may be affected by this difference in resources, and those who contribute money may have a claim on the successful candidate for services rendered. The problem of finding a balance between allowing candidates the necessary freedom to attempt to convince the electorate, but at the same time to avoid corruption, is an ever-present one in a democracy. In the United States a number of rather ineffectual attempts were made to deal with this problem, but the Watergate affair, with its revelations about the activities of the Committee to Re-elect the President, led Congress to pass the Federal Election Campaign Act (FECA) in 1974. The Act laid down strict rules regarding the reporting of campaign contributions and expenditures, and also set limits to the amounts that could be contributed by an individual ($1,000) or an organisation ($5,000), to any one candidate.

The Act also set limits to the amount a candidate might spend on his or her own election, but this provision was declared unconstitutional by the Supreme Court. These restrictions, however, are not as effective as they might seem. There was no limit set to the number of 'organisations' that might contribute to a candidate's expenses, and as a result large numbers of 'Political Action Committees' (PACs) were set up to contribute to the funding of candidates' campaign expenses – another aspect of the way in which interest groups, rather than the political parties themselves, are the essential channels of political action in America.

The 1974 Act, however, failed to prevent the continuing increase in the growth of campaign expenditures, in part because of a loophole in the law which allowed 'soft money' to be contributed to the campaign by individuals or organisations. 'Hard money' was the term used to describe the contributions made directly to named candidates, which were regulated by the Federal Election Campaign Act. However, the Act did not prevent individuals or organisations from making contributions to a *political party*, and this money could be used to pay for television advertisements supporting or attacking particular policies; this became known as 'soft money'. Television and other advertisements paid for by soft money could even refer to a candidate by name, provided that the advertisement did not contain the phrases 'vote for' or 'vote against'. In the election of 2000 a total of $495 million in soft money was raised by the parties.

As a result of the outcry against this use of soft money the Bipartisan Campaign Reform Act (BCRA) was passed in 2002. The Act prohibited national political parties from raising or spending soft money and it came into effect before the presidential election of 2004 but, as we have seen, the amount spent in that election reached record heights. In part this increase was due to a loophole in the BCRA. Although the Act outlawed the raising of soft money by political parties, it did not prohibit the raising of soft money by other types of organisation that might be aligned with one party or the other, and many such groups were indeed formed to raise money. These became known as advocacy groups, or '527 groups', after a section of federal law which exempts from taxation the raising of money for political purposes. $435 million was raised in this way in 2004 and so the saga continues. Money, large amounts of it, remains indispensable to the working of the American electoral system.

The 1974 Act also initiated an interesting approach to the problem of 'fairness' in the electoral system by introducing the public funding of presidential election campaigns. At the stage of the presidential campaign proper, after the candidates have been chosen, they may opt to finance their campaigns from the Presidential Election Campaign Fund. The federal government provides money for the national conventions of each of the major parties, and funds are also available to pay part of the cost of primary election campaigns for candidates from major and minor parties. Of course part of the original rationale of this provision of taxpayer's money to fund political parties was to offset the restrictions which were being placed on their ability to raise money directly. In spite of the fact that the restrictions enacted in the FECA and the BCRA have been largely ineffectual, the public funding of elections continues. In 2004 the two major party nominees received $74.6 million each in public funds to conduct their election campaigns; to help finance the organisation of the national conventions the two major parties received $14.9 million each from the US Treasury.

It can now be seen just how far the electoral machinery in the United States emphasises the geographical and sectional influences in its politics, but at the same time allows pressure groups and individuals to influence the outcome of elections through financial contributions, with all the dangers inherent in that activity. In Western democracies the use of geographical constituencies provides a built-in tendency to stress regional differences of interest rather than class or pluralistic factors. In the United States the constitutional provisions that decentralise power and authority powerfully reinforce this tendency. In other countries ideological and organisational forces have modified, sometimes almost obliterated, the built-in emphasis upon geography in the electoral system, but in the United States the party system and the electoral system have tended to reinforce each other's decentralising tendencies. Only the presidency acts as a centralising force and the selection and election of presidents are by no means free of sectional influences. Thus the party system and the electoral system discharge one vital function: they select the candidates to fill political office. But because of their sectional nature they are relatively poor at performing another function vital to the political system: the formulation of policies. The job of partly filling this gap is performed by the next set of political structures to which we shall turn our attention – the interest groups.

Further reading

Abramson, P.R., Aldrich, J.H. and Rohde, D.W. (2003) *Change and Continuity in the 2000 and 2002 Elections*, Washington, DC: CQ Press.
Mieczkowski, Y. (2001) *The Routledge Historical Atlas of Presidential Elections*, London: Routledge.
Nelson, M. (ed.) (2005) *The Elections of 2004*, Washington, DC: CQ Press.
Polsby, N.W. and Wildavsky, A. (2003) *Presidential Elections: Strategies and Structures of American Politics*, 11th edn, Lanham, MD: Rowman and Littlefield.
Pomper, Gerald M. (ed.) (2001) *The Election of 2000*, London: Chatham House.

Websites

Dave Leip's Atlas of US Presidential Elections: www.uselectionatlas.org
Federal Election Commission: www.fec.gov
US House of Representatives, Election Information: http://clerk.house.gov/members/electionInfo

5 Pressure politics

Group pluralism

Arriving at political decisions involves complex processes that vary according to the issues, the circumstances at the time the decisions are being taken, and many other institutional and personal factors. Three major sources can be determined from which the eventual solutions to problems are generated: the institutional machinery of government itself, the party system, and interested groups. Most decisions will involve all three of these structures in some degree or another, but as we have already seen the role of political parties in terms of policy formation is relatively weak, and a vacuum is created to be filled by the complex structure of interest groups. This separation of the functions of selecting leaders, and of initiating and influencing policy, gives to the American political system its peculiar flavour and complexity, which will become fully apparent only when we look at the behaviour of Congressmen and Senators and their relationship with the president and the administration. Party politics and pressure politics criss-cross and merge to produce an ever-changing pattern of legislative and executive behaviour.

But how do we distinguish between the party system and the structure of interest groups? After all, many of the persons involved in one of these patterns of behaviour will be involved in the other as well. Formally, the difference between political party and interest group is that the former organisation nominates candidates for public office, and the latter does not. If a group attempts to put up its own candidates for election, it becomes a political party and subject to all the legal provisions that in the United States regulate the operations of political parties. Yet this relatively straightforward distinction does not mean that in practice a sharp, clear line can be drawn between the two forms of political organisation. Holders of elective office, wearing a party label, may be very closely associated with particular interest groups, and although such groups do not formally nominate candidates they may publicly endorse a particular party or its candidate, contribute to campaign funds and either secretly or openly work to elect or defeat particular individuals. The membership of party and group may overlap to the point where a particular group may be little more than one 'wing' of a political party; on the other hand, a group may be at pains to remain aloof from both parties in order to be able to appeal to them both on an equal basis. Thus interest groups may be seen either as alternatives to the political parties or as complementary to them. The complexity of the American party system gives added significance to this characteristic of interest groups, for a particular group may be identified more closely with a political party at state or local level than at the federal level, or have a closer relationship to the presidential party than to the congressional party. A group of individuals may emerge and re-emerge in different guises at different times, as the occasion demands. Thus, although for analytical purposes it is useful to describe the party system and the structure of interest groups as if they were quite distinct entities, the realities of political life are more complex.

This blurring of the distinction between parties and interest groups is paralleled at the other end of the spectrum by the way in which the structure of interest groups merges into the machinery of government itself. Thus some groups, the American Farm Bureau Federation, for instance, achieved a position that made them almost an essential party to any government action affecting their interests: groups formally outside the government can become appendages to it. In the same way, parts of the government machine itself may behave like interest groups in order to safeguard their own position. Thus for many years the Air Force was a powerful interest group exercising influence on Congressmen in opposition to the policy of the Defense Department and other branches of the armed services. The National Guard, a part-time reserve military organisation, was extremely successful in obtaining its aims through traditional interest group methods, particularly through the efforts of the National Guard Association.

Bearing these complexities in mind, it is true to say that the importance of interest groups in the American political system has given rise to a theory of politics in which the interaction of groups becomes the essence of democratic government. Group pluralism is perhaps *the* American theory of politics, finding its roots in James Madison's theory of the Constitution in 1787, and providing an alternative both to the Marxist class theory of politics and to the nineteenth-century individualistic theories of democracy. This theory of government is based upon the assumption that individuals as such can have little or no impact upon the way in which decisions are taken. The group is the significant unit of the political system. In a free society innumerable groups will form and re-form to express the diverse and changing interests of their members. Such groups are not a threat to the traditional channels of government action but a necessary complement to them. The groups perform the functions of supplying information about the enormous range of complex activities in which government becomes involved, and of giving expression to a range of opinions of far greater diversity than the normal representative machinery of government could cope with.

Two things are necessary for the successful operation of this type of political system. First, there must be a broad consensus of agreement about the basis and aims of the society so that no group will attempt to force its views upon the rest to the point where civil war might ensue. As we have seen, this consensus is one of the characteristic features of the American ideological scene. Second, there must be a set of political mechanisms through which inter-group bargaining can be conducted in such a way that some sort of equilibrium can be attained between the competing demands. Perhaps the first requirement of this system of government is that it should be flexible. The pattern of demands is continually changing as new economic, social and military developments take place, and a stable political system must be able to accommodate them. Changing group aspirations, such as those of blacks and other minority groups today, will disturb the established distribution of authority or wealth, and a new position of equilibrium, a new compromise, must be attained, a new bargain struck. This flexibility, the ability to adapt to changing circumstances, is one of the outstanding characteristics of the American *political system*, in contradiction to the oft-laboured clichés about the inflexibility of the American *constitution*.

This description of the working of the political system undoubtedly over-emphasises the pluralistic features of American government, certainly failing to give sufficient weight to the policy-making functions of the presidency. Nevertheless, it is by no means negligible as an explanation of the general working of American politics. As we shall see, on many issues the Congress of the United States becomes something of a marketplace in which the pressures of party, constituency and interested groups, including in the last category departments of the federal administration, are assessed, balanced and reconciled to produce compromises that seem in the eyes of the members of the legislature to be as satisfactory as possible to the interests involved. Given the diversity of American society, these interests can be effectively represented only by a wide variety of competing groups with overlapping membership. This last consideration, the way in which the membership of different groups overlaps, is an important factor in the operation of group bargaining, making the processes of the reconciliation of competing demands far easier than if the groups concerned were ossified into completely distinct and separate sections of the community.

The flexibility of the political system flows to a considerable extent, therefore, from the way in which interest groups work the cumbrous machinery of American government. The constitutional devices of federalism and the separation of powers, which together serve to decentralise both the government and the parties geographically, and to disintegrate them vertically, create the conditions in which interest groups can flourish and indeed become essential to the operation of government. Interest groups, unlike political parties, are not bound to particular geographical constituencies. They can organise themselves across states or sections, or across the whole nation. They can adopt a unitary or a federal structure, as circumstances demand. A retail drug-store owner in a small Southern town can ally himself with fellow drug-store owners in New York City or Los Angeles to achieve common aims even if his views on all matters other than retail prices are completely at odds with those of other members of his profession. Interest groups thrive upon the fragmented character of the government system. A group that is frustrated at one level or in one department of the government can quickly switch its efforts to another level, or to another point of access, in order to try to get its views adopted. Thus it could well be argued that it is interest groups rather than political parties that bring into some sort of coordinated relationship the various branches of the government – federal, state and local – although it could also be argued, with equal justification, that it is the conflicting demands of interest groups operating through different levels and branches of the government that generate the sharp conflicts that arise between the parts of the government machine.

However, this description does not give full expression to the complexity of group politics. It suggests that there are clearly identifiable groups in the population each with its common interest, but this is not really the case. How does one define or designate an 'interest'? The black community might seem to be a group with an obvious interest in common, and yet that community is represented by a wide range of organisations, some more militant than others, with differing aims, varying from the desire to integrate blacks fully into American life to the intention to set up a separate black state or states. Similarly, there are sharp divisions of opinion within the business community or between labour unions, or within a group of professional people such as schoolteachers, about the way in which their aims should be pursued. Thus we must turn our attention from the existence of different groups of people in the community at large who can be labelled as economically, racially or socially similar in interest to the actual organisations, in their enormous number and variety, that figure on the political scene.

Interest groups and organisation

We have seen that the existence of a distinct group in the electorate, such as the black community, may be an important factor in the outcome of political battles at election time. But politics is a continuing process, in which interested groups may wish to be involved at every stage of government activity, and in order to achieve this they must be organised. Thus, the importance of the black community does not lie simply in its potential voting power, but also in the numerous organisations that capitalise upon that potential by bringing pressure to bear upon government agencies to further the black interest as they see it. The associations and organisations that come into existence to express new demands or to defend old positions vary considerably in the form and durability of their organisational life. Some are ephemeral operations which come into existence in response to a particular stimulus, say the threat of government regulation of the affairs of a particular section of the community, and expire as soon as a decision has been taken or a problem solved. At the other extreme there are those organisations that exhibit a formidable degree of stability, homogeneity of purpose and expertise, which makes them more significant elements in the process of policy-making than the great political parties. The National Association for the Advancement of Colored People (NAACP) and the National Rifle Association (NRA) are examples of the latter type of organisation, and are continually involved in political situations. Between these extremes there is a bewildering variety of organisations with differing aims which may from time to time become involved in political decisions and which are therefore potentially participants in the political process.

The list of such organisations is endless, and their concerns are equally various. Many of them are to be identified with an interest only in the very broadest sense, for example, the League of Women Voters or the National Federation of Business and Professional Women's Clubs. Nor do groups have to be associated with economic interests in order to be effective, as the Marxist analysis would suggest. Perhaps the most famous of all interest groups was the Anti-Saloon League, which played an important part in bringing about the passage of the Eighteenth Amendment prohibiting the manufacture or sale of alcohol in the United States. Religious denominations, many with representatives in Washington, maintain organisations to keep an eye upon governmental affairs that interest them; such are the National Council of Churches of Christ, the Board of Temperance of the Methodist Church, and the United States Conference of Catholic Bishops. The Christian Coalition of America is the national organization of conservative Christians; the American Israeli Public Affairs Committee concerns itself with American policy in the Middle East, and exercises an influence on government out of proportion to the Jewish population; the American Muslim Taskforce on Civil Rights and Elections is an umbrella organization representing fifteen Muslim associations. Associations of ex-servicemen such as the American Legion or the Veterans of Foreign Wars concern themselves both with pensions and with wider political issues such as the activities of the United Nations and its impact upon American interests. Professional associations such as the American Medical Association (AMA) and the American Bar Association (ABA) exercise very considerable influence over the areas of government action in which they can claim a special expertise. The activities of the AMA in combating President Clinton's proposals for health care reform, together with the Health Insurers Association of America (HIAA), represents perhaps the best known interest group campaign of recent times, in which the HIAA and the AMA used every tactic available to highly organised interest groups to influence public opinion and members of Congress. Other professional bodies, such as the American Federation of Teachers, represent the concern of their members with salaries and conditions of work. In the field of civil rights there is a bewildering variety of groups, ranging from the NAACP and the Congress of Racial Equality to the Nation of Islam, whose leader, Louis Farrakhan, in 1995 mounted a demonstration in Washington, 'The

Million Man March'. The official estimate of attendance was 875,000 black men. And then, almost as appendages of the great political parties, there are those groups whose interest is ideological rather than economic or social; the Americans for Democratic Action on the one hand or the John Birch Society on the other. There is thus a great spectrum of groups with differing degrees of political involvement, with different organisational biases and using different techniques in the search for influence upon government. But there are four major complexes of interest groups that demand more detailed attention: the representatives of business, of labour and of agriculture, and 'cause groups' claiming to represent the public interest.

Business interest groups

Business and politics are inextricably interwoven. Great decisions of national policy on matters of foreign affairs or defence will have an immediate effect upon the business community. The decisions of the federal government on space programmes, aircraft production and the methods of prosecuting foreign aid programmes or military operations involve the expenditure of billions of dollars for contracts with American firms. The war in Iraq and the subsequent need for rebuilding that country's infrastructure initiated a scramble for government contracts, and considerable criticism of the way in which they were allocated and controlled. The tax policy of federal and state governments is of immediate interest to every business corporation in the country as well as to a host of small businessmen. Business interests may seek to promote or to prevent government action, to gain a competitive advantage over other businesses, or to defend themselves against legislation promoted by labour unions to improve wage rates or working conditions. The United States at the end of the nineteenth century pioneered attempts to deal with the monopolistic tendencies of modern industry, and to legislate against restrictive pricing agreements. The Wagner and Taft–Hartley Acts embody a comprehensive scheme of government control of collective bargaining, and the federal government sets a minimum wage and maximum working hours for all workers engaged in interstate commerce (a definition that has been expanded by the Supreme Court to include a high percentage of all American workers). An impressive range of federal agencies, the independent regulatory commissions, enforce legislation regulating many areas of business activity. The Federal Trade Commission (FTC) is charged with the promotion of free and fair competition by controlling false and misleading advertising and other business practices. As early as 1887 the Interstate Commerce Commission was established to regulate the rates and operations of railways, and later to take over the regulation of interstate trucking companies; it was abolished in 1995 as a result of moves to deregulate industry. The Securities and Exchange Commission, the Federal Communications Commission, the Federal Energy Regulation Commission, the Federal Trade Commission – all exercise extensive authority over businesses engaged in their field of interest, and there are many other federal agencies engaged in the regulation of business activity. The fifty states also have a wide variety of regulatory functions, and the concentration of some types of business in a few states, for example the insurance business in the Northeast, renders the activities of these states particularly important in certain fields. State and local regulation of road hauliers has been of particular importance in the past because of the great variety of state laws concerning the taxation of road transport and the standards that hauliers must meet in the construction and operation of their vehicles. Local businesses are subjected to an enormous variety of state and local regulations covering, for instance, health regulations on the production of milk.

There is, therefore, enormous scope for business groups to interest themselves in, and to become involved in, the legislative and administrative operations of government. Furthermore, the large volume of legislation on the statute books that involves business operations, in a country where legislation is subject to judicial review by the courts in order to test its constitutional validity, means that businesses are quite frequently involved in litigation to determine the extent of their rights and obligations under the law, right up to the level of the Supreme Court of the United States. The size and power of some of the corporations that thus come into contact with the government is awesome – a few of them seem even to rival the government itself in the size of their operations and the extent of their influence. Giants such as General Motors or the American Telephone and Telegraph Company conduct their own relations with the government, using all the paraphernalia of modern public relations techniques.

The business community in general is represented in its contact with government agencies by associations that specialise in representing their members' interests. A few of these, in particular the National Association of Manufacturers, the Chamber of Commerce of the United States, and the Business Roundtable, are nation-wide organisations claiming to speak for the business community as a whole. But each branch of industry and commerce has its own trade association to represent its interest. By 1961 there were 1,800 national trade associations in the United States, 11,000 state, regional and local associations, and 5,000 local chambers of commerce. In 2004 there were 34,000 trade associations listed at state and national level. The more inclusive an association attempts to be, the less likely it is to be able to develop clear policy positions, except on a very few matters of common interest, or to exercise leadership in business affairs; and when an association does take a stand on a matter of importance the views of the leadership may be quite unrepresentative of the membership of the association. Thus the larger and more inclusive the group becomes, the more likely it is to suffer from the same disabilities as those that beset the political parties themselves.

The operation of inter-group bargaining and the divisions within the business community are illustrated by the way in which the battles over retail price maintenance and the control over the production of natural gas were conducted. Retail price maintenance is the use of legislation to outlaw price-cutting by retailers, in order to maintain a common minimum price for a product. The group most interested in the continuation of retail price main-tenance legislation was the National Association of Retail Druggists (NARD), who over a long period fought off attempts by the federal administration, the courts and price-cutting competitors to outlaw price-fixing agreements. The NARD was successful in getting legislation supporting its position adopted by Congress and by many state legislatures. In the 1930s, in its effort to obtain the passage of the Miller–Tydings Amendment, which exempted price-fixing agreements made under state law from the prohibitions of the anti-trust laws, the NARD established 'contact committees' of local retailers in every congressional district, choosing acquaintances and friends of congressmen to staff them. The Amendment was passed despite the opposition of the president and the FTC. At the state level the Association was extremely suc-cessful in getting states to pass the necessary legislation, and the model law that it supported was passed by eleven states before a typographical error in the draft was noted. The success of the NARD in these years, although resale price maintenance has succumbed to other forces since, illustrates one very important aspect of business in politics in the United States. It is not only the giants of the 'military-industrial complex' that can successfully exercise pressure upon government; one of the most persistently successful interests in getting help from government has been the small businessman.

The battle over the regulation of the production and distribution of natu-ral gas during the Eisenhower administration is illustrative of the way in which different business groups can line up against each other using the dif-ferent levels of federal and state government to attempt to achieve their aims. This was a dispute over whether the states or the federal government should control the output and pricing policy of the natural gas industry. The producers were fearful of federal control and formed a Natural Gas and Oil Resources Committee to keep control in the hands of the states. The local gas distributing companies, however, hoped for lower prices with federal control, and, allied with labour, municipal and consumer groups, they fought to assert federal power. A Council of Local Gas Companies allied with a committee of mayors pleaded for the consumer before Congress. The oil and gas industry was reported to have spent over $1.5 million to 'educate' Senators. The gas producers scored an initial success by getting the legislation that they wanted passed by Congress, but allegations of improper lobbying, in particular the revelation by Senator Case that a large sum of money had been paid into his campaign fund in connection with the legislation, led President Eisenhower to veto the Bill.

The business community has adapted itself to the working of pressure politics in America in two ways. Business corporations have used Political Action Committees to channel money to those candidates for political of-fice whom they wish to support. Trade associations and other lobbyist or-ganisations have formed into coalitions in order to pursue common aims on particular issues coming before government. This has enabled them to take a more aggressive attitude towards government policy, pursuing more positive aims, rather than simply defending themselves against attack.

Labour and politics

The paradoxical position of labour in the United States has been expressed by V.O. Key as 'a numerically great force in a society adhering to the doctrine of the rule of numbers, yet without proportionate durable political power as a class'. We have already seen some of the special factors in American history that have contributed to the spectacle of a highly industrialised society in which socialism has been of negligible importance – the lack of any true feudal tradition, the open character of American society in the nineteenth century, the influence of the moving frontier of settlement. Yet although these factors help to explain the absence of any significant *socialist* party, they only serve to explain in part the weakness of labour as a political force. Part of the explanation lies in the general dispersion of constitutional authority and political power, which has militated against the growth of *any* national political organisation based upon an appeal to a single principle or a single group. Similarly, the diverse make-up of the American population, the great variety of ethnic and religious elements, has tended to fragment the labour force and to prevent the development of any cohesive attitudes or organisations based upon a specifically *labour* approach to politics. The lack of any ideological impulse on the part of the working class was reinforced by the absence of any truly conservative attitudes at the other end of the social scale, at least until the post-Second World War period. The acceptance of change was built into the American philosophy, so that there was no need for a political force based upon the demand for change as an end in itself. All these factors helped to create a situation in which labour became a series of interest groups rather than a political party.

It is not only that labour has not wanted to become an independent political force, however; for American unionism has also, in one sense, failed even as a movement with the aims of improving wages and working conditions. Union membership has declined steadily over recent decades. In 1980 the proportion of the working population represented by unions was 21 per cent, but by 2005 only 12.5 per cent of wage and salary earners were union members; in a few states the proportion of workers in unions was very small indeed – in South Carolina only 2.3 per cent and in North Carolina only 2.9 per cent. The union movement has also failed in other ways which have affected its political influence. Some sections of the movement have been associated with racketeering and criminal activities, which have brought organised labour into disrepute, the extreme example being the Longshoremen's Union in New York and Jersey City, which for many years was virtually run by racketeers, enforcing their authority by gangsterism and maintaining their position through their connections with local political machines.

Furthermore, the labour movement has been riven by internal dissension and personal rivalries. The American Federation of Labor (AFL) was formed in 1886 as a federation of unions largely organised upon a craft basis, and for much of its history it was firmly opposed to the intervention of government in labour matters. It favoured laissez-faire, and was squarely capitalistic in philosophy. With the growth of mass production industries, however, and in particular the car industry, industrial unions became increasingly important, and resulted in the establishment of the Congress of Industrial Organisations (CIO) in 1938.

The built-in conflict between the principles of craft and industrial unions naturally led to great hostility between AFL and CIO, but they differed also in terms of their philosophy of government. The CIO, born of mass production industry and the years of the Depression, was more dependent upon government support than the AFL and consequently was in favour of government intervention in labour affairs. In 1943 the CIO established a Political Action Committee to provide for the organisation of labour's political arm. Whereas the AFL had avoided outright endorsement of presidential candidates, the CIO executive endorsed Truman as the Democratic candidate in 1948 and four years later the AFL followed with their endorsement of Adlai Stevenson.

The weakness of the labour movement as a political force was demonstrated in 1947, when Congress passed the Taft–Hartley Act with provisions restrictive of organised labour, including a clause that allowed state governments to outlaw the closed shop. The passage of the legislation, which was supported by the National Association of Manufacturers, emphasised the disruption of the unions, for the AFL and the CIO were at odds about the strategy for opposing the Bill, and internal dissension within the CIO threatened that organisation itself. In 1955 the two federations combined into the AFL–CIO, but this remains a loose federation of unions each with autonomous powers. The new federation set up a Committee on Political Education which worked on behalf of candidates who received its endorsement, particularly by carrying out registration campaigns, coordinating the collection of campaign contributions and organising canvassing on behalf of the candidates it chose to support. However, again the weakness of union power is illustrated in that the federal minimum wage has not been raised since 1997 and stands at a mere $5.15 an hour.

The orientation of the unions towards Democratic presidential candidates in recent years is clear enough, but officially the AFL–CIO has a non-partisan approach towards legislative elections, a policy that is described as rewarding labour's friends and punishing its enemies whatever their party label. In practice, only very few Republican senatorial or congressional candidates receive union endorsement, compared with the large number of Democratic candidates who do so. However, endorsement by the unions is not an automatic matter for Democrats, and the views and record of the individual candidate become crucial. Similarly the unions make large contributions to the campaign funds of Democratic candidates, but the political aims of the unions remain limited. They wish to further the interests of their members through political action and to defend themselves against attempts by business interests to attack their position, but they do not wish to govern, or to bring about fundamental changes in American society. The American labour movement is not opposed to capitalism, it simply wishes to promote the interests of the workers within a capitalistic economy.

The farmers and the government

Agriculture in the United States provides an example of the way in which an important minority group can achieve political power out of all proportion to its numbers. The farm population is much less significant in numbers than the unions and less wealthy than the business community, yet it seems able to fight off all attacks upon government programmes and supports that have evolved to help the farming community as a result of earlier depressed conditions. Farm groups, allied with congressmen and with the sections of the administration that operate the farm programmes, seem to have created, in the words of one observer, a private system of government in which decisions on agricultural matters are taken exclusively by the agricultural interests themselves. Since the 1930s the power of the farmer has become institutionalised in the close integration of agricultural organisations with the government machine to the point where it is difficult to draw a line between public agency and private group. Much of their power, however, stems from the peculiar characteristics of the farm vote. The farm vote is, even in American terms, both highly independent and highly variable. Farmers tend to switch to the party that is currently supporting them more readily than do other groups. Split-ticket voting is frequent, and the turnout of the farm vote is more changeable than that of other sections of the population. This makes the farm vote an unpredictable and potentially very important factor in elections. Congress is, therefore, particularly sensitive to the reactions of the farmer.

However, the success of farm groups does not mean that agriculture is free of the divisive forces that fragment business and labour interests. The organisations representative of agriculture are very numerous. The variety of crops and products, many of them in competition with each other, produces its own crop of associations to represent producers, for example, the American Dairy Association, the National Cotton Council of America, and the National Association of Wheat Growers. However, three major organisations claim to speak for agriculture as a whole: the National Grange, the American Farm Bureau Federation and the National Farmers' Union. Each tends to be strongest in a particular area of the country, however, and they can come into conflict with each other. The Farm Bureau Federation has maintained close contact with government agencies since the New Deal period, when it was associated with the creation of agricultural programmes to combat the

Depression. It has been said of the AFBF that its support is necessary for the success of any legislation relating to agriculture, and the Federation can, if it wishes, put enormous pressure on Washington.

Public interest and cause groups

The 1960s and 1970s saw a remarkable change in the structure of interest groups in the United States. As we have seen, hitherto most interest groups had been representative of particular social or ethnic groupings, or had been the spokesmen of business, labour or agriculture. A few organisations, such as the League of Women Voters, had claimed to be concerned with the interest of the public in general, or with promoting 'good government'. In the 1960s, however, a large number of organisations sprang up whose aim was to protect the consumer, to promote efficiency in government, and to protect – or indeed to improve – the environment. One of the best known of these is Common Cause, whose aim is 'to change political structures so they will be more responsive to social needs and to produce a major reordering of national priorities'. The Public Citizen Foundation is dedicated to the protection of consumer interests, particularly by revealing safety defects in products. The Izaak Walton League, the National Audubon Society and the Sierra Club fight pollution and scrutinise construction projects to assess their impact on the environment and to oppose those schemes that they consider to be harmful.

A distinct but related development has been the growth of a number of new groups devoted to furthering particular causes. A plethora of groups promote women's rights (including the unsuccessful attempt to obtain an Equal Rights Amendment to the Constitution). The National Organization for Women works for the liberalisation of laws on abortion, and numerous pro-life groups such as the National Right to Life Committee fight to restrict or remove the availability of legally authorised abortions. Groups such as Greenpeace, which oppose nuclear power, have been increasingly active, pressurising Congress and the administration and developing public campaigns to mobilise opinion on their behalf, stimulating the formation of organisations, the Nuclear Energy Institute for example, representing the interest of the nuclear power industry. The development of the modern media of communication has enabled like-minded citizens across the country to collaborate on matters of common interest in a way that would have been impossible even thirty years earlier. The American Association of Retired People, with 35 million members, has become one of the most formidable groups on the political scene. The decline of the mass political parties as vehicles for policy development reduced their function as a channel for the expression of concerned public opinion. Public interest and cause groups have therefore become the medium for the activities of those who in earlier times would have joined the Progressive Movement or worked through the Democratic Party for the New Deal. These groups have had considerable success in promoting improved safety regulations, particularly for automobiles, and in securing the passage of legislation on pollution and consumer protection. For a time they seemed almost to have replaced the labour unions as the main anti-business force in the pluralistic politics of the United States, and they have certainly been one of the reasons why business interests themselves have become more aggressive in their behaviour. President Carter was criticised when making appointments to his administration for having paid too much attention to the claims of the new public interest and cause groups, and too little to those of the traditional labour and ethnic groups.

Interest groups at work

How do interest groups operate? The almost infinite flexibility of this type of political structure is reflected in the wide variety of the methods open to the interest group to try to achieve its aims. Groups can attempt to influence public opinion through all the media of communication available in modern society – through the press, television, radio and internet – and using all the modern techniques of the public relations industry. Or they can use more direct methods of gaining the attention of the public, organising protest marches or going to the extreme of sit-down strikes or even riots. When these extremes are reached, of course, the groups concerned are close to rejecting the whole basis of the equilibrium theory of democracy through group interaction in favour of a different type of politics: the politics of extremism. The basis of pluralist democracy is agreement on fundamentals and upon the necessity of using the 'normal channels' of the institutional machinery to achieve group aims. When a group feels that its minimum demands are unacceptable to the society in which it exists, it may opt out of the system, cease to be an interest group, and attempt to become a revolutionary force. As with so many of the distinctions used in the analysis of political activity, it is not always possible in practice to draw hard and fast lines in order to label particular groups as part of the interest group structure or place them outside it. Many groups hover on the fringes of the equilibrium system of politics – the use of company police in the 1920s to quell strikers, the Minutemen, the advocates of 'black power'. It is one of the characteristics of the American political system and of its ideological basis that there is a sizeable part of the population that is potentially ready to step outside the framework of compromise politics to further its interest by violent means if necessary. Thus the same group of people may be behaving at one moment as an interest group and at another as a conspiracy. It is at this point that the government ceases to be merely the neutral mechanism through which competing group demands are reconciled and becomes again both the instrument of law and order and the instrument for the imposition of policy, whether at Little Rock or at Waco.

The normal channels of group activity, of course, relate very closely to the institutional structures of government through which decisions are taken

– groups may attempt to exert influence on elections, on the process of legislation, on the way in which government programmes are administered, or on the courts. Groups may attempt to influence the selection of candidates for office at all levels of government, both in primary and general elections, and in particular since the passage of the Federal Election Campaign Act of 1974 by the means of Political Action Committees. Thus labour unions and other groups attempt to secure the election of candidates responsive to their demands. The Congress of Racial Equality in 1967 pledged itself to secure the return to Congress of the black Congressman Adam Clayton Powell who had been barred from taking up his seat. In 1952 oil-producing interests made it clear to delegates at the Democratic National Convention that Adlai Stevenson's attitude towards state control of offshore oil deposits was hostile to their interests. Groups may contribute to party funds, help with canvassing, aid party organisation, and provide speakers and literature to help in a campaign. The effectiveness of such activities, and the extent to which the interest groups benefit from the later behaviour of candidates who achieve office with their support, vary, of course, from negligible to very considerable, but it is very difficult to give any precise indication of the results of pressure politics at any stage of the governmental process. Congressmen who benefit from the support of a particular group at election times are probably predisposed towards their point of view in any case, and would normally assist them as far as seemed practicable in view of all the varying interests of their constituents. Perhaps the most that such groups can hope for, at federal level at any rate, is to maintain close contact with legislators through their supporting activities and thereby to have easier access to the Member of Congress or Senator at critical times. Interest groups attempt to influence the behaviour of the legislators in a number of ways. They may arrange to deluge them with letters and telegrams from constituents urging their point of view, or they may arrange for groups of voters to present their views to their representatives at the Capitol. Rather more subtly, and perhaps more effectively, they may prepare detailed briefs to deliver as evidence before congressional committees or to convince individual members of the legislature of the rightness of their case. Many interest groups maintain permanent offices in Washington, or in state capitals, in order to keep up close personal contact with legislators and administrators; other groups use the services of a professional lobbyist who may represent a number of groups who cannot afford to maintain their own representative. The use of a lobbyist who will pursue a group's interest in the legislature is by no means new. In 1846 a certain A.J. Marshall was hired by the Baltimore and Ohio Railroad to obtain from the legislature of the state of Virginia the grant of a right of way through the state to the Ohio River. When offering his services to the company Marshall emphasised that he was not proposing to use corrupt methods in dealing with legislators. 'My scheme is to surround the Legislature with respectable and influential agents, whose persuasive arguments may influence the members to do you a naked act of justice. That is all.' The modem lobbyist must be skilled in producing 'persuasive arguments', and many are equipped with staff and research facilities to enable them to do this. They must be capable of producing draft legislation that a sympathetic Congressman or Senator will be prepared to introduce into the legislature and to sponsor its passage. Much legislation of importance on the statute books of the United States today originated in the offices of interest groups.

The importance of lobbying activities, and some past scandals, led Congress in 1946 to pass the Regulation of Lobbying Act (superseded by the Lobbying Disclosure Act of 1995); a large number of state legislatures also have regulatory legislation on their books. The federal Act requires persons or organisations who engage in paid lobbying activities to register and to file reports upon money spent in pursuance of attempts to influence the passage or defeat of legislation in Congress. Inevitably, the activities of interest groups who wish to influence the legislature will shade off from the purely laudable functions of providing valuable information for Congressmen and channelling opinions to the legislature, to the outright use of bribery and inducements. In 2004 the whole question of the role of lobbyists was heightened by disclosures about the activities of a prominent lobbyist in Washington, Jack Abramoff, who was accused of making payments of various kinds to a number of Senators and Congressmen in order to get support for the legislative aims of his clients. In January 2006 Abramoff pleaded guilty to a number of charges, including conspiracy to bribe public officials, and investigations into the behaviour of a number of legislators were begun. A group of Senators and Congressmen, both Republican and Democrat, proposed new legislation including a ban on gifts, free meals and privately financed travel for members of Congress.

The importance to interest groups of making a direct impact on the decisions of the legislature follows from the fact that, as will become clear later on, the Congress of the United States exercises more effective decision-making power than any other Western legislature. But the concern of interest groups with government decisions does not end with the legislature. Administrative agencies, and particularly the independent regulatory commissions, daily make decisions of great importance, in some cases involving the fate of commercial activities amounting to millions of dollars. On the decision of a government agency depends the granting of a licence for a television station or to operate an airline, the prices to be charged by companies producing electric power or running a railroad, or the authority to make a large issue of securities. Inevitably, the groups interested in such decisions attempt to ensure that their interest is represented to the authority concerned. Equally inevitable is the feeling that these agencies, set up to regulate an industry, in practice become too closely associated with it and too responsive to its needs rather than to those of the general public. Charges have been made of excessive entertaining of members of government commissions by companies with an interest in the decisions to be made by these members, of the provision of free transport by airline companies, of gifts of television sets by broadcasting companies, and in one case at least of the payment of an outright bribe.

Finally, interest groups must involve themselves in the work of the courts and represent their point of view as strongly, although by using different techniques, to the judges as to legislators or administrators. In the United States the courts are a part of the political process in its widest sense, for the courts make decisions that in other countries are usually made by the elected or appointed officials of the other branches of government. At state and local level the judges cannot be completely absolved from charges of corrupt practices, but at the federal level, where the judiciary is of very high calibre, the tactics of the interest group must be to argue its case before the courts as persuasively as possible. If a group fails to block undesired legislation in Congress it can fight it in the courts on various grounds, including its constitutionality. It is also possible to use the courts as a means of furthering positive political aims. The most striking use of this technique was the success of the NAACP in using litigation as a long-term programme in the fight against segregation, both in state and federal courts. The Supreme Court of the United States allows the filing of briefs by amici curiae, 'friends of the Court', who can support one or other side of the dispute before the Court. In this way organisations, as well as the federal or state governments, can lend their support to the individuals involved in a case to the extent that cases before the Court come sometimes to look like inter-group battles rather than a judicial dispute between individual antagonists. In this way the pluralistic battles of American politics are initiated and fought through the machinery of government.

Inevitably, the emphasis upon the pressure politics of interest group interaction leads to an impression of confusion, almost of anarchy in American political life, to which are added overtones of corruption and the exercise of undue influence. Yet it must be recognised that the structure of interest groups performs an essential function in a diverse society. It provides for the representation and the expression of opinions and interests that the party system – any party system – would be incapable of providing. Alongside the political parties, interest groups articulate and channel demands to those elected and appointed officials who make the decisions which bear the imprint of the authority of government, whether federal, state or local. Pluralist theorists argue that this is the essence of democracy in a modern society. However, it is also the case that those groups which have the most resources, in particular the resource of money, are more likely to be successful in the pluralist battle, and this does not necessarily reflect truly 'democratic' outcomes.

Further reading

Cigler, A.J. and Loomis, B.A. (eds) (2002) *Interest Group Politics*, Washington, DC: CQ Press.

Rozell, M.J. and Wilcox, C. (1998) *Interest Groups in American National Elections*, Washington, DC: CQ Press.

Spitzer, R.J. (1995) *The Politics of Gun Control*, Chatham, NJ: Chatham House.
Truman, D. (1971) *The Governmental Process*, 2nd edn., New York: Knopf.

Websites

American Israeli Public Affairs Committee: www.aipac.org
Christian Coalition: www.cc.org
Handgun Control: www.handguncontrol.org
National Organization for Women: www.now.org
National Rifle Association: www.nra.org
National Right to Life Committee: www.nrlc.org

6   Congressional politics

The Congress of the United States is, without doubt, the most powerful representative assembly in the world today. This is not merely to reiterate the fact of the power and wealth of the United States – it is also recognition of the fact that, as a *legislature*, Congress continues to exercise a degree of independent decision-making power far greater than that retained by the other legislatures of the Western democracies. It is true that, like all legislative bodies in the complex modern world, its power has declined relative to that of the so-called 'executive branch' of government. Increasingly, it is the president and his administration that initiate policy and provide leadership in legislative affairs, but the Congress makes effective decisions upon domestic and foreign policy, upon the role of government in society, and the way in which government activities will be financed. The president can initiate policy, and he can urge it upon Congress with all the resources at his command, but he cannot *determine* what legislation shall pass, when it will be passed, or in exactly what form it will pass. Once legislation has been introduced into the British House of Commons by the government it is virtually certain that it will be passed, but one can only predict what *might* happen to legislation in Congress, and such predictions, however well-informed, may well turn out to be wrong.

The parameters of congressional power

The power of Congress as a policy-making body is, of course, the result of the whole context of the constitutional and political forces within which it operates. The internal structure of power and the organisation of the Congress reflect this context. We have seen that the Constitution of the United States gives to each of the two Houses of Congress a high degree of legal autonomy, in relation both to each other and to the president. The president has no power to dissolve Congress, nor does he have any direct legislative authority. He can send messages to Congress requesting action, and he has a limited power of veto over congressional acts of which he disapproves. The two Houses of Congress have equal power under the Constitution, except that the Senate is given the function of ratifying treaties on behalf of the United States, and of confirming the appointments to senior federal executive and judicial posts. The Constitution also provides that all bills for raising revenue must *originate* in the House of Representatives, but the Senate retains the right to amend or reject such proposals. Just as important for congressional autonomy, however, is the fact that the decentralised party system provides no basis for the effective disciplining of Senators or Congressmen. No single person or group of leaders at the national level can endanger the political career of a legislator simply because he has refused to follow their leadership. From time to time Congressmen are disciplined by their congressional party. Representative John B. Williams, a Democrat from Mississippi, supported the Republican candidate for the presidency in 1964, and as a consequence the caucus of the Democratic Party in the House stripped him of his seniority in the party. But no one in Congress or in the administration could prevent, or even consider attempting to prevent, his re-election to Congress in 1966. The method of selecting candidates, in particular the system of primary elections, places the effective power of discipline in the hands of the local party, or of the Congressman's constituents, and not in the hands of national leaders. The diversity of the local political systems that we have surveyed and the truly local basis of power in those systems are the fundamental guarantee of congressional autonomy.

The most important consequences of this constitutional and political context are, first, that there is no single united source of leadership in Congress comparable to that exercised by the government in a parliamentary system. Second, Congress has organised itself to allow full play to the sectional and local interests that dominate the fates of its members, and to the group pressures that fill the vacuum left by the absence of strongly party-oriented programmes. Third, the changing patterns of voting in Congress on the issues that come before it are determined by a very complex interaction between local, sectional and pluralistic influences, by the individual characters of Congressmen, and by the influence of the president and the administration. Thus the individual Senators and Congressmen stand at the centre of a great web of relationships, constitutional and political. Some of these relationships greatly strengthen their ability to exercise judgement independently of the overriding authority of any person or group, but of course the exercise of this judgement is a matter of the highest political sensitivity. Members of Congress can exercise their judgement only in a political context, which has a number of dimensions. Members of the same party as the president will feel the pull of allegiance to the national leader of the party; but they will also have a loyalty to the congressional leadership of the party in the House or the Senate. The extent of the loyalty owed to these two types of party leader will depend upon a number of factors, and they will not always coincide. The Senators and Representatives will be particularly concerned with their perception of constituents' attitudes, and also with the views of interest groups that may put those views to them with varying degrees of importunity.

They will be concerned also with the positions adopted by other members of Congress with whom they have some affinity, the other members of the committees upon which they sit, the other members of the state delegation of which they form a part, or the views of other members whom they respect as authorities upon particular subjects.

This is the context within which senators and representatives operate, and their exact reaction to a particular legislative proposal will depend upon the relative importance of these differing factors in the light of their own personal circumstances. Often the cues that they receive from party leaders, constituency, or pressure groups will conflict, and they must make up their minds which to respond to. This decision may depend upon how near they are to re-election, the relative strengths of the reactions from these differing sources, or their perception of the importance of a particular issue. Potentially the study of congressional behaviour is the description of how 535 men and women, each in a different political context, will react to particular situations. Fortunately for us, however, the patterns of congressional behaviour are not random or haphazard, and we can discover the political and institutional structures that give a relative stability to the way in which the legislature goes about its business. We shall look at the influence of parties, and at the other determinants of congressional voting behaviour, then at the organisational structure of power in Congress, and finally at some concrete examples of the way in which the complex decisions on modern legislation are taken.

Party discipline and party unity

The extent to which the American system of government allows the individual members of the national legislature to make up their own minds and to vote accordingly on the issues that come before them can be measured in two ways. First, by the extent to which individual Senators or Congressmen follow the dictates of the leaders of their parties; second, by the extent to which the members of the president's party in Congress follow the lead of their nominal head, or the extent to which members of the other party oppose him. By looking at the way in which members of Congress voted in the 1997 session of the legislature, we can gauge the extent of party unity, and the reality of party discipline (or the lack of it) in the Congress. In fact in that particular year, the first year of President Clinton's second administration, party unity in Congress was not as high as it had been in the immediately preceding years, but ideological and policy differences between the two parties were still sharp. The Republicans had kept the control over both Houses of Congress that they had gained in the mid-term elections of two years earlier, in spite of the fact that President Clinton had won re-election by a large majority over his Republican opponent, Bob Dole. The congressional Republicans had fought the election on the basis of the 'Contract with America' of House Speaker Newt Gingrich, setting out their legislative programme, and they wished to show that, in spite of the fact that they did not control the presidency, they were the effective government of America. The Democrats in Congress wished to demonstrate their support of the first Democratic President to gain re-election in twenty-eight years.

Both congressional parties wished to demonstrate their unity. It may be surprising, then, for those used to a European style of politics, to observe the extent to which the voting discipline of Senators and Congressmen fell far below the kind of party unity normally to be found in parliamentary systems of government. In the latter, party discipline would normally be measured by the extent to which the voting support of members of a political party for the policies of its leaders fell below the 'norm' of 100 per cent. When British political parties fail to achieve this norm there is a great deal of comment and analysis. However, very few votes in the United States Congress would come near to this standard of party cohesion. In the 1970s party unity was very low, in the 1980s there was a gradual increase in partisanship, but it was in the 1990s that the battle between the parties became more intense.

Nearly 50 per cent of the recorded votes – roll-call votes – taken in the 1997 session were actually *bipartisan* votes, that is votes in which a majority of the Republicans were voting the same way as a majority of the Democrats, opposed by minorities from both parties. Only half the votes taken, therefore, were 'party votes'. The *Congressional Quarterly*, from which these figures are taken, defines a party vote as one in which a majority of the Republicans is opposed to a majority of the Democrats, which is thus a test of party unity. Even in the case of these 'party' votes, however, the cohesion within each of the two parties was far from complete. In 1997 the average Democrat in the House of Representatives voted with a majority of his or her own party on only 82 per cent of the recorded votes taken during the session, and the average Republican 88 per cent of the time. Individual Congressmen and Senators varied greatly in the degree of their support for the party majority. In the Senate five Republicans voted with a majority of their party on fewer than 50 per cent of the votes taken, and Senator D'Amato of New York voted with a majority of his party on only 33 per cent of the votes taken. Two Republican members of the House of Representatives, both from New York State, voted with the majority on only 30 per cent of the votes taken; to put it another way, they voted *against* their party 70 per cent of the time. The opposition of Senators to the policies of their own parties reflected strong regional and ideological divisions within the party. The Republican Senators who voted most against their party's position came from the Northeast. The sectional element in American politics is far from dead, and it is most visible in congressional politics.

The first term of President George W. Bush should have signalled an increase in party unity in the legislature. There were three factors in the election of the year 2000 that suggested a new approach to party discipline and to a greater degree of loyalty to the president from his party in the Congress. First, alongside the election of a Republican president, the Republicans maintained a majority in the House of Representatives (221 Republicans; 212 Democrats) and in the Senate the two parties were initially equally balanced with 50 seats each. The long experience of 'divided government' seemed to be ending. However, in May 2001, Senator Jeffords of Vermont announced that he was leaving the Republican Party to become an independent and would vote with the Democrats on the organisation of the Senate, giving the Democrats the slimmest of majorities in the Senate. In the mid-term election of 2002 the Republicans took control of both Houses of Congress. The attack on the Twin Towers in 2001 and President Bush's reaction to it had raised his public approval rating to 90 per cent and, contrary to the usual expectation that the president's party will lose ground at mid-term, the Republicans gained seats in the House and won back control of the Senate. The second factor was the continued realignment in the politics of the South and the increasing grip of the Republicans on the Southern Senate seats. A major consequence of this development is the concentration of conservatives in the Republican Party and the diminution of intra-party strife among the Democrats. Finally, the dominance of the neoconservatives in the administration and in a number of congressional seats gave an unusually strong ideological coherence to the Republican Party, which influenced a number of the less ideological Republicans to go along with their leaders' policies. Surprisingly, however, the coming together of all these factors did not result in a significantly higher degree of partisanship in Congress than during the Clinton administration. In the Senate, on average, Republicans voted with a majority of their party only on 84 per cent of the party votes, and Democrats on 83 per cent. In the House, party unity scores were higher but only marginally. As always, Southern Democrats were most likely to vote against a majority of their own party. One Democratic Senator from Georgia, Senator Zell Miller, voted with a majority of his party only on 40 per cent of the party votes in which he participated. As the next election loomed, Senator Miller announced that, although he intended to remain a Democrat, he would vote for George W. Bush in 2004.

The second aspect of the nature of party loyalty and identity that we can observe is the extent to which the president, who is a party leader as well as head of state and chief executive, wins the support of Congress for his policies. One measure of this support is the presidential success rate calculated by the *Congressional Quarterly*. This measure is based upon the number of votes taken in the Congress upon issues where the president has clearly stated his position, so that it can be seen whether the majority of Senators and Representatives have accepted his recommendations. This measurement of the relations between president and Congress has its limitations. It deals only with those issues on which the president has made a clear public expression of his position, and it takes no account of those issues upon which the president and the administration have abandoned all hope of convincing the Congress, and have therefore decided not to press their views. Nevertheless, the presidential success rate gives a useful insight into the extent to which presidents are able to get their way.

The clearest evidence of the extent of party support for presidential policies can be seen during the administrations of presidents who have faced a majority of their own party in both Senate and House. This is the situation most closely comparable to parliamentary government. Such a situation existed under John F. Kennedy, Lyndon Johnson, Jimmy Carter, Bill Clinton during the first two years after his election in 1992, and George W. Bush after 2002. Of these, President Johnson had the greatest success rate. In 1965, 93 per cent of the votes on which he had taken a clear position went his way. In other years he was less successful, falling to a success rate of 75 per cent in 1968, the final year of his presidency. President Kennedy, for all his charisma, could not rise above 87 per cent of the votes going in his favour, and some of those that went against him were of much greater significance than those that he won. President Carter's success rate never even climbed into the 80 per cent range. President Clinton, working with a Democratic Congress in 1993 and 1994, achieved a success rate of 86 per cent, but when the Republicans gained control of Congress in the 1994 election his success rate fell to little more than 36 per cent in the following year.

The other side of the coin is that presidents faced with a majority of the opposing party in Congress can still achieve some of their aims, a situation inconceivable in a parliamentary system. The experience of President Reagan in the 1981 session of Congress is particularly interesting. Here was a Republican president with a Republican majority in the Senate, but a Democratic majority in the House of Representatives. Nevertheless, in 1981 President Reagan had a success rate of over 81 per cent, indicating that, on those issues on which he had expressed a clear view, the Congress had agreed with him four times out of five. Thus the Republican President Reagan, on this measurement, was more successful over all, facing a Democratic House and a Republican Senate, than Mr Carter, who had only had to cope with both Houses of Congress dominated by his own party. True, the Republican Senate had agreed with Mr Reagan on more occasions (87.5 per cent of the votes) than the Democratic House of Representatives (72 per cent of the votes), but this situation indicates very clearly the fact that party, though important in the American political system, is by no means the only important element in its operation.

Influences on congressional voting behaviour

It is very clear from the evidence that issues that come up for decision by Congress are not simply decided on party lines. Each vote is the result of the complex of pressures acting on Congress, and the patterns of voting differ from issue to issue. Coalitions within Congress form and re-form to decide particular questions of policy. Party allegiance is an important, but by no means determining factor in the way in which these patterns form. The effect of party loyalty is at its greatest on procedural or organisational votes: for example, the election of the Speaker, or the control over committee assignments. On substantive issues of policy, however, the alignments in Congress depend upon the issue under consideration, and the importance of party membership as an influence upon voting behaviour will depend upon the nature of these issues. What then *is* the significance of party on the way in which Senators and Representatives vote?

It is impossible to give an answer to this question in a straightforward way that would suggest a simple causal relationship between party membership and voting. It has been shown that there is a greater statistical correlation between party and congressional voting patterns than between the latter and any other single factor. Yet we have shown above that Senators and Congressmen habitually vote against the majority of their party without any adverse effects, either from the leadership of their party or from their constituents. Why then should party allegiance affect voting at all? There are a number of reasons. First of all, particularly for members of the House, there is an important relationship between constituency attitudes and party image. Representatives do not have the publicity exposure of Senators. They must rely to a large extent upon the image that the electorate has of their party. Often particular Congressmen can rise above this and make a personal impression on the electorate, but they are bound to be concerned with the party attitudes that many of their constituents have. This image will vary to some extent from one part of the country to another, but the behaviour and policies of the president will be an important component of that image. When there is no strong constituency opposition to the president's policy, therefore, the member of Congress will tend to go along with the party leader. If, however, constituency attitudes are clearly opposed to the president's policy, then the member of Congress will put constituency loyalty first and party loyalty second. On very many issues that come to a vote in Congress the members' constituents will be ignorant or apathetic, and in such circumstances legislators are free to listen to the urgings of pressure groups, or to vote the way the administration or congressional leaders wish. The president has inducements to offer – patronage or support for federal expenditures in their states or districts – and congressional leaders can provide publicity, good committee assignments, help at election time, and special facilities on Capitol Hill. Thus there will be a natural tendency for the members of the legislature to go along with their party, unless there is some strong reason to the contrary.

Groups of Congressmen of the same party who come from similar constituencies will naturally tend to react in the same way to the issues that confront them. The most important result of this is the way in which intra-party blocs form on overlapping sectional and ideological lines in Congress. The relative freedom of members of Congress from party discipline means also that coalitions can be formed *across* party lines by groups of Senators or Representatives who take the same view on an issue in spite of the fact that they are from different parties. These coalitions form and re-form according to the issue, and they may be strong enough and stable enough over time to flout the views of party leaders and to defeat the aims of the president and his administration. The most famous of these is the so-called 'conservative coalition' of Republicans and Southern Democrats, which for many years was able to check the passage of legislation on civil rights. These legislative proposals originated from Democratic presidents such as Kennedy and Johnson, at a time when both Houses were under Democratic control, but the coalition between many of the Republicans and the Southern Democrats who were opposed to the administration's policies was powerful enough to defeat them.

On many issues, however, the administration will not even state a position, or try to influence the vote. The administration cannot dictate to Congress, and if it tried to use its persuasive powers all the time they would soon become ineffectual. Thus it is rather misleading even to think in terms of 'party discipline' in Congress. When a president badly wants a measure to be passed every weapon will be employed. An appeal may be made to constituents over the head of Congressmen. But the president will not, and could not, conduct a continuous and consistent effort to direct congressional voting behaviour on every issue. Equally, congressional leaders must attempt to persuade rather than wave a big stick. Thus the statistical correlation between party and voting does not mean that senators and representatives are forced to vote the party line. It usually means that it is their natural inclination to do so. But when other factors enter into the picture then party loyalty may soon be forgotten.

The most important factor that can disrupt party voting is the Congressman's perception of the attitudes of constituents. Congressmen are highly responsive to what they believe their constituents desire. They go to great lengths to test opinion in their constituency, by taking public opinion polls on issues, by extensive personal contacts and by paying close attention to the huge deliveries of mail every Congressman receives. Undoubtedly, when national party policy conflicts with constituency opinion, as they perceive it, they will choose the latter. This is particularly clear in the field of civil rights, where Congressmen are very sensitive to constituency opinion. On other issues constituency opinion may be irrelevant because it is largely non-existent.

There is a third component, however, and that is the influence of pressure groups. The power of pressure groups to influence congressional voting is easy to explain in two types of case. First, when there is no particular constituency interest involved, and when the administration takes up no position on an issue, then a Congressman must look somewhere for the information and the 'cues' that will determine his or her vote, and these the pressure groups can provide. Second, when the appeals of a pressure group *reinforce* constituency interest, the Senator or Congressman will be completely deaf to appeals to party loyalty or to duty to the administration. The more difficult case to explain is what happens when the constituency interest is neutral and there is a sharp conflict between the party leadership and powerful pressure groups. Very often in such battles the Congressmen seem bemused by the conflicting demands being made upon them. In such circumstances they may look to other groups in Congress with whom they have shared interests – the other members of the congressional delegation from their home state, the members of the committees on which they serve, or other individuals in Congress whose opinions they respect because of their expertise or experience.

Finally, the importance of personality must not be overlooked. It is true that on the vast majority of the issues that come before Congress the attitudes of its members are determined by administration pressure, or by constituency or group attitudes, but there are always mavericks whose behaviour is unpredictable. In many cases, where the considerations of party, constituency and group pressures are nicely balanced, the Congressmen's or Senators' personal inclinations may be decisive in determining the way they cast their votes.

This then is the overall picture of congressional voting behaviour. It suggests a rather anarchic situation, but this is only a half-truth. Congress is in fact a highly organised, highly structured body. Indeed, if it were not, then anarchy would certainly reign. It is the fluidity of the voting patterns and the slackness of party ties that make the organisational structure of Congress so significant, and which give to the committee system in particular its vitally important role.

The structure of Congress

The task that Congress has to perform imposes upon it the necessity of a highly organised procedure for dealing with legislation. Priorities have to be determined between conflicting claimants for limited congressional time; procedures have to be devised to enable legislation to be dealt with in an orderly manner; and the requirements of adequate representation of the interests involved have to be met. In a parliamentary system it is usually the government that undertakes the task of determining the legislative programme for the session and ensuring that it is seen through complex legislative procedures. But there is no government in Congress. The constitutional separation of powers, as it has been interpreted since the early days of the Republic, prevents the president or his advisers from participating in the formal processes of legislation other than by transmitting messages to Congress. They cannot vote, or even speak in debates, and they are not allowed to have seats on the floor of the House. Of course, a wide range of informal contacts supplements the formal relationships between Congress and administration, but it remains true that the leadership that a president must attempt to exercise over the operations of Congress must be conducted from outside that body.

This lack of a directive government inside the legislature has meant that Congress has evolved its own leadership. The organisation of Congress, the control over its procedures and the legislative programme are all decided upon within Congress. The division between the presidential party and the congressional party is, therefore, highly institutionalised; although the two sets of leaders usually work tolerably well together, they retain their distinct points of view, and occasionally come into sharp conflict. Furthermore, the decentralised character of American politics is fully reflected in the organisation of Congress. Congressional leadership is decentralised, some might say fragmented, with groups of leaders drawing their strength from differing sources. The legislative procedures, especially the role of standing committees in the passage of legislation, give full opportunities for the local, sectional and pluralistic forces in American politics to have their say.

The extent of the decentralisation of power in Congress is epitomised by the very existence of the United States Senate. Here is a legislative chamber that is at first sight an anachronism. It is composed of two representatives of each state of the Union regardless of population. It is a second or upper chamber that has survived in an age that has seen a decline in the power of second chambers. Yet the Senate is the more powerful, and certainly the more prestigious, of the two chambers of the American legislature. Its power relative to that of the House of Representatives has increased rather than diminished. Since it has fewer members than the House, the individual Senator has a prestige and position that very few members of the popular chamber can hope to attain. Senators have terms of office three times as long as members of the House; the Senate's procedures are less restrictive of individual members; it has special functions in relation to foreign affairs and nominations; and it has equal legislative powers with the other chamber. Thus not only is political leadership in the United States divided between president and Congress, it is also divided within Congress between Senate and House, and the leaders of the two Houses will not always see eye to eye. Furthermore, within each House of Congress the leadership is decentralised and divided.

Congressional leadership

The leadership in each House of Congress is divided into two distinct but overlapping groups. The first group consists of party leaders – the Speaker in the House of Representatives, the majority and minority leaders in both houses, the majority and minority whips, the chairmen of the party caucus or conference, and party committees; the second group of congressional leaders are the chairmen of the standing committees.

Party leaders are elected by the party caucus – or conference – consisting of all the members of the party in the House or Senate. There was a time, notably during the first administration of President Woodrow Wilson (1913–16), when the party caucus, by a two-thirds vote of its membership, could bind the party to support policy decisions and to vote accordingly in the legislature. Today, however, the more fragmented nature of the parties rules out any attempt on the part of the caucus to determine policy issues, for to do this would be more likely to provoke disintegration than to promote unity. It is on organisational questions that party allegiance plays a vital role. Congress must be organised, party leaders elected and committees constituted, and the parties show the highest degree of cohesion on these questions of the distribution of congressional offices.

However, the power of the party caucus has increased, particularly in the Democratic Party in the House of Representatives. The chairmen of standing committees used to be chosen through the 'seniority system'. Committee chairmen play an extremely important role in the legislative process, as we shall shortly see, and until 1971 a Senator or Representative became chairman by virtue of being the member of the majority party with the longest record of *continuous* service on that committee. The role of the party caucus was simply to rubber-stamp the outcome of this process of natural selection. Since 1971, however, there has been something of a revolution in this area of the American political system. In the House of Representatives both parties changed their rules to ensure that the majority of the party caucus can exercise effective control over appointments to committee chairmanships, disregarding the claims of seniority. In January 1975 the chairmen of three important House committees were deposed by the Democratic caucus and replaced by more junior Congressmen. As a result of the reforms following the election of 1994, a limit of six years was set to the term of office of House Committee chairmen; in the Senate also both parties have taken steps to limit the operation of the seniority system.

The Speaker

The role of the Speaker in the House of Representatives is very different from that of the Speaker in the British House of Commons. True, the American Speaker has the responsibility, as presiding officer, of regulating the procedures of the House in a manner that will be fair to both sides. At the same time the Speaker is also the foremost leader of the majority party in the lower chamber, actively and continuously furthering its interests. With power to interpret the rules of the House, and control over its procedures, the Speaker wields considerable influence over its members: a discretionary power to recognise those who wish to speak from the floor, and in doubtful cases the ability to determine to which committee proposed legislation shall be sent. The size of the House of Representatives, and the volume of work it has to get through, turns these into formidable powers in the hands of a skilful Speaker. When the president and the majority in the House are drawn from the same party, the Speaker is perceived to be the most devoted supporter of the president's programme in the House. This does not mean that the president's policies are accepted uncritically; rather, the Speaker is the main instrument for effecting compromises between the president and the party in the House, when they can be obtained. The Speaker can tell the president what is possible and what is not. At the extreme, a Speaker who fundamentally disagreed with the president might resign, but usually the president will respect and accept the Speaker's views about policy in the House, because the Speaker is a personage to be reckoned with. However, when president and Speaker are from different parties, then the relationship is very different, for the Speaker becomes the leader and spokesman of 'the opposition', with whom the president must deal almost on terms of equality. Newt Gingrich, the Republican Speaker who came into office as a result of the congressional election of 1994, was determined to take over control of the programme of legislation, and to impose it upon the incumbent Democratic President Clinton, and had some degree of success in this endeavour.

The majority and minority floor leaders

The Constitution appoints the vice-president of the United States as the presiding officer of the Senate, although not normally presiding over its proceedings, attending only when it is expected that there might be a tied vote. There is no direct equivalent of the Speaker in the upper chamber. The president of the Senate *pro tempore*, usually the longest-serving member of the majority party, presides over the Senate's proceedings, but without the political weight of the Speaker in the House. The senior party leaders in the Senate are the majority and minority leaders. When the president's party has a majority in the Senate the majority leader is the link between the chief executive and the upper chamber, and has the responsibility of furthering the president's programme. There is a majority leader also in the House, who is the lieutenant of the Speaker, although as always in Congress there will be occasions when they disagree. The minority leaders in both Houses are also important in the legislative process, particularly when the leadership of the majority in Congress is of the opposite party from the president. The leaders on both sides tend to be drawn from the more moderate, middle-of-the road members of the legislature, for essentially their function is to act as brokers between the various wings of the party, and to elicit the greatest possible degree of agreement.

As in the British Parliament there is a system of whips in Congress but, as is the case with the Speaker, the whips in the House and Senate perform a role very different from their namesakes in the House of Commons. Like the British whips, they are two-way channels of communication, informing the leadership of the views and voting intentions of members of the party, and passing down information on the position of the leadership on legislative issues. In the House there is a system of assistant whips, organised on a regional basis. The whips also have the task of trying to get members of the party on to the floor to take part in voting, but they cannot exercise any disciplinary authority, or hope to pressure members of Congress into following the wishes of the leadership, if those members are determined to oppose them. Indeed, the opinion of the individual whip may deviate considerably from the position of the floor leaders.

The congressional committee system

The most effective work in Congress is done away from the floor of the House or Senate in the standing committees. It is difficult to exaggerate the importance of these committees, for they are the sieve through which legislation is poured, and what comes through, and how it comes through, is largely in their hands. The importance of standing committees in the legislative process is well illustrated by the significant difference in the positioning of the committee stage in Congress compared with the committee stage in the British House of Commons. In the latter body the formal first reading of a Bill is followed by a full-scale second-reading debate. The vote at the end of the second-reading debate signifies that the House has accepted the principles of the Bill, and the function of the committee to which the Bill is then sent is to make an effective and unambiguous piece of legislation within those principles. Standing committees of the House of Commons have no power to question the principles of the legislation or to propose major amendments to it. In the United States Congress, however, the committee stage follows immediately after the formal introduction of the Bill, before the chamber as a whole has an opportunity of considering it. Thus the committee is not in any way inhibited in its approach to the Bill. It can propose amendments that alter the whole character of the proposal, or it can even strike out everything after the enacting clause and substitute a completely new Bill. It can report a measure to the House or Senate with or without amendments or simply pigeonhole it by failing to take any action on it. The latter fate is that of most Bills, for Senators and Congressmen introduce far more legislation than could possibly be enacted. Indeed, some legislation is undoubtedly introduced by Congressmen as a gesture of good will to interested groups, safe in the knowledge that the committee will never let it go any further. But similar treatment can also be accorded to important legislative proposals originating in the administration if the committee does not wish to report them out. A committee can be discharged from further consideration of a Bill if it refuses to act on it, but the discharge procedure is a difficult one to operate.

The standing committees of Congress are specialist committees to which legislation concerning their particular field must be sent. The number of these committees varies from time to time; in 2006 there were twenty in the House and sixteen in the Senate. Some of the most important Senate committees are: Budget; Foreign Relations; Appropriations; Armed Services; Judiciary; Homeland Security and Governmental Affairs; Agriculture, Nutrition, and Forestry; and Commerce, Science, and Transportation. The most important of the House committees include the Rules Committee; Budget; Appropriations; Ways and Means; Judiciary; Homeland Security; Banking and Financial Services; Agriculture; Commerce; and Transportation and Infrastructure. There are also a number of joint committees of both houses that coordinate the supervision of administrative agencies or make representations to Congress on specific topics. Many of the standing committees are divided into a number of subcommittees, each with its own responsibility for a specialised area of the committee's field of interest. Some of the larger committees have a considerable range of specialised subcommittees – ten subcommittees of the House Appropriations Committee, eight subcommittees of the Senate Judiciary Committee.

The standing committees, and their subcommittees, hold hearings at which members of the public, representatives of interested groups, or members of the administration can give evidence in support of, or in opposition to, proposed legislation. The witnesses may be cross-examined by members of the committee; for members of the administration this can be quite an ordeal, far more searching and detailed than the questions asked at question time in a parliamentary system. Witnesses may prepare complex, detailed briefs to submit to the committee, and these together with a transcript of the proceedings are made public. Until 1973 the public was excluded from the 'executive sessions' of committees, in which most of the real work was done, and in which a Bill could be changed out of all recognition. Today, in general, committee sessions in both House and Senate are open to the public, with the exception of sessions in which issues concerning national security are being discussed or those which would 'tend to defame, degrade or incriminate any person'.

The committees can become extremely expert in their field of interest, as members of Congress may serve continuously on a committee for many years. They are provided with a specialist staff, which, although it cannot compete with the resources of the departments of the administration with which the committee must deal, can brief the members on the subjects to which it must give consideration. This expertise, and the fact of working together over long periods, tends to build up a corporate spirit on a committee, which may transcend party loyalties. The committees are the principal arenas in which compromise takes place, and by the time the members of a committee have hammered out a compromise they will be reluctant to see it upset either by the leadership of their own party or by amendments from the floor. Some committees, notably the Senate Foreign Relations Committee, have managed to develop considerable internal unity, regardless of party. The activities of the committees make it possible for a large proportion of the business conducted on the floor of the House or Senate to be dealt with by 'bipartisan majorities' – that is, votes in which a majority of each of the two parties joins to decide an issue. It is usual for approximately half the roll call votes in a session of Congress to be taken by bipartisan majorities. Conversely, if a committee is opposed to the passage of a bill it is very unlikely to be acceptable to the chamber as a whole. Thus, although standing committees are composed of members of both parties in proportion to party strength in the House, the practical result of their operations is to provide another focus of loyalty that cuts across party lines.

The chairman of a standing committee has considerable influence over the fate of legislation. Over the years he or she will have built up a network of influence and will know how the system works and exercises control over the calling of the committee and over its agenda. It used to be the case that committee chairmen were chosen on the basis of the seniority system, which meant that they were almost inevitably from safe seats, and, when the Democrats were in control, a disproportionately high number came from the Southern states. In 1966 the chairmen of more than half of the Senate committees came from former Confederacy states, while six came from Western states and one from West Virginia. There were no committee chairmen from New England or New York, none from great Eastern states like Pennsylvania, or from industrial states like Michigan or Illinois. In the House eleven of the twenty chairmen were from the South. Inevitably, the Southern committee chairman, who had been in Congress representing a safe constituency for many years, tended to be somewhat out of touch with, and unresponsive to, the interests of the great cities of the North. Yet it is these cities that are so significant in the election of the president and where so many of the pressing problems of America today are to be found. However, since 1970 there has been a steady decline in the hold of the South over committee chairmanships. Nevertheless, in 2006, with the Republicans in the majority, five of the sixteen Senate committee chairmen came from the Deep South; in the House, however, with its stricter control over the selection of committee chairmen, only three of the twenty committee chairmen came from Southern states.

The influence of the committee chairman is by no means finished when the committee has reported out a Bill. The committee appoints a floor manager for each Bill, often the chairman, whose role is to see the Bill through to the final vote. In the House of Representatives the Rules Committee will have allotted a certain amount of time for the Bill, which will be divided equally between its supporters and its opponents, and the floor manager and a senior member of the committee in opposition to the Bill will allocate this time among those who wish to speak. Usually the members of the committee will dominate debate on the floor and will greatly influence the extent to which the measure is amended.

Conference committees

The two Houses of Congress consider legislation independently of each other, so that a Bill passed by one House may fail to pass the other. Usually on important matters identical Bills are introduced into both Houses, but by the time they have been through the legislative process it is unlikely that they will still be identical, and it will be necessary to iron out the differences between the Senate and House versions of the legislation. Sometimes these differences may be reconciled by the supporters of the legislation securing similar amendments in both Houses, but if important differences persist then a conference committee must be set up, with members from both Houses, to hammer out a compromise. This is a rather contradictory consequence of the autonomy of the two Houses of Congress, for after each of them has spent a great deal of time and effort working on a Bill, they must turn the final decisions over to a small number of their members, working in secret, to produce a draft that may differ considerably from the version so recently enacted by them. It is true that the conference committee simply submits a report to both Houses, which must be accepted by them if the legislation is to pass, but the power of the committee lies in the fact that each House must accept or reject its report outright. Any attempt to amend the Bill as reported by the conference committee would necessitate another conference, and the agreed compromise upon which the conference report was based might be shattered.

Thus conference committees have considerable power, and appointment of the managers, as they are called, to represent each House on an important piece of legislation is crucial in determining the sort of compromise that will be reached. Formally the power of appointing managers lies with the Speaker and the President of the Senate, but they usually follow the wishes of the chairmen of the committees concerned with the Bill. The members of conference committees tend to be the more senior members of either House, and the influence of the two standing committee chairmen in the proceedings of the conference committee is bound to be considerable. There is thus a danger that, when the more senior members of the committee have been forced on the floor of the House to accept amendments of which they disapproved, the offending amendments may be quietly dropped in conference, on the grounds that it was necessary to do so in order to get agreement with the managers from the other House. Even at this late stage in the legislative process, the president, congressional leaders or interest groups, and in particular the administrative agencies concerned with the legislation, may try to influence the outcome of the negotiations in the conference committee.

Party committees

There are a number of party committees in each House of Congress: campaign committees, policy committees, and committees on committees. The last-named are very important, for it is they who assign members of the party to the standing committees of Congress. The standing committees are of varying degrees of importance and, therefore, of varying degrees of desirability. Members hope for assignment to the plum committee positions in order to impress their constituents, and also in order to be able to influence the most important decisions in the legislature. In the Senate this function is performed by the Democratic Steering Committee and by the Republican Committee on Committees; in the House, by the Democratic Steering and Policy Committee and by the House Republican Committee on Committees.

The working of these committees varies according to political conditions. Thus, House committee assignments used to be made by the Democratic members of the House Ways and Means Committee, who were accused of favouring conservative and Southern Representatives. When Lyndon Johnson was Senate majority leader he used his position to dominate the steering committee in order to secure compliance with his policies in the Senate.

Thus, in addition to the party caucuses and conferences, there are party policy committees in each House, but their leadership role on policy matters is severely limited. They are able to make strong pronouncements on policy only on the rare occasions when there is virtual unanimity in the party. Their major function is to consult with the party leadership on problems of scheduling the legislative programme. There is, therefore, a sizeable group of people in the two Houses who exercise some degree of leadership. The Speaker in the House and the majority leader in the Senate are by far the most important of these, but neither of them is anything like as powerful as a party leader in a strongly disciplined legislative party. They must work mostly through persuasion and with the relatively few sanctions available to them. They must attempt to steer the legislative programme through Congress even though the process of legislation is only partially under their control. They must work with the standing committees, which dominate the legislative process, and they must also cope with two extra difficulties – the power of the Rules Committee in the House, and the operation of the filibuster in the Senate.

The House Rules Committee

In order to understand the importance of the Rules Committee in the House it is first necessary to outline briefly the process by which legislation goes through Congress. Senators and congressmen introduce Bills, and after a formal first reading they are sent to the standing committees for consideration. A large number of standing committees are working simultaneously on many pieces of legislation, and when they have dealt with them they are reported to the House or Senate for debate on the floor, preliminary to their passage or rejection. Thus there arises the question of which of the many Bills that are reported by standing committees should be taken first. Given the limited time available in a session of Congress, the determination of priorities is all-important, for Bills that are not given time on the floor will die with the end of the session.

It is here that the Rules Committee of the House of Representatives exercises its authority. Bills must be given a 'special rule' by the Rules Committee if they are going to be given priority for consideration on the floor of the House. As the House Calendar may contain thousands of Bills a special rule is necessary in order to ensure that important legislation is given a hearing. The rule will allocate a certain length of time to the Bill, and may lay down conditions for the consideration of amendments. Thus the Rules Committee is the funnel through which all legislation must pass, and it may attempt to delay consideration of a particular measure, or to block its passage altogether by refusing to grant a rule.

The vital function of establishing the priorities of the legislative programme may be influenced by the Speaker or the elective leadership of the House, but in the end it is the Rules Committee that makes the decision. The Rules Committee is *not* a party committee but one of the standing committees of the House. It is composed of majority and minority party members, the former numbering twice the latter. The committee and its chairman play an essential part in the processes by which the House deals with the president's legislative programme, but there is no guarantee that the Chairman of the Rules Committee will be sympathetic to the president's programme; when the party with a majority in the House is of the opposing party, there is a built-in conflict between them.

In the years following the Second World War this potential for conflict was fully realised. Because of the operation of the seniority rule, and because the method of making committee assignments tended to favour conservatives, the Rules Committee became dominated by the conservative coalition in Congress. The chairman of the Rules Committee, Judge Howard W. Smith of Virginia, became, in effect, the leader of the conservative coalition in the House, and his key position on the Rules Committee gave him a power out of all proportion to the votes that the Southern Democrats could muster in the House itself. When President Kennedy was elected in 1960 the Rules Committee was considered to be the major obstacle to the passage of the legislation that he intended to propose to Congress, and a change in the composition of the Committee seemed an essential prerequisite for the passage of his programme. Speaker Sam Rayburn therefore conducted an operation in the House to expand the Committee from twelve to fifteen members, making possible the appointment of some liberal Democrats.

However, although the power of the conservative coalition on the Committee was moderated, the Rules Committee still failed to grant rules for twenty pieces of legislation in the years 1961–3, and in 1965 a further diminution in its power was decreed by the House. Previously the only way around the power of the Rules Committee to block legislation had been the procedure of 'discharging' the Committee from further consideration of a Bill. But a discharge petition requires the signatures of a majority of the total membership of the House, so that it was very difficult to operate the procedure. In 1965, however, 'the twenty-one-day rule' was introduced, which gave to the Speaker the power to call up a Bill for consideration on the floor if the Rules Committee had failed to grant a rule after twenty-one days. Then, by the vote of a majority of those present, the House could adopt its own rule for the discussion of the bill. Thus the Rules Committee was brought more closely under the direction of the elective leadership of the House. The twenty-one-day rule was used to discharge the Rules Committee six times in 1965 and twice in 1966. Perhaps more important was the fact that the very existence of the new procedure probably induced the Committee to grant rules in a number of other cases. Even so, the failure of the Rules Committee to act killed seventeen Bills in 1966, some of which had been requested by the president and the administration, and in 1967 conservatives were able to gain the repeal of the twenty-one-day rule. Today the Speaker and other party leaders in the House have a much greater influence over the decisions of the Rules Committee, although from time to time the latter will assert its independence.

The filibuster in the Senate

The problem of determining priorities for legislation, upon which the power of the House Rules Committee is based, gives little difficulty in the Senate. In that more relaxed chamber the majority leader, in consultation with a *party* committee, the Policy Committee, and with the cooperation of the minority leader, arranges the legislative programme. The strict control that is exercised over debates in the House, however, does not exist in the Senate, so that the increased power of the leadership to schedule legislation is offset by its almost complete inability to control the actual length or relevance of debates on the floor of the Senate. The privilege of unlimited debate has traditionally been the pride of the Senate, conferring upon the individual Senator the power to dramatise the importance of an issue by staging a long performance on the floor of the Senate, during which time all other business is held up. In 1953 Senator Wayne Morse of Oregon held the floor, without a break, for twenty-two hours and twenty-six minutes, and in 1959 Senator Strom Thurmond of South Carolina spoke for twenty-four hours and eighteen minutes against the passage of a Civil Rights bill.

In defence of unlimited debate, it is argued that in a heterogeneous country like the United States, which is in a sense, 'composed' of minorities, no group should be forced against its will to accept legislation that it considers destructive of its vital interests. No individual Senator can hope to block legislation through the use of this privilege, but a relatively small group of eight or ten Senators who are determined to prevent the passage of a Bill can hold the floor in turn indefinitely, and so force the leadership of the Senate to abandon a measure. This is the filibuster, and it is a technique that was successful in preventing the passage of civil rights legislation for many years. Even the threat of a filibuster can be enough to deter the leadership from introducing a Bill on to the floor of the Senate if it is going to disrupt the work of the whole session. Although the main beneficiaries of the procedure were Southern Senators, who were prepared to fight civil rights measures in this way, many other Senators are loath to see limits put on debate, because in the future it might be *their* minority interests that would benefit from this type of defensive action.

Until 1917 there was no means of bringing debate to a close in the Senate so long as a single Senator wished to continue speaking. However, as a result of the filibuster that was conducted by a handful of Senators against a proposal to arm American merchant ships, a closure rule was introduced. The present rule, adopted in 1975, provides for closure of a debate if three-fifths of the entire Senate vote for it, that is sixty Senators. Before 1975 a vote of two-thirds of the Senators present and voting was required to end debate, so that just over one-third of the Senate could prevent the passage of a bill if they were determined enough. Senators are reluctant to vote for closure, and filibusters have been difficult to prevent. Between 1917 and 1975 closure motions were introduced 104 times, but only twenty-four filibusters were ended in this way. The new rule made it easier to end debate, but still gave a determined minority a good deal of power. The final blow to President Clinton's unsuccessful attempt to reform the health care system was the threat that a filibuster would be mounted to prevent the passage of the legislation.

Filibusters, and threats to filibuster, are very much alive today. In 2003 and 2004 Democratic senators used the filibuster to block a number of President Bush's nominations for judgeships in federal appellate courts. A number of contentious issues, such as immigration control and stem cell research, provoke threats of filibusters. However, in January 2006 an attempt by Democratic Senators, led by John Kerry and Edward Kennedy, to mount a filibuster against the confirmation of Samuel Alito as a Supreme Court Justice failed, and the Senate voted to close debate on the nomination by seventy-two votes to twenty-five. Nineteen Democratic senators joined the Republican majority in voting for closure.

The presidential veto power

Once legislation has passed both Houses in an identical form, it is sent to the president for signature. The president can veto the Bill by returning it to Congress, with a message giving reasons for refusing to sign. If, however, the Bill is not vetoed within ten days while Congress is in session, it becomes law without the presidential signature. The president also has a 'pocket veto'; if, after Congress has adjourned, the president fails to sign a Bill within ten days, excluding Sundays, then it lapses. This can be quite a significant power in practice, because many Bills are passed in a hurry at the end of the session, and the president can use the pocket veto without having to give his reasons, and without fear that his veto will be overridden. President Carter used the pocket veto to nullify four Acts of Congress right at the end of his administration, even after having been defeated in the presidential election.

The veto power is an important weapon in the presidential armoury, for the threat of the use of the veto can be used to gain amendments to legislation. However, it is also a somewhat clumsy weapon; the president can only accept or reject a measure *in toto*, for there is no power to veto particular items in a Bill. Congress sometimes uses this fact to add 'riders' to Bills they know the president will not veto. Clauses unrelated to the main subject matter of the Bill are included, because Congress knows that the president would veto them if he could. In 1996, however, the Republican-dominated Congress passed the Line Item Veto Act, which authorised the president to cancel individual spending items in Bills. A complex procedure made it possible for Congress to reinstate the vetoed item, but if the president persisted in this course of action in the end it would necessitate a two-thirds majority of both Houses to override his veto. The introduction of a line item veto had been discussed for over a century, and in 1984 President Reagan called for a constitutional amendment to this effect. It was also included in the Contract with America that the Republicans made the basis of their congressional election campaign of 1993. Ironically, it was the Democratic President Clinton who had the first opportunity to exercise the line item veto. In August 1997 Clinton vetoed three spending items totalling over $600 million, and the opposition to the new veto power grew. In February 1998 a Federal District Court declared the Line Item Veto Act to be unconstitutional, and this judgement was later confirmed by the Supreme Court, thus returning to the situation where the president must veto the whole Bill or allow it to become law.

Presidential vetoes can be overridden if both Houses of Congress pass the Bill again by a two-thirds majority of each House. Only a small proportion of presidential vetoes are overridden, because the president can usually expect to muster over one-third of the votes in each House of Congress. Another weapon in the congressional armoury is the so-called 'legislative veto', which was adopted by Congress in order to exercise greater control over the executive branch of government. Many statutes incorporated provisions that gave authority to one or both of the Houses of Congress to overrule particular decisions made by government agencies under the legislation. For example, in 1974 the Immigration and Naturalization Service (INS) exercised its discretion to allow an East African Asian, Jagdish Chadha, to remain in the United States although his visa had expired. The Act that the INS was administering contained a legislative veto provision, and the House of Representatives overruled the decision and ordered Chadha to be deported. Members of Congress who were anxious to combat the power of the administration inserted more and more such provisions into legislation, and Congress gave authority for one House, both Houses, or even a congressional committee or the chair of a committee to overrule individual decisions of a regulatory agency or department. Presidents, of course, resisted the use of the legislative veto, and asserted that it was unconstitutional. In 1983 the Supreme Court in the *Chadha* case held the legislative veto to be unconstitutional, but it did not prevent the Congress from continuing to make use of similar provisions to control the actions of the administration.

This, then, is the complex legislative procedure of Congress. It can be seen that it allows a great deal of freedom to individuals and groups in Congress to affect the outcome of the legislative process. True, most important legislation originates with the administration, although not all of it. But Congress retains the power to refuse to pass legislation or to amend it significantly during passage. Sustained pressure by the administration over a number of sessions of Congress will usually eventually build up enough support to pass measures that a president is committed to, but in the process it may be necessary to accept considerable modifications to proposed legislation. Furthermore, the timing of legislative policy is often as important as its content, and this is more in the control of Congress than of the president. Examples of the complex procedures involved in the legislative process are given in Chapter 11 below, where the fate of proposals for health care and welfare reform by the Clinton Administration are described.

Congressional control of finance

Ultimately, in all government activities, it is finance that is the controlling factor. Laws must be enforced, policies must be implemented, and they always cost money. The raising and spending of money provides the ultimate control by Congress over the administration, and it provides also an area of American government that exemplifies the paradoxical relationship between president and Congress. The broad outlines of the annual budget are fixed by circumstances and previously adopted policies, and are, therefore, to a considerable extent outside the control of both president and Congress. But at the margin, and it is a margin involving billions of dollars, there is a game of tug-of-war between the two branches of the government that illustrates both their weaknesses and their strengths. The initiative in financial matters must come from the administration, and the attempt to use the financial operations of government as an instrument of overall economic policy must also largely be made by the president and the administration. Nevertheless, this is an area of government over which Congress has been most tenacious in its bid to retain the ultimate control, rejecting all proposals that would loose its hold on the purse strings. Furthermore, it is in the field of financial planning that the administration has over the years made its biggest bid to achieve internal coordination, even if not wholly successfully; yet it is in the financial sphere that the *decentralised* character of congressional power is most apparent.

Estimates of expenditure required for the forthcoming year are prepared by the departments and agencies and sent to the Office of Management and Budget to be coordinated. The budget is submitted to Congress in February, and immediately the effect of the decentralised power structure of Congress comes into operation. The process of providing funds for government is dominated by the built-in tensions of the legislative process, for appropriation bills must go through much the same procedures as ordinary legislation. The Congress is concerned to safeguard the expenditure of public money, but it is also responsive to constituency and interest pressures. Thus at one and the same time it may attempt to cut back some administration requests and to appropriate more than the administration wishes in other directions. The House and the Senate may differ quite considerably on the amount to be appropriated for different purposes, and these differences have to be reconciled in conference committees. The legislative committees of Congress, each with their pet programmes, may come into conflict with the appropriations committees, which have the primary responsibility for ensuring an economic use of public funds. Finally, the appropriations committees are themselves divided up into a large number of subcommittees, each of which has its own views on the appropriations for the government departments for which it is responsible.

The House of Representatives has always claimed a pre-eminence in the financial field, and all money bills originate in the House, although in fact the Constitution insists on this point only in respect of bills for raising revenue. Furthermore, the House usually tends to take a more restrictive view of the needs of the government for funds. The normal pattern is for the House to reduce the total requested by the president by a substantial amount, for the Senate to propose an appropriation considerably in excess of that suggested by the House, although still lower than the presidential request, and then for the conference committee to approve finally an amount about half-way between the House and Senate figures. Of course, the administration is well aware of this general tendency, and no doubt it adjusts its requests to the expected behaviour of Congress – some observers rather cynically suggest that after all the effort expended by Congress the administration usually gets just about the amount it had originally aimed at.

However, although this is the broad pattern of the financial operations of Congress, it would be a mistake to think that the outcome of the battle over particular appropriations can always be forecast in this way. Sometimes Congress appropriates more money than the president has requested for a particular programme, either in an attempt to force a particular policy upon the administration or as a result of the desire to benefit constituents. One of the most consistent examples of the appropriation by Congress of more money than requested has been the way in which, over a period of ten years or so, Congress appropriated more for the maintenance and development of the manned bomber force than the president wished. This action reflected a dispute within the administration between air force generals, who wished to prevent cuts in the bomber programme, and the officials of the Defense Department, who wished to rely to a greater extent upon missiles. At times this dispute was painfully open. In 1956 General Curtis LeMay, Chief of the Strategic Air Command, was successful in getting Congress to add $800 million to the defence appropriation for the production of B-52 bombers against the opposition of President Eisenhower's Secretary of Defense, Charles Wilson. In 1964 General LeMay, then Air Force Chief of Staff, again persuaded Congress, against the opposition of another president and another Secretary of Defense, to appropriate $52 million for research into a 'follow-up' bomber to replace the ageing B-52s. There are many more recent examples; in 2006 the House of Representatives voted to increase President Bush's request for money for the purchase of vehicles for the army by $1,330 million.

Another area in which Congress tends to appropriate more money than requested is in the field of so-called 'pork barrel' legislation, in which money is appropriated for public works expenditures that will bring work and business, and other benefits, to the Congressman's home district. Particularly important in this respect are the construction of dams and flood control projects and irrigation schemes. Many of these are projects that will be carried out by the US Army Corps of Engineers, a particularly powerful administrative agency, nominally under the control of the army, which works closely with members of Congress. In 1966 Congress appropriated money to start work on sixty-three new water construction projects, although only twenty-nine had been included in the president's budget. In other fields, however, the tendency has been for Congress consistently to cut down presidential requests below what might be considered the normal removal of padding.

The House Ways and Means Committee and the Senate Finance Committee share a similar responsibility for recommending tax measures, as do the appropriations committees for recommending expenditures. These four committees tend to be even more autonomous than the other standing committees of Congress. In particular, the House committees have great prestige and a reputation for considerable expertise. The House almost always accepts their recommendations; it is also relatively rare for the Appropriations Committee of the House to make amendments to the reports of its numerous subcommittees, which deal with the appropriation bills for various departments and agencies. Before 1974, although the chairmen of these committees attempted to coordinate activities within their own spheres of responsibility, there was no one body in Congress that was in a position to take an overall view of financial affairs. Attempts were made, without success, to get these four committees to work more closely together, or to introduce procedures that would give greater continuity to the appropriations process over a number of years. However, Congress successfully resisted any attempt to diminish its annual control over the raising of revenue and the authorisation of expenditure.

As a result of President Richard Nixon's attempts to circumvent congressional control of finance, the Congressional Budget and Impoundment Control Act was passed in 1974, establishing a congressional budget system to give to Congress an effective control over the national budget. Budget committees were created in both Houses of Congress and a reconciliation process was established to enable Congress to coordinate the government's spending and revenue operations. It was intended that Congress should take overall control of the budget away from the administration and produce a congressional budget to effect the policies that the legislature wanted. The procedure established in 1974 lay dormant until 1980, when the Senate and House budget committees combined various spending and taxing proposals in a single budget. On taking office in 1981 President Reagan requested extensive cuts in government spending along with reductions in taxation, and this meant that the budget committees of the Senate and House would have to impose cuts upon the appropriate committees who were dealing with the various branches of expenditure. The process was completed successfully and the final legislation, when signed by President Reagan, reduced government expenditure by $35 billion below the levels projected by the previous administration.

By far the most dramatic intervention by Congress in the field of financial control came, however, in 1985 with the passage of the Balanced Budget and Emergency Deficit Control Act, known as the Gramm–Rudman–Hollings Act. When President Reagan was elected in 1980, he promised to balance the federal budget, but in succeeding years the budget deficit rose to gargantuan proportions, reaching $207 billion in 1983. The failure of the president and Congress to agree on ways of removing this massive deficit led Congress in 1985 to adopt a legislative solution which, if effective, would have extraordinary results on the working of the government of the United States. The Act set yearly targets for the elimination of the deficit, which would result in achieving a balanced budget in 1990. The president was required to submit annual budgets not exceeding these targets; but, if president and Congress could not agree upon the financial measures needed to meet the targets, a sequence of *automatic* cuts in expenditure were required by the Act to reduce government spending to the required level. The Congressional Budget Office and the Office of Management and Budget were jointly to provide the estimates upon which these cuts were to be based and then they were to be automatically enforced. Such a revolutionary method of determining the level of government spending would virtually remove control over individual programmes from both president and Congress alike, placing it effectively in the hands of non-elected officials. Soon after its passage, the Supreme Court invalidated essential parts of the Act, and it proved to be unworkable, but it well illustrates the determination of Congress to maintain its influence over financial policy, and not simply to bow to the wishes of the executive branch of government.

Other control functions

Congress conducts many investigations of the activities of the federal government in an attempt to keep control of this vast machine. Each year the appropriations committees and subcommittees investigate departmental operations, and standing committees conduct inquiries relevant to their sphere of legislative responsibility. The most notorious committee investigations were those of the House Un-American Activities Committee and the investigatory subcommittee of the Senate Government Operations Committee, chaired in the early 1950s by Senator Joseph McCarthy. Senate committees and some House committees have the power to subpoena witnesses and documents, and if witnesses refuse to answer questions put to them they may find themselves in jail, convicted of contempt of Congress. The House Un-American

Activities Committee was the main source of citations for contempt of Congress, many of them for failing to answer questions or produce documents about supposed communist activities, though few of these contempt citations actually resulted in convictions in the courts. In 1966 seven leaders of the Ku Klux Klan were cited for contempt for refusing to give the committee records of the Klan's activities, and the Imperial Wizard of the Klan was convicted by a federal court and sentenced to a year's imprisonment.

At its worst the investigatory power of Congress can be used to harass individuals who offend against the political opinions of committee members, or to further the political ambitions of members of Congress. At its best it can be a valuable instrument for investigating the activities of the government in order to prevent abuses of power, both public and private. Investigations have been directed at the Ku Klux Klan, interstate criminal activities, racketeering in labour unions, the invasion of privacy through the use of electronic devices and lie detectors, and the allocation of government defence contracts.

The Senate has special power under the Constitution to confirm or reject the nominations to office of executive and judicial officers made by the president, including members of the cabinet and federal judges. Many nominations are made each year, and most of them are quickly confirmed. Very few nominations are actually rejected, although the president may withdraw a nomination when opposition is manifested in the Senate. Occasionally, a nomination can lead to a protracted battle, with a public investigation of the nominee by a Senate committee and heated debates on the floor of the Senate about the nominee's record and qualifications. Sometimes objections are made to nominees because of the policies they are expected to pursue, and sometimes on personal grounds. The president usually avoids serious difficulty by consulting congressional leaders on appointments, and in one respect must be quite meticulous in this process of consultation. The convention of 'senatorial courtesy' ensures that the president will clear every nomination with the Senator of the president's party (if any) from the state from which the nominee comes. If the president fails to do so, the Senator concerned may state on the floor of the Senate chamber that the nominee is 'personally obnoxious', and the Senate will normally reject the nomination. An exceptional case of the refusal to confirm the nomination of a member of the cabinet was the rejection of Lewis L. Strauss as Secretary of Commerce in 1959. President Eisenhower nominated him at a time when there was a Democratic majority in the Senate. Strauss had formerly been the chairman of the Atomic Energy Commission, and Senator Clinton P. Anderson, chairman of the Joint Atomic Energy Committee, led the fight against his nomination. The battle lasted nearly six months, with the president throwing all his weight behind the attempts to secure confirmation of the nomination. Democratic Senators opposed Strauss because of his conservative attitudes, because of some of his decisions as AEC chairman and because of his role in the J. Robert Oppenheimer case in 1954. The final vote in the Senate was

forty-nine against confirmation and forty-six in favour. Two Republican Senators voted against their president's nomination. If they had voted the other
way the nomination of Strauss would have been confirmed.

President Bush's nomination of John Bolton as Ambassador to the
United Nations in 2005 was strongly opposed by Democrats in the Senate,
who mounted a filibuster to prevent his confirmation. Twice the Republican
leadership attempted to close debate on the nomination, but failed to get
the necessary sixty votes. However, under Article II of the Constitution the
president may fill vacancies in such offices during the time when the Senate
is in recess. Such appointments expire at the end of the next session of the
Senate. So, when the Senate took its recess in August 2005 President Bush
appointed Bolton as Ambassador to the United Nations. Unless confirmed by
the Senate in the meantime, Bolton would lose his post at the end of 2006.
Because of their importance in the development of constitutional law, appointments to the Supreme Court are scrutinised very closely by the Senate;
the details of this process are discussed in Chapter 10.

Another field in which the Senate is given special powers is that of foreign
policy. The Constitution requires that treaties made on behalf of the United
States shall be subject to ratification by two-thirds of the Senators present
and voting. Perhaps the most shattering exercise of the power of the Senate
was the rejection in 1919 of the Treaty of Versailles, which had been largely
moulded by President Woodrow Wilson. By so doing the Senate prevented
the United States from becoming a member of the League of Nations. The
power of the Senate in this field has declined, however, owing to the practice
of concluding 'executive agreements' between the president and foreign governments, agreements that do not require senatorial confirmation.

Traditionally, the conduct of war was an area that Congress left almost
exclusively to the president. The Constitution gives Congress the power to
declare war, but in practice this has been far overshadowed by the president's
role as Commander-in-Chief, and the consequent ability to order troops into
action in any part of the world. This aspect of presidential power is discussed
in Chapter 12 below.

Congress and policy-making

The structure and operation of the Congress of the United States closely
reflect the decentralised and heterogeneous character of the American political system. All the threads of class, pluralistic and sectional politics can
be found in the operation of its committee system and in the changing patterns of voting as different issues come up to be decided. The sectional element in the American political scene is exaggerated in Congress by the
way in which Congressmen and Senators react to the views of a majority of
their constituents, although a sizeable minority in the region may have a
different opinion. The representative system in Congress does not claim to
produce a proportional representation of opinion throughout the country,

but neither does it produce a stable, continuously coordinated government, which is usually represented as the great boon of the Anglo-Saxon system of single-member, simple-majority electoral systems. The tendency towards multi-party politics that we found earlier is barely restrained by the needs of organising Congress and by the advantages of maintaining control of certain key congressional positions. Thus policy-making is haphazard and discontinuous. Congress approves programmes and then refuses to appropriate money for them; it demands economy and then spends more money than ever on projects that will benefit constituents. The nature of Congress and the working of the legislative process raise the whole question of ensuring governmental responsibility for policy: how can the citizen affix responsibility for governmental policies, or the lack of them, if faced with a continually changing kaleidoscope of coalitions in Congress? And yet in a very real sense there is more genuinely responsible government in Congress than in most of the party-dominated legislatures of the world. For we have seen that there is nothing that ultimately is of more importance to members of Congress than the views of a majority of their constituents. However, the pluralist nature of Congress makes it unlikely that it will be able to provide the kind of leadership that is necessary in the modern state. That leadership can only come, if it is to come at all, from the president.

Further reading

Foley, M. and Owens, J.E. (1996) *Congress and the Presidency: Institutional Politics in a Separated System*, Manchester: Manchester University Press.
Loomis, B. (2000) *The Contemporary Congress*, New York: St. Martin's Press.
Mayhew, D. (2000) *America's Congress*, New Haven, CT: Yale University Press.
Schickler, E. (2001) *Disjointed Pluralism: Institutional Innovation and the Development of the U.S. Congress*, Princeton, NJ: Princeton University Press.

Websites

Congress: www.congresslink.org
Library of Congress: www.thomas.loc.gov
US Senate: www.senate.gov
US House of Representatives: www.house.gov

7 Presidential politics

The description of the American political system that we have developed to this point is one of enormous variety and diversity: a set of sectional, class, pluralistic and individualistic forces which can only with difficulty be compressed into a few broad categories. The institutional structures that we have examined have fully reflected and expressed this diversity: the federal system, the structure of pressure groups, the political parties, the working of Congress – all of these give full rein to multifarious interests, each intent on furthering its economic aims, defending its social position or gaining a hearing for its point of view. Each of these structures channels and articulates these demands, gradually contributing to the process of bargaining and compromise that decision-making requires. Yet the very nature of all these structures emphasises their own pluralistic character, for pluralism is built into all of them as a dominant characteristic. It is only when we come to the presidency of the United States itself that we reach a part of the political structure where a single will must be expressed, a single mind made up. This is not to say that all the enormous pressures of the pluralistic political system do not reach expression in the presidency. They are indeed felt, and their impact is very considerable, as we shall see. But here at least there is the *possibility* of a unity, which exists nowhere else in the system, and consequently the possibility of the exercise of leadership. It is in the area of leadership that the American political system may be thought to be most defective, and it is the function of the president to try to remedy that defect. Given the nature of the American system, and of the political culture that sustains it, the task of the president is a superhuman one, almost inevitably doomed to failure before it begins. This is the challenge of the presidency, its fascination and its tragedy.

When the president is greeted at a public function on arrival at an airfield or a military parade, the band strikes up the familiar tune 'Hail to the Chief'. The president *is* a chief in many senses – chief of state, party chief, commander-in-chief of the armed forces, chief administrator and chief initiator of legislation. At the same time, the president embodies the power and authority of the nation. On this solitary individual, for four years or more, is placed the final responsibility for the external, and much of the internal, affairs of the United States. But just how powerful is a president? What are the tools that are available for the discharge of political functions of the office? What are the built-in limitations on presidential power? These are the questions we shall look at in the present chapter.

Of course, it is true to say that the nature of the presidency at a particular moment depends considerably upon the incumbent of the office – great men make great presidents. But although the personality of the president may make a considerable difference to the course of day-to-day policy-making, there are very real institutional limitations on the president – things that can be done and things that cannot, as well as things that cannot be escaped. In certain circumstances a president may set the country on a new course, achieving a new economic policy, setting off in a new direction in foreign affairs, initiating great social changes. But all the time the president is subject to very real constitutional and political limitations. In recent years in Britain there has been much discussion of the extent to which the office of prime minister has been moving more and more towards a presidential form, and by implication the discussion is usually cast in terms of the extent to which the British prime minister is becoming more like the American president, and consequently becoming a more powerful and dominant political figure. But the comparison between these two great offices is in fact by no means as simple as this. The recognition of the increasing power of the prime minister *in relation to other members of the cabinet* does seem to make the holder of the office more like the American counterpart as head of the government, but in relation to other parts of the political system the comparison is much more complex. In order to assess presidential power we must look at the presidency from every angle, regarding internal affairs and external, considering its relationship to the cabinet, to other advisers, to Congress, to the party system, to pressure groups and to the courts. For the working of the presidency fluctuates between two poles: on the one hand, an awesome exercise of power, power that is personal and seemingly unchecked; on the other hand, an impotent inability to gain acceptance for major policies which the president considers essential to the well-being of the country, or even for relatively minor aims which seem desirable. It is the ever-changing complex of interrelationships between these two poles that constitutes presidential politics, the ramifications of which we shall now explore.

The political functions of the president

The president has a number of *constitutional* powers which we shall look at shortly, but the way in which they are exercised is largely dictated by the political context. At the same time, the provisions of the Constitution do constitute a very real framework for the exercise of presidential power, for they provide the legal weapons which other political actors can use in their struggle with the president.

The president has four main political functions. First, like Congress, although necessarily in a very different way, to act as a broker between the contending interests that make demands upon the government. No president can afford to ignore the demands, some trivial, some gargantuan, that develop in the political system. The president may be looking towards re-election or simply attempting to secure political support in matters of vital concern to the administration's policies, but in either case the political game must be played. The president is potentially the ultimate target, direct or indirect, of every individual or group that wishes to promote or defeat legislation, to obtain the exercise of a presidential power or to affect the operation of the administration. In a multitude of matters of governmental concern the attempt to gain the ear of the president will not be worth the effort and no attempt will be made. The decision to attract presidential attention will not necessarily depend simply upon the intrinsic importance of the matter at issue, but also upon the politics of access to the president. Individuals or groups who potentially have support to offer the president, whether it be the likelihood of voting support in a congressional battle or simply the friendship of someone whom the president may trust, will be in a privileged position as far as access is concerned. Whether this results in actual presidential support for the policy is quite another matter – but access in itself is a vitally important factor when a single person must cram so much into a working day. In many matters of vital concern to interest groups, presidential intervention or the refusal to intervene, may be decisive, although presidential support for a particular point of view is by no means a guarantee of success. Thus the presidency is a pluralistic institution like the other parts of the system, although in a very different dimension.

The first political function of the president, then, is to reflect and react to pluralistic pressures, but the second function, paradoxically, tends to cut across and even contradict this line of action. The second political function is to attempt to interpret and pursue the national interest as the president sees it. The idea of the national interest is fraught with difficulties for the student of politics. Indeed, those who see the political system in extreme pluralistic terms deny that the concept can have any meaning. Objectively, it is true, there may not be any policy, or set of policies, that can be unequivocally designated as being in the interest of the whole nation, except perhaps when one can isolate a situation that would lead to its complete destruction. Nearly every policy will help or harm different groups in varying degrees. The decisions of governments inevitably strike some sort of balance between the advantages and disadvantages that they anticipate will result from alternative policies, so that the national interest can almost always be resolved into sets of conflicting pluralistic interests. Nevertheless, whatever the *objective* realities of the national interest may be, the person who holds the office of president must do more than simply attempt to strike compromises between contending interests. Policy goals must be identified that seem to provide the best long-term prospects – economic, social and strategic – for the overwhelming majority of the American people, and attempts must be made to attain these goals. For the pluralistic jumble of interests that faces the president will not necessarily and automatically cancel out into some rational and successful pattern. The implicit assumption that it will do so lies behind much of the extreme adherence to the philosophy of pluralism, and represents a considerable danger in assessing the operation of modern political systems. It leaves no room for leadership, seeing the role of government merely as that of an umpire between contending interests.

A full explanation of, and understanding of, the presidency requires more than simply seeing the office as a neutral machine for registering public opinion. Presidents can, and must, be leaders, even if that leadership proves to be a merely negative force. They stand at a fulcrum of the American political system, using levers that can, in many circumstances, although not all, turn the tide of events in one direction or another. There is no escaping this responsibility, even though in attempting to carry it out a president will often succumb to sectional pressures or to political expediency.

The third function is closely related to the first two. The president must try to act as the focal point of loyalty for this diverse American society, at one and the same time giving to each distinct group the sense that its interests are being defended against internal attacks and attempting also to give at least a minimal sense of unity to the whole country, particularly in relation to the rest of the world. No other single individual can ever lay claim to represent the whole of the American people. As head of state as well as head of the administration, the president must be seen abroad, and to some extent at home as well, as in some sense embodying the power and authority of the whole of the United States. It is this that in large degree has led the presidency increasingly to take on a charismatic quality, giving to the president an almost mystical aura, sometimes seeming to be endowed with the awesome quality of a monarch, but combined with the real hard-headed power of a skilled politician. Yet here again, the built-in complexity of the system produces another paradox. The president speaks for the nation, but must also speak as a party leader and, necessarily having to pursue controversial policies, sometimes speaks simply as a leader of a faction. The line between the national leader giving voice to the aspirations and demands of the whole people, and the party or factional leader pursuing policies that many fellow countrymen bitterly oppose, is indeed a difficult one to maintain. It is usually easier for a president to pursue these potentially conflicting roles when the administration's foreign policies remain essentially uncontroversial. When foreign policy becomes a matter of bitter internal dissension, as in the case of the Vietnam War, then the president's task becomes a formidable one indeed.

The fourth, and perhaps the essential, political function of the president is to be 'coordinator-in-chief' – indeed, almost the only coordinator – of the innumerable semi-autonomous parts of the governmental machine, both legislative and executive alike. The extraordinarily fragmented nature of the

American governmental structure should by now be apparent to the reader, but there are two further dimensions which will be looked at in more detail in later chapters – the loosely integrated character of the American administrative machine, and the powers of the courts to affect the outcome of political situations. The president must, by an extreme act of will, attempt to get acceptance of a set of policies by this vast and complex body of people. In the last analysis the standing of a president depends upon the success with which this function is performed. To evolve and initiate policies is of little use if the acquiescence of Congress, and of state and local governments, is not obtained; and the passage of legislation, or the exercise of presidential authority, will be of little real value if the president's intentions are frustrated by members of the administration. The president is by no means lacking in weapons with which to tackle the problem of coordination, in its widest sense, and most of the reforms that have been made in the presidency in the past thirty years have been directed at improving the president's performance in this area. However, in performing this function the president faces two most formidable obstacles.

In the first place there are the benefits, and also the considerable disadvantages, of the loosely organised party system, with its consequent lack of party discipline. The advantage is that the president can hope to attract support for some policies from the members of both parties in Congress, but by the same token the president's own party cannot be depended upon to give unequivocal support for the administration's legislative proposals. Furthermore, the effects of this lack of party cohesion go beyond the sphere of the relations of the president with Congress. They reach into the administration itself. The president is not able to assume that party allegiance will assure ready compliance among the senior members of the administration, even when they are members of the same party, which is not always the case. The president may meet almost as much opposition, of a rather different kind, it is true, from within the administration as from outside it. Second, the president faces an array of constitutional obstacles to the attempt to coordinate the action of government. Much of the politics of the presidency consists of the efforts of the president to overcome these barriers to the smooth exercise of power. Let us look then at the constitutional position of the president.

The powers of the president

As in other respects, the Constitution's grant of power to the president is in very general terms, the main provision being: 'The Executive Power shall be vested in a President of the United States of America.' The content and meaning of this bald statement has been filled in since 1789 by the accumulation of practice, and by the decisions of the Supreme Court. The Constitution did, however, expand a little on the role of the chief executive. The president was also to be commander-in-chief of the army and navy of the United States, and of the militia of the several states when called into the service of the

United States. The president could require the opinion, in writing, of the principal officer of each of the executive departments, and was also given power to grant reprieves and pardons for offences against the United States except in cases of impeachment. The other important powers granted by the Constitution were the power to make treaties, subject to their ratification by a two-thirds majority vote in the Senate, and to nominate ambassadors, other public ministers and consuls, judges of the Supreme Court and all other officers of the United States, subject to the confirmation of the Senate. However, Congress was given the power to allow the president, acting alone, to make appointments 'of such inferior officers as they think proper', and the vast majority of official appointments are today made in this way.

In accordance with the Founders' belief in the separation of powers, the president was given no positive role in the legislative process other than the duty, from time to time, to give to the Congress information on the state of the union, and to recommend to its consideration such measures as considered necessary and expedient. The president has also the power to convene both Houses of Congress in emergency session, and to adjourn them if they disagree with respect to the time of adjournment (the last eventuality has never yet arisen). The president has no power to dissolve Congress and so lacks what is sometimes considered to be the ultimate disciplinary weapon in parliamentary systems of government. As a check to the legislature, however, a veto power over legislation was granted, subject to the ability of Congress to override the veto by a two-thirds majority vote in both Houses.

By this grant of power the Founding Fathers in 1787 certainly did not intend to establish an office of the power and importance that has become the hallmark of the modern presidency. Many of them may have wanted 'a mere executive', one who would faithfully carry into effect the orders of the legislature; others wanted a more powerful president who would be able to check the dangerous tendencies of a democratic legislature; but none could have foreseen that the president would become the main initiator of policy, working with every weapon at the administration's disposal, constitutional and political, to further those policies, and to lead the country in the direction that the president considers desirable. Some modern presidents, President Taft for example, have tended towards the 'weak' view of the President's function, but the transformation of the office by Theodore Roosevelt, Woodrow Wilson and above all Franklin D. Roosevelt into a dynamic centre of policy-making was a reaction to the demands made upon governments in the modern world, which they were unable to ignore.

Checks to presidential power

The Constitution thus gives little *direct* authority to the president to control the affairs of the nation, and sets considerable obstacles to the achievement of this aim. In legislative and financial matters the president is constitutionally almost entirely dependent upon Congress, and the Senate has a veto on appointments and treaties. The Supreme Court also stands as a potential check to the power of the president, with the ability to pronounce presidential actions unconstitutional, as it did in 1952 in the steel seizure case. The Constitution provides that the president may be impeached and removed from office if guilty of treason, bribery or 'other high Crimes and Misdemeanours.' Impeachment was a procedure used in Britain to remove the King's ministers, and abandoned at the beginning of the nineteenth century. For a president to be impeached a resolution has to be passed by the House of Representatives setting out the charges. The Senate with the Chief Justice presiding then tries the president, and it requires a two-thirds vote of the members present to convict. Two presidents, Andrew Johnson in 1868 and Bill Clinton in 1999 have been impeached; the latter because of sexual scandals and the consequent charges that he committed perjury and abused the powers of his office. Andrew Johnson escaped conviction by one vote and the proceedings against Clinton failed because there was no majority of Senators to convict him. The threat of impeachment is taken very seriously by presidents. Richard Nixon resigned in 1974 when impeachment seemed imminent, and Ronald Reagan was threatened with possible impeachment over the Iran–Contra affair.

The revelations of the illegal and improper behaviour of President Nixon in the Watergate affair led Congress to pass the Ethics in Government Act of 1978. The Act provided that if a complaint of irregularity is made to the Attorney General a Special Prosecutor, or Independent Counsel, can be appointed to investigate the complaint and report to the Congress. The Act covers the behaviour of the president, vice-president, members of the cabinet and other senior officials, some seventy offices in all. After President Clinton's election in 1992 accusations were made about possible financial irregularities in a land transaction in Arkansas when he was governor. An Independent Counsel, Kenneth Starr, was appointed to investigate the matter, and this led into an examination of Clinton's private life and his sexual behaviour. Starr's investigation took four years until he reported to the Congress in September 1998, and it was his report that led to the impeachment of the President.

Party chief and national leader

If the presidency is to exercise the leadership in national affairs that modern conditions demand, its constitutional authority must be used in the context of the *extra*-constitutional position of the president as a national and party leader, in order to play a role not foreseen in the Constitution. The two sources of extra-constitutional power available to the president are the allegiance of party supporters in Congress and in the country as a whole, and 'public opinion'. These two sources of power sometimes complement each other and sometimes conflict. A skilful president may ring the changes of differing combinations of public and party support, sometimes depending upon the latter to attain limited aims which do not enjoy wide popular support, and at others using public opinion to override contrary opinions in the party. In essence, presidential politics consists of the attempt to walk this tightrope, and it brings the presidency to its lowest ebb when presidential policies come up against strong opposition both in the country at large and in the president's own party. Equally, however, when a president enjoys wide popular support and is backed by a relatively united party, the power of the presidency is impressive indeed.

As in so many other respects, however, these two sources of power are by no means simple and straightforward, either in their composition or in their usefulness as weapons in the presidential armoury. The president's position as a party leader is an equivocal one. In office the president is necessarily the titular head of the party, at least until a successor is nominated at the national convention. As the party is the organisational structure through which candidates are nominated and election campaigns conducted, there is a constant tendency to emphasise party unity. This desire for unity in the party works both ways, however. It gives the president some sort of claim to party allegiance, but it also imposes a considerable restraint, in that the attempt must be made to avoid making demands that will seriously divide the party. The claim of party loyalty on state and local political leaders is necessarily a limited one. They will often make considerable efforts to maintain a semblance of unity, perhaps with considerable embarrassment in the context of their local politics, but the claims of party loyalty alone cannot override really strong local pressures. A party leader who is also president of the United States has, however, more to offer to those whose support is required than the satisfaction simply of being a good party person. In return he may offer support for projects that a legislator or party chieftain wishes to further. Presidential approval of legislative proposals, or presidential commitment to the expenditure of money on public works in a state or locality, are powerful incentives to be a good supporter of the head of the party. In spite of the drastic curtailment of the spoils system, in which appointments to government positions all the way down the civil service hierarchy were potential political inducements, the president still has some thousands of offices to fill, and they include many plum positions, highly desirable to the friends and supporters of local politicians, and sometimes to those politicians themselves. The appointment of ambassadors and judges provides an important but by no means inexhaustible source of presidential bounty. This patronage is *not* channelled through those members of the president's party who consistently oppose the administration's policies.

Another of the weapons the president may use in his role as party leader is publicity. What the president does or says is automatically newsworthy, and the way in which public appearances are managed, the references made to party colleagues, the people invited to appear on platforms or at public events – all these seemingly innocent considerations can be the subject of the most intense political manoeuvring. Presidents, and presidential aspirants, may also become involved in the dangerous sphere of local political disputes, throwing their weight behind one faction or another, and hoping to benefit one day from the gratitude of the successful contender, although they may equally reap the bitter enmity of the opposing and not necessarily defeated faction. The dangers, and the likely lack of success, of too deep an involvement in local politics are illustrated by the experience of Franklin Roosevelt in the elections of 1938, when he attempted to intervene on behalf of Democratic congressional candidates without success, but a more subtle and continuing use of presidential influence is an inescapable part of a successful president's armoury.

The president may hope, therefore, to call upon party support, however engendered, for administration policies, but cannot rely upon it. Often, in order to get Congress to accept proposed legislation, the president must turn to a wider and more inclusive source of support, the American people. It is, of course, difficult to distinguish clearly these two roles of the president. Usually, in appealing for support to the people, the president is attempting to demonstrate to the party in Congress that they would be unwise to flout presidential leadership. At the same time the president may be appealing to members of the opposing party or to political independents for support on a national, non-partisan basis, for the good of the country as a whole, and on many issues it will be possible to achieve such support both in Congress and in the country. The president's appeal to public opinion has become of considerable political importance. The prestige and prominence of the office, the fact that the president alone can claim to speak *for* the nation, gives a special right to speak *to* the nation. With the development of the mass media, the president has tended to appeal for support more and more to a unique constituency, the nation, against the members of Congress who can be seen with some truth as an assembly of local politicians. Franklin Roosevelt first used the radio as an effective political weapon in his 'fireside chats' in the 1930s, in which he told the American people what he was attempting to do and asked for their support. The use of the radio (President Bush still makes a weekly radio address) has been surpassed in importance by presidential appearances before the television cameras, and the presidential press conference has become an institutionalised part of the machinery of government.

Woodrow Wilson, who established regular press conferences, first put the direct dialogue between the president and the representatives of the press on a regular basis. Franklin Roosevelt further developed this medium of communication in which the president could give background information and explain his policies to reporters, on the clear understanding that he would be quoted directly only when he gave his permission. In this way the president hoped for an understanding of, and representation of, his policies that would go beyond his public announcements. The presidential press conferences were then held in the intimacy of the president's office in the White House, but President Truman gave them a rather different character by transferring them to a much larger room where hundreds of correspondents from all over the country, and indeed all over the world, could attend. This proved to be the initial step in transforming the press conference into something quite different. In 1955 President Eisenhower allowed his press conferences to be filmed for television, and instead of a cosy, off-the-record discussion, the press conference became an unprecedented opportunity for a president to answer, before a national audience, the questions put to him by reporters. President Kennedy took this process one vital stage further. Whereas the Eisenhower conferences were filmed and edited before transmission, Kennedy instituted the live press conference, in which he stood before the television cameras giving his views on a wide range of subjects direct to the American people without the intervention of time or editors. The impact of this method of communication is difficult to measure, but its significance for presidential leadership must surely be enormous. The president is, of course, thoroughly briefed by his press secretary, by the State Department and by other advisers upon likely questions and the answers to be given. At one time he was in a position of considerable superiority over his questioners, who treated him with deference and did not attempt to cross-question him. However, the effect of the Watergate scandal was to transform the attitudes of the press and television reporters to the presidency. In 1998 President Clinton was subjected to the humiliation of being questioned about his relationship with Monica Lewinsky every time that he gave a press conference at which his intention was to make pronouncements on matters of national or international importance. Even when the press conferences were held in foreign locations, such as Moscow or Dublin, the American reporters pursued him mercilessly and embarrassingly on the subject of his sexual behaviour.

Therefore, as in the case of the president's role as party leader, the endeavour to project an image as a national leader in order to persuade opponents in Congress not to oppose too actively has its limitations. To obtain public sympathy and understanding for the administration's position is one thing, but to translate this into *active* support, which will make a positive impact upon Senators and Congressmen, is quite another. Furthermore, the obverse of the president's power to persuade through the mass media is the revelation of weaknesses or the inadequacies of policies or character. A misjudged attempt to persuade may quickly have the reverse effect from that which was intended. The intelligent use of the media of communication must avoid saturating or boring the public with presidential exhortations. A dramatic appeal by the president might generate considerable public support, but dramatic appeals six times a week are likely to have a very different result. Presidential leadership can be exercised in part, therefore, through the management, almost the manipulation, of public opinion, but the danger is that it can also make the president into the prisoner of public opinion, for, if the effort to persuade fails, it is extremely unlikely that success will be achieved in any other way.

The institutions of the presidency

Up to this point we have treated the *presidency* as if it consisted simply of the president alone. The dominant position of this individual should not, however, blind us to the fact that the presidency is an institution, and that the modern presidency involves an extensive structure of offices and functions. It is to this aspect of the presidency that we now turn, to look first at the role of the cabinet, and then at the Executive Office of the President.

The Cabinet

The Founding Fathers' attachment to the principle of the separation of powers in 1787 ensured that they would reject the system of cabinet government that was then in an embryonic stage of its development in Britain. They saw the British cabinet as a means of the maintenance of a royal dominance over the legislature and they did not wish to put such a weapon into the hands of the president. Some of the Founders, however, wished to establish some form of council to advise the president, and the first proposal that was submitted to the Constitutional Convention, the Pinckney Plan, incorporated such a body. However, the Constitution as finally submitted for ratification to the states contained no reference to a council, cabinet or other collective body to work with or advise the president. It simply stated that the president might 'require the opinion, in writing, of the principal officer in each of the executive departments, upon any subject relating to the duties of their respective offices'. Thus the Constitution left the president in a solitary pre-eminence in the executive branch of government.

However, from the very beginning of the Union George Washington took to consulting his heads of departments collectively as well as individually, and as early as 1793 the term 'Cabinet' was being applied to this group of advisers. Under President George W. Bush the cabinet consists of the Vice-President, the White House Chief of Staff and the heads of the fifteen executive departments: the Secretaries of Agriculture, Commerce, Defense, Education, Energy, Health and Human Services, Homeland Security, Housing and Urban Development, Interior, Labor, State, Transportation, Treasury, and Veterans Affairs, and the Attorney General. Cabinet-level rank also has been accorded to the Administrator of the Environmental Protection Agency, the Director of the Office of Management and Budget, the Director of National Drug Control Policy and the US Trade Representative. The heads of agencies without cabinet rank may be asked to attend from time to time for the discussion of particular subjects.

Until President Eisenhower's term of office, the cabinet worked on an extremely informal basis. There was no cabinet agenda and no minutes were recorded. The business was conducted as the incumbent president wished. Eisenhower formalised cabinet meetings, holding them weekly and introducing an agenda and minutes. He appointed one of his Special Assistants to the President as Secretary to the Cabinet. President Kennedy, with a completely different approach to the organisation of his administration, abandoned frequent meetings of the cabinet and abolished the cabinet secretariat. The cabinet virtually ceased to have any collective function, giving way to ad hoc meetings with the president of those members concerned with a particular problem.

Presidents have used the cabinet as an organ of consultation and advice, but it has never enjoyed the role of a collective decision-taking body like that of the British cabinet. There are a number of reasons for this, quite apart from the silence of the Constitution on the subject. The whole atmosphere of the American political scene is opposed to the idea of the collective responsibility of a tightly knit, cohesive cabinet along the lines that used to be the ideal of cabinet government in Britain. The cohesiveness of British cabinets rested upon two interrelated characteristics of the British system: parliamentary government and the party structure. The former makes it imperative for the cabinet to maintain a unified front in order to safeguard its majority in the House of Commons, without which it must resign. The latter, based upon closely disciplined, ideologically oriented party organisations, produces a relatively like-minded body of men and women at the head of a political party, whose approach to the problems of government will be quite similar. Although the foundations of this party system may be crumbling in Britain today, and the concept of collective responsibility has lost much of its earlier significance, the members of a British cabinet still tend to be very close to each other in their political ideas and ideals, compared with the attitudes of the opposing party. Furthermore, they will be a group of men and women most of whom have shared the same long apprenticeship in the House of Commons, working their way up from the back benches, through junior and then more senior ministerial positions, until they reach the cabinet. They will also have shared the years of political wilderness in opposition. This forges a bond that is not lightly broken. None of these considerations applies to the American cabinet.

First, the American cabinet is not formally responsible to Congress. In a constitutional sense its responsibility is to the president alone, but in terms of practical politics the heads of the great departments must pay almost as much attention to what Congress wants as to the president. It is congressional legislation that empowers them to act, it is money granted by Congress that finances their activities, and it is the committees of Congress that keep a vigilant watch on their performance. Thus cabinet members look to the president who hired them, and could fire them, and to the Congress, particularly to the chairmen of those committees with whom they must deal, but they do not look much to their cabinet colleagues, except perhaps as potential rivals for presidential favours and congressional funds.

Second, the relationships between the president and the members of his cabinet may be very close, and yet they are of a different quality from those of a prime minister and his or her colleagues. The president may appoint to the highest offices in the administration individuals who were personally unknown until a few days before their appointment. The president may, rarely it is true, appoint members of the opposing party to important positions in the administration. Although regard must be shown for the representative

nature of the cabinet, ensuring that the regions of the country are represented and that no section of the community feels itself to have been slighted, the
president is virtually unfettered in terms of the actual individuals appointed.
There is no 'Shadow Cabinet' in the American political universe, and so no
clear expectations to be satisfied, unless the president has given hostages to
fortune during the electoral campaign. The tendency is to appoint experts
to cabinet posts, in the sense of finding people qualified to do the jobs to
be done, rather than looking for any other qualification. They may be businessmen, academics, former state governors, congressmen, judges, lawyers,
engineers, or from any other walk of life, and after they have finished with
the administration they will probably return whence they came. Thus their
loyalty, their first allegiance, is to the president who appointed them.

It is not, however, their only loyalty. As we have seen, they must look also
to important figures in Congress, and they must also look to their 'clientele'. Each of the great departments, even the Department of State, has a
clientele, the people they serve and regulate, and to whom they develop a
sense of responsibility. Sometimes the identification with a section of the
community can become so strong – in the case of the Departments of Agriculture, Commerce and Labor, for example – that their aim seems to be to
promote a particular interest to the government, rather than to represent
the government itself. This is yet another divisive characteristic, forcing the
members of the cabinet to seek individual and confidential contact with the
president in order to ensure support. Thus there is an important distinction
to be made between the cabinet as a collective body and the individuals who
compose it. It is often emphasised, quite rightly, that it is the president who
has the final responsibility for decisions. Even if the cabinet were to be unani-
mously opposed to a presidential policy they could not outvote the president,
or veto the policy. It is true also that the president appoints the members of
the cabinet and can dismiss them. Yet to see the individual members of the
cabinet as the mere creatures of the president is a mistake. They can and do
disagree with their master. If the president is determined to overrule them,
they will be overruled, but they all operate in a political context. Department
heads have their sources of support distinct from the president, and each has
many decisions to make, so that the most active and well-informed of presidents cannot be aware of all of them, or afford to try to exercise a continual
personal surveillance over them. Individual cabinet members can attain a
political influence that may be of some embarrassment to the president, and
a very few have even rivalled the president's authority in their own sphere.

Given the nature of the American cabinet, it seems difficult to understand
why it should have persisted at all as a collective entity, and yet, although it
seems at times almost to have ceased to function in this way, there would appear to have been a continuous need for a body of this sort. Presidents need
to indicate in some way that the administration is working as a team, and
to demonstrate collective support and approval for policies, particularly at
times of crisis. A meeting of the cabinet, with its members representing their
differing clienteles, authenticates the process of consulting the pluralistic

interests that go to make up the American polity, but it represents very little in terms of actual decision-making, for the decisions are taken elsewhere. Similarly, the cabinet fails to make any significant contribution to the solution of that problem of coordinating the activities of the governmental machine that is so critically important in modern government. To help the president to perform this function, therefore, a quite distinct set of institutions has been evolved.

The Executive Office of the President

The president heads an administration that includes some 2,750,000 federal civil servants, as well as 1,500,000 members of the armed forces. In addition to the fifteen executive departments, there are over forty independent agencies of the federal government together with a plethora of advisory boards, committees and commissions. The president stands in a solitary position of overall responsibility for the acts of this enormous machine and must direct and coordinate its activities, and to do this requires information about its operations, assessments of policy needs, and a means of ensuring that presidential decisions, and those of the Congress, are carried out effectively and in the spirit in which they were intended. The problem of channelling information and advice upwards to the president and of transmitting commands down through the machinery of government, as well as the complex problems of liaison with the Congress, have inevitably increased with the enormous expansion of the functions of the federal government. The size of the presidential staffs gradually increased in a rather haphazard fashion until the New Deal programmes of Franklin D. Roosevelt imposed an intolerable strain upon the existing machinery. In 1937 the President's Committee on Administrative Management emphasised the need to equip the president with an organisation to control and coordinate the administration effectively. As a result, Congress passed the Reorganization Act of 1939, and empowered President Roosevelt to establish the Executive Office of the President. This he did by Executive Order 8248, in September 1939. Clinton Rossiter has described this as an innovation that saved the presidency from paralysis and the Constitution from radical amendment. The Executive Office has become the heart of the administration, providing the president with information and advice, attempting to foresee future trends in government and to forecast future problems for the government. It conducts the president's relations with the Congress, with the press and the general public, and supervises the implementation of presidential decisions.

Under President Bush the Executive Office consists of eleven subdivisions to advise and assist the president, including the White House Office, the Office of Management and Budget, the Council of Economic Advisers, the National Security Council, the Office of National Drug Control Policy, the Office of Science and Technology Policy, and the Office of the United States Trade Representative.

The White House Office

The nerve centre of the Executive Office, and indeed of the presidency, is the White House Office. Included in the White House Office are the Domestic Policy Council, the Homeland Security Council, the National Economic Council, the Military Office and a number of other bodies as well as the Office of the First Lady. The White House Office has a staff of hundreds, but the twenty or so men and women who work closest to the president are the Chief of Staff, the Senior Adviser to the President, and Assistants to the President covering various areas such as National Security Affairs, Legislative Affairs, Economic Policy, Domestic Policy and Homeland Security. There is also the Press Secretary, the Special Counsel to the President, and the Director of the Military Office. The White House Office also includes the president's physician, a personal secretary and a social secretary. The exact nature and role of this group of people depends entirely on the president, who has a completely free hand in their selection. At one extreme they could be merely a set of errand-boys running messages or carrying out routine tasks; but in fact the Assistants to the President have become the most coherent group of people in the administration, taking a major part in the process of innovation and policy-making. John F. Kennedy surrounded himself with a group of talented men from different areas of national life, whose role was described by one of them, Theodore Sorensen, in the following way:

> Two dozen or more Kennedy assistants gave him two dozen or more sets of hands, eyes and ears, two dozen or more minds attuned to his own. They could talk with legislators, newsmen, experts, Cabinet members and politicians – serve on inter-departmental task forces – review papers and draft speeches, letters and other documents – spot problems before they were crises and possibilities before they were proposals – screen requests for legislation, Executive Orders, jobs, appointments with the President, patronage and Presidential speeches – and bear his messages, look out for his interests, carry out his orders and make certain his decisions were executed.

The allocation of work among these members of the White House staff is again a matter of presidential taste. Assistants may be detailed to cover particular fields – foreign affairs, defence or liaison with Congress – or simply used as generalists or trouble-shooters. The potential importance of the advisers who are closest to the president lies in the nature of the void that they fill in the system of government, a void that the cabinet is quite unfit to fill. With a powerful, dominant personality like that of Kennedy in the president's chair they may be influential but clearly subordinate, but what if the president is not so dominant, or is physically weak? Is there not a danger that an unelected, unrepresentative official or group of officials could wield excessive power? Some critics of the Eisenhower administration levelled this charge against one member of the President's staff, Sherman Adams. President Eisenhower appointed Adams as 'Assistant to the President' a title that had been created under the administration of his predecessor, President Truman. Adams was given a broad grant of power that led his critics to label him 'the Assistant President'. Access to the president was channelled through Adams, who saw his function as that of 'shielding the president from problems that could be settled on the lower echelons', and ensuring that work of 'secondary importance' should be kept off the president's desk. Although Adams strongly denied that this position represented in any way a usurpation of presidential authority, it inevitably meant that it was *his* judgement that determined what was, and was not, of secondary importance. In effect, every president since Eisenhower has had a chief of staff in the White House Office to act as the main coordinator of his advisers, and as the channel of communication between the president and his administration.

President Nixon's Chief of Staff, H.R. Haldeman, together with John Ehrlichman, Nixon's Domestic Policy Adviser, were known as the 'Berlin Wall' because they controlled access to the president and helped insulate him from public opinion. Both Haldeman and Ehrlichman received jail sentences for their part in the Watergate scandal. Another member of the White House staff to be indicted and convicted was Vice Admiral John Poindexter, who became National Security Adviser to President Reagan. Poindexter was convicted of criminal conspiracy with Colonel Oliver North, a member of the staff of the National Security Council. Poindexter and North were convicted in 1990 for their role in the Iran–Contra affair, the trading of arms for the release of American hostages. President Reagan denied all knowledge of these activities of members of his staff.

The relationship of the White House Office to the cabinet is, therefore, of critical importance. The cabinet, which should contain the main administrative lieutenants of the president, has been consistently downgraded, and a new, potentially extremely powerful apparatus has been created around the president. The evolution of this relationship during the ill-fated presidency of Richard Nixon is particularly instructive. On taking office in 1969 President Nixon, concerned with the problem of coordinating government policies in the field of urban affairs and economic policy, created two new important posts in the administration and two new coordinating bodies. The post of Counselor to the President was established in the White House Staff, with the prime responsibility of coordinating the development of domestic policies and programmes. The President appointed Dr Arthur Burns to this position, and gave him cabinet rank, thus putting him at a level never formally held by a member of the White House Staff. The President also appointed to his staff an Assistant to the President for Urban Affairs, Dr D.P. Moynihan. There were created alongside the National Security Council two new cabinet-level organisations, the Council for Urban Affairs and a Cabinet Committee on Economic Policy. In July 1970 President Nixon effected an even more fundamental change in the relationship between the cabinet and the Executive Office. A Domestic Council was established in order to coordinate the activities of the departments and agencies operating in the domestic field. The Council consisted of the president, the vice-president and the heads of the departments, with the exception of the Secretaries of State and Defense, but it included also the two members of the White House Staff with the title of Counselor to the President, as well as other presidential aides and the chairman of the Council of Economic Advisers. Most of the White House Staff working on domestic affairs were absorbed into the staff of the new Council, which was intended not to operate as a single entity, but to divide into a number of committees each dealing with a particular area of policy. The development had begun of a new kind of cabinet, constructed in part out of some members of the traditional cabinet and in part out of the White House Staff, who were to assume formally responsibilities that they had exercised before, if at all, only informally.

At the beginning of his second term, President Nixon pressed on further with this line of development. In January 1973 he announced the establishment of a 'Super-Cabinet', in which the dividing lines between the cabinet and the White House Office disappeared almost entirely. Although the Super-Cabinet was never really to operate because of the vast upheaval of the Watergate affair, it is worth some study since some similar structure may yet emerge again in response to the need for coordination at the top of the federal government.

Nixon established five Assistants to the President to work under him, 'to integrate and unify policies and operations throughout the executive branch of the Government, and to oversee all of the activities for which the president is responsible'. The five assistants were H.P. Haldeman (White House administration), John D. Ehrlichman (domestic affairs), Henry Kissinger (foreign affairs), Roy L. Ash (executive management) and George P. Schulz (economic affairs). Schulz, to be appointed an Assistant to the President in the White House Office, was to retain his Cabinet post as Secretary of the Treasury. Three other cabinet members, in the field of domestic policy, were to be given broad coordinating functions over their cabinet colleagues and other divisions of the administration. These three members of the cabinet were also to become members of the White House Staff as Counselors to the President and to become chairmen of the committees of the Domestic Council dealing with their area of policy. Furthermore, the three domestic coordinators were to report to the President through the Assistant to the President, John Ehrlichman.

How this system would have worked had it not disappeared in the Watergate holocaust it is impossible to say. It is significant, however, that it formed the White House Office and the cabinet into a single hierarchy of control under the president, and so blurred the distinction between cabinet members and presidential assistants that it hardly seemed any longer a guide to the significance of an individual; what was important was his position in the hierarchy. President Ford returned to the pre-Nixon relationship between the cabinet and the White House Office, and soon after taking office President Carter stressed that he intended to strengthen the working of 'Cabinet government'. He was, he said, 'very much opposed to having a concentration of large numbers of people in authority in the White House Staff. I much prefer that Cabinet officers make their own decisions, manage their own departments, and that the co-ordinating effort rests with me.' The Domestic Council was abolished and replaced with a Domestic Policy Staff in the White House Office. As a result of the Watergate affair, therefore, the concept of a 'strong' cabinet was reasserted as a reaction to the abuse of power by Nixon and the arrangements that he made to strengthen his control over the administration. Nevertheless, the problem of coordinating the work of the American government remains, and it cannot be done by one individual. In 1985 President Reagan reiterated his commitment to cabinet government when creating two new cabinet-level bodies, the Economic Policy Council and the Domestic Policy Council, to work alongside the National Security Council in the coordination of policy in their respective fields. As with the earlier attempts to create effective coordinating machinery, these new councils were to consist of a mixture of the heads of executive departments and members of the White House Staff.

The National Security Council

The conduct of defence policy presents special problems for the American administration. The president is commander-in-chief, and as in other fields the final decisions are the president's, but the unity of command implicit in this constitutional principle must be translated into reality in an extremely large and diffuse government machine. The cabinet, as we have seen, is of no use for this purpose, and as a result Congress created a special 'defence cabinet' in 1947, the National Security Council. The Council has the duty to 'consider policies on matters of common interest to the departments and agencies of the government concerned with the national security and to make recommendations to the President'. The National Security Council is chaired by the president. Its regular members (both statutory and non-statutory) are the Vice-President, the Secretary of State, the Secretary of the Treasury, the Secretary of Defense, and the Assistant to the President for National Security Affairs. The Chairman of the Joint Chiefs of Staff is the statutory military adviser to the Council, and the Director of Central Intelligence is the intelligence adviser. The Chief of Staff to the President, Counsel to the President, and the Assistant to the President for Economic Policy are invited to attend any NSC meeting. Under President Eisenhower the Council met frequently to discuss current problems of foreign policy; the staff prepared policy papers to keep the members of the Council abreast of new developments in matters such as weapon technology; and there was a complete substructure of interdepartmental committees. Under Presidents Kennedy and Johnson, however, the Council met less frequently, problems being dealt with much more by the president in collaboration with groups of advisers. Like the cabinet itself, the National Security Council cannot make decisions for the president, but can only provide the information and advice on which to base decisions. Certainly it would seem that few major decisions at times of crisis have actually been made in the Council. Under the control of the National Security Council, nominally at least, is the Central Intelligence Agency. Its major function is to coordinate the intelligence activities of the government and to evaluate the intelligence that is received. However, in the wake of the Watergate scandal, disclosures about CIA activities led to investigations of its activities by Vice-President Rockefeller and by Congress. The extraordinary revelations of its operations, culminating in bizarre, James Bond-like plots to assassinate foreign heads of state, raise profound questions about the nature of the American governmental machine. Whether CIA activities are characteristic of the secret services of other states we cannot know – they do not allow their legislatures to investigate secret activities in the way in which Congress has done. The more important question, however, is the extent to which these almost unbelievable plots were evolved with or without the knowledge of responsible members of the administration. The fragmented nature of the American administrative machine will be stressed later in this book, and the problems to which it gives rise are well known. However, what is merely 'uncoordinated action' in one part of the government machine can in another lead the whole world into disaster.

Homeland Security

The problem of the coordination of the government machine, and the propensity of American government to spawn new agencies was highlighted by the situation that developed after '9/11'. One of the consequences of the attack on the World Trade Center in New York in 2001 was a review of the organisation of the federal government to foresee, prevent and deal with terrorist attacks and other disasters that might occur. The immediate response was to create new government agencies. The Department of Homeland Security was established in 2002 with the task to 'prevent and deter terrorist attacks and protect against and respond to threats and hazards to the nation. We will ensure safe and secure borders, welcome lawful immigrants and visitors, and promote the free-flow of commerce.' The Homeland Security Council was set up in the Executive Office of the President, alongside the National Security Council. On 1 March 2003, the Federal Emergency Management Agency (FEMA) became part of the Department of Homeland Security. Its mission was 'to lead the effort to prepare the nation for all hazards and effectively manage federal response and recovery efforts following any national incident.' It wasn't long before FEMA was tested by the onslaught of Hurricane Katrina on New Orleans. We shall look more closely at this disaster in a later chapter.

The World Trade Center disaster also raised questions about the efficiency of the American intelligence services. Inevitably, the question was asked, 'Could this have been prevented?' The major agency involved in collecting and evaluating intelligence was the Central Intelligence Agency, but there were, and still are, fourteen other separate intelligence agencies in various departments of the federal government, including the Department of Justice and the Department of Defense. The coordination of the activities of these separate bodies to provide effective intelligence and an appropriate response came under examination and was found to be wanting. President Bush appointed the National Commission on Terrorist Attacks Upon the United States to enquire into the circumstances leading up to the attack on the Twin Towers and to make recommendations about how to prevent future attacks from occurring. In its Report the Commission stated that 'The agencies cooperated, some of the time. But even such cooperation as there was is not the same as joint action.' The Commission made a number of recommendations, including the creation of a Director of National Intelligence to coordinate the work of the fifteen intelligence agencies, including the CIA. Despite the opposition of a number of people inside the administration, in 2004 Congress passed the Intelligence Reform and Terrorism Prevention Act. President Bush appointed John Negroponte as Director of National Intelligence and implemented most of the Commission's recommendations. This involved the creation of the National Counter-terrorism Center to 'assist in analyzing and integrating foreign and domestic intelligence acquired from all U.S. government departments and agencies pertaining to the war on terrorism. The Center identifies, coordinates, and prioritizes the counterterrorism intelligence'. The Domestic Nuclear Detection Office was established to provide 'a single federal organization to develop and deploy a nuclear-detection system to thwart the importation of illegal nuclear or radiological materials'. The Privacy and Civil Liberties Oversight Board was appointed 'to further help ensure that privacy and civil rights are not eroded as we fight the War on Terror' and the Terrorist Screening Center was set up 'In order to consolidate terrorist watch lists and provide around-the-clock operational support for Federal and other government law-enforcement personnel across the country and around the world'. To add to this bureaucratic nightmare, in March 2006 President Bush created a Center for Faith-Based and Community Initiatives in the Department of Homeland Security, to 'identify barriers to faith-based and other community organizations' participation in our programs and activities, and propose ways to remove these barriers and to better integrate the community into our efforts. As a result, the department will more effectively channel the unique resources and capabilities of faith-based and other community organizations in times of crisis, and on an ongoing basis, in preparing for catastrophes of all types'. As is so often the case, the felt need to coordinate government activities led to the creation of further agencies, so aggravating the problem of coordination.

The Office of Management and Budget

The problem of financial control in the American system is a difficult one indeed: Congress is jealous of its prerogatives, and the departments of the administration use all their guile to retain the maximum possible financial autonomy. The instrument that the president uses to maintain control over the financial operations of the government is the Office of Management and Budget. It is important to realise that the United States Treasury Department is very different in function from the British Treasury or most other European finance ministries. The US Treasury has never had the role of supervising in detail the expenditures of government departments, or of relating government expenditures in general to government revenues. Before 1921, indeed, there was no national executive budget (a term that is applied to proposed expenditures, not to proposed taxation). Each department prepared its estimates for submission to Congress, and the duty of the Secretary of the Treasury was simply to compile them into a single book of estimates. In 1921 the Budget and Accounting Act provided that the president should submit an annual budget of the United States to Congress, and it established the Bureau of the Budget to aid him. The Bureau was nominally established in the Treasury Department, but the Act provided that the Director of the Bureau should report directly to the president. This rather anomalous position was ended in 1939 when the Bureau was transferred to the newly created Executive Office of the President.

The Act of 1921 gave to the Bureau the authority 'to assemble, correlate, revise, reduce, or increase the requests for appropriations of the several departments and establishments'. As a result of its strategic position in regard to finance, and the fact that its functions involved it in the activities of all the agencies of the executive branch, the Bureau was the natural instrument for presidential attempts to coordinate the activities of the administration and to promote administrative efficiency. So, in addition to its functions in relation to the preparation and administration of the budget, the Bureau was charged with the task of conducting research into better administrative management and advising the departments upon better administrative organisation and accounting practices, coordinating departmental advice on proposed legislation, and coordinating and improving the government's statistical activities. In July 1970 the Bureau of the Budget was absorbed into the newly established Office of Management and Budget in the Executive Office of the President.

Potentially, the Office of Management and Budget is the most powerful coordinating device available to the president. It has knowledge of, and extensive contacts with, every part of the administrative machine. Its power to revise estimates is ultimately the power over policy. The Director of the OMB has direct access to the president, and at the same time has the major responsibility of seeing that presidential policy is carried through. However, the practical significance of the Office must be assessed within the political and administrative context in which it operates. It is unlikely ever to have the degree of control over executive departments that the British Treasury wields, simply because the American administrative machine is much more loosely knit. Furthermore, the power of its head ultimately depends upon the extent to which the president is prepared actively to give support to the Director. If a president is determined to use the Office as an instrument of policy, rather than as a mere accounting device, and makes it clear that the Director's point of view will be upheld, then control over the estimates can become a reality. But with the best will in the world a president inevitably faces the difficulty that there is only a limited amount of time and effort that can be devoted to these matters and for the Director it becomes a political problem of how far, and how often, an appeal can be made for direct presidential support in conflicts with departments. Finally, of course, the Office has to take account of Congress, and of the influence wielded by chairmen of committees over the bureaus and agencies of the government and on their behalf. The Director and the president too must live with the knowledge that Congress might reverse their decisions. They do not, therefore, have the same authority in the settlement of disputes within the administration that a Chancellor of the Exchequer has in the British administrative machine, for the latter is virtually certain that Parliament will pass the estimates in the form that is proposed.

The Council of Economic Advisers

The function of the Office of Management and Budget is to control and co-ordinate the activities of government through the supervision of departmental expenditures, but modern governments must concern themselves with economic policy in a wider context. They must attempt, at whatever level of sophistication, to control the general direction and pace of economic development, to control inflation, prevent slumps, and sustain economic growth. The broad acceptance of this philosophy by Congress in the immediate post-war period led to the passage of the Employment Act of 1946, which set up the Council of Economic Advisers. The function of the Council is to advise the president on future economic trends, to develop and recommend to him policies that will 'maintain employment, production, and purchasing power', to conduct studies of the economy and to recommend policies that will contribute to this aim. The Council, consisting of a chairman and two other members, together with its staff, has the task of preparing for the president an Annual Economic Report for presentation to the Congress, setting out the administration's view of what is likely to happen during the year in the economic sphere, and making recommendations on economic policy. Even more perhaps than other parts of the presidential entourage, the Council must be seen essentially as an advisory body. It has been described as the 'economic conscience' of the administration, serving as a counterweight to the Treasury

Department and the Office of Management and Budget with their more restricted and more immediate responsibilities. Undoubtedly, it has served as an invaluable educative influence on presidents and their staffs, working for more flexible and farsighted economic policies. It has meant that the influence of skilled economists has been brought to bear right at the apex of the American administrative machine.

The vice-president

Throughout most of the history of the United States the vice-presidency was an office of little significance. John Garner, vice-president to Franklin D. Roosevelt, said of the office: 'It isn't worth a bucket of warm spit!' The Constitution gives two functions to the vice-president – to preside over the Senate, a task normally delegated to a senior Senator, and to succeed the president if the president dies in office, is removed by impeachment or resigns. The latter is by no means an insignificant matter. No fewer than nine vice-presidents have succeeded to the office of president: four presidents died in office, four were assassinated, one resigned. Whilst the president continues in office the actual role of the vice-president depends entirely on what the president asks, or allows, the vice-president to do. Some presidents have virtually ignored the vice-president, or treated him as a possible rival. Some vice-presidents have been entrusted with responsibilities of some importance. Al Gore, Clinton's vice-president, had a higher profile than most holders of the office. He was given the task of advising the president on government waste and on environmental questions, and was prominent in promoting the Kyoto Treaty on carbon emissions, although the Senate rejected the treaty in a unanimous vote.

It is, however, Vice-President Richard Cheney who is considered in the words of American scholar, Stephen Hess, to be 'the most powerful Vice-President we've ever had.' It appears that Cheney has been a hard-liner on foreign policy in the administration, and advocated the invasion of Iraq in order to remove Saddam Hussein and to destroy his 'weapons of mass destruction'. He played a leading role in trying to exempt the CIA from the McCain Anti-Torture Amendment, outlawing torture by US personnel. His Chief of Staff, I. Lewis Libby, was indicted in October 2005 on charges of perjury and obstruction of justice for allegedly having lied to a grand jury about conversations with reporters concerning a CIA operative, Valerie Plame, whose identity was revealed by the press. The magazine *Time* said of him, 'Cheney makes his own rules, he decides what intelligence matters, what secrets are worth keeping, and what force is worth using'.

The problem of the presidency

In September 1974 Richard Nixon became the first president of the United States to resign from office. He did so after it became clear that he would be impeached if he did not resign, and after some of the most extraordinary events in the history of the United States had taken place, events that were revealed in the most exhaustive detail to the whole world by the newspapers and by congressional investigations. An attempt will be made at the end of this chapter to put this, the lowest point ever reached by the institution of the presidency, into perspective. Here we are concerned to explore the nature of presidential power, its extent, its bases and its limitations. The end of the Nixon presidency gave a bizarre colouration to this picture, but the underlying nature of the problem of the presidency remains the same.

The central problem of the presidency is its solitary character. The cabinet rarely acts in any collective sense, and the final burden of decision taking, or of the extent to which it will be abdicated to others, rests upon the shoulders of one person. The creation of the Executive Office in 1939 initially eased this problem, but now it can be seen to have created new and perhaps more fundamental problems. What then is the nature of this power that the president wields?

The parameters of power

There are two rather contradictory statements used to describe presidential power. On the one hand, it is asserted that the president of the United States is the most powerful elected official in the world; on the other hand, it is argued that the power of the president is, in effect, simply the power to persuade. As we have seen, this power is certainly hemmed in by constitutional boundaries, but it is a mistake to try to characterise the power of the president in a single, well-turned epigram. The reality is much more complex. We are now in a position to analyse the nature of presidential power, and to explore its boundaries. Of course, we cannot say anything about the nature or extent of presidential power in *any particular* future situation, for so much must depend upon the exact circumstances, or upon the nature of public opinion at the time; what is unthinkable at one moment may be practical politics the next. What we can do is to define the parameters of presidential power, the constants within which it must develop and be exercised according to the political context. We can distinguish three sets of conditions of this sort, which overlap and combine into differing qualities of *potential power*. Given a certain level of public and party support, therefore, the potential power of the president will vary according to the way in which these factors add up in a particular instance.

The potential power of the president to act will vary in the following ways:

1*a* if the action involves persuading Congress to confer new statutory powers on the administration;
  b if the action can be taken under an existing congressional statute;
  c if the action can be brought within one of the directly granted constitutional powers of the president;

2*a* if the action depends entirely upon the immediate appropriation of money by the Congress;

 b if the action requires the appropriation of money by Congress in the relatively near future;

 c if the action requires no expenditure of money other than the normal running expenses of the administration;

3*a* if the action lies in the field of domestic policy;

 b if it lies in the field of diplomacy;

 c if it involves the exercise of military power.

   Thus, *with a given level of popular support*, one can generalise that the potential power of the president will be least if Congress must be persuaded to grant new powers before action can be taken, if the required action needs the appropriation of money, and if it is in the field of domestic policy. The president's potential power will be the greatest if the policy can be implemented independently of congressional approval, in an area requiring little or no immediate expenditure of money, and in the field of the responsibilities of commander-in-chief. In between these extremes there will be a considerable number of different degrees of potential power according to the combination of factors involved.

   The president and the administration exercise enormous statutory powers granted by Congress over the years. Today this authority extends into a wide variety of fields of activity, touching the life of every citizen of the United States. Every statutory authority granted to the administration is potentially a weapon of presidential policy, for powers originally granted for one purpose can sometimes be turned to the support of other policies. Furthermore, the authority granted by Congress may be used to the hilt or drawn upon very little. The way in which the administration uses its powers depends in the last resort on the president. Thus the power to help minorities to exercise their rights as voters may be very actively pursued, or allowed to languish. It is the president who will instruct the Attorney General to pursue one policy or another, or at least give the latter support. In almost every field of government activity there are such powers which can be implemented in differing ways. Furthermore, the modern administration has a considerable reservoir of delegated power, the power to fill in the administrative details of legislation, and to legislate itself within the authority granted by Congress. The principle of delegated legislative power, which seems on its face to offend against the doctrine of the separation of powers, has long been accepted by the judiciary, provided that the grant of power is not so wide as to be invalid through vagueness, or is incapable of being policed by the courts. However, there are clearly limits to these possibilities. The administration is bound by the law and must justify its acts if challenged in the courts, so that where there is doubt, or where a quite new programme is to be initiated, the president must go to Congress and persuade it of the need for further legislation.

   Even when explicit powers have been granted to the administration, however, the president's position is not wholly secure. What has been given can be taken away, and the congressional grant of power may have been explicitly hedged with all manner of conditions and limitations. The president's potential power is greatest, therefore, in those areas where there exists independent power to act based directly upon the Constitution, although in practice these constitutional powers will usually have been filled out and augmented by federal legislation. Most of these powers are to be found in the field of military affairs and diplomacy, but they also have internal aspects. The president can call the state militia – the National Guard – into federal service and use them to maintain law and order, usually, but not always, at the invitation of the governor of a state. The president can use federal marshals or, in an extreme case, federal troops to enforce federal law and the decisions of the courts. The intervention of President Eisenhower in Little Rock, Arkansas, in 1957, and of President Kennedy in Alabama in 1961 and in Mississippi the following year, are good examples. From time to time presidents have claimed 'prerogative powers' to act without statutory authority where the safety of the nation is involved – usually, it is true, moving quickly to gain *ex post facto* congressional approval of their actions.

From time to time presidents have tried to extend their power beyond the framework set out above. In time of war, presidents have claimed an authority to act in ways reminiscent of the prerogative powers of the Crown in Britain, prerogatives which the Founding Fathers were at pains to deny to the president. Abraham Lincoln suspended habeas corpus during the Civil War and spent money without congressional authorisation. Franklin Roosevelt made executive agreements with foreign powers during the Second World War that usurped the authority of the Senate over treaties. During the Korean War, President Truman tried to assert executive authority during a war situation by nationalising the steel industry without the approval of Congress. President Nixon used his power as commander-in-chief in the Vietnam War to conduct secret operations in Laos and Cambodia. These presidential actions have been justified by what has come to be known as the doctrine of the 'unitary executive'. This is the assertion that the president has as much right to interpret the Constitution in his sphere of competence as the Supreme Court has, a doctrine which goes back to the early days of the debates about the distribution of governmental powers between the branches of government.

George W. Bush has invoked the doctrine of the 'unitary executive' to assert his right to adopt policies which are not approved by Congress, or in order to avoid the supervision of the courts. Bush has used 'signing statements' to attempt to modify or avoid the effect of laws passed by Congress. When signing a bill passed by both Houses of Congress the president may make a statement about how the act will be executed. Thus in signing the McCain Anti-Torture Bill of 2005, designed to outlaw the use of torture by American troops or other agencies, Bush stated that:

> The executive branch shall construe ... the Act, relating to detainees, in a manner consistent with the constitutional authority of the President

to supervise the unitary executive branch and as Commander in Chief
and consistent with the constitutional limitations on the judicial power,
which will assist in achieving the shared objective of the Congress and
the President . . . of protecting the American people from further terrorist attacks.

In other words the President was saying that he would interpret the Act in the
way that suited him. Bush also evaded the terms of the Foreign Intelligence
Surveillance Act of 1978, when in response to the attacks of 11 September
2001 he authorised the National Security Agency 'to intercept international
communications in to or out of the United States of persons linked to al-
Qaeda or an affiliated terrorist organization'. The Attorney General, in 2006,
justified such wiretappings without the authorisation of a warrant. 'Among
the President's most basic constitutional duties is the duty to protect the Nation from armed attack. The Constitution gives him all necessary authority
to fulfill that responsibility'.

These, then, are ways in which the president's potential power is dependent upon the extent of existing authority to act, and upon the basis of
that authority. But this is not the only dimension. The problem of finance
must be considered. An existing authority, statutory or constitutional, is of
little significance if the money to implement it is not forthcoming. Some
statutory powers can be exercised with little or no expenditure of money,
whereas others require large appropriations by Congress before they can be
implemented. Congress keeps quite distinct the two operations of *authorising*
a programme and *appropriating* money for it. It is by no means unknown for
it to do the former and to balk at the latter. Furthermore, Congress insists
upon the annual appropriation of funds, although the authority to pursue
a particular policy may have been on the statute book for many years, so
that the administration must continually justify its demands and persuade
Congress to give it the money it needs. Thus the use of federal troops or of
the National Guard to maintain order is a very different financial proposition
from running an anti-poverty programme, even though the latter has been
fully approved by Congress. Similarly, the decision to implement the Voting
Rights Act with greater vigour may initially involve only a redeployment of
the resources of the Department of Justice, but in the long run it will depend
upon congressional willingness to maintain a large force of attorneys and
federal marshals.

The third dimension of presidential power is the arena in which action is
contemplated. The general considerations set out above about the character
of the sources of power, and the financial implications of policy decisions,
apply to the fields of domestic and foreign policy alike, and also to the problems of the military sector. Thus the foreign aid programme is one where
congressional control is felt very strongly, because of the need both for statutory authorisation and for the annual appropriation of large sums of money.

But there are a number of considerations that tend to enhance the power of the president when moving from strictly domestic concerns into the field of foreign affairs, and even more so when acting as commander-in-chief of the armed forces rather than as chief diplomat. These considerations overlap our first category of the nature of the sources of power, for in the area of foreign relations the president has far more directly granted powers to conduct the affairs of the nation. The major restriction is the requirement that treaties must be ratified by a two-thirds majority of the Senate, but, since the refusal of the Senate to ratify the Treaty of Versailles, presidents have resorted much more to the use of executive agreements with foreign countries which do not require ratification.

The major difference between the diplomatic and domestic roles of the president is that the president is strategically in a much more powerful position in foreign affairs *in relation to internal American political forces*. The role of national leader is here most potent, and the claim to represent the whole nation against sectional forces the most persuasive. As the president and only the president must make the final decisions in matters of foreign policy there is a natural tendency to allow the president to know best in this field. It does not mean of course that decisions will not be challenged, and indeed hotly contested in some quarters; but there is almost the presupposition in the attitude of the general public that the president should be supported. This attitude is buttressed by patriotic sentiments, which can be extremely powerful in American politics, which suggest that the president should be supported when under attack from foreigners. It is possible for the president to move with greater freedom in foreign affairs than domestic politics, partly because of the original constitutional powers of the office, partly because of the initial strength given by public opinion. Furthermore, it is in the field of foreign affairs that the institutional power of the presidency carries most weight. In internal affairs the president must function much more as a power broker between contending interests and the machinery of presidential decision-making is very closely bound up with the pluralist structure. There are interest groups in foreign affairs, of course, and some are very important, but usually their significance is less than in internal affairs. The information and advice that the president gets from White House advisers, cabinet members and officials will therefore be of greater significance than in the domestic field. The overwhelming difference between external affairs and internal politics is the potential power of the president to commit the country to a course of action, which, once embarked upon, is extremely difficult to repudiate or reverse. The president's powers as commander-in-chief are the extreme example of this. By being able to order American troops to take up positions abroad, or even to commit them to hostilities, the Congress and the people are presented with a fait accompli, where they must choose between repudiating their president, and so perhaps endangering their own troops, and supporting the commander-in-chief.

The Twenty-Second Amendment

The growth of presidential power in the twentieth century, and in particular in the period 1932–45, called forth a large volume of criticism and demands that it should be curbed. There were two major lines of attack, one unsuccessful (the Bricker Amendment) and the other a successful move – the Twenty-Second Amendment to the Constitution. The length of the president's tenure of office is a matter of great importance for his power and influence. An incumbent president is in a strong position (though not an impregnable one) to gain re-nomination and re-election. As we have seen, the ability of a president to secure agreement for the administration's policies depends very much upon a number of factors involving the use of the president's position as party leader and national leader, as well as the constitutional and statutory powers of the office. If it is known that the end of the president's period of office is in sight, much of the president's armoury falls away. Soon someone else will be wielding these powers and dispensing patronage. It is true that even late in a term of office the president's position is still awesome enough to confer considerable influence within the party. Witness the way in which President Johnson was apparently able to affect the decisions on the party programme at the Chicago Convention in 1968, but the ability to secure congressional support for proposed policies inevitably declines as the term of office nears its end. The influence of an incumbent president will therefore be likely to be greater as long as there is a chance of being re-elected.

Given the power and prestige of the incumbent in the White House there has been a persistent fear, throughout the history of the Union, that a strong president might try to become a permanent president through continual re-election, and attain a position not far removed from that of a dictator. However unreal this might seem, it has been a continual fear, which increased as a consequence of the considerable growth of the power of the president during the twentieth century. The Founders of the Constitution decided against writing into that document a limitation upon the number of terms the president might serve, but George Washington, who of all presidents might have hoped for life tenure of the office, declined to stand again when he had almost completed his second term, explicitly warning against the dangers of too long a period of office. This attitude hardened into a two-term tradition that remained unbroken until 1940, although presidents who had been elected for two terms persistently hoped for a third term of office. None, however, was successful until President Franklin Roosevelt, a man of unrivalled popularity in a time of great tension, was nominated for a third term, and four years later for yet another. After the war this remarkable achievement, together with the fears that Roosevelt's policies engendered, led to demands for curbs on presidential power. The Republican-dominated Eightieth Congress in 1947 proposed an Amendment to the Constitution limiting presidents to two terms. It was ratified in 1951 and became the Twenty-Second Amendment. It has the effect of diminishing the influence and authority, in the second term, of the most effective of presidents, for it removes whatever doubt might have remained of the likelihood of the incumbent president running for a third term. It may also have a potentially more drastic effect upon the term of office of a vice-president who succeeds to the presidency. A vice-president who succeeds to the presidency and serves more than two years of the unexpired term (presumably even if only a few hours more), cannot be elected to the office in his own right more than once. Almost as soon as he is elected the speculation will begin about his successor.

The other attempt to limit the president's power was first introduced into Congress in 1951 by Senator John Bricker of Ohio, who proposed to amend the Constitution in order to subject executive agreements made by the president to the same control by the Senate as treaties, and to ensure that treaties would not be enforceable except through federal legislation, which would be subject to the same constitutional limitations as other legislation. The Bricker Amendment was proposed to Congress in a number of forms, and a much less restrictive Amendment was proposed by Senator Walter George in 1954, but none of them was successful in gaining the necessary two-thirds majority in Congress.

The power of the presidency

The presidency is then the centre of the American political system, an institution that concentrates great power in the hands of one person, but subjects that person also to the humiliations of utter defeat. It is a single point in a great sea of ever-moving, ever-changing political forces of the most varied character, which threaten to engulf and beat the president down, but a point that provides the one central, stable focus of authority which can, for a time at least, dominate, lead and innovate. By 1974, however, the presidency was at its lowest ebb. The impact of the Vietnam War on American society, closely followed by the Watergate affair, shook the confidence of the American people in their institutions, and led them to look very closely at the relationships between president and Congress that lie at the very heart of their system of government. The resignation of President Nixon, coming as it did barely in time to forestall his impeachment, together with the conviction of some of the most powerful members of his administration and the apparently endless revelations of criminal or corrupt activities by those in government service, underlined the claim by congressional leaders that the presidency was out of control and should be subjugated to a reinvigorated Congress. To the outside observer, perhaps the most striking aspect of this episode in American history is the fact that the Constitution and the political system managed to survive these extraordinary events, and to remove highly placed wrongdoers so effectively. Few if any other systems of government in the world would have made it possible to relentlessly expose the misdeeds of those still actually engaged in the exercise of power, and to remove them, without violence, through proper legal procedures. Naturally enough, however, the scandals produced a strong reaction against what Arthur M. Schlesinger Jr has labelled 'the Imperial Presidency'.

However, the desire to reduce the power of the presidency was an over-simple reaction to an extremely complex situation. The Watergate affair, though not of course in any sense inevitable, represents an extreme possibility inherent in the way in which an eighteenth-century constitution has evolved under the strains of twentieth-century conditions. The proximate cause of Watergate was, no doubt, the character of President Nixon and of the aides with whom he surrounded himself, but to understand the more fundamental causes it is essential to see these events within the context of the long-term trends in the American political system.

The American political system is extremely intricate. It has evolved in response to the needs of a society that was expanding rapidly in quite unique circumstances. In comparison with other nations, the United States was able to establish itself in an environment that was in some ways very favourable – an 'open' society with the possibility of expansion, a wealthy society, and one that was for most of the nineteenth century free of foreign entanglements and able to devote its energies to the solution of the problems of settling and developing the continent. As a result, the political system that emerged is able to do certain things very well indeed, and copes with other problems much less efficiently. The structure of the electoral system, of the parties and pressure groups, the organisation of the Congress – all these are superbly adapted to the task of registering and reflecting the interests and opinions of innumerable groups throughout the country and of aggregating those interests in a way that will facilitate the emergence of compromise policies, that often represent the lowest common denominator of interested opinion. As a mechanism for this purpose the system is unsurpassed in the modern world. The other side of this coin, however, is that the compromises that work so well in so many fields are potentially disastrous in those areas that demand coordinated and continuous policies. The compromise politics of consensus give to interested groups the opportunity to delay, and to modify substantially the policies that eventually emerge. In this way minorities defend themselves from attack, but at the same time they gain the ability to veto effective action on behalf of other minority groups. When confronted by a head-on clash of interests, the political system, instead of being able to resolve such conflicts, can only shelve them. The president, or the Supreme Court, can exert considerable leverage, and by a courageous act of leadership may sometimes move the political situation. Their autonomy, somewhat apart from the pluralist battle, and their prestige, endows them with this possibility, but in the process they must often subject themselves to vicious attack. Their ability to exercise this leadership is limited by their personal courage and skill, and by the institutional factors that hem them in.

The limitations on the power of the president are considerable. As powerful as the president is in the field of foreign affairs, a very different situation exists in regard to domestic policy. The president may be frustrated by Congress on those matters the administration considers essential to the national interest, and unable to ensure the passage of legislation, whether trivial or vital in importance. To pursue a vigorous policy in respect of domestic legislation requires a tremendous commitment on the part of the president, backed by all the charisma that can be mustered. A John F. Kennedy can put all his enormous appeal into his relations with Congress and the public, and then fail miserably. A Lyndon Johnson can use all his ability as a wheeler-dealer to get a large legislative programme through Congress, only to see the results dissipated in the impossible complexity of the administrative arrangements necessary to win congressional approval. An Eisenhower without the urge to build great domestic programmes can withdraw to the golf course; a Nixon can withdraw to an aloof, remote world apart. For all of them the temptation to spend more and more of their time and effort on foreign policy is almost overwhelming.

The roots of this situation are to be found in the institutional and political developments that dominated the twentieth century. There was a vast centralisation of government authority and an increase in the power and functions of the federal government in that period. There was also a consequent expansion in the statutory powers and functions of the president. It is to the federal government, and hence to the president, that Americans looked increasingly for the solutions to the problems of their society. However, at the same time as this centralisation of constitutional and legal authority was taking place, there was under way an increasing *decentralisation* of political power, making it more and more difficult for the federal government to exercise effectively the authority that it had accumulated. *The most significant fact of American government during the twentieth century was that the centralisation of government authority took place without a corresponding centralisation of political power.* On the contrary, the power base of the president, the only truly national political figure in the country, was seriously weakened. Congress became more and more a collection of individuals, Senators and Congressmen who did not feel committed to support the president, even a president of their own party. This decentralisation of political power resulted from the ending of the patronage system, from the evolution of the American welfare state and the disappearance of machine politics, and from the introduction of primary elections. The whole basis of the coherent political structure that was relevant to the problems of politics in the nineteenth century was removed, but was not replaced by any other coherent organising principle of politics. A president with a strong character could battle against this system and try to dominate it by sheer force of character; a weak person had to turn to other means of ego-maintenance.

The opening years of the twenty-first century saw an apparently new situation: a Republican president allied with a Republican majority in the House of Representatives, and also in the Senate after 2002. There was a more ideological orientation to inter-party conflict and an increase in partisanship in the Congress, suggesting that the president was more likely to get his way than in most recent administrations. The events of 11 September 2001 emphasised the role of the president as the leader of the nation in time of crisis. However, Bush's second term saw him come up against increasing resistance from his own party in Congress, partly because the problems of the war in Iraq resulted in his public approval rating dropping to 36 per cent, partly because some of his policies disappointed important sections of the Republican Party. They were unhappy about the reform of the Social Security system, the changes made to Medicare and the president's proposals on immigration. In 2006 the president was faced with a serious revolt by the Republican Party in the House of Representatives over the administration's approval of the intention of a company based in Dubai to take over control of a number of US ports, including the Port of New York. Opposition to the plan was voiced in Congress, on security grounds, but President Bush announced that he would veto any legislative proposals to block the takeover. The reaction in Congress was intense. The Appropriations Committee of the House voted sixty-two to two against the plan. The situation was retrieved only by the Dubai company announcing that it would withdraw from its planned takeover. Significantly, however, this event triggered expressions of considerable dissatisfaction with the way in which the White House had treated Republicans in both House and Senate. It might be, therefore, that the general characteristics of the American political system were reasserting themselves.

Finally, the organisational changes that have been made since 1939 to help the president in attempting to deal with Congress and to coordinate the administration have resulted in greater isolation from the day-to-day political life of the country. The machinery of the White House Office can be a vital tool with which a president can direct a national campaign to implement the administration's policies – at the other extreme it can be a wall between the president and those who wish, quite legitimately, to influence the federal government. In the period 1971–4 all these factors, long-term and short-term, institutional and personal, combined to create a situation in which the president, isolated and aloof from the political life around him, allowed or encouraged his closest political aides to undertake acts that led them to convictions and prison sentences, and led to his own resignation. The same was true of the Iran–Contra affair during the administration of President Reagan. Similar concerns have been expressed about the working of the White House under President George W. Bush in his dealings with the Congress. The problems of policy formulation and execution in this situation will be explored in later chapters.

Further reading

Gould, L.L. (2003) *The Modern American Presidency*, Lawrence, KS: The Press of the University of Kansas.
Jones, C. (1994) *The Presidency in a Separated System*, Washington, DC: Brookings.

Neustadt, R. (1991) *Presidential Power and the Modern Presidents: The Politics of Leadership from Roosevelt to Reagan*, New York: Free Press.
Schlesinger, A.M. Jr. (1974) *The Imperial Presidency*, New York: Houghton Mifflin.
Schlesinger, A.M. Jr. (2005) *War and the American Presidency*, New York: Norton.

Websites

Grolier Encyclopedia On-line: http://ap.grolier.com
Miller Center of Public Affairs: www.americanpresident.org
The White House: www.whitehouse.gov

8 The media and politics

The nature of the American media

Communication is vital to all systems of government in the modern world, but nowhere more so than in the pluralistic politics of the United States, with its frequent elections, groups ceaselessly competing for influence over policy, and a complex institutional structure. The print media – newspapers, broadsheets, journals and books – were important features of American colonial societies in the seventeenth and eighteenth centuries, and remained the only medium of communication, other than word of mouth, until well into the nineteenth century. The situation began to change with the development of the telegraph and the use of the Morse code, so that messages which would previously have taken days to carry by horse or train could be sent from one side of the continent to the other in minutes. The invention of the telephone made possible direct communication from one individual to another across the country. It was the invention of radio, however, that really inaugurated the era of 'the mass media' so that President Franklin D. Roosevelt, with his 'fireside chats', could potentially reach every citizen. After the Second World War television began to transform the role of the media in politics. In the late twentieth century the development of the internet brought a new dimension of person-to-person communication, the impact of which on the conduct of politics is only now becoming apparent.

The importance of the media in the modern state raises a number of questions. What effect do the media have on the outcome of elections and how do they affect policy decisions? Do the media simply report the news or do they make it? Do the media reflect public opinion or do they shape it? Are the media manipulated by government or do they control it? We may not be able to give satisfactory answers to these difficult questions, but at least we may hope to throw some light on the impact of the media on the political system of the United States.

Newspapers

In a country the size of the United States, newspapers were inevitably local in origin, most of them founded before the development of the technology which now makes it possible to reach readers thousands of miles from the point of origin. Newspapers were centred on cities and towns across the country, founded as the growth of settlement opened up new areas. Even today, although there are over 1,400 daily newspapers, there are few national newspapers in the sense in which there are national newspapers in (much smaller) European countries, such as Britain. The *New York Times* and the *Washington Post*, with the status of national institutions, are still not available for sale in newsagents or supermarkets in many small towns, although they are now accessible daily on the internet, along with many other newspapers. The only newspaper readily available almost everywhere is *USA Today*, useful but without the extensive coverage of the great traditional dailies. Although many newspapers were founded by individuals who ran them as personal fiefdoms, today the majority of daily newspapers are owned by large corporate chains. Alongside the newspapers, weekly magazines such as *Time* and *Newsweek* have considerable influence, with large circulations, and for the political and business elite there are a number of specialist news magazines, such as *U.S. News and World Report*, *National Review* or *New Republic*.

The news media show the same pattern as the general characteristics of American society – initial high decentralisation, followed by increasing nationalisation and the increasing influence of 'big business'. At their height newspapers had considerable influence on the course of American politics, and in some cases decisive influence. It was the investigatory journalism of Bob Woodward and Carl Bernstein of the *Washington Post* that revealed the scandal of Watergate, and led eventually to the resignation of Richard Nixon. However, with the rise of television and the internet the relative influence of the press declined.

Radio

The first commercial radio station in the United States was established in Pittsburgh in November 1920 and began broadcasting with a report of the election results of the presidential election of that year. The development of broadcasting was rapid, with hundreds of stations being established in the 1920s; in 2005 there were over 10,000 commercial radio stations. Congress passed the Radio Act of 1927 to introduce order into the system by allocating wavelengths; the Federal Communications Commission was set up by the Communications Act of 1934 for that purpose. Although radio stations were established as independent businesses, and still are, networking soon became desirable so that news programmes, commentaries and some entertainment and sports programmes could be generated by the network and distributed to affiliated stations across the country. Four large networks were created: the National Broadcasting Company, the Columbia Broadcasting System, the American Broadcasting System and the Mutual Broadcasting System; the last of these has now ceased to exist. The affiliated stations and the networks are all commercial operations dependent on income from advertising; public service broadcasting did not begin to operate until well after the Second World War, and it was not until the passage of the Public Broadcasting Act of 1967 that government funding of public service broadcasting began. However, public service broadcasting has not been free from the need to attract funds from commercial sponsors by offering limited advertising opportunities.

The development of the radio networks made possible the 'fireside chats' which President Franklin D. Roosevelt initiated in 1933 and delivered until 1944, shortly before his death. Radio became the main source of news for millions, but the rise of television after the Second World War reduced the appeal and influence of radio. However, radio experienced a revival with the development of 'Talk Radio'. Most radio stations had come to broadcast continuous popular music, occasionally interspersed with weather forecasts and networked news bulletins. In the 1990s, however, the talk radio movement burgeoned after a legal requirement that controversial issues should be presented in an honest, equal and balanced manner was repealed. Radio talk show hosts could now make extreme statements of opinion without having to allow any response. Initially this opportunity was exploited by conservative presenters, such as Rush Limbaugh. Commenting on those taking part in the demonstrations on immigration that took place in April, 2006, Limbaugh stated on his radio show:

> There are countless leftists, socialist, Marxist, communist, what have you, who are filled with their own self-loathing. They're generally losers. They don't matter much to anybody, and they recoil at success, dominance, achievement, and power, and their objective is to tear it down. They live under the illusion that capitalism has created by design a certain set of winners and a certain set of losers and it's the winners who determine who the other winners are and who the losers are going to be. They are in the losing side. So they have this false notion that that's inherently unfair and we must all be equal, but the real objective is not equality.
>
> The real objective is not quality lives for the people they claim to represent. The real objective is not happiness and the pursuit of happiness for the downtrodden of the world. It is simply a desire to destroy a country like the United States of America, however possible. They fully well understand that destroying the distinct American culture is a classic way and perhaps an easy way of destroying this country. So they glom onto any subject that they think will advance that objective of theirs. This is a perfect opportunity for them. It's a perfect opportunity to stand with their Democrat socialist brethren and to promote them, and it's a great opportunity to once again condemn this country.

Liberal talk show hosts also emerged, but they have been less success-ful in drawing audiences. Prominent also are religious broadcasting stations numbering several hundreds, but more important perhaps are the television evangelists such as Jerry Falwell and Pat Robertson; the latter stood as a candidate for the presidential nomination of the Republican Party in 1988.

Television

Although public television broadcasts began in Britain in 1936, the develop-ment of television was slower in the United States, where television broad-casting began in 1939. However, television was virtually suspended during the war years and it was not until 1946 that the television age really began. Television stations followed the pattern of radio in that they were commer-cial, drawing their revenue from advertising; the three great radio networks moved into television adopting the same pattern of working with affiliated stations across America, joined later by the Fox network. Although televi-sion stations are required by federal law to 'afford equal opportunities' to all candidates for an elective office who wish to make political broadcasts, the candidates have to pay for the air time they use, adding to the costs of elec-tion campaigns. The heavy cost of using the networks resulted in the produc-tion of 'soundbites', statements in support of a candidate or a party lasting perhaps only a few seconds, during which time no coherent argument could be developed. The use of television for political campaigning was rather slow to evolve, but when it did it transformed elections and helped the decline in the power of party organisations that had been gathering pace since the introduction of primary elections.

Television has changed the way in which the public is influenced by the media in a number of ways. Doris Graber has pointed out in *Mass Media and American Politics* how the immediacy of television news broadcasts increases their importance over other media in crisis situations. In the immediate af-termath of the attack on the World Trade Center there was a considerable increase in public reliance on television news. The extent of news coverage on the major networks is limited, usually with little concern for foreign news, although naturally when American troops are involved in warfare, as in Iraq, the balance shifts considerably. However, the development of channels such as Fox News and CNN devoted almost exclusively to news and comment pro-vides the opportunity to view news stories as they break for those who are interested.

Negative campaigning, the use of television advertising and other media to convey negative information about an opponent's character or record, has been a feature of American electioneering for many years, going back to the 'mudslinging' era of the 1884 election in which Democrat Grover Cleveland was accused of having fathered a child out of wedlock, and the Democrats were portrayed as the party of 'Rum, Romanism and Rebellion'. The election of 2004 had a fair share of negative campaigning. The Swift Boat Veterans for Truth (SBVT) was formed during the election campaign in order to discredit

John Kerry's claims about his Vietnam War service. Kerry served in the Navy during that war and was decorated with the Purple Heart and other medals. He had operated in Swift Boats, or Fast Patrol Craft, small armed boats designed to operate in shallow waters. After his return from Vietnam he had played a part in the anti-war movement including joining the organisation Vietnam Veterans Against the War. In the period leading up to the 2004 election campaign Kerry had used his war record to give credibility to his claim to be able to lead the nation in its 'war against terror', and when arriving on the podium at the national convention to accept the Democratic nomination he gave a military salute and said 'Reporting for duty'. The SBVT consisting of war veterans, including one who had served alongside Kerry, was registered as an advocacy, or non-partisan 527 group, and during August 2004 placed four advertisements on television denigrating Kerry's war record and his later anti-war activities, describing him as dishonest, unreliable and unfit to lead. Allegations were later made that the Bush campaign had links with SBVT, and that prominent Republicans had funded the group. The development of cable television has again changed the media landscape and its relevance to politics. To the three great networks of the immediate post-war period have been added not only further networks but also hundreds of cable channels. The availability of so many channels makes it very much more complex for politicians to reach their target audience.

The internet

The increasing popularity of the internet since it became available for use by the public in the 1990s has inevitably led to its being used for political communication. Its use by candidates for political office was slow to develop, but the election campaign of 2004 was evidence, in the words of Matthew Kerbel, 'that the Internet can help to shift the balance of political power in a long contest by organizing volunteers, boosting morale, influencing the spin in mainstream media, and of course raising money.' Kerbel describes the Internet as the most democratic medium in American history and one which can genuinely engage the voters in the political process:

> After decades of being sedated by television, many people have come to regard politics as a spectator sport. To blog about the accomplishments of political action, to feel inspired by a politician, or to occasionally do something to further a campaign is out of step with how politics is portrayed on television, but it is a perfectly natural reaction on-line.

The politician who made the most use of the internet in 2004 was the Democrat, Howard Dean. He made extensive use of 'weblogs', posting his speeches on Blog for America. He was able to raise large sums of money by soliciting small contributions from supporters on the web. In the end he did not secure the Democratic nomination, but he set a precedent which few future candidates are likely to ignore. Potential candidates for the nomination in 2008 are already devoting a great deal of time to blogs, discussing issues, answering questions put by bloggers.

The attraction of the internet to political campaigners is that it can have a more personal touch than radio and television advertising and it is a lot cheaper. The multiplication of television channels makes it more difficult to get a candidate's message across, whereas email messages can be downloaded daily to the target audience and podcasts can deliver videos directly to voters. In 2006 the Federal Election Commission ruled that almost all political activity on the internet would be exempt from the restrictions of campaign finance laws. The effect of the internet is likely to be an even greater decline in the coherence of the political organisations, in particular political parties, as it puts more power into the hands of individuals to exercise influence over the political process.

The influence of the media

Doris Graber concludes that 'the mass media play a major role in political socialization and in learning and accepting the beliefs, norms and rules that govern political life'. Socialisation is a process which begins early in life and continues over a long period, as political attitudes become well-established. But the media can also affect public opinion on particular issues as they arise, by the way in which they are presented, and the fact that individuals have evolved particular beliefs about politics and particular political leanings does not mean that public opinion is set in cement and cannot be changed. Thus President George W. Bush had an approval rating of 80 per cent in January 2002, 58 per cent in January 2004, 50 per cent in January 2005, down to 33 per cent in March 2006. This slide in popularity had a number of causes, but among them have to be the television pictures of the continuing violence in Iraq, the press reports of the deaths of American military personnel, the press assessments of the success or failure of the establishment of democracy in Afghanistan and Iraq, the television pictures of New Orleans in the aftermath of Hurricane Katrina. Clearly the media have a great deal of influence, but how objective is their reporting?

There is no such thing as complete objectivity; every writer, every commentator is influenced to some degree by his or her own political views, by the circumstances of the time, by the perceived impact of their work on their employers, on the government, on the public, on interested groups. To present a news story or an analysis of events involves the selection of some facts rather than others, giving greater or lesser weight to differing aspects of these events, offering opinions about what is or is not important. It is almost inevitable, therefore, that a news presentation or current events programme will give a particular 'slant' to the situation; the real problem is to decide when selection, which is inevitable, tips over into deliberate distortion.

The media and elections

The role of the media, particularly television, in elections is enormously enhanced by the nature of the American political system. The presidential election focuses attention on the single most important election in the world, so that it can become a drama, involving very high stakes. The weakness of the political parties means that the voting behaviour of the electorate is much more independent than in most countries of the world. Above all, the fact that the voters are so closely involved in the choice of party candidates through primary elections makes personality, or the voters' perception of personality, a vitally important factor in the process. To win, a candidate has to project an image that will inspire confidence that he or she is suitable for the office, whether it be for city councilman or president of the United States. What better medium than television for this purpose? Television focuses on the personality of the candidate in a way that no other medium can: the gesture, body language, the facial expression. Thus television has concentrated more on personalities than on policies; the latter can better be dealt with in the print media, particularly the 'quality press', although this reaches a much smaller number of people.

Although President Eisenhower made use of television in the election of 1956, the first occasion on which television made a considerable impact on a presidential election was that of 1960, the contest between John F. Kennedy and Richard Nixon. Kennedy was virtually unknown nationally and not popular with the Democratic Party leaders; his Catholicism was thought to be a disadvantage and his stance on civil rights policy not popular in the South. But Kennedy's personality came through to the ordinary voter on television in a way that would not have been possible otherwise. The campaign was notable also for the staging of the first television debate between rival candidates, in which famously Nixon's 'five o'clock shadow' compared unfavourably with the rugged, handsome appearance of Kennedy. Kennedy won the election by a hair's breadth, and it is difficult not to attribute his victory in large part to the influence of television.

After 1960 no further television debates were held until 1976, in the contest between Jimmy Carter and Gerald Ford, but since then they have become a regular feature of election campaigns, not only at the presidential level, but at congressional and state levels as well. The fairness of the way in which these debates have been staged is in some doubt. In 1996 the Republican candidate for the presidency, Robert Dole, was able to exclude Ross Perot, the candidate of the Reform Party, from the debates; in the election of 2000 two 'third-party' candidates, Ralph Nader and Patrick Buchanan, were excluded. In both cases it was the fear of the major party candidates of the effect that the minor party candidates might have on the vote if they were allowed to enter the debates that resulted in their exclusion.

It is difficult to generalise about the effect of television on the outcome of elections. Undoubtedly television has an influence, but the exact effect will vary from election to election. In a landslide election, television and the media as a whole may have little influence on the result, but in close elections it may be decisive. The election of 2000 was as close as they get. However, neither of the candidates' performances on television was particularly impressive, and a new perspective on the effect of television on the voters is emerging. Marjorie Hershey has argued that 'the idea that presidential candidates ought to be evaluated on the basis of their entertainment value had become well entrenched in media coverage as well as in public opinion.'

Freedom of the press

The First Amendment to the Constitution, passed in 1791, states:

> Congress shall make no law respecting an establishment of religion, or prohibiting the free exercise thereof; or abridging the freedom of speech, or of the press; or the right of the people peaceably to assemble, and to petition the government for a redress of grievances.

During the eighteenth century the English courts, interpreting the common law, had established that the government had no right to censor printed matter *before* publication, although the authorities could sue authors or publishers for 'seditious libel' after publication. The English common law was 'received' in the American colonies, where it was seen as a bulwark against the domination of the royal governors. With the establishment of the Federal Constitution, however, the former colonists feared possible oppression from the federal government and the Bill of Rights was passed in order to protect their freedoms, including the freedom of the press. The Bill of Rights was intended as a restriction on the powers of the federal Congress, not of the state governments, which many saw as the defenders of the rights of their citizens. It was not until the twentieth century that the Supreme Court applied the Bill of Rights as a check on the powers of the states in the field of the regulation of press freedom, as in other areas of civil rights.

In the early years of the Republic the freedom of the press did come under attack from the federal government in the form of the restrictions embodied in the Alien and Sedition Acts, but these expired in 1801 and it was not until the First World War that restrictions on press freedom by the federal government became an issue again, although the states and local governments could, and did, pass laws restrictive of the freedom of the press. In 1917 and 1918 Congress passed the Espionage Act and the Sedition Act, designed to meet the threat of actions subversive of the war effort, and later used to meet the perceived danger of communism. These Acts made it a crime to 'disrupt or discourage recruiting or enlistment service, or utter, print, or publish disloyal, profane, scurrilous, or abusive language about the form of government, the Constitution, soldiers and sailors, flag, or uniform of the armed forces'. The Acts were upheld by the Supreme Court, which held that free speech had never been an absolute right (*Schenck* v. *United States*, 1919). However, it was in this case that Justice Wendell Holmes formulated the test which was to become the basis of later decisions of the Supreme Court and provided protection for press freedom and for free speech generally. Holmes argued that restrictions on freedom of speech and the press could be justified only if there was a 'clear and present danger' that the words used would 'bring about the substantive evils that Congress has a right to prevent. It is a question of proximity and degree.' During the Second World War and afterwards the record of the protection of freedom of the press was much better than in the earlier conflict, and in 1971 the Supreme Court decided a case of great importance for the freedom of the press. Daniel Ellsberg, an employee of the Department of Defense, leaked to the press what came to be called the 'Pentagon Papers'. These papers were in fact a 7,000-page history of the Vietnam War, a top-secret internal document of the Department including many classified documents. The *New York Times* began to publish excerpts from the documents and the federal government attempted to prevent further publication by obtaining an injunction. In the case of *New York Times* v. *US*, the Supreme Court ruled that the federal government could not prevent publication of the documents.

Having ruled that the protection afforded to the press by the First Amendment against actions of the federal government applied also against the actions of state and local governments, the Supreme Court in the 1960s turned to the ways in which state and local authorities limited the freedom of expression. The Court overruled a Massachusetts law used to declare an eighteenth-century novel, *Fanny Hill*, obscene and to ban it (*Memoirs* v. *Massachusetts*, 1966). Perhaps the most important decision for the press, however, concerned the law of libel. The law of libel is much less strict in the United States than in English law. In English law the truth of an accusation is the critical point at issue in a libel case; to justify a potentially defamatory statement the publisher has to show it to be true. In the United States, until 1964, the law of libel was considered to be a matter exclusively for the states, but in that year in the case of *New York Times* v. *Sullivan* the Supreme Court ruled that a public official who had been criticised concerning his official conduct could not recover damages for libel unless it could be shown that the publisher had been guilty of 'actual malice' in making the accusation. Showing that the facts were false was not in itself sufficient to win a case for libel. This judgement allowed journalists to be openly critical of public figures without fear of libel actions, although the Court later narrowed the journalist's privilege somewhat by requiring that the publication complained of must involve a matter of public concern, if it was to escape the penalties of the law of libel.

Journalists feel strongly that they should be able to protect the sources on which they rely for information, much of which may be given on the basis of confidentiality. When they come under pressure to reveal their sources, particularly if some element of illegality is involved, they have claimed the right to remain silent, based on the First Amendment's assertion of the freedom of the press. However, the Supreme Court has held that reporters who are issued with a subpoena to give evidence before a grand jury about the source of their information cannot refuse to give evidence. In 2004 Judith Miller, a journalist on the *New York Times*, was subpoenaed to give evidence concerning what she knew about the press having revealed that Valerie Plame was a CIA agent; revealing the identity of an agent is an offence under federal law. Valerie Plame is the wife of a former American ambassador who had criticised the George W. Bush administration over the war in Iraq, and it has been suggested that Plame's identity was revealed by someone in the administration as a reprisal against her husband. Although Miller had not herself written about Plame, it was thought that she had evidence about the case, but she refused to reveal her source. She justified her actions by telling the judge: 'My motive here is straightforward. A promise of confidentiality, once made, must be respected, or the journalist will lose all credibility and the public will, in the end, suffer.' Her plea was rejected and she was committed to jail for contempt of court. She was in jail for eighty-five days before agreeing to reveal the name of I. Lewis Libby, former chief of staff to Vice-President Cheney, but only after obtaining Libby's agreement to the disclosure of his name. A number of states have enacted 'shield laws' that provide a degree of protection for journalists against prosecution for refusing to reveal their sources.

The management of the media

So far we have considered the effect of the media on the way politics is conducted, but there is a reverse side of the coin – the way in which politicians, usually the ones in office, try to manage or manipulate the media. To some extent this represents a very necessary function of government; to provide the information on a vast range of issues that is necessary for the public to be able to understand what government is doing and why. But, as with all the double-sided aspects of the media, there is a point at which providing information tips over into providing disinformation, misleading the public in order to achieve political ends that cannot be achieved in any other way. Again this can take many forms, some relatively harmless. It has become common for political protagonists to put 'spin' onto the presentation of a policy or the way a government is performing. 'Spin' does not necessarily involve lying; rather putting forward the best possible interpretation of the situation by being 'economical with the truth', that is suppressing important aspects of a policy or performance and emphasising other aspects to the point where truth is distorted. At the extreme it does mean making statements that are knowingly untrue, presumably in the hope that in the short term this will achieve the desired end and that in the long term it will be forgotten.

Obviously the administration needs an organisational structure to liaise with the media; there is a large organisation that performs this function. Within the White House Office a Counselor to the President is Head of Communications and responsible for overseeing the Press Office and the Offices of Communications, Media Affairs, and Speechwriting. A high-level official may be in charge of coordinating the strategy of presenting the administration's policies, such as Karl Rove when he held the post of Deputy Chief of Staff for George W. Bush. The White House Press Secretary is the most high-profile person, responsible for making regular appearances at press conferences. The government's concern with the media, however, goes far beyond the straightforward provision of information. There are many ways in which the news is embellished. Presidential 'news events' are carefully staged for television broadcasts; the official line is distributed to radio, television and the press in a highly coordinated way; presidential messages are prepared on tape for distribution to local radio stations with the content adapted to local circumstances. However, the 'management' of the news sometimes, often in the most critical areas, spills over into deliberate distortion.

The history of the use of deception by American presidents as a means of advancing, or concealing, their policies is a long one. Eric Alterman has described some of the examples of official deception, from the lies told by Franklin Roosevelt over the Yalta conference through John F. Kennedy's handling of the Cuban missile crisis, Lyndon B. Johnson's misrepresentation of the Gulf of Tonkin incident and Ronald Reagan's role in the Iran–Contra scandal to George W. Bush and the war on Iraq. A number of Republicans, notably Richard Cheney, Donald Rumsfeld and Paul Wolfowitz, had linked Saddam Hussein's regime in Iraq to the possession of weapons of mass destruction in order to urge 'regime change' in that country long before they became important members of George W. Bush's administration. After the events of 11 September 2001 the administration focused upon the existence of these weapons and the linking of Saddam Hussein with terrorist groups, as a justification for the use of force in Iraq. Alterman concludes: 'The case Bush made to convince the nation to embark on its first ever "preventative" war was riddled with deception from start to finish.' Although there was intelligence which supported the view that Saddam Hussein did have weapons of mass destruction, there were also warnings from a number of sources that this was not so, but such warnings were systematically ignored. Later attempts to bolster up the allegations, by claiming that the government of Iraq was attempting to purchase uranium in Africa or that trailers had been found in Iraq which had been used for the production of biological weapons, were discredited. In 2006, Paul R. Pillar, a former CIA senior intelligence analyst responsible for the Near East, asserted that the Bush administration 'had used intelligence not to inform decision-making, but to justify a decision already made. It went to war without requesting – and evidently without being influenced by – any strategic-level intelligence assessments on any aspect of Iraq.' The administration used its relationships with news reporters to present its distorted view of the situation in Iraq to Congress and the American public.

Although there are limits to the freedom of the American media, it is undoubtedly the freest in the world. There is a multiplicity of media in the United States, all with some importance in the political process. The media is as pluralistic as the rest of American society. There is, therefore, the opportunity for extensive criticism of the political leadership of the country, which may be attacked simultaneously by different groups of many political colours. Government may attempt to manage or manipulate the media, but its pluralist character, the multiplicity of the outlets, and the fact that ultimately government cannot *control* the press, radio or television mean that, in the end, lies or distortion will be revealed. The addition of the internet to the range of information sources available makes it even more likely that, however much administrations may stray from the truth, in the end, truth will out.

Further reading

Alterman, E. (2005) *When Presidents Lie: A History of Official Deception and Its Consequences*, New York: Penguin Books.

Graber, D.A. (2006) *Mass Media and American Politics*, 7th edn, Washington, DC: CQ Press.

Hershey, M.R. (2001) 'The Campaign and the Media,' in G.M. Pomper (ed.) *The Election of 2000*, New York: Chatham House.

Kerbel, M.R. (2005) 'The Media: The Challenge and Promise of Internet Politics,' in M. Nelson (ed.) *The Elections of 2004*, Washington, DC: CQ Press.

Tedford, T.L. and Herbeck, D.A. (2005) *Freedom of Speech in the United States*, 5th edn, State College, PA: Strata Publishing.

Western, J. (2005) *Selling Intervention and War*, Baltimore, MD: Johns Hopkins University Press.

Websites

Blog for America: http://blogforamerica.com
Daily Kos: www.dailykos.com
D.C. Bloggers: http://DCbloggers.com
Rush Limbaugh: www.rushlimbaugh.com

9 Politics and the administration

So far we have been concerned largely with the complex manoeuvres and manipulations related to the formulation of government policy through its various stages, from the electoral process to the point where president and Congress issue their authoritative decisions. All of this has been eminently 'political', but in this chapter we turn to an area in which the importance of political influences is just as great but not so obvious. *Administration* may suggest simply the putting into effect of decisions taken elsewhere, and some civil servants and reformers in the past have argued that politics and administration should be kept in quite distinct compartments. According to this view the civil service should simply be the neutral instrument of the democratically elected politicians, and should not itself have a policy-determining role. There have been attempts in the United States to implement this view, in particular in the case of those agencies that have been given regulatory functions in the industrial and commercial field. The proponents of this view argue that, once its goals have been set for it, the only function of the bureaucracy is to pursue those goals with the maximum efficiency, free from the considerations of personal gain or political advantage that would cloud their judgement or affect their behaviour if they were involved in any way in political intrigues. But this simple view of the nature of administration just will not do. The executive is deeply involved in politics at many levels. Much of the legislation that eventually is enacted into law is first formulated in the departments and agencies of the government, and pressure groups and members of Congress are of course well aware of this, and may attempt to influence administration proposals at a very early stage. The exact way in which the constitutional and statutory powers of the government are exercised may make a very considerable difference to these policies in practice, because so much discretion is inevitably left to those who implement the law. The officials who form the administration may well be overtly involved in politics both by attempting to influence Congress in matters relating to their agencies, particularly appropriations, and by being influenced by Congressmen in the way they carry out their administrative duties. Furthermore, the departments of the government may battle with each other where their interests, or the interests of their 'clients', conflict, and even within a single department such conflicts may arise and become very sharp indeed. Thus the idea that the administrative agencies of government can be isolated from political problems is a chimera, and in America there are a number of social and political factors that increase the extent to which the officials of the government may become involved in political issues.

Nevertheless the demand for efficiency in government is a continuing and powerful force for reform, and it must be admitted that, up to a point, the demand that administration should be taken out of politics has improved the quality and the performance of the federal bureaucracy. But how far should it be taken? If the administrative machine is too insulated from the political battle might it not become out of touch with the needs and aspirations of the people? In a democracy should not the civil service be representative of, and responsive to, all the differing interests and points of view that make up the society? And if the president is to get the administration's policies effectively translated into actions, is it not essential that those who actually direct this work should be fired with enthusiasm for them? This tension between technical efficiency and democracy can be seen throughout the working of the American governmental machine, and the exact balance that has been struck is the subject of the present chapter.

The structure of the administration

The major characteristics of the American political system, which we have seen working their way through every aspect of the structure, have their impact also upon the organisation and operation of the executive branch of government. Indeed, rather than presenting a picture of a unified, hierarchical, highly coordinated administrative machine, the American administration is decentralised, fragmented, some might say almost anarchic. The separation of powers as it has evolved in its American version, far from creating an administrative instrument subservient to the presidential will, has in practice given to Congress the power, and the inclination, to interfere in the day-to-day working of the administration. The structure of the federal system, necessitating as it does that the federal administration must work with state and local officials across the continent, subjects the operation of the machinery of the federal government to a great variety of pressures which are felt both by the bulk of civil servants, most of whom work outside Washington, and by those executives who have to cope with Senators and Congressmen, as well as the governors and state and local politicians who flock to the capital to put their views to the president and the administration. In fact, the pluralism of American politics is amply reflected in the structure and practice of the administration. The administrative apparatus of the federal government is divided up into three broad categories: the executive departments and agencies, the independent agencies, and government corporations.

The executive departments

As we have seen, the president's cabinet is composed largely of the heads of the executive departments, and these form the core of the administration, the part most under his control. They have gradually increased in number as the functions of government have expanded. In 1789 the federal government was inaugurated with the Department of State, the Treasury Department and the Department of War. President Washington included the Attorney General in his Cabinet, but the department that the latter leads today, the Department of Justice, was not created until 1870. In 1798 the Department of the Navy was added, and with the Department of War was the continuing focus of much inter-departmental service rivalry. The emergence of the air force in the twentieth century was not acknowledged with departmental status until 1947, when it was detached from the army, but only two years later all three service departments were subordinated to the newly created Department of Defense. The Secretary of Defense became a member of the cabinet; although the service departments continue to be called such, and have Secretaries at their head, these officers are not in the cabinet. The Postmaster General became a member of the cabinet in 1829, but the Post Office became a fully fledged executive department only in 1872. In July 1971, however, the Post Office was turned into a government corporation and the Postmaster General no longer has cabinet rank. The other departments set up in the nineteenth century were Interior (in 1849) and Agriculture (in 1889). Since then no fewer than nine executive departments, in addition to the Department of Defense, have been created, reflecting the great expansion of government functions. A Department of Commerce and Labor was created in 1903, and was then divided into the Department of Commerce and the Department of Labor in 1913. The government activity resulting from the New Deal policies of President Roosevelt during the 1930s meant the creation of numerous agencies and commissions, some squarely within the executive branch, others with a greater degree of independence; but no new executive departments were created during this period. In 1953, however, many of the agencies that had been created to administer social security and welfare programmes were amalgamated into a new department, the Department of Health, Education and Welfare. In 1980 this in turn was divided into two departments, the Department of Health and Human Services, and the Department of Education. Further expansion of the responsibilities of the federal government resulted in the creation of the Department of Housing and Urban Development in 1965, the Department of Transportation in 1966, and the Department of Energy in 1977. The Department of Veterans Affairs was created in 1989. Following on the terrorist attack on the World Trade Center the Department of Homeland Security was created in 2002.

The attainment of full departmental status with a seat in the cabinet represents for most of the departments the culmination of a long process of the creation and amalgamation of lesser agencies and bureaus, sometimes as part of other departments, sometimes as independent executive agencies directly responsible to the president. Some have gone through a complex process of development; for example, a Bureau of Labor was created in 1884 as part of the Department of the Interior. It later became an independent agency, but not of department status, only to lose its independence by becoming part of the Department of Commerce and Labor, and finally to re-emerge in 1913 as a fully fledged Department of Labor. At any one time, therefore, a number of very important agencies may operate outside the structure of the departments, headed by an administrator or director who is responsible to the president and not to a cabinet officer. Some of these agencies may be very large and important, for example the National Aeronautics and Space Administration. From time to time the amalgamation of agencies into a department tends to simplify the general structure of the administration, but there are always a number of such independent agencies, and there is a continual pressure to create new ones to solve problems as they arise.

In form the departments follow a hierarchical pattern, with the secretary at the head, supported by an under secretary or deputy secretary. Assistant secretaries head the major administrative sections of the department, and below these are the operative units of the department, the bureaus or offices, headed by a director or a chief. This level of bureau chief is a critical one in the administration. Many bureau chiefs are career officials, whereas above this level nearly all are political appointments. Yet the bureau chiefs become the focus of political pressure by congressmen or lobbyists because it is at this level that the vital operative decisions are taken. Indeed, the apparently straightforward chain of command from the president downward is highly misleading. The president can, in most cases, obtain compliance from subordinates in the departments provided that the time, the energy and the information to exercise such control are available. But clearly the president cannot be everywhere at once, and the nature of the cabinet hardly makes it an effective coordinating body. Indeed, some presidents have encouraged conflict within the administration as a means of ensuring their own pre-eminence, or to help work out within the administrative structure the solutions to the different political problems with which it must contend. But conflict is by no means confined to relations *between* departments. The apparently monolithic structure of the department is deceptive. Many bureaus are relatively independent of higher control, both formally and in practice. Two outstanding instances are the Federal Bureau of Investigation in the Department of Justice and the US Corps of Engineers in the Department of the Army.

Congress has contributed to the fragmentation of power in the administration by reinforcing the powers and independence of bureaus. It has given specific authority by statute to bureau chiefs to exercise powers independently of the control of president or secretary; it has written detailed administrative procedures into law which may make the practice of a bureau quite different from the rest of the department; and it has 'interfered' in the working of departments by appropriating money in such detail that the head of the department has little discretion over the way in which his department uses its funds. The committees of Congress, particularly their chairmen, tend to develop direct relationships with the bureau chiefs, and the latter may use the political leverage given by the support of influential Congressmen and Senators against the authority of their superiors in the administration. Thus the political problems involved in the implementation of policy may well prevent the exercise of effective control by the president or cabinet members over the detailed operation of their own administrative machine. The fragmenting effect of politics on the administration has considerable impact upon the departments, at its core, where presidential control is theoretically at its greatest. The diffusion of authority and power goes much further than this, however, for in a number of vitally important fields of government action Congress has deliberately decreased the power of the president by setting up agencies which are very much more free of direct supervision, the independent regulatory commissions.

The independent regulatory commissions

The regulatory commissions have been described as a 'headless fourth branch' of the United States government. These powerful and important bodies are *in* the executive branch, but not of it. They carry out functions laid down in statute, but have a very complex set of formal and informal relationships with president and Congress of a quite different kind from the normal executive departments. The commissions perform a wide range of regulatory functions over major areas of industrial and commercial life. The first regulatory commission, the Interstate Commerce Commission, was established in 1887 to regulate the railways, but in the wake of the deregulation movement it was abolished in 1995. However, many important regulatory commissions continue to operate. The Federal Maritime Commission controls the practices of the shipping industry. The Federal Communications Commission regulates interstate and international communication by radio, television, wire, satellite and cable. The Federal Trade Commission has a general oversight of business practices including unfair and restrictive practices, control of advertising and labelling of goods, and a number of other aspects of business regulation. The National Labor Relations Board regulates collective bargaining, supervising the activities of trade unions, preventing unfair labour practices, conducting secret ballots among employees to determine who shall represent them, and dealing with jurisdictional disputes between unions. Public utilities are regulated by the Federal Energy Regulatory Commission and the Nuclear Regulatory Commission, and the whole field of banking and finance is dealt with by the Federal Reserve System and the Securities and Exchange Commission. The Food and Drug Administration regulates drugs and medical matters as well as food safety.

Congress has placed this enormous amount of regulatory power over the economic life of the country in the hands of a number of commissions whose authority is derived from statute. They report directly to Congress and their responsibility to the president is far from clear. Any president is bound to be concerned with the way in which these bodies regulate economic life, but what power does the president have over them? A board, averaging five members, who are appointed by the president for fixed terms of office, heads each of the commissions. Thus a new president taking office will be faced with a whole complex of agencies whose heads have been appointed by the previous president. It may be two or three years before the process of retirement makes possible the reappointment of a majority of members of each of the commissions. Furthermore, the president does not have the power to dismiss members of the commissions, as is the case with senior officials in the normal executive departments. This was settled by the Supreme Court in 1935, when it ruled in the case of *Humphrey's Executor* v. *US* that President Roosevelt did not have the power to dismiss a member of the Federal Trade Commission appointed by President Hoover, except on the grounds of 'inefficiency, neglect of duty, or malfeasance'. The Court reiterated this view in 1958. However, it must be noted also that the turnover among members of the commissions is very high, and a president will not have to wait till all the members have completed their terms of office before their posts fall vacant. One further limitation on the president written into the legislation regulating the composition of the commissions is the requirement that the members should be drawn from both political parties.

Why did Congress set up agencies enjoying this degree of independence? Undoubtedly there were a number of motives. A desire to place limits on the increasing power of the president during the New Deal period, when some of the major commissions were established, no doubt played a part, but there were other and more complex reasons. In one sense the regulatory commissions were the response to a new type of industrial society and to the unprecedented role that the government was called upon to play in regulating the economic affairs of private industry. It was felt necessary to break away from the traditional machinery of government, with its normal division into three parts, and to create a new instrument for this purpose, which would be an industrial pattern of organisation to meet the needs of an industrial society. Another reason for making these commissions independent was the fact that they are by no means simply 'executive' agencies. Their regulatory role requires that they should exercise a rule-making power; that they should decide in a judicial fashion whether these rules were being broken in particular cases; and also that they should administer and police the rules. Thus in lawyers' language, in addition to their administrative functions, they exercise quasi-legislative and quasi-judicial powers. These reasons reinforced the point of view of those who believed that it was time administration was taken out of politics and recognised as a distinct technique, which could be objectively and efficiently applied to the solution of largely technical problems.

However, the hope that agencies whose decisions could make fortunes for some and deny them to others, and that might affect the whole economic climate of the nation, could be insulated from politics was inevitably still-born. Presidents have made strenuous attempts to exercise a much closer control over the commissions than Congress ever intended. As we have seen, the turnover of membership is such that the president is able to make many more appointments during his term than was envisaged. The president's power to re-appoint members might influence their behaviour and other influences can be brought to bear. President Eisenhower's assistant, Sherman Adams, when asked whether he had found it necessary to ask commissioners to hand in their resignations, replied, 'If you insist on the question I should have to answer it in the affirmative.' Professor Bernard Schwartz has provided a great deal of evidence of the informal links between the White House and the commissions, and it can also be shown that members of Congress have brought pressure to bear on the commissions in much the same way, using the ultimate legislative power of Congress over the commissions as the threat to gain compliance. One commentator on the working of the Federal Communications Commission, Susan Oberlander, has described the way the system operates:

> There is almost always another arena in which to challenge an FCC decision. Parties can find an audience on Congressional committees, or industries can complain to friends on the White House staff or in the media, they can challenge FCC interpretations in court, and if courts rule against them, they can return to the legislature.

Pressures from president and Congress, however they might conflict with the theory behind the commission form of government, are perhaps to be excused more than the pressures that come from those being regulated: business and labour interests. A few cases of actual corruption have come to light, but the problem is more one of the personal relationships between those who make decisions on the commissions and those who can offer them much higher rewards in industry when they leave their government posts. There are examples, perfectly legal, of serving members of the commissions openly offering their expertise to the highest bidder. Thus the commissions are neither truly independent nor subject to the control and direction of the president to the extent that is the case in the executive departments. They disappoint those who would like to see them making their decisions free from all pressures, and equally those who believe that a president should have effective control of his administration's economic policy.

Government corporations

It should already be clear that laissez-faire, if that is interpreted as complete freedom from interference by government in economic affairs, is certainly not characteristic of the United States. The American government undertakes extensive regulation of many aspects of economic life, but there is yet another administrative dimension to add to the executive departments and the independent regulatory commissions – the government corporations. Although it is true that the United States avoided the nationalisation of private industry that took place in Britain and elsewhere, the federal government nevertheless become involved in conducting numerous activities that are commercial or industrial in nature. For this purpose the government corporation was chosen as the appropriate form to enable these activities to be carried out according to the dictates of commercial or industrial needs. It was intended in this way to give to those directing public enterprises the same sort of freedom to act with the same flexibility that directors of private enterprises enjoy. The best-known of these corporations is the Tennessee Valley Authority; proposed by President Franklin Roosevelt and set up by Congress in 1933, the TVA built dams, hydro-electric plants and later nuclear power stations, supplying electricity to over 8 million people in the Tennessee Valley. Other public corporations include the Saint Lawrence Seaway Development Corporation, Amtrak, the rail network and the US Postal Service. However, as with public corporations in Britain, the attempt to give the necessary autonomy to government corporations to run their affairs along purely commercial lines has not been wholly successful. The corporations have been subjected to increasing legislative and administrative supervision, and the passage of the Government Corporation Control Act of 1945 integrated them more closely into the normal machinery of the executive branch.

This then is the picture of the administrative machinery of American government. As we have seen, it is a complex organisation, which has grown in a haphazard and sporadic fashion. The 'Great Society' programmes of President Johnson's administration added new accretions to the system, and its growth continues. The problem of coordination and control that this structure presents has increasingly been the subject of study by academic students of government and administration, and by government commissions. Before we turn, however, to their recommendations we must look at another aspect of the administrative machine, the characteristics of the civil service.

The federal civil service

We have seen some of the structural problems that the development of 'big government' has created in the United States. The same dilemmas are reflected in the field of the personnel of the federal government. How far should political considerations enter into the choice and promotion of those who must run the government? Is efficient government best served by utilising the services only of neutral career civil servants or by politically committed people who will wholeheartedly dedicate themselves to presidential policies? In the early years of the Union, President Washington attempted to establish that ability should be the major criterion of appointment to office under the federal government, provided that loyalty to the new Constitution was ensured. Succeeding presidents, who like Washington were 'aristocrats', broadly followed his example, although Thomas Jefferson, after taking office in 1801, ensured that the Republicans were well represented in the federal service to an extent that his Federalist predecessors had not. In 1829, however, with the election of Andrew Jackson as a man of the people, a different principle of making appointments was explicitly recognised. Jackson claimed the right to reshape the civil service to conform more closely to the composition of American society, and to remove from office the 'unfaithful or incompetent'. The era of the 'spoils system' had begun. The justification of political appointment to government jobs was that the civil servants must be in sympathy with the policies of the administration. At the same time the triumph of the spoils system was the result of a grass roots political movement which aimed at using the government service as a means of maintaining political power through patronage at state and local level, and then in the federal government. Although the spoils system is today much reduced in its overall impact on the structure of government, these two rather mixed motives continue to play a part in the way in which the system is operated. It is a means of satisfying the demands of the party faithful, and at the same time assuring that an important part of the civil service is strongly motivated towards supporting the president, either out of personal loyalty and gratitude, or because they believe passionately in his policies.

During the mid-nineteenth century the spoils system became firmly established and increased in importance. When Lincoln took office in 1861 he made almost a clean sweep of the top-level positions and his successors generally followed suit. In the post-Civil War period there was a rising tide of corruption, which became associated with the patronage system, and as a result there developed a demand for reform of the civil service, and in particular for the introduction of a 'merit system' of appointment and promotion. After a number of abortive measures, including the appointment of a short-lived Civil Service Commission in 1871, the Civil Service Act of 1883 (the Pendleton Act) was passed into law. This legislation, which forms the basis of the present civil service system, was essentially an adaptation of the British system of recruitment and tenure established as a result of the Northcote–Trevelyan Report and the Macaulay Report of 1854. The Pendleton Act established a Civil Service Commission, since renamed the Office of Personnel Management, to conduct competitive examinations for entry to the service, and gave a degree of security of tenure to civil servants. However, the Americans did not follow the British precedent altogether. The American examinations were to be 'practical in character', unlike the system that emerged from the British reports, with its emphasis on languages and mathematics. The American system provided also for freedom of entry to the service at all levels. Only certain classes of employees were included in the new merit system, representing initially only 10 per cent of the total federal civil servants, the rest remaining under the patronage system.

In that part of the civil service untouched by the reforms, the spoils system continued with undiminished vigour, but the gradual classification of positions on a merit basis had extended to over 40 per cent by the beginning of the twentieth century. By 1932 the process of reform had progressed to the point where 80 per cent of the service was taken out of the realm of political appointment; although the New Deal and the war brought about a resurgence of the number of unclassified posts, during the post-war years the merit system forged ahead to the point where it now includes 85 per cent of federal posts. Of the remaining 15 per cent, however, many posts could, in their nature, not be brought under the system – posts abroad and temporary or part-time posts, for example. There remain a substantial number of posts, including many of the most important jobs in the executive branch, that are at the disposal of an incoming president. Estimates have varied from 7,000 to 15,000 jobs; although this represents only a fraction of 1 per cent of the total size of the civil service, it represents quite a formidable task of selection for an incoming administration. Furthermore, there is constant pressure upon presidents to increase the amount of patronage available, particularly when there is a change of party in office. President Eisenhower gave way to such pressure in 1952 by declassifying some thousands of positions that had recently been given security of tenure by the previous administration.

President Eisenhower also introduced a new category, a buffer zone, as it were, between the great mass of career civil servants and the top-level political appointees. It was argued that the new Republican administration found it difficult to exercise control over policy-making posts near the top of the service because they were filled with career officers who had been appointed under the Democratic presidents of the preceding twenty years. A large number of key posts were transformed into 'semi-political appointments': posts occupied by advisers on policy, confidential assistants to the heads of agencies, or people whose job was publicly to defend controversial policies. Thus it is important to realise that the personnel of the federal government is not divided simply into a thin layer of political appointees at cabinet level directing the activities of the professional civil servants. Political appointments reach well down into the upper layers of the administrative hierarchy, but to different levels in different areas. Indeed, within the same department some appointments may be made under civil service rules, while others of a similar grade may be political or semi-political in character.

The American civil service differs from the British, therefore, in that the higher levels are not wholly professionalised, but it differs also in another important way from the service that was established in Britain in the nineteenth century. The British service was divided into a number of different classes, and the most senior of these – the administrative class – was composed of officers who were generalists, able to move from one department to another, advising ministers on policy and supervising its execution. Because the service was fully professionalised, these civil servants became a permanent, coherent body of top administrators, forming a distinct caste in the hierarchy. The United States civil service was not divided in this way. It is a unified structure, with a number of salary grades within which appointments are made, although there are also the 'political' posts, normally requiring confirmation by the Senate. American students of administration have sometimes used the British civil service as a model for the reform of their own system, arguing that it should be politically neutral, but others, who would deplore excessive use of patronage, nevertheless are worried about creating a 'neutral' service, without a deep commitment to presidential programmes.

Congress and the federal service

We have already seen, at various points, how Congress affects the working of the administration and the people who compose it. Congress sets up the administrative structure by legislation or by approval of presidential reorganisation plans. The president's nominations to senior positions must be confirmed by the Senate, and must, therefore, be cleared with influential Senators. The legislature provides the funds by which the administration operates, and may scrutinise estimates very closely, probing the working of departments and agencies at committee hearings. Congressional committees continually call civil servants before them and subject them to very close questioning.

Although individual members of the civil service may form quite close connections with members of Congress, there is a built-in distrust of 'bureaucrats' among Senators and Representatives. Most legislators, as we have seen, feel a very close affinity to the people in their constituencies, sometimes over 2,000 miles away from Washington, DC. They have much sympathy with the state and local governments with whom they will have been in close contact throughout their political careers. The federal government, therefore, remains in some sense the enemy still, even when they themselves become members of the national legislature. Most of them resent, and are fearful of, big government, and the power that it gives to a vast, impersonal and permanent bureaucracy. Few members of Congress, therefore, resist the temptation to attack civil servants when the opportunity arises, and the period since the Second World War has provided on occasion extreme examples of this tendency.

The internal and international strains of the post-war period, the Cold War and the fear of communism provided the backdrop for the phenomenal rise to prominence of Senator Joseph McCarthy. McCarthy, as chairman of the Permanent Sub-committee on Investigations of the Senate Government Operations Committee, pursued a vendetta against civil servants, accusing them of communist sympathies and causing a number of them to resign or be dismissed. He particularly attacked civil servants in the Department of State, the Central Intelligence Agency and the Department of the Army. The extent and bitterness of McCarthy's attacks eventually led to a reaction against him, and after the extraordinary public battle between McCarthy and the army in 1954 he was censured by the Senate. This was an extreme example of an attack on the service, but the House Committee on Un-American

Activities (later renamed the Internal Security Committee) concerned itself actively over a period of thirty-seven years with the loyalty of federal government employees until its abolition in January 1975. It exemplified the way Congress, in certain circumstances, is able to exercise considerable influence on the administrative process.

The separation of powers between the legislative and executive branches of government in the American system has, however, other more positive aspects to it. The determination of members of Congress to exercise as much control as possible over the administration has led to a more open system of government than anywhere else in the world. In addition to the battery of investigatory committees and hearings that the Congress brings to bear directly on the administration, the legislature has also attempted to make available to the general public as much information as possible on the decisions taken by the executive, and the basis for those decisions.

In 1966 Congress passed the Freedom of Information Act, which as amended in 1974 opened up government files for public inspection. Any individual can ask to see the files held by any government agency on a particular matter, and the agency must produce the file within ten days or state its reasons for not doing so. The Act covers the whole field of government including law enforcement agencies such as the FBI and national intelligence agencies such as the CIA. The agencies and departments can withhold information on certain limited grounds, such as a threat to national security, but their decisions to refuse information can be challenged in the courts. Approximately 1 million requests for information are received each year under the Act, and the facility is used extensively by newspapers, businesses and indeed foreign governments. Opponents of the Act argue that much of the information that is obtained is used by businesses to gain unfair advantage over competitors, and that in a number of cases foreign intelligence agents have obtained information harmful to the national interest. However, the Freedom of Information Act remains as a remarkable tribute to the openness of American democracy.

Presidential control of the administration

To the problem of attempting to coordinate the legislative and executive policies of the federal government is added the problem that the president faces in attempting to control his own administration. The fragmented character of the administrative structure that we have described presents a challenge of vast proportions to a president attempting to direct the government. This question of control has received a great deal of attention as the size of government has grown, and the problem of coordination has escalated. The report of the Hoover Commission in 1949 put the problem as follows.

> Responsibility and accountability are impossible without authority – the power to direct. The exercise of authority is impossible without a clear

line of command from the top to the bottom, and a return line of responsibility and accountability from the bottom to the top.

This concern for stronger, more effective presidential direction of the administration has been a recurrent theme of official studies. In 1937 the Committee on Administrative Management (the Brownlow Committee) recommended that the administrative and legislative functions of the independent
regulatory commissions should be transferred to the executive departments,
leaving the commissions only the judicial part of their duties. However, when
Congress passed the Reorganization Act of 1939, implementing some of the
Committee's proposals and giving to the president the power to formulate
reorganisation plans for submission to Congress, it withheld from the president the power to reorganise the independent commissions. In 1949 the
Hoover Commission on the Organization of the Executive Branch, after an
exhaustive survey of the machinery of government, laid great stress on the
need for greater coordination and control in the administrative structure,
and in the same year a new Reorganization Act gave new power to the president to propose reforms in the administration. This time the independent
regulatory commissions were not excluded by the Act. Successive presidents
submitted a large number of reorganisation plans to Congress, perhaps the
most important being the one creating the Department of Health, Education
and Welfare in 1953.

In 1955 the Second Hoover Commission went further than its predecessors and recommended that the problem of the regulatory functions of the
commissions should be dealt with by the creation of an Administrative Court
to take over their judicial role. Before taking office in 1960, President-elect
John F. Kennedy asked James M. Landis to report on the problem of controlling the independent agencies. He submitted a report that proposed that
the Executive Office of the President should have a coordinating authority
over the commissions, with three offices responsible for transport, communications and energy policy. In addition, an Office of Oversight over all the
regulatory agencies would be created in the Executive Office, the authority
of the chairmen of the commissions would be strengthened, and they would
be more directly responsible to the president. After taking office, President
Kennedy included some of these recommendations in a series of Reorganization Plans that he submitted to Congress. There was a powerful reaction in
Congress against the strengthening of presidential power over the commissions, and the President failed to get his proposals for three of the commissions accepted. The ideas that Landis put forward for making the Executive
Office into a general supervisor of the commissions were dropped.

Thus, although there has been a good deal of reform, and much concern
for the greater integration of the administrative machine, the fundamental
problems remain. Indeed, the changes that have been made have not kept
pace with the problem. Every new burst of government activity sees the proliferation of new agencies, and the problem of the presidency becomes more
and more formidable.

Administration and the federal system

The interrelationships between politics and administration are not, however, restricted to the internal operations of the federal government; for, as we have seen in every other sphere of the American political system, the fact of federalism introduces another dimension, the effect of state and local politics on the national government. It is necessary to realise at this point that, just as the *politics* of national and local affairs are inextricably interwoven, so also the administration of American government is a vast complex of national, state and local programmes, most of which involve more than one level of government. Only in a very few areas do federal programmes have no implications for the states and localities, for in many fields of domestic policy Congress has deliberately chosen to administer federal programmes through, and in cooperation with, state and local authorities. In many areas of social policy the federal government provides money in the form of grants-in-aid, sets standards for the states to comply with, and supervises the administration, but the states and localities carry out the programmes and also provide money from their own resources. Even when no cooperative programme is in operation, there is usually a state programme running alongside the federal one, so that the two levels of government may be in competition with each other, or may complement each other.

This network of administrative relationships necessitates that federal, state and local officials will constantly be coming into contact with each other, and the way in which government programmes are carried out will depend very much on the quality of the cooperation between them. However, it is important to emphasise the word 'cooperation'. Although the federal government may have provided most of the money for a programme, and have laid down quite precise conditions about the way in which it should be carried out, it cannot give orders to state and local governments. Its major sanction is the withdrawal of funds, and this is sometimes done. But this type of action is politically hazardous for federal administrators to adopt. The state officials can call upon political support from their superiors in the state government; Congressmen and Senators can be mobilised to put pressure on the federal department concerned; and as a last resort Congress can, and sometimes does, act to reverse the decisions of federal officials taken under legislation in which Congress itself had previously acquiesced. Thus administrative relationships between the levels of government are very political, and sometimes highly sensitive.

The problems that face the federal administration in dealing with state and local authorities are intensified by the very nature of state and local administration. In the first place, the structure of most state administrations is even more fragmented than that of the federal government itself. A governor is usually much less in control of the state's administrative machinery than the president is of the federal machine. The former has to contend with senior members of his administration who are separately elected by the people, and who may not share his views on policy. State legislatures have been even more assiduous than Congress in creating a multitude of independent agencies hardly subject at all to gubernatorial authority. Furthermore, many local authorities enjoy a high degree of autonomy, and are not easily controlled by the state government, so that, where two or more levels of government are involved in administering a programme, overall federal control may be very remote. It is true that in recent years the federal government has tended to bypass state authorities in some programmes, and to work directly with local authorities, particularly with city governments in urban renewal programmes, but this has political drawbacks as well, for it tends to arouse resentment in the state administration, which does not relish direct federal–local relationships.

Another complication in this situation is that the merit system has not been accepted to anything like the same extent for state and local employees as it has for the federal civil service. Patronage, either openly or in disguised forms, is still characteristic of great areas of state and local government. The impact of state and local political situations upon politically appointed officials is, therefore, likely to be considerable, and at one remove the federal administrators will be aware of these pressures. In such circumstances the administrative machinery becomes the vehicle through which political compromises are worked out. The federal legislature may be following a policy that is only grudgingly accepted by the state legislature because of its desire to attract the federal grants that go with the programme. In such circumstances federal and state administrators have to work out a modus vivendi that will not offend their respective political masters, and in practice the federal officials may be in a position to be much more flexible than their state colleagues. Indeed this is almost inevitable, for federal programmes must be implemented across the whole continent in widely differing conditions, and without such flexibility it is unlikely that it would be possible to administer such a programme at all.

Further reading

Peters, B.G. (2002) 'Bureaucracy and Public Management,' in G. Peele, C.J. Bailey, B. Cain and B.G. Peters (eds) *Developments in American Politics 4*, Basingstoke: Palgrave.

Stillman, R.J. (2003) *The American Bureaucracy*, 3rd edn, Belmont, CA: Wadsworth.

Wilson, J.Q. (2000) *Bureaucracy: What Government Agencies Do and Why They Do It*, New York: Basic Books.

Websites

The Administration: www.whitehouse.gov/government
Federal Agencies: www.lib.lsu.edu/gov/fedgov.html

10 Politics and the judiciary

It may seem strange to link the description of the structure and functions of the judicial system with the further elaboration of the working of American politics; but in fact no proper understanding of the political system can be attained without a clear realisation of the role of the judges, and in particular of the justices of the Supreme Court of the United States, in the way in which policies are made and implemented. Politics, in the broadest sense, has an impact at all levels of the American judicial system, and equally the courts play a vitally important part in the way in which the government of the country is carried on. This is not to suggest that judges are necessarily politically motivated, in a narrow partisan sense, in coming to decisions. A large section of the American judiciary, certainly most federal judges, are of an extremely high calibre, but they cannot escape the responsibility of making decisions which in most countries are usually taken by the legislature or by executive officials. Some of the most significant decisions in American political history have been taken not by president or Congress, but by the Supreme Court, acting in its judicial capacity to settle disputes arising under the laws and Constitution of the United States. The extent of this power, the way in which it is exercised, the motivations and opinions of the men who exercise it, and its results for the American polity, are all factors that the political scientist must attempt to assess.

The Supreme Court and judicial review

The Constitution of the United States briefly sets out certain broad, and rather vague, principles for the organisation and operation of government. It set up three branches of the government: a legislature, a chief executive and a judiciary; it recognised a division of power between federal and state governments and set out broad categories of federal power; it guaranteed certain rights to the individual, and set certain limits to the exercise of power by the federal and state governments. These rules still stand today, hardly altered at all in formal terms, yet applying to a country that has changed dramatically since 1787. However, these rules by their very nature are virtually meaningless without interpretation. What is the exact meaning of 'No person shall be ... deprived of life, liberty or property, without due process of law', a provision of the Fifth Amendment to the Constitution adopted as part of the Bill of Rights in 1791? What exactly is entailed by 'due process of law'? Or take the Commerce Clause of the Constitution, which gives to Congress the power 'to regulate commerce with foreign nations, and among the several States, and with the Indian Tribes'. What exactly is 'commerce'? Does it include the manufacture of goods or simply trading in the finished products; does commerce include ships, trains and aeroplanes, banks, insurance companies and atomic energy plants? The problems are endless. Who then should decide what the Constitution means and then apply that interpretation to specific cases? The Constitution makes no direct reference to this problem other than the provision of Article III that 'the judicial power shall extend to all cases, in law and equity, arising under this Constitution, the laws of the United States, and treaties made, or which shall be made, under their authority.' However, in the Federal Convention in Philadelphia in 1787 and in contemporary writing there is evidence that the members of the Convention were aware that the Supreme Court would have the power to interpret the Constitution and to declare null and void congressional acts that conflicted with the Constitution. Alexander Hamilton, in number 78 of the *Federalist Papers*, published in 1788 before the ratification of the Constitution, gave a very clear explanation and defence of the right of the Supreme Court to act as the arbiter of the constitutionality of the acts both of the legislature and of the executive, concluding that the duty of the Court 'must be to declare all acts contrary to the manifest tenor of the Constitution void.'

The power of the Supreme Court to exercise this 'judicial discretion', in Hamilton's words, by no means went unchallenged. The Court was accused of aspiring to judicial supremacy, and bitter attacks were made upon it. Even its power to invalidate the acts of state legislatures was contested, in spite of the Supremacy Clause of the Constitution, which provides that the Constitution and laws of the United States 'shall be the supreme law of the land ... the laws of any State to the contrary notwithstanding.' Gradually, however, the Court asserted itself. In *Chisholm* v. *Georgia* in 1793, and *Fletcher* v. *Peck* in 1810 it established its authority to set limits to the power of state governments. In 1803 in *Marbury* v. *Madison*, the Court for the first time announced that the federal Congress had acted unconstitutionally. In later cases the Supreme Court made clear that it would enforce the Constitution against the acts of federal and state officials and would uphold the rights of the individual, as it interpreted them, against the power of government. Thus did the Court establish a form of judicial supremacy over the parts of the government; but, as we shall see, this does not mean that the Court is completely unchecked by these other parts. There is, of course, the ultimate power to amend the Constitution, vested in Congress and the state legislatures, or state conventions. Even then, however, the interpretation of constitutional amendments and their application to judicial disputes is in the hands of the

Court. Thus the Court came to exercise a formidable power through which non-elective justices can overrule the decisions of the elected representatives of the people. There are, however, practical and political limits to the power of the Court. Its composition, and to a great extent its jurisdiction, are controlled by Congress. The justices are nominated by the president, and appointed after confirmation by the Senate, holding their office 'during good behaviour'. Congress can remove the justices through the cumbersome method of impeachment, their authority can be restricted, or, indeed, the Court could be abolished by constitutional amendment. These methods of controlling or influencing the Court have been attempted, and it inevitably operates, therefore, in a political context. As its decisions often have far-reaching political implications, the justices can hardly be unaware, at one level of consciousness or another, of the role that they play in the political system. What then is that role?

The Supreme Court as policy-maker

The Supreme Court has made decisions affecting every aspect of American life, decisions that have shaped the course of development of every sphere of government activity. It has been the instrument of a great expansion of the power of the federal government; it has imposed restrictions upon the powers of the states; it has reached deeply into the economic affairs of the nation and regulated the social relationships between individual citizens. Yet the instruments that it has used for this work have been very few. Its major weapons have been the Commerce Clause, the General Welfare Clause and, in recent years, the Fourteenth Amendment. The Court has used other provisions of the Constitution to change the balance of powers between federal and state governments, and between president and Congress, or to place limits on all of them. These are the War Power, the Treaty Power, the First, Fourth and Fifth Amendments and the general enabling clause which gave to Congress the authority 'to make all laws which shall be necessary and proper for carrying into execution' the powers enumerated in the Constitution.

The Commerce Clause, quoted above, provides the most striking example of the way in which the Court has taken a brief, vague grant of power and transformed it into something of which the Founding Fathers could not have conceived, enabling the federal government to deal with the economic problems of the modern state. In the early years of the Union the Court was called upon to decide whether the power to regulate commerce put the ferries that plied between New York and New Jersey under the control of the federal government. In 1824, in *Gibbons* v. *Ogden*, it decided that it did. Over a century later, the gradual extension of the Commerce Clause culminated in the application of federal power to manufacturing industries, to banks, insurance companies and stock exchanges, to television and radio, to the production of atomic energy – indeed, to almost every aspect of economic life that Congress wishes to regulate.

By 1985, in the case of *Garcia* v. *San Antonio Metropolitan Transit Authority*, the Supreme Court had come to the conclusion that the commerce power virtually gave unlimited authority to the Congress to legislate on matters of national interest without the states having the power to challenge the exercise of federal authority in the courts. Effectively, therefore, the Court seemed to have removed federalism from the sphere of constitutional debate into the political arena alone. As Justice Blackmun wrote, 'State sovereign interests . . . are more properly protected by procedural safeguards inherent in the structure of the federal system than by judicially created limitations on federal power.' However, in 1995 the Court took a new direction in relation to the power of the federal government to control areas of life traditionally in the sphere of the states. In *United States* v. *Lopez* the Court struck down a federal statute which attempted to outlaw the possession of guns in a local school zone. A student in the twelfth grade arrived at a high school in San Antonio, Texas, carrying a concealed .38 calibre handgun and five bullets. He was charged under the federal Gun-Free Zones Act of 1990. The Supreme Court, in a five-to-four vote, ruled that the Act exceeded the authority of Congress under the Commerce Clause, because the fact that the student was carrying a gun could not substantially affect interstate commerce. Delivering the Court's judgement, Chief Justice Rehnquist argued that accepting the federal government's view that the possession of a gun could be controlled in this way would mean that it would be difficult 'to posit any activity by an individual that Congress is without power to regulate.' Congress would be able to regulate the educational process, and to set a curriculum for local elementary and secondary schools. This would be to conclude that there would be no distinction between what was 'truly national and truly local. This we are unwilling to do.' The Court therefore stepped back, and gave notice that there were still constitutional boundaries to state and federal powers. In subsequent decisions the Court reiterated their view of the limits to federal power over the states. In the case of *Alden* v. *Maine* in 1999, the Court stated that:

> Under the federal system established by the Constitution, the States retain a 'residuary and inviolable sovereignty'. They are not relegated to the role of mere provinces or political corporations, but retain the dignity, though not the full authority, of sovereignty.

In 2000 in the case of *US* v. *Morrison* the Court held that Congress did not have the constitutional authority to provide a civil remedy for victims of 'gender-motivated violence'. Christy Brzonkala, a student at the Virginia Polytechnic Institute, alleged that she was raped by two other students and sued them under the federal Violence Against Women Act of 1994. The Supreme Court held that the Commerce Clause did not provide Congress with authority to pass the legislation, because 'gender-motivated crimes of violence are not, in any sense, economic activity'. Thus boundaries were set against the ability of Congress to legislate on social issues that it wished.

Other federal constitutional powers have been broadly interpreted by the Court. The power of Congress 'to lay and collect taxes ... to pay the debts and provide for the common defense and general welfare of the United States' is the basis for the social welfare and security programmes of the federal government, which are both extensive and expensive. The Fourteenth Amendment, ratified in 1868, provides that 'no State shall make or enforce any law which shall abridge the privileges or immunities of citizens of the United States; nor shall any State deprive any person of life, liberty or property, without due process of law; nor deny to any person within its jurisdiction the equal protection of the laws.' On the basis of this Amendment the Court has moved into the whole sphere of civil rights, outlawing racial segregation in the schools and other public facilities, regulating state police and court proceedings, and attempting to assure political equality to the citizens of the United States. In these, and in many other areas, the Court has to give an authoritative interpretation of the Constitution, albeit one that may change from time to time. Let us look at the Court's functions in the American political system by reviewing four important cases through which the Court influenced policy-making in the period after the Second World War.

Brown *v*. Board of Education of Topeka, 1954

The Fourteenth Amendment was incorporated into the Constitution after the Civil War in order to ensure that the newly freed slaves would be recognised as American citizens and accorded their proper rights by the governments of the states. As we have seen, the Amendment provided, among other things, that no state might 'deny to any person within its jurisdiction the equal protection of the laws'. However, this broad instruction could be interpreted in differing ways. The Southern states in particular wrote into their statute books laws that provided for segregation of the white and black races in the schools, on public transport, and in other areas of social life. Did such laws conflict with the Amendment? In 1896 the Supreme Court considered this problem in the case of *Plessy* v. *Ferguson*. The state legislature of Louisiana had required all railroads to provide 'equal but separate' accommodation for the two races. The Supreme Court upheld the constitutionality of the Louisiana statute, arguing that, although the Fourteenth Amendment had ensured the *political* equality of the black and white races, it was impossible to ignore the *social* inequality of blacks and whites, and concluded that it could not say that 'a law which authorises or even requires the separation of the two races in public conveyances is unreasonable.' Although the Court was dealing in this case with public transport, it made reference in the decision to segregation in education, and over the following half-century *Plessy* v. *Ferguson* was the constitutional basis for all kinds of state-enforced racial segregation. Provided that the state laws required separate but equal facilities, the Constitution offered no barrier to the segregation of the races.

In the period following the Second World War, however, the National Association for the Advancement of Colored People developed a growing campaign against segregation. The NAACP had been working towards a judicial confrontation on this issue for many years, and in a carefully planned scheme of attack the NAACP gradually set the scene for reconsideration by the Supreme Court of the basic constitutional principle upon which segregation was established. In a series of cases the Court whittled away the supporting argument for segregation by refusing to accept the 'separate but equal' formula in the field of university and professional education. Then, in 1954, the Court squarely faced the question of segregation in the elementary schools. The Court considered a number of cases from various states in which the black plaintiffs argued that segregated public schools were not equal and could not be made equal, and that therefore the equal protection of the laws, which the Fourteenth Amendment was intended to guarantee, was far from being a reality.

In the *Brown* case the Court reviewed the history of the Amendment, relied heavily upon psychological and sociological evidence of the effect of segregation upon black children, and then proceeded explicitly to overrule *Plessy* v. *Ferguson*. The unanimous Court, speaking through Chief Justice Warren, found that segregated schools, even if physical facilities and other tangible factors were equal, deprived the children of the black minority of equal educational opportunities. 'Separate educational facilities are inherently unequal' and therefore a denial of the equal protection of the laws. Thus, without any legislation having been passed by Congress, and without any presidential initiative, the judiciary instituted a new policy. The Court did not order an immediate desegregation of all schools, and the process of desegregation by judicial action went on slowly over the years after 1954, but the implications of this case for American politics can hardly be exaggerated. It was the forerunner of Court decisions that outlawed segregation in other walks of life. It brought down upon the Supreme Court the wrath of the defenders of segregation, and it opened an era of more and more insistent demands for the recognition of civil rights.

In the years following the *Brown* decision the long slow progress of desegregating the schools was pursued as case after case came before the federal courts. Detailed plans were prepared for each school district, involving the daily transporting of white children to schools which had previously been exclusively black and black children to schools which had previously been exclusively white. This process of 'busing', in which children might spend long periods each day on the school buses, was deeply unpopular with many parents, particularly the parents of white children, who protested, sometimes violently. It also led to 'white flight', the movement of the white population out of cities to areas where their children would not be subject to busing, and thus in practice to further residential segregation. In 1992 the Supreme

Court recognised the difference between *de jure* segregation and *de facto* segregation, that is the difference between segregation required by state law, which is unconstitutional, and segregation resulting from the fact that different communities choose to live in different areas. In *Freeman* v. *Pitts* in 1992 the Court decided that, provided the school district had done all that it could to end deliberate discrimination according to law, 'Once the racial imbalance due to the de jure violation has been remedied, the school district is under no duty to remedy imbalance that is caused by demographic factors.' Although 'forced busing' still continues in some areas, its impact has been greatly reduced.

Baker *v.* Carr, 1962

Few cases decided by the Court have had such far-reaching political implications as that of *Baker* v. *Carr*. As we saw in Chapter 4, the state legislatures, which control their electoral law and also provide the framework of the federal electoral system, had allowed themselves to become unrepresentative because of the wide disparities in the sizes of the electoral districts in many states. Usually far greater weight was given to rural areas than was justified on a population basis. The gerrymandering of district boundaries in order to gain party advantage had reached the point where, in the words of Justice Clark, the apportionment of state legislatures had produced 'a crazy quilt without rational basis.' Because these unrepresentative state legislatures also determined the boundaries of federal congressional districts, a similar, though less extreme, misrepresentation was to be found at the federal level. The entrenchment of rural interests had been challenged in the courts on a number of occasions before 1962, but the Supreme Court had avoided ruling on the matter. In 1946, in *Colegrove* v. *Green*, a majority of the Court refused to interfere in the way in which the state of Illinois had drawn the boundaries of the congressional districts within the state, although the largest district contained over eight times as many people as the smallest. The majority on the Court was not agreed on the reasons why it refused to deal with this problem, but Justice Frankfurter argued that 'Courts ought not to enter this political thicket.' Frankfurter pointed out that legislative apportionment is heavily 'embroiled in politics, in the sense of party contests and party interests.' He concluded that this was a problem best left to the executive and legislative branches to deal with, subject to the vigilance of the people in the exercise of their political rights. The Court had always declined to interfere in a rather miscellaneous collection of 'political questions' involving for the most part matters concerning foreign affairs, or international boundaries or disputes. The labelling of a question as 'political' did not mean, of course, that the Court normally avoided a problem just because it was controversial. This would rule out most of the Court's constitutional business, but Justice Frankfurter maintained that legislative apportionment was a question in which the

Court should not intervene because to do so 'would cut very deeply into the very being of Congress.'

In 1961 and 1962, however, the Court was faced with a challenge to the composition of the legislature of Tennessee, which had not been reapportioned since 1901. The state's electoral districts had remained unchanged in spite of considerable shifts in population within the state, so that there were great inequalities in the representation of counties in the state legislature. After long deliberation the Court decided that the equal protection of the laws clause of the Fourteenth Amendment laid on the federal courts the duty of ensuring that the states made provision for a fair representation of the electorate. What constituted fair representation and how it would be enforced was not made clear in *Baker* v. *Carr*, but the decision immediately provoked an outburst of litigation, in which the constitutionality of state electoral laws was challenged. The courts were faced with the problem of determining whether state legislatures were fairly apportioned and of passing judgement upon schemes for the redistricting of state legislatures. This led the courts into an incredibly complicated area of the legal and political structure. If a state's legislative apportionment was challenged and found to be unconstitutional, the legislature then had to produce a scheme for its own reapportionment satisfactory to the federal courts. If the new scheme was not satisfactory the Court could reject it and demand that a new one be prepared. The nature of the judicial process is such that, although the courts could continually reject such schemes until a satisfactory one was forthcoming, they did not themselves have the power, or the ability, to produce their own plans for legislative apportionment. An example of what then happens is illustrated by the case of Florida. In 1964 the Supreme Court found the districting provisions in that state to be unconstitutional. In the following year the Florida legislature reapportioned the state, but its plan was ruled unconstitutional. In 1966 the Florida legislature again adopted a reapportionment scheme, and in January 1967 the Supreme Court again rejected it as unsatisfactory. This process continued until the Court was satisfied that the state had complied with its ruling.

Since the original decision in *Baker* v. *Carr* the Supreme Court went on to tighten up very considerably its view of the requirements of the Fourteenth Amendment in this field. In later cases it laid down that the basic rule of 'one man one vote' must be implemented for primary elections as well as for general elections, for both the upper and lower houses of state legislatures, for elections for state executive offices, and for the House of Representatives at the federal level. In the case in which this basic principle was first adopted, *Reynolds* v. *Sims* in 1964, the Court said that it would not insist on mathematical exactness in applying this rule, but in two cases in 1969, *Wells* v. *Rockefeller* and *Kirkpatrick* v. *Preisler*, the Court insisted that the states must 'make a good faith effort to achieve precise mathematical equality' in apportionment. Thus the Supreme Court grapples with the complexities of state politics, for its decisions may be of vital importance to the groups contending for control of state legislatures. Justice Brennan, when delivering the Court's opinion in the *Baker* case, acknowledged that 'what is actually asked of the Court is to choose among competing theories of political philosophy.' Having chosen, the Court is then faced with the task of putting that philosophy into practice.

The steel seizure case: Youngstown Sheet and Tube Co. *v.* Sawyer, 1952

The rather humdrum title of this case conceals one of the most dramatic, cliff-hanging episodes in the history of the Supreme Court. In 1951, during the Korean War, the steelworkers' trade union began negotiations for an increase in wages as part of a contract with the steel companies due for renewal the following year. The managers of the steel mills were not prepared to increase wages unless there was a simultaneous increase in the price of steel. President Truman and his administration had two major concerns in this dispute. They wished to keep the steel mills in production to maintain supplies for the armed services, but they wished also to keep the price of steel down in order to check inflation. In order to press their demands the union threatened strike action, but repeatedly called the strike off until eventually they announced that they would strike on 9 April 1952. At 10.30 p.m. on 8 April President Truman appeared on television and announced that he intended to take possession of the steel mills and to keep them in operation. The President explained that he considered that the unions' wage demands were fair, and that the steel companies had refused to grant this increase without a price rise, which, the President said, was 'about the most outrageous thing I ever heard of.' The seizure of the steel mills was effected by Executive Order no. 10340 under the president's authority as chief executive and commander-in-chief. But did the president have such authority? The steel companies immediately filed a complaint in the federal district court, and the legal battle continued until the Supreme Court announced its decision on 2 June. While the lawyers argued, the steel mills were operated under the direction of Charles Sawyer, the Secretary of Commerce, in the midst of a political furore. Members of Congress introduced bills to withhold appropriations from the Department of Commerce to prevent it from implementing the executive order. The unions announced that they would strike immediately if the steel mills were returned to the companies. A turmoil of political and constitutional debate raged around the president. In this highly charged political atmosphere the Supreme Court handed down its decision, ruling by a majority of six to three that the president had exceeded his constitutional powers by attempting to take possession of the steel industry without statutory authority. The president does not have the power to make laws, the Court said, for this function was entrusted by the Constitution to the Congress. 'In the framework of our Constitution, the President's power to see that the laws are faithfully executed refutes the idea that he is to be a lawmaker.' Thus the

Court, in a time of crisis, reasserted the nature of limited government in the United States, and its own authority to set limits to presidential power. The president immediately returned the mills to the owners; the men went on strike and remained out for seven weeks.

Roe *v.* Wade, 1973

Few social issues are more contentious than the role of government in the control of abortion, and it is perhaps surprising that it was the Supreme Court under the relatively conservative Chief Justice Warren Burger that moved into this political minefield, and in a way which dismayed conservatives. Until 1973, the control of abortion remained almost exclusively in the hands of the governments of the states. Some states, such as Massachusetts and Connecticut, had straightforward prohibitions on all abortions. In the majority of the states, there were restrictive laws that limited legal abortions, either to situations in which the mother's life was in danger, or to a very limited list of other circumstances. Two such laws, those of Texas and Georgia, were challenged in the courts, and in 1973 in the case of *Roe* v. *Wade* the Supreme Court by a majority of seven to two handed down a decision which profoundly changed this aspect of American life.

The Court ruled that the Fourteenth Amendment to the Constitution conferred on women a right of privacy that could be encroached upon by government only when other policy considerations became, in the eyes of the Court, sufficiently significant to limit that right. Justice Blackmun, a Nixon appointee, delivered the decision of the Court. He ruled that state governments had no right to prohibit abortions during the first three months of pregnancy. In the second three months, the state might intervene to make rules, principally with the intention of protecting the woman's health, but in the final ten weeks of pregnancy the state 'may go so far as to proscribe abortion . . . except when it is necessary to preserve the life or health of the mother'. Thus the laws of Texas and Georgia, and of forty-four other states, were ruled unconstitutional. The states could pass new legislation on abortion, provided that the new laws were consistent with the Court's ruling.

The most remarkable aspect of *Roe* was that the Court's opinion was not based on a long exposition of the history of the right to privacy, and its relation to abortion. The right to privacy had itself been invented by the Court only eight years earlier in *Griswold* v. *Connecticut*, a case involving a state statute which aimed to prohibit the use of contraceptives by married couples! There was no other case law on which to base the decision of the majority of the judges of the Supreme Court. Justice Blackmun's opinion in *Roe* was notable, in Robert McKeever's words, for 'its concern for the detailed balancing of what it perceived as the different interests involved', and resembled therefore the kind of compromise that normally emerges from the legislative process. It certainly is true that the pluralistic struggle that characterises the working of the Congress and the administration has come also to play a part in the judicial process, particularly when social issues are being considered, with numerous interest groups on both sides of the argument submitting amici curiae briefs.

Having got into this difficult area of social regulation the Court had no option but to grapple with its complexities. State legislatures passed laws that were intended to modify the effects of *Roe* without challenging it head-on. A Pennsylvania statute required that a woman seeking an abortion should be fully informed of the consequences of her decision, that she should be required to undergo a twenty-four-hour waiting period before the abortion was effected, and that married women must notify their husbands of their intention. In 1992 the Supreme Court upheld the first two provisions of the statute, and struck down the third (*Planned Parenthood* v. *Casey*). As a result of this decision thirty-eight states passed laws setting conditions on the access of women to abortions. Pro-life groups, such as Operation Rescue, conducted campaigns against abortion clinics, blocking access to them and disrupting their operation, in order to discourage women from using them. Some pro-life protesters adopted more violent means, and murders were committed in the vicinity of abortion clinics in Florida and Massachusetts. The Supreme Court was then faced with deciding on the legality of local laws designed to protect women attending clinics and the medical staff who worked there.

Whether or not one approves of the stand that the Court took in *Roe* v. *Wade*, it is a remarkable example of the way that judges can make law contrary to the views of the elected representatives of the people. The *Roe* decision met with the bitter opposition of the Catholic Church and other groups, and persistent attempts have been made to reverse it. A number of attempts have been made to pass legislation through Congress to overthrow it or to limit its effect. So far those attempts have failed, but this issue remains one of the most controversial political and legal questions in American politics today. A number of abortion cases in recent years have been decided by five-to-four majorities of the justices. The decisive 'swing vote' was cast by Justice Sandra Day O'Connor, who retired in 2006. Her resignation, together with the death of Chief Justice William Rehnquist in 2005, gave President George W. Bush the opportunity to nominate two new justices to the Court. With these new appointments a review of *Roe* v. *Wade* would seem to be inevitable.

The nature of judicial review

Undoubtedly, then, the Supreme Court makes policy in a variety of fields, and it is therefore involved in politics, because in many instances it is the Court that decides the policies that are put into effect. But there have been differing views about the nature of the function that the Court performs when it decides that Congress, president or state legislature has acted constitutionally or unconstitutionally. One view of the role of the judiciary is that stated as long ago as 1748 by Montesquieu, when he said that the judges should be 'no more than the mouth that pronounces the words of the law, mere passive beings, incapable of moderating either its force or rigour.' In its modern form this view of the function of the judges can be described as the *mechanical* theory of jurisprudence. The judges are seen simply as highly skilled experts in the law, who learn a complex body of rules and then deduce almost automatically the application of the law to particular cases. From this point of view the judge is a neutral instrument; he does not interpose his personality between the general rules of the law and the solution of the practical problems that he must solve. Justice Roberts made the best statement of this view by a modern judge in 1936:

> When an act of Congress is appropriately challenged in the courts as not conforming to the constitutional mandate the judicial branch of the Government has only one duty – to lay the article of the Constitution which is invoked beside the statute which is challenged and to decide whether the latter squares with the former. All the Court does, or can do, is to announce its considered judgement upon the question.

But is there a higher law that can be discovered, studied, and applied by the judges independently of their personal ideas and attitudes? The school of legal realism challenged the view of the nature of law as simply an exercise in deductive logic. This school of jurisprudence argued that it is impossible to deduce unequivocally the application of legal rules in particular cases from very general and vague statements like those to be found in the Constitution. The exact decisions made, and therefore the general development of the law, depend on the way in which the judges exercise their discretion to choose one possible interpretation rather than another. This is not to say that the judges would simply decide cases in an arbitrary, erratic fashion. They would be, and should be, influenced by developments in society, by the needs of the time and the attitudes of society to the way in which they should be satisfied. This *sociological* view of the evolution of the law tends to foster a more flexible approach to the activity of judicial review, leading eventually to the acceptance by the Supreme Court of sociological and psychological evidence as relevant to the solution of judicial problems.

A view of the role of the judges in the political system that is at the other extreme from that of the mechanical view of jurisprudence has been developed by the *behaviourists*. These students of judicial motivation approach the way in which decisions of the courts are arrived at neither by looking at the internal logic of the law nor by simply observing the influence of the broad developments of social forces upon the law. They attempt to explain judicial behaviour, as other types of political behaviour, by the analysis of the personal characteristics of the judges, their social background and education, or their party orientation and ideological attitudes. The voting records of the judges and their personal characteristics are studied by statistical and mathematical techniques in the same way as the behaviour of members of the legislature. If it could be shown that judges with similar personal characteristics consistently vote in a particular way in cases involving disputes between employers and labour unions, in civil rights cases, or in cases relating to individual freedom, then the explanation of the nature of law will be very different from either of the other types of explanation we have discussed. The role of politics in the working of the judicial system is clearly quite different according to which explanation you choose.

The true description of the judicial processes is probably a construction of all three of these conceptions. The structure of legal rules and institutions does have an internal logic and a function in the political system that places considerable restraints upon the judges who have the responsibility for maintaining them. A judiciary that failed to be influenced by the essential changes that take place in society would soon be bypassed or replaced. At the same time individual judges, *within the limits that the system allows*, must surely be influenced, marginally at the very least, by their personal experience and deeply held convictions. From the interplay of these three factors the American judicial system has been able, for two centuries, with varying degrees of success, to keep the structure of constitutional rules broadly in line with the enormous changes that have taken place in the society to which they are applied.

Nevertheless, the policy-making aspect of the work of the courts is bound to focus attention upon the motives of the judges, particularly by those opposed to their decisions. Critics of the way in which the Supreme Court overruled congressional legislation in the 1930s accused the Court of being 'a third chamber of the legislature', or pictured them as nine irresponsible judges exercising an arbitrary power to overrule the popular will. Members of the Court themselves have had different views of their function, some stressing the responsibility of the Court to act positively in defence of the principles of the Constitution, others stressing that it is the function of the executive or legislative branches of the government to make policy and to solve social and economic problems. These two attitudes, *judicial activism* and *judicial restraint* respectively, have in the history of the Court been reflected in the attitudes of different groups of justices, sometimes one gaining the ascendancy, sometimes the other. Judicial activism can lead, as in the 1930s, to the Court striking down innovatory moves by the Congress; or it can lead, as in the period since 1954, to the Court itself initiating policies at a time when the legislature is relatively quiescent or even actively opposed to such policies. Such activism can call down upon the Court the anger of very different groups; on the one hand, those who wish to see the legislature pursue strong and effective policies, and on the other, those who wish the status quo to remain undisturbed. The fact that the Court has been under attack at different times, or even at the same time, by progressive and conservative forces alike, is in fact a major source of its great strength.

We have established, therefore, the political role of the Court and the sense in which it must be understood. We shall look more closely at this connection between politics and law in the American judicial system, but it is necessary now, in order fully to understand the processes of decision-taking, to describe the judicial system as a whole and the nature of the judicial process.

The structure of the judicial system

We have concentrated so far upon the role of the Supreme Court of the United States, but that august body stands at the head of a complex judicial system in which is reflected the overall characteristics of American government, and in particular its federal structure. There are in fact more than fifty judicial systems in the United States: there are the federal courts headed by the US Supreme Court, and a separate judicial hierarchy in each of the states, each with its own state Supreme Court, as well as the courts in the District of Columbia and Puerto Rico. The relationship between these judicial structures, and between the laws that they administer, is complex indeed. As far as structure is concerned the federal system is relatively simple. There are three levels of courts: at the bottom are the district courts, ninety-four of them across the continent including the District of Columbia, each consisting of from one to twenty-seven district judges. Above the district courts are the courts of appeal, arranged in eleven circuits plus the court of appeal for the District of Columbia, each with from three to fifteen justices. Above these the Supreme Court with its nine justices forms the apex of the federal system. In addition, there are special federal courts to deal with customs and patents, military cases, and claims against the United States. The Supreme Court has original jurisdiction only in a few important types of case. For the most part cases reach it on appeal either from the lower federal courts or from the Supreme Courts of the states.

The state judicial systems tend to be much more complicated, and vary very considerably from state to state. The states are responsible for passing and enforcing the major part of the criminal and civil law in America. For every prisoner in federal prisons there are ten in state prisons. Basically, the function of the federal courts is to apply federal laws, and that of state courts is to apply the laws of that state, but the relationships of the systems are much more complex than this. They are not completely separate and distinct. The federal Constitution lays the duty upon all courts, federal and state alike, of enforcing the Constitution of the United States and the laws made under it. The Constitution is the supreme law of the land, and when state laws conflict with it, or with federal laws made under that Constitution, then the state laws must give way. State courts must, therefore, take account of federal statutes and decisions of federal courts, in so far as they affect the cases that come before them. If, however, no 'federal question' is involved, the matter will be dealt with entirely in the state system, and the final court of appeal will be the Supreme Court of the state. Issues involving federal law will normally be initiated in the federal district court and appealed up to the United States Supreme Court. However, particular cases will not fall neatly into one or other of these categories. Federal laws and decisions of the federal courts overlap very considerably in many areas with state law, and state law must always be applied in a way that is consistent with the Constitution as interpreted by the Supreme Court. Where a dispute exists between citizens of different states, the federal courts may have jurisdiction of the dispute even though no federal law is involved.

Cases may be initiated in a state court, decided by the state Supreme Court, and then appealed to the Supreme Court of the United States on the grounds that the state has decided the matter in a way that conflicts with the Constitution or with federal law. A case may be started in the federal courts on the ground that a state or one of its officials has infringed the Constitution or a federal law; and a case started in a state court may be transferred to a federal court. The broad outlines of the American judicial system are illustrated by the chart in Figure 10.1.

Such a complex system inevitably involves difficult questions of jurisdiction and, as we shall see later, it raises also the problem of the way in which the decisions taken by the highest court in the land are put into effect in lower courts. It leads to rather similar consequences in the judicial sphere to those in other aspects of the federal system. The federal and state courts work together, but they are also in competition with each other, and in extreme cases litigants can attempt to play off one system against the other, which leads sometimes, in the words of Dean Griswold, 'to a sort of legal battledore and shuttlecock, with cases bouncing back and forth almost endlessly between the State and the Federal jurisdictions'.

An essential part of the judicial system is the legal profession, which has in the United States a particular importance. The complexity of the law, the

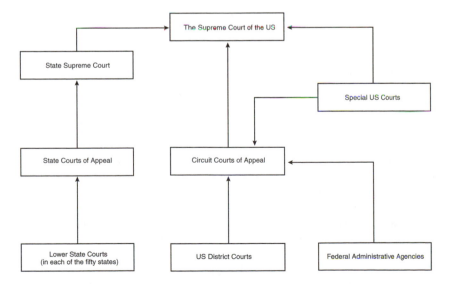

Figure 10.1 The judicial system of the USA

fact that court decisions have such vital significance for government, and the general litigious tendencies of Americans all give much work to lawyers. The legal profession is also the path to public office in the other branches of government: half the members of the Congress are lawyers. Furthermore, the legal system provides unique opportunities for combining the practice of law with a political career. An essential stage in the process of law enforcement is that of deciding when enough evidence has been accumulated in a particular case to warrant a prosecution. This function is entrusted to the district attorneys, who are therefore able to exercise considerable discretion in deciding whom to prosecute, and are potentially in a position of considerable political power and influence. In the states these officers are usually elected, and they can and do use their office for electoral purposes. The crusading district attorney and the district attorney who is subservient to local political interests may be stereotypes of fiction, but they are by no means unknown in real life. Many political careers are begun at this level, and the state governor's mansion, the Senate or the House of Representatives, even the Supreme Court itself, may be the eventual haven of a former prosecutor. As well as deciding which cases to prosecute, the district attorney's office is also responsible for the actual conduct of the prosecution in the court, providing an opportunity for a dramatic public performance.

At the federal level, the enforcement of law is in the hands of the Department of Justice headed by the Attorney General. In each federal judicial district there is a United States attorney who, unlike his counterpart at the state level, is an appointed official. The Solicitor General supervises the work of the United States attorneys and represents the federal government before the Supreme Court. The Federal Bureau of Investigation performs the police functions of the federal government, and other sub-divisions of the Department of Justice supervise various areas of law enforcement such as civil rights, anti-trust actions and the laws regarding immigration.

The judicial process

Considerable emphasis has been placed in the present chapter on the policy-making role of the American judiciary, and its importance is indeed considerable; however, it must be noted that there are considerable limitations upon the ability of courts to perform this function. The nature of the judicial process restricts the courts to a rather different role from that of the other branches of government. The courts cannot initiate action. They must wait for cases to be brought before them for decision. If the constitutionality of a particular piece of legislation is not challenged in court, then the courts cannot pronounce upon it. The courts do not have the resources for gathering and assessing information that are available to the legislature or the executive, but must depend upon the briefs that litigants submit to them. On the other hand, they are not subject to the same overt pressure as other branches of government. This is not to say that pressure groups ignore the courts – far from it – but it means that the 'politics of access', as David Truman has termed it, has to be conducted in a very different way. The long involved process of the law can lead to the passage of years before a case is finally decided, although on occasion the courts can move with remarkable speed.

Perhaps the greatest advantage of the judicial process as a decision-making mechanism, in particular in a highly pluralistic political system like that of the United States, is that, although the courts may become the centre of great political controversy, the way in which they go about their work gives their decisions a prestige and a disinterested quality very different from that of the other branches of government. On the other hand, the facts that the Supreme Court reaches its decisions by majority vote, that quite often very important decisions are reached by a five-to-four majority, and that the dissenting justices may write powerful and persuasive opinions, indicate that the judicial process is by no means a completely mechanical one. Informed and learned judges can reach widely differing conclusions about the law.

One very important aspect of the judicial process is that the courts do not operate by pronouncing general abstract rules in advance of particular situations. They decide specific cases; although in doing this they formulate general rules, interested parties can still argue that *their* particular case is rather different and should be decided differently. If they are prepared to risk the costs involved they may fight their case in the courts and possibly right up through the system to the Supreme Court. At the very least this can provide them with a powerful delaying tactic. Thus a general pronouncement against segregation like that contained in the *Brown v. Board of Education* decision does not result in the immediate desegregation of all segregated schools. It results instead in a large number of cases in the courts, fought out over a long period. It can be argued that this leads to an intolerably slow and patchy application of the law, much less efficient than the administrative process applying statutory rules. On the other hand, it can be argued that this method allows for a very flexible application of the law, enabling local conditions and special circumstances to be given full weight.

Another dimension of the way in which the courts apply the law is the way in which lower federal courts and state courts enforce decisions of the Supreme Court. Although the rule of *stare decisis* applies to the lower courts, requiring them to observe Supreme Court rulings, in practice it is very difficult for the Supreme Court to ensure compliance with its decisions in the thousands of cases that come before courts all across the country. The only weapon it has is its power to overrule lower court decisions on appeal, but the Supreme Court can review only a tiny percentage of cases. Even lower federal courts may modify and moderate the application of Supreme Court decisions because of their closeness to the political situations involved in judicial decision-making, but state courts, particularly where the judiciary is elective, are naturally even more responsive to the local political atmosphere. State appeal courts may be more sympathetic to the lower state courts whose decisions they must review than to the federal Supreme Court whose rulings they should apply.

Nevertheless, it must be said that, given the pressures of state politics upon the judiciaries, particularly in the case of civil rights in the Southern states, state courts have followed federal precedents reasonably well, and would certainly seem to have been more sympathetic to the protection of the rights of minorities than other branches of some state governments.

The overall picture of the judicial process is one of slow development and flexibility in the way in which decisions are applied. This is profoundly disturbing to those who look for clear and unambiguous decisions, applied promptly and uniformly. But in the United States the complexity of the political system and the diversity of local political situations make it quite impracticable, and impolitic, to impose a rigid administrative policy in many areas of government activity. This consideration leads us back, then, to look a little more closely at the way in which politics affects the work of the judiciary.

Politics and the judges

The extreme view of the judges as simply politicians in robes is an untenable one; nevertheless, the policy-making role of the judiciary does involve it in overtly political manoeuvres. Nowhere is this more evident than in the selection of judges, both federal and state. Federal judges are nominated by the president and confirmed by the Senate. These positions, with life tenure and a prestige above that of any office of the government other than that of the presidency itself, are the choicest patronage plums that the president has at his disposal. During a four-year term a president may, on average, expect to appoint two Supreme Court justices and make perhaps fifty to a hundred appointments to district and appeal courts. No president can afford to ignore either the partisan advantages of such appointments or the fact that the men and women he nominates will be able, to say the least, to give a particular emphasis to the way in which policy is carried out. Party allegiance is certainly a very important factor in the selection of candidates for judicial office. The overwhelming majority of appointments to the Supreme Court are made from supporters of the party of the appointing president, and in the case of the lower federal judiciary the proportion is even greater. Over 95 per cent of the appointments that President Eisenhower made to district court judgeships were of Republicans, and over 90 per cent of the appointments that President Kennedy made during his three years of office were of Democrats.

In making their nominations to the Supreme Court, presidents are almost inevitably influenced by their estimate of the attitude of the nominee to the kind of policies of which the president approves. The character of the Supreme Court was changed considerably by the appointments that President Roosevelt made from 1937 onwards. President Carter had an unprecedented opportunity to mould the character of the federal judiciary, appointing 258 judges to federal courts during his four-year term of office. These nominees included record numbers of women, black people and Hispanics, and contributed a large number of judges with a liberal activist view of the role of the judiciary. After President Reagan took office in 1981, a sustained effort was made to reverse this liberal activist character of the federal judiciary and to secure the appointment of judges whose ideology would reflect the conservative views of the administration. Before making nominations, the President's staff undertook intensive studies of the nominees' previously expressed views to try to ensure that their future judicial decisions would reflect the values held by the Reagan administration. President George W. Bush in nominating justices to the Court came under unprecedented pressure to nominate conservatives, and particularly to nominate justices who might take an anti-abortion stance. In the event, Bush's nominations of John G. Roberts as Chief Justice and Samuel A. Alito as Associate Justice were confirmed. However, the president's power to influence the course of judicial decisions should not be overestimated. Once appointed, the justices are by no means the mere creatures of the men who appointed them, and many presidents have been incensed by the opinions of justices that they had raised to the supreme bench.

The Senate's power to reject judicial nominees is not something that can be taken lightly; the administration must consult with senatorial leaders, and in the case of lower court appointees the approval of the senior Senator of the president's party from the nominee's home state must be obtained. The president delegates the selection of lower court judges to the Deputy Attorney General, but the selection of Supreme Court justices will be a matter for his personal attention. Although the Senate treats the President's nominations with respect, it exercises its right to reject them. There was a bitter contest over the nomination of Justice Brandeis in 1916, and in 1930 John J. Parker was rejected by the Senate. The most spectacular exercise of the power of the Senate occurred in 1968, when it forced President Johnson to withdraw the nomination of Justice Abe Fortas for the position of chief justice. President Nixon was subjected to defeat on two successive nominations, those of Clement F. Haynsworth and G. Harold Carswell. President Reagan's nomination of Judge Robert Bork in 1987 became the object of a bitter battle in the Senate. The Republican President had nominated a judge with a very conservative record; the Democrats had a majority in the Senate, and the more liberal members were strongly opposed to Bork. His nomination was defeated by fifty-eight votes to forty-two. The Senate was the stage for another fight when President Bush nominated Clarence Thomas in 1991, only to have the judge's former colleague, Anita Hill, publicly accuse him of sexual harassment; Thomas was nevertheless confirmed.

The president's nominations are considered in the first place by the Senate Judiciary Committee, which holds public hearings where the nominees are questioned by members of the Committee about their views on the issues that come before the Court, about their previous careers, and in the cases of judges, the decisions they have made and the opinions they have written. The committee then makes its recommendation to the Senate. Evidence is heard from the nominee and from representatives of groups who may endorse or oppose the nomination. The Committee on the Federal Judiciary of the American Bar Association investigates the nominee's record and grades him or her as 'exceptionally well-qualified', 'well-qualified', 'qualified', or 'not qualified', and gives evidence before the Judiciary Committee.

Appointment to the Supreme Court is seen as the climax of a political or legal career – one chief justice, Taft, had previously been president of the United States. The main routes to appointment on the Court are membership of the Senate or House of Representatives, a Cabinet post, lower federal or state courts, and state legislative or gubernatorial office. Some justices have had what would be described as a political career, rather than a straightforward legal background, before appointment. Indeed, a few of the greatest justices who have sat on the Court had had no previous judicial experience at any level.

The political nature of the state judiciaries is more explicit. In over two-thirds of the states the judges are elected, either directly by the electorate or by the state legislature. Studies of the decisions of elected judges have suggested that political considerations may affect the sentences that they impose, for in varying circumstances either a harsh or a lenient sentence may arouse considerable popular support. What then are the factors that determine judicial decisions?

As far as the Supreme Court is concerned the existence of blocs or coalitions on the Court has long been known and understood. As with legislative coalitions, they can be shown to form and re-form according to the issues to be decided, with differing judges exhibiting differing degrees of consistency in their voting behaviour. On some issues certain justices can almost always be found on one particular side of the question, whereas the behaviour of others may be less predictable. Thus in the 1957 term of the Court, Justice Douglas voted for litigants claiming protection for their civil rights on forty occasions, while Justice Clark voted against on thirty-nine occasions. However, it should not be assumed that the evidence leads to the simple conclusion that the judges simply use their high office to pursue narrow political ends.

Justices are subjected to cross-pressures when their views of the merits of a particular issue come into conflict with their respect for norms of judicial behaviour such as *stare decisis*. Justices are clearly influenced by their wish to respect earlier Court decisions even though they had not originally supported them. When in 1992 the Court came to reconsider the *Roe* v. *Wade* decision which had authorised abortion, there was almost certainly a majority on the Court which was opposed to *Roe*, but they refrained from overturning it because of the damage this might do to 'the Court's legitimacy, and to the Nation's commitment to the rule of law' (*Planned Parenthood of Southeastern Pennsylvania* v. *Casey*). Some justices, as Robert McKeever has said, 'may feel cross-pressured, since the judicial restraint which demands the reversal of *Roe* also counsels respect for precedent.' Thus the institutional forces that make the Supreme Court so much more than a mere group of legal politicians give it also the power to assert itself against the executive and legislative branches, and at times to brave public uproar in defence of constitutional principles in which they believe. The years since 1954 have been a period in which the Court has used this institutional power to the full, and from time to time incurred the deep anger both of the Congress and the president.

Judicial activism and judicial restraint

In the early years of the New Deal the Court actively used its power to block congressional action on a wide range of matters affecting the economic life of the nation. In two years, 1935–6, the Court invalidated seven major statutes that had been intended to deal with the economic problems of the Depression, and the president's programme lay in ruins. The attack upon the Court, and the new appointments made by Roosevelt, led to the dominance of the philosophy of *judicial restraint* on the Court until the *Brown* v. *Board of Education* decision in 1954 ushered in a new era of *judicial activism*. In view of the political repercussions of the desegregation decision, the Court might well have rested on its laurels and not ventured into other controversial areas, but instead it undertook to innovate in a number of other extremely politically sensitive fields of constitutional law. Having incensed Southern Senators and Congressmen, the Court proceeded to anger both conservatives concerned about the threat of communism, and all those across the country who were fearful of further federal intrusion into the affairs of the states.

In a series of decisions in 1956 the Court moved further into the field of civil rights. It held that defendants in criminal cases, against whom FBI agents had testified, should be given access to the Bureau's files to enable them to check for discrepancies between the testimony and the reports upon which it was based (*Jencks* v. *US*). It placed restrictions upon the investigatory powers of congressional committees in a decision specifically directed at the Un-American Activities Committee of the House of Representatives (*Watkins* v. *US*). The Court reversed the convictions of fourteen leaders of the Communist Party convicted under the Smith Act that was aimed at persons conspiring to teach the violent overthrow of the government (*Yates* v. *US*). The Justices freed a university professor who had been convicted under a New Hampshire law for refusing to answer questions concerning his political beliefs (*Sweezy* v. *New Hampshire*). Finally, the Court invalidated the laws of forty-two states directed against subversive activities, on the grounds that Congress had legislated in that field to the exclusion of state power (*Pennsylvania* v. *Nelson*). In the following year the Court turned its attention to safeguarding other rights of the individual against the power of government. It invalidated legislation that revoked the citizenship status of naturalised citizens who had offended the government (*Trop* v. *Dulles*); and it overturned the decision of the State Department to withhold the passports of those it wished to prevent from travelling abroad (*Kent* v. *Dulles*; *Dayton* v. *Dulles*). In a string of cases the Court invalidated sections of congressional statutes that it considered infringed the civil rights of the citizen, in particular sections of the Nationality Act of 1940 and the Smith Act. In 1965 the Court invalidated an Act of 1959 which disqualified members of the Communist Party from becoming officers or employees of a labour union (*US* v. *Brown*). The Court was even more active in striking down state laws and controlling state court procedures. It ruled that the states may not prescribe prayers in the public schools (*Engel* v. *Vitale*), or Bible readings at the beginning of the school day (*School District* v. *Schempp*). In the 1960s the Supreme Court used the Fourteenth Amendment to 'nationalise' the procedures and safeguards that have long been applied in the federal courts, by ruling that they must be applied also in state courts, and applying strict tests to police procedures. Citizens must be protected against unreasonable search and seizure (*Mapp* v. *Ohio*), against cruel and unusual punishments (*Robinson* v. *California*), and must be provided with counsel by the state if unable to afford it themselves (*Gideon* v. *Wainwright*). These developments culminated in the case of *Miranda* v. *Arizona* in 1966, which applied the procedures to the activities of state police that the FBI had used in federal cases. The Court asserted the right of an individual under interrogation to have a lawyer present, and laid upon the state the duty of supplying one at state expense if the person under interrogation could not afford it.

The role of the Court today

The Supreme Court under Chief Justice Warren was undoubtedly responsible for a greater degree of active judicial policy-making than in any period other than the New Deal years. Today, in a number of critical policy areas the courts are still working out the consequences of those decisions. However in 1969, right at the beginning of his presidency, Richard Nixon had the opportunity of nominating a successor to Earl Warren as Chief Justice, and as a result a much more conservatively minded man was appointed, Warren E. Burger. Over the next two years three more Nixon nominees were appointed: Blackmun, Powell and Rehnquist. In 1975 President Ford nominated Justice John Paul Stevens. No further appointments were made until 1981 when the first woman to serve on the Supreme Court, Justice Sandra Day O'Connor, was nominated by President Reagan.

The radical policies of the Warren Court in the 1950s and 1960s had been carried through by a group of justices that included two who had been nominated by President Franklin Roosevelt in the 1930s: Hugo L. Black and William O. Douglas. The resignation of Earl Warren in 1969, and the departure from the Court of Black in 1971 and of Douglas in 1975, transformed its approach to constitutional questions. The liberal activist majority of the Warren Court was replaced by a less cohesive, more cautious group of justices, without any dominant philosophy of constitutional interpretation. The Court became much more respectful of the powers and policies of the federal government, and much less ready to assert its own powers. As Justice Rehnquist expressed it, in 1981, the Court adopted a 'healthy deference' to

Congress when reviewing its decisions, particularly on national security and foreign policy questions. The Burger Court did not reverse the policies of its predecessor. Rather, it moderated them. It by no means gave up its right to invalidate Acts of Congress, as for example in 1976 when it decided that an attempt by the federal government to control the minimum wage regulations for the employees of state and local governments was unconstitutional (*National League of Cities* v. *Usery*), but it adopted a more tentative approach to its task, deciding issues according to the shifting majorities on the Court, avoiding either a strongly conservative or strongly liberal approach.

In the years from 1981 to 1988 President Reagan had the opportunity to appoint three Justices, Sandra Day O'Connor, Antonin Scalia and Anthony Kennedy, and to promote Justice William Rehnquist to Chief Justice. President Bush nominated David Souter and Clarence Thomas to the Court. Thus these two Republican presidents were able to change the balance of power on the Court, bringing about a more conservative direction to the course of judicial review. The Reagan administration took on an active role in urging on the Court a new attitude towards a number of policies, and the Court responded, although perhaps not to the extent that Reagan would have wished. In the implementation of desegregation in schools the Court retreated from the activism of earlier years, leaving more discretion to the states and local school districts (*Freeman* v. *Pitts*, 1992). The Court adopted a less clear stand on abortion (*Planned Parenthood* v. *Casey*, 1992). President Clinton had the opportunity to appoint two Justices in his first term of office – Ruth Ginsburg in 1993 and Stephen Breyer in 1994. Although both are at the liberal end of the spectrum, the balance of power on the Court did not change, and its decisions reflected this. In the field of affirmative action the Court outlawed the use of quotas to give preference in employment to minorities (*Adaran Constructors* v. *Pena*, 1995), and in the area of federalism has been much more protective of states' rights (*US* v. *Lopez*, 1995; *US* v. *Morrison*, 2000). It remains to be seen whether the Court under Chief Justice Roberts will adopt a new, more coherently conservative line or continue to follow the centrist position of the Rehnquist Court.

Congress and the Court

In the space of fourteen years, the Supreme Court under Chief Justice Warren initiated new policies in a wide variety of ways, all of which were likely to offend conservative elements in the community. As a result the Court came under fierce attack both outside and inside Congress. The Constitution had provided for an independent judiciary by providing that the judges should hold office during good behaviour; that is, they could be removed only by impeachment. However, the Constitution gave Congress a potential power to discipline the Court, either through legislation or by proposing constitutional amendments. From time to time throughout its history the Court has come into conflict with the legislature. Congress has increased and decreased the number of judges. On one occasion the legislature passed a statute withdrawing jurisdiction from the Court while a case was actually under consideration by the justices. However, most of the attacks upon the Court have failed, though some only by a very narrow margin. They have taken the form of the introduction of proposed constitutional amendments which would have required a two-thirds majority, or some other high proportion of the Court's membership, before a state or federal statute could be declared unconstitutional. Broad attacks have been mounted on the Court's appellate jurisdiction, which would have removed large areas from the Court, or would even have removed altogether its power to overrule the decisions of state supreme courts. Thus, the Detainee Treatment Act of 2005 purported to remove from the jurisdiction of federal courts any cases concerning the prisoners held in detention at Guantánamo Bay. Attempts have been made to fix a retiring age for the justices, to make their positions elective, or to give them short fixed terms of office. Other proposals would have made the Senate into an appellate court to review Supreme Court decisions, or would have given to Congress the power to set these decisions aside.

These attacks have come at the Court from every direction. In its early years the Jeffersonians attacked the Court for its centralising influence; the abolitionists attacked the Court for its support of the property rights of slave-owners; after the Civil War the Radical Republicans wished to curb the power of the Court because of its apparent sympathy for Southern complaints about arbitrary arrests and restrictions upon freedom of speech; in the last quarter of the nineteenth century the Progressives attacked the Court because of its support for business and commercial interests; in the 1930s liberals attempted to transform the Court because of its attack upon the New Deal legislation; in the years following 1954 Southerners and conservatives bitterly attacked the Court because of its decisions on segregation, apportionment and abortion.

President Reagan's administrations saw the emergence of a battle between the chief executive and the Supreme Court on a scale unknown since the attack by President Roosevelt on the Court in the 1930s, but from a very different ideological standpoint. Roosevelt attacked the Court for its activism in striking down his liberal policies aimed at ending the Depression, and his attack on the Court was a demand for judicial restraint, allowing the legislature to make decisions demanded in the national interest. Reagan also attacked the activism of the Supreme Court, but his complaint was that the Court was too liberal in its approach to social policy and his demands for ' judicial restraint' amounted to the requirement that the Court should reverse its decisions on such questions as abortion, school busing and school prayers, although on none of these issues could he get Congress to legislate the policies that he would have liked to see implemented.

The Court and public opinion

The Supreme Court wields considerable power in the American political system, and it plays a vital policy-making role in the government. What then is the place of the Court in a democracy? How is it that nine unelected judges with life tenure can wield this power in the most election-conscious nation in the world? Undoubtedly, the Court has been able to exercise a degree of leadership, because of its prestige and its relative aloofness from the hurly-burly of political life. Nevertheless, the power of the Court depends in the last resort upon its success in refashioning the rules of the Constitution in a way that the informed public, and in particular those who are responsible for the operation of the machinery of government, are prepared to accept. To some extent the Court, like other parts of the system of government, moderates its policies when they meet fierce opposition or when its own position is seriously threatened. After each of the Court's periods of controversial activism it has, to a greater or lesser degree, retreated from its most exposed positions and made its judgements more palatable. However, the explanation of the Court's power is not to be found simply in terms of its ability to gauge public opinion accurately. Its role has to be seen in the general context of the pluralist political system of the United States. The Court is able to exercise its power because it rarely comes squarely into conflict with a truly united opposition, either inside or outside the formal institutional structure of government. Such a coalition of interests determined to attack the Court has not yet had the continuity or cohesion that would be required to put through the legislation or constitutional amendment that would be necessary to curb the Court. Every attack that has been made upon the Court so far has been based upon the current dissatisfactions of those outraged by its decisions, but they have not overcome the reservations of the rest of the community who fear the long-term results of reducing the Court's power. Many of the problems that the Court is able to tackle appear to be quite intractable as far as actions by the more overtly political branches are concerned. Thus the Court remains, and is likely to remain, at the centre of the policy-making process in the United States.

Further reading

McKeever, R.J. (1995) *Raw Judicial Power? The Supreme Court and American Society*, 2nd edn, Manchester: Manchester University Press.

McKeever, R.J. (1997) *The United States Supreme Court: A Political and Legal Analysis*, Manchester: Manchester University Press.

O'Brien, D.M. (2005) *Storm Center: The Supreme Court in American Politics*, 11th edn, New York: Norton.

Websites

Cornell Law School: http://supct.law.cornell.edu
FindLaw: www.findlaw.com
Supreme Court Reports: www.supremecourtus.gov

11 The making of American domestic policy

The uniqueness of American society, and of its political system, lies in the combination of stability and change that has characterised American life since the end of the eighteenth century. Today the American system of government is in a very real sense the most 'modernised' political system in the world, less inhibited than any other by traditionalist modes of behaviour, and yet it operates within a constitutional framework of unparalleled stability and strength. By the end of the Second World War, the political system seemed to have set firmly into the mould created during the long domination of the presidency by Franklin Delano Roosevelt. Today, however, the political system has evolved into something very different from the 'Roosevelt System' which then characterised the processes of decision-taking. In order to understand the way in which decisions are taken today it is necessary to chart the developments that have taken place since 1945 and observe the way in which the system of government that President Roosevelt bequeathed to the United States has been transformed.

The Roosevelt system

The dominant characteristic of the Roosevelt system was a pluralist political system in which a number of traditional groupings – labour, business and agriculture – operated through the channels of the government machine. Federalism, the division of power between the national government and the states, was well adapted to the working of this system of pluralism. Pressure groups brought about the compromises on policy decisions that were necessary for the government of the country. The political parties remained a vitally important structure through which political offices were allocated. The Roosevelt coalition of the Northern cities and the predominantly rural South seemed to have established a mechanism by which the national government could, through the medium of the Democratic Party, pull together ite parts of the nation. Under Roosevelt the presidency had been entral driving force in the system of government. The need for l leadership during the years of the Depression and throughout the war seemed to show that only the president could provide the coherent initiatives in internal and external policy that were required to deal with the complex problems of the modern world. More and more it seemed as if the legislature could only follow where the president led. Furthermore, under Roosevelt a new liberal establishment had been created in Washington, with the federal civil service evolving policies in the fields of employment, social welfare, transport and a hundred other areas, which were then to be implemented by the state governments, sometimes reluctantly, on conditions laid down by the federal government.

The Roosevelt system, then, represented an attempt to bring the United States into the twentieth century by developing new social and economic policies, but it was dependent in the last analysis upon the same political infrastructure that had supported the system of government since the Civil War. Roosevelt, though an innovator, depended upon the party bosses and political machines that had formed the substructure of American politics for many decades; but many of his own policies were to undermine that system and help to transform American politics into something very different.

The new political system

Most of the basic characteristics of the Roosevelt system have now been changed almost out of all recognition. Although American politics is still very much characterised by the interplay of group politics, the nature of those groups has changed considerably. To the older groups have been added new ones concerned with issues such as environmental protection, pollution control, social issues such as women's rights and abortion, and many others. The quality of the pluralistic battle has changed also because of the decline of the importance of the party system. As a result of the extension of primary elections, particularly presidential primaries, and the new rules for the selection of delegates to the national conventions, professional politicians, particularly in the Democratic Party, came to play a much-diminished role in the organization and operation of the national political parties. In effect, the Democratic Party's selection procedure for the choosing of Democratic presidential candidates was taken over by pressure groups, who have a formal position in the party, and who are represented in it as of right. Thus the old linkages, corrupt as they often were, between bosses at the state and local level and national politicians, were broken. This in itself might have been highly desirable, but nothing has replaced these former linkages, and there remains largely a void. National nominating politics has become a matter of personalities, of the ability of presidential candidates to attract to themselves an organisation to promote their candidature, and above all a matter of the use of the mass media to project the candidate's image across the nation, using soundbites.

This new style of politics has been accompanied by a change in the presidential candidate that is successful, and also by an undoubted de the power and importance of the presidency. In spite of the attention that has been given to the idea of an 'Imperial Presidency', firstly after the Vietnam War and more recently in the wake of the invasion of Iraq, there has in fact been a continual decline in presidential power since the time of Roosevelt.

The new American nationalism

The explanation of this new political system can be found only by an examination of the nature of American society, and by an examination of the stage of development that the United States has reached in its perception of its own national identity. The unique character of American nationalism lies at the heart of the political system in the United States. Americans have had to develop a sense of national identity over a much shorter period than most European states, and in quite different circumstances. The United States is a country of immigrants and the descendants of immigrants and at the outset of the new nation there were doubts about whether a sense of national identity would ever emerge. As late as the middle of the nineteenth century there were those who were prepared to give their total allegiance to one section of the country, rather than to the nation as a whole. The American system of federalism grew out of this conflict between local loyalties and loyalty to the nation.

Today, however, the United States exhibits a kind of nationalism that is quite unique in the modern world. America differs from any other large nation, European or Asian, because it is in a very real sense an artificial construction of the modern age. European nations have been created as the result of the bringing together through conquest of tribal units, which have been forged into a single society. But such societies are never fully integrated. The tribal and sub-national divisions within them reappear, because they are associated with a historic territory, a homeland, a language or some other ethnic characteristic that can form the basis of nationalist sentiment. Thus, since the end of the Second World War, nationalist movements have sprung up in Britain, France, Spain and other European countries where ethnic groups look back over many centuries to an earlier national identity, real or imagined. Although the United States is a country composed of an enormous diversity of ethnic origins, there are really no important historic communities in the United States that have a close association with a particular region or area. The old loyalties to New England, the sense of community in Louisiana – none of these has the kind of importance in day-to-day American politics that the Scots have in the United Kingdom, or the Basques in Spain. The closest analogy to such European loyalties to be found in North America is that of Quebec in Canada, although many Mexican-Americans do now look upon California in a rather similar way.

During the twentieth century the development of rapid transport, the expansion of settlement into new areas such as California and Alaska, the spread of industrialisation into the South – all these things tended to produce a population that has many diversities within it, but is spread out across the whole face of the United States without the kind of local or regional differentiation that one would find in Europe. In one sense, therefore, America is more of a single, united nation than any other in the world. The loyalties of the population have no other focus than that of the United States. Old sectional and regional loyalties persist, but they are no longer strong enough to have any real claim to the allegiance of Americans.

Such a situation might be thought to lead to a highly centralised political system, in which a powerful national government was the only effective political force. Clearly this is not the case. The nature of American society in the post-industrial age is such that there is no desire for a strong, powerful central government. Individualism remains a very strong element in the make-up of the American electorate. A large proportion of the population resists the centralisation of power and the extension of government activity. As a result of these two factors – the peculiar uniformity of American nationalism, and the resistance to big government – there has resulted a strangely unstructured, decentralised system of government and politics. The institutions of state and local government are used in order to prevent the centralisation of political power, without their being themselves the focus of strong loyalties.

Political power is diffused across a large but an increasingly undifferentiated country. Political parties have provided little structure to the system, at least until recently. After the congressional elections of 1994 when Newt Gingrich became the Speaker of the House of Representatives the increasingly ideological nature of the Republican Party, combined with the change of allegiance from the Democrats to the Republicans made by many Southern whites, resulted in politics becoming more partisan, but that partisanship is still not as intense as in most European countries. It did not prevent President Clinton being re-elected in 1996 alongside a Republican majority in both Houses of Congress. In spite of the Republican control of both presidency and Congress since 2002, the constitutional separation of powers and the electoral system still hold out the distinct possibility of a return to divided government, with a president of one party faced by a majority of the opposing party in one or both of the Houses of Congress.

Democracy in the United States

The American political system is a combination of pluralist, class, elitist and individualist influences. In a sense, that must be true of any political system, for in the real world no actual system of government will fit exactly into any single intellectual category. The special quality of the American system is the way in which all these different elements are kept in balance, through a constitutional system the main purpose of which is to prevent the accumulation of power in the hands of any single individual, section or group. Politic
America is group politics, and the process of achieving compromises betv

contending group interests is at the heart of the system. Nevertheless, a simple-minded pluralist view of American politics cannot be sustained. Clearly, certain groups have more influence, more financial muscle, better organisation and more effective access to the centres of decision-taking, and can therefore expect to win more often than others. Elite groups of industrialists, the military, bureaucrats or judges can have a decisive effect at the right time in the right circumstances. Although one can search in vain for the power elite that determines all important matters in the United States, any study of American politics that *ignored* the significance of elites would be inadequate.

'Class politics' is also an essential fact of life in America, but it is emphatically *not* the class politics of the Marxist analysis. That analysis centres on the concept of a small ruling class that dominates and exploits the masses, and in many societies that was, and is still today, a fair representation of the situation. In America, however, we see a very different position. America is overwhelmingly and increasingly a middle-class society. It is this middle class, and not the industrial proletariat or the bourgeoisie, that is the fly-wheel of the political system. In some senses this makes for a more insoluble problem than that posited by the Marxist critics of the system. In a society where a small, powerful and wealthy minority exploits the vast majority of the citizens, some relief might come from revolution, but the American situation is one in which perhaps 80 or 85 per cent of the people are satisfied with the system and have more to lose than to gain from radical change. The remainder, who are underprivileged and live in relative poverty in an affluent society, can see little prospect of attaining the levels of wealth of the more prosperous sections of the community. It is therefore more a case of 'majority tyranny', and much more difficult to resolve. It is here that the major threat to the stability of American life lies.

Above all, America remains a country in which individuals can have an impact, at all levels, on the outcome of political decisions. The relative lack of ideological restraints and of strong organisational structures makes it possible for the individual, if sufficiently determined, to influence the outcome of decisions by the local school board, or even to defeat the intentions of the president of the United States. The policy outcomes of this system, its results, are not necessarily 'good' or 'desirable', for the people who make up the system are unfailingly human. However, the 'openness' of the American political system, the fact that no single person or group can control the flow of information within it or impose upon it a single all-inclusive organisational structure, ensures that it comes closer than any other modern state to being a representative democracy.

The American political system was deliberately fragmented by the Founding Fathers, distributing authority between the federal government and the states, separating legislative, executive and judicial powers, and creating a genuinely bicameral legislature, in which the two Houses of Congress both exercise considerable power. Congress was created as a legislature in its own right, not dependent on the president, but as a rival. Later developments in the organisation of Congress further fragmented political power among congressional committees and, by adopting procedures such as the filibuster in the Senate, gave significant power to individual members of the legislature. The political party system, instead of coordinating the disparate parts of the system, is itself decentralised and weak, reinforcing its disintegrative character. The system of pressure groups sprang up to fill the vacuum in policy-making that was created. The making of policy, therefore, is not centrally controlled or coordinated. There is no single pattern to decision-making. The process depends upon four factors:

- the nature of the issue that is to be decided;
- the particular groups that are interested in the outcome of that issue;
- the bearing of 'public opinion' on the issue, and the perception of Senators and Congressmen of its importance to their prospects for re-election;
- the circumstances of the national or international political environment at the time that the issue comes up for decision.

Thus the processes by which individual policy decisions are made differ considerably. Each issue is unique; they are decided by changing coalitions of interest groups, with the involvement of governmental agencies; different weights are given to the influence of the president or congressional party leaders; some issues depend almost entirely on decisions of the courts, others are not susceptible to solution through judicial procedures.

In this chapter we will examine a number of areas of domestic policy-making in order to illustrate the various factors that influence outcomes. The first of these is the attempt to reform the American system of health care, a subject that dominated the first two years of President Clinton's first term of office.

Health care reform

The major source for the provision of health care cover is private insurance. Insurance companies and Health Maintenance Organisations (HMOs) issue policies. The premiums are paid by employers to provide benefits for their employees, by individuals to provide cover for themselves or their families, or by a combination of these. The HMO or the insurance company pays the hospital bills, the doctors, and the cost of drugs, accommodation, etc. The problem with this kind of private provision is that it is very variable in its coverage. Limits may be set by the insurers to the total amount that can be claimed over the period of a person's life span. Policies differ in the extent to which they cover chronic or catastrophic illness, mental illness or pregnancy, and the extent to which family dependents are covered, and of course the insurance system does not provide automatic coverage for the unempl———
the disabled and the elderly. The system also suffers from adm
complexity and soaring fees for hospitals and doctors, and is subje

– it has been estimated that as many as 10 per cent of health care claims are fraudulent.

The shortcomings of the private insurance system led the federal government in 1965 to introduce Medicare, an insurance programme to cover the elderly and some disabled persons. Medicaid was also introduced to cover the very poor. The states, in combination with the federal government, finance health care for low-income groups and those receiving public assistance, such as the blind and the disabled. However, Medicaid is tied in with the state's welfare system, so that entitlement varies from state to state. The states differ in the arrangements they make for their citizens. Hawaii created a government-run scheme similar to the British National Health Service; other states have attempted to go it alone, without becoming ensnared in the complex federal regulations attached to Medicaid. Oregon adopted a policy of rationing health care in order to provide a programme that covers a much larger proportion of the needy population.

The richest country in the world, with magnificent health care facilities, does not provide basic care for many of its citizens. In 1992 some 35 million Americans were not covered by any of these plans, and millions more were underinsured. Sixteen per cent of Americans under the age of sixty-five were uninsured, with much higher percentages in minority groups such as blacks (21 per cent) and Mexican-Americans (35 per cent). During the 1992 presidential election campaign Bill Clinton had repeatedly promised that he would reform the nation's health care system, and public opinion seemed to be in favour of some initiative to overhaul it. Five days after his inauguration in January 1993, Clinton appointed his wife Hillary to head a Task Force on National Health Care Reform. This was an unprecedented move. The wives of Presidents had in the past exercised considerable influence, particularly in cases of presidential illness. Edith Wilson was apparently in charge of the government of the United States after President Woodrow Wilson suffered a stroke in 1919; Nancy Reagan played an important part in running the White House when her husband was shot; but this was the first formal appointment of a First Lady to a government post. It caused a good deal of controversy, although Mrs Clinton soon impressed Congress and the public with her grasp of the complexities of the health care problem.

The Task Force took four months to complete its work. It did not seek simply to provide a solution which was politically acceptable to the interests involved, but set out to devise a plan which would meet the basic objectives that the president had espoused, in particular universal health care coverage for all Americans. From the day, 22 September 1993, that Clinton unveiled his plan before a joint session of Congress, critics said the proposal was too complicated. In November the Bill was introduced into Congress. Clinton planned to provide permanent health care coverage to all Americans by requiring employers to pay 80 per cent of the cost of a basic package of benefits for their employees. He proposed to control skyrocketing health care costs by capping the amount that insurance premiums could increase annually. He also proposed that new large purchasing groups be formed, called alliances, to provide health care.

The proposal was met by a barrage of negative advertisements in the press and on television, and an onslaught of news stories that left the public bewildered. The Health Security Bill, embodying the recommendations of the Task Force, ran to 1,342 pages. The health insurers and the drug companies attacked the Bill, and the confusion was confounded by the way in which the Congress dealt with the proposal. During the first half of 1994 five major committees and a host of secondary committees struggled to draft their own versions of health care reform. Congressional leaders were unable to resolve the competition among the congressional committees that wanted to take charge of the legislation. In the House, the Ways and Means Committee, the Energy and Commerce Committee, and the Education and Labor Committee all claimed the right to consider the proposals. Secondary aspects of the Bill were referred to seven other committees. In the Senate the Chairmen of the Finance and Labor Committee, Patrick Moynihan, and the Human Resources Committee, Edward Kennedy, both prominent Democrats, could not agree on which committee should have jurisdiction. Each of these committees drafted their own alternative Bills, so that there were now six different versions of the proposed legislation under consideration, the Clintons' Bill and the five committee versions. None had enough support to pass. In an attempt to break the deadlock, House and Senate leaders set out to draft their own versions of the reform legislation; in late July and August, the Democratic Leaders in both House and Senate introduced further Bills.

As a result of the complexity of the issue, and the confusion in Congress, the public was unclear about its attitude to the legislation. The opponents of the Bill, the health insurers, the drug companies, and the doctors, mounted a strong campaign in the media. On television a series of short clips portrayed a middle-class couple – Harry and Louise – perplexed and worried about the cost and quality of health care if the Clinton plan was passed. Even Clinton's supporters had to accept modifications to the grand plan, such as allowing the health care plans of trade unions to be exempted from the scheme. At this point the president's party, the Democrats, had a sizeable majority in both the House of Representatives and the Senate, but the leader of the Republicans in the Senate, Bob Dole, was more in tune with opinion in the legislature than was the president. 'Our country has health-care problems, but not a health-care crisis,' he argued. 'The President's idea is to put a mountain of bureaucrats between you and your doctor.' He proposed 'common-sense solutions', piecemeal answers to particular issues, such as a guarantee of uninterrupted coverage when moving from one employment to another, and no bar to coverage due to previous medical conditions. This 'incremental approach', so characteristic of the policy-making process in America, was more attractive to legislators than the blueprint offered by the Clinton administration. Towards the end of the 1994 session of Congress, it became clear that there was no majority for any of the various Bills then under consideration. There was a threat by the Republican minority to mount a filibuster in the Senate if an attempt was made by the Democratic leadership to put a Bill through, and there was no prospect of finding the necessary votes to end such a filibuster. The health care reform legislation, which had absorbed so much time and effort by the Clinton administration, simply expired.

The failure of the Clinton Plan was the result of a combination of factors: the decision by the Clintons to attempt a root-and-branch reform in a country where such exercises are viewed with suspicion; the weakness of a president unable to depend upon the loyalty of his party in Congress; the power of well-financed pressure groups; and the increasing resistance of the public to 'big government'. Following the victory of the Republicans in the congressional elections of November 1994, the incremental approach to reform was pursued in a bipartisan fashion. An Act was passed in 1996 as the result of the collaboration of Republican Senator Nancy Kassebaum and Democratic Senator Edward Kennedy. The Kassebaum–Kennedy Act introduced a number of changes that enabled the automatic transfer of health care insurance from one job to another, and prevented the exclusion of the insured person from health care coverage on the grounds of a pre-existing medical condition. This was followed by an Act that extended state health care to children in working families whose employers did not provide health care for dependents. Thus the alternative programme which had been advocated by Senator Dole was enacted after the defeat of the president's grand plan. These incremental changes did little, however, for the millions of people not covered by the health care system at all, the original objective of the Clinton reform proposals.

President Clinton had to abandon his attempt to provide inclusive health care, and since the election of George W. Bush in 2000 the picture has got worse. By 2004 the number of American citizens not covered by any kind of medical plan had risen to 45.8 million, 15.7 per cent of the population, drawn from all sections of the public.

Welfare reform and divided government

As in other Western democracies the decade of the 1990s began with increasing concern about the rising costs of the welfare system, and with a desire to reform it. The emphasis was to end the dependency of the poor on welfare payments, and to get them back to work. Although it was the Republicans who were most insistent on the need for reform, the demand was by no means limited to them. During his 1992 campaign for the presidency Bill Clinton had pledged 'to end welfare as we know it', but for his first two years in office the president's concern with health care reform precluded any serious attempt to fulfil this campaign promise. The victory of the Republicans in the congressional elections of 1994, however, gave them the initiative and put the president on the defensive, both in the case of welfare reform itself and in the concurrent attempts by the Republican leaders in Congress to cut back on the Medicaid programme. The result was Clinton's reluctant assent to the Personal Responsibility and Work Opportunity Reconciliation Act of 1996, and the biggest upheaval in the working of the American federal system for sixty years.

In 1935, as part of the New Deal programme of President Franklin Roosevelt, Congress passed the Social Security Act. One part of the Act set up programmes for the disadvantaged which would be financed jointly by the federal and state governments and administered by the states under conditions set by the federal government. This programme, typical of the 'cooperative federalism' initiated by Roosevelt, provided federal grants-in-aid for the states and set tight conditions that the states had to meet to receive this federal money. Under the Social Security Act one of these conditions was that those families who met the eligibility requirements for assistance were automatically entitled to benefit, and the states could not deny it to them. This became, therefore, an open-ended commitment for the states, taking away from them control over their own expenditures. A similar situation was created in 1965 when President Lyndon Johnson signed the Medicaid programme into law. This legislation provided automatic entitlement to medical care for claimants who met the eligibility requirements for welfare benefit, and it was financed in the same way, a conditional grant-in-aid programme administered by the states, with approximately half the cost coming from state funds. The requirement of automatic entitlement, together with the rising costs of both programmes, led Republican state governors to urge that the states be given more control over these programmes, particularly Medicaid, which is extremely costly. Welfare reform was one of the aims set out in the Republican 'Contract with America' on which the election of 1994 was fought.

Although President Clinton had committed himself to some form of 'welfare-to-work' reform, the proposals introduced into Congress by the Republicans in 1995 went much further than he would have wished. He was opposed to the Republican proposal to end automatic eligibility for Medicaid; he also rejected plans to limit the entitlement to 'food stamps' by the poor, to deny certain benefits to legal immigrants, and to give the states control over a range of other welfare programmes for women and children. The president vetoed two bills on welfare reform passed by Congress, one in December 1995 and the second in January 1996, but as the 1996 election campaign got under way both parties were under pressure to show that they had made progress in this area. In 1996 bills were again introduced into Congress providing for reform in the welfare and Medicaid programmes. The link between welfare and Medicaid was the key issue that would determine the fate of the reform legislation. As long as the proposal to cut back on eligibility for Medicaid benefits remained as part of the package the likelihood of a presidential veto of any Bill that was passed by Congress remained high. In July 1996 the Republican leadership in Congress decided to drop the Medicaid provisions, and to present the president with the straight choice of either assenting to or vetoing a welfare reform bill.

The development after 1932 of New Deal policies, particularly in the field of social welfare, had centralised political power, forcing the states to accept the policy of the federal government and to provide a large part of the finance for them. For many years Republican presidents had talked of swinging the balance of power back towards the states and away from the federal government. Richard Nixon had proposed a 'New Federalism', and Reagan and Bush had each attempted to find a different basis for the distribution of functions between the two levels of government. They had had little real success in this endeavour, so it was ironic that it was the Democrat, Bill Clinton, who was obliged to sign a bill which for the first time achieved a really significant shift of power to state governments. The problem of a Democratic president facing a Congress dominated by the Republicans is clear in the voting patterns in Congress when the critical vote was taken on the legislation. The Republicans, although they had had to give up their attempt to reform Medicaid, were virtually unanimous in support of the Bill – only two Republicans in the House of Representatives and no Republican Senators voted against. The situation in the Democratic Party was very different. President Clinton had announced that, although there were parts of the Bill to which he was deeply opposed, nevertheless he would sign it. Thus a vote for the Bill was a vote in favour of the president's policy. But only half the Democrats in the House could bring themselves to vote for the Bill – ninety-eight in favour and ninety-eight against. In the Senate the situation was little better; twenty-five Democratic Senators voted in favour of the welfare reform proposal, and twenty-one against. Particularly noticeable was the fact that a majority of the Democratic Senators representing Northern states opposed the Bill, whereas all but one of the Southern Democrats supported it. Black and Hispanic congressional representatives were overwhelmingly opposed to the Bill. The president had been forced to participate in a process of reform that was never in his control and that deeply divided his own party.

The mechanism that was adopted in the legislation was the use of block grants. The grants-in-aid made by the federal government to the states under the Social Security Act had been accompanied by very explicit conditions, leaving little discretion to the states in the way that the programmes were administered, or in the amount of their own revenue that they had to contribute. Under the new legislation block grants were made to the states totalling $16.4 billion a year, leaving the states to decide on levels of benefit and eligibility requirements for participants, and requiring the states to contribute significantly less from their own resources than before. One major effect of the new law was to increase the extent to which welfare programmes could differ from state to state, reflecting the political philosophies of state legislators. The State of Wisconsin adopted a radical approach to welfare, abolishing the entitlement to benefit unless the recipient of the welfare payment undertook some kind of work. Other states adopted their own ways of reforming their welfare programmes. The result was that state governments regained a much higher degree of control over their actions than at any time since the 1930s. The trend towards giving states greater flexibility continued under the presidency of George W. Bush with the passage in 2006 of the Deficit Reduction Act which gave the states the power to scale back Medicaid benefits. The Act also increased charges to patients and required the states to check the citizenship of recipients before providing medical care.

Immigration

Immigration is a delicate political issue in many countries, but the United States is in a unique situation; it is a country of immigrants, so it is in some ways bound to be more sympathetic to potential migrants than many other countries, but at the same time its wealth has made it a goal for so many millions who want to enjoy its lifestyle that severe tensions are almost certain to come to the surface. There was a vital need for immigrants throughout the nineteenth century, in order to people the western lands that were wrested from the native American tribes, bought from the French or ceded by Spain and Mexico, and then to fill the factories that were multiplying in the cities of the North and East. In the twentieth century there was an influx of people from all over the world, nearly 47 million legally admitted immigrants, plus many further millions who entered illegally. Legal and illegal immigration continues in the twenty-first century with over 1 million legal immigrants entering in each of the years 2001 and 2002.

During most of the nineteenth century entry into the United States was virtually unrestricted. Specific restrictions were imposed; for example the Chinese Exclusion Act of 1882 forbad the entry of further Chinese immigrants. The flow of Chinese had begun with the California Gold Rush and continued with those who worked on the Trans-Continental Railroad, which was completed in 1869. The Chinese Exclusion Act was not repealed until 1943. Health tests for immigrants were implemented in the 1880s with the opening of Ellis Island as an immigrant control centre. Concern for the impact of immigration on the employment of American workers led to the passage of legislation, the National Origins Act of 1924, which severely restricted immigration by setting national quotas for immigrants. These quotas favoured northern Europeans over those from southern and eastern Europe and virtually excluded Asians. The next important piece of legislation was the Immigration and Nationality Act of 1952 (the McCarran–Walter Act), passed over the veto of President Truman, which retained quotas and also set preferences both for ethnic groups and for those with particular skills and qualifications. Senator Pat McCarran, a Nevada Democrat, one of the authors of the legislation, was chairman of the Senate Internal Security subcommittee that took upon itself the task of rooting out 'subversives' in government, and the 1952 Act gave wide powers to the Attorney General to deport subversives. National quotas were ended in 1965, but the McCarran–Walter Act, although amended many times, remains the basis of US immigration law today. Preference is given to aliens related to citizens of the United States and to other categories such as aliens who are members of the professions holding advanced degrees, or aliens of exceptional ability, skilled workers, professionals and other workers.

The events of 11 September 2001 changed the politics of immigration like so many other things. The administration of the immigration service, which had been part of the Department of Justice, moved to the newly established Department of Homeland Security. Security was to become an increasingly important influence on immigration policy, as for so many other aspects of government. However, another problem was to become salient in 2005–6 – illegal immigration. It has been estimated that there are nearly 12 million illegal immigrants in the United States, although some people would put the number much higher. Much of the influx of illegal immigrants is from Mexico, where every day thousands cross the border illegally. Many are caught and returned to Mexico, approximately 1 million arrests each year, but many others get through, and many of those returned to Mexico make attempted crossing after attempted crossing. One estimate of illegal Mexican immigration places the current figure at 485,000 per year. The extent of this problem necessitated the formulation of new policies, but the difficulties of achieving a consensus over such an emotive issue then became apparent. There are three aspects to the problem – the way in which to control the Mexican border, the more stringent enforcement of immigration laws and the question of what to do about the large number of illegal immigrants, many of whom had been living in the United States for years.

The first move to deal with this issue was made by the Republican chairman of the House Judiciary Committee, F. James Sensenbrenner, who in December 2005 introduced a bill entitled the Border Protection, Antiterrorism and Illegal Immigration Control Act. The proposed Act was directed towards toughening the law on illegal immigrants, making unlawful presence in the US a crime on conviction of which would make millions of 'undocumented immigrants' ineligible for citizenship. The Bill made no provision for an amnesty for illegal immigrants, and no special provision for the many seasonal workers on whom many American farmers depend. Other aspects of the Bill were the provision for the construction of a fence along part of the US–Mexican border and strengthened control procedures at entry points. If this Bill were to become law, the outcome might be that most, if not all, of the illegal immigrants in the country would be eligible for deportation. The White House issued a statement supporting the Bill, with some reservations, and the Bill was quickly passed by the House of Representatives; 203 Republicans and thirty-six Democrats voted in favour, 164 Democrats, seventeen Republicans and one Independent voted against.

In March 2006 the Senate began consideration of a more liberal approach to the immigration issue. A number of versions of this proposed legislation were introduced, including the possibility of the legalisation of the status of many undocumented persons living in the US, a guest worker programme and less punitive measures for being in the country unlawfully. Objections by conservative senators to the original draft legislation proposed by the chairman of the Senate Judiciary Committee, Arlen Specter, led to an attempt by the Republican Majority Leader, Senator Frist, to come up with bipartisan compromise proposals. Frist proposed that illegal immigrants should be divided into three categories: those who had been in the United States for five years or more could be granted citizenship under certain conditions; those who had been in the country for two to four years could apply for legal status, but they would have to return to a border crossing in order to apply; the remainder would be deported. However, the compromise proposal failed to get acceptance, and by April 2006 there was deadlock. President Bush indicated that he supported a further compromise which would involve a guest worker programme but not an amnesty. However, he faced considerable opposition from many Republican Senators and Congressmen. The prospect of large-scale deportations led to unprecedented demonstrations in many cities by hundreds of thousands of Latinos, not just Mexicans, but legal and illegal immigrants from many South American countries, some waving foreign, mostly Mexican, flags. Whilst urging Congress to pass legislation to control immigration, President Bush in May 2006 decided to order 2,500 National Guard soldiers to the Mexican border to give support to the border patrols.

The failure of the federal government to find a solution to the illegal immigrant problem led many states to try to deal with the issue themselves. As long ago as 1994 the voters in California approved a referendum proposal, Proposition 187, denying taxpayer-funded goods such as free education and free hospital treatment to illegal aliens. There was anger in many states over the fact that illegal aliens often received government-funded health care, education benefits and subsidised housing. Georgia passed a law imposing fines on employers who hire illegal immigrants, and other states are following suit. Arizona, which is one of the states bordering Mexico, is considering a number of proposals, from requiring proof of citizenship in order to vote or to receive welfare benefits, to building an eighty-mile fence along the border. Private citizen groups have taken initiatives, such as the Minuteman Project, a volunteer group that patrols the United States–Mexico border.

The death penalty

Some policies are made in the United States with almost no input from the president or the Congress; the law concerning the death penalty has been developed, for the most part, by the legislatures of the states and by the judiciary, in particular by the Supreme Court. Most of the criminal law in America is state law and most criminal prosecutions are made by state law enforcement authorities; in 2000 there were over 1,194,000 prisoners in state jails compared with only 111,000 in federal jails. Murder is a crime that is largely subject to state law, except for those murders committed on federal property, such as army bases, or committed in the course of federal crimes such as drug-trafficking, kidnapping or acts of terrorism. Until 1972 the Supreme Court had not given consideration to the constitutionality of the death penalty, although the Eighth Amendment to the Constitution, passed in 1791, had forbidden 'cruel and unusual punishments'. The states had been free to adopt capital punishment or not, and free to adopt the means of execution and the conditions attached to it. In 1972 thirty-nine states and the District of Columbia had laws enforcing capital punishment, including sixteen that provided for the death penalty for rape as well as murder. Of the sixteen states that punished rapists with the death penalty, thirteen were Southern states, where there are a high proportion of blacks. The federal government also provided for the death penalty for a number of crimes, including treason, espionage, train-wrecking and aircraft piracy.

In the case of *Furman* v. *Georgia* in 1972, the Supreme Court ruled by a majority of five to four that the death penalty was unconstitutional. However, among the five justices who took this view there was no consensus on the grounds for outlawing the death penalty. Two justices, Brennan and Marshall, were of the view that the death penalty was inherently unconstitutional, because it was a 'cruel and unusual punishment'. In the words of Justice Brennan:

> Death is today an unusually severe punishment, unusual in its pain, in its finality, and in its enormity. No other existing punishment is comparable to death in terms of physical and mental suffering . . . Since the discontinuance of flogging as a constitutionally permissible punishment death remains as the only punishment that may involve the conscious infliction of physical pain. In addition, we know that mental pain is an inseparable part of our practice of punishing criminals by death, for the prospect of pending execution exacts a frightful toll during the inevitable long wait between the imposition of sentence and the actual infliction of death.

Justice Brennan concluded:

> Today death is a uniquely and unusually severe punishment. When examined by the principles applicable under the Cruel and Unusual Punishments Clause, death stands condemned as fatally offensive to human dignity. The punishment of death is therefore 'cruel and unusual,' and the States may no longer inflict it as a punishment for crimes. Rather than kill an arbitrary handful of criminals each year, the States will confine them in prison.

Three justices, however, White, Stewart and Douglas, held that the death penalty *as currently operated* was unconstitutional. Their objections centred on the arbitrary and discriminatory nature of the judicial processes involved. The discriminatory effect of state laws was described by Justice Thurgood Marshall:

> A total of 3,859 persons have been executed since 1930, of whom 1,751 were white and 2,066 were Negro. Of the executions, 3,334 were for murder; 1,664 of the executed murderers were white and 1,630 were Negro; 455 persons, including 48 whites and 405 Negroes were executed for rape. It is immediately apparent that Negroes were executed far more often than whites in proportion to their percentage of the population.

The Court found that the states that provided for capital punishment gave juries broad discretion to decide whether or not to impose the death penalty, making it an arbitrary procedure. The death penalty was therefore invalidated in those states and by implication in federal cases also. Even before the *Furman* decision there had been a temporary moratorium on executions, and now they were outlawed. But the fact that there was no united majority on the Court meant that *Furman* would not be the last word on the death penalty. It was clear that a majority of the justices would accept the death penalty on certain conditions. Furthermore, a majority of the American public was in favour of capital punishment for murder. In the wake of the *Furman* decision thirty-five states adopted new laws which embodied sentencing procedures that eliminated the discretionary provisions to which some of the Supreme Court justices had objected. So, when in 1976 the Supreme Court was faced with a decision on these newly fashioned capital punishment laws, it restored the death penalty by a majority of seven to two, provided that certain standards were met in sentencing procedures (*Gregg* v. *Georgia*). Marshall and Brennan maintained their view that the death penalty was unconstitutional per se, but the majority upheld the newly revised laws of Georgia, Texas and Florida, which they considered to embody procedures which eliminated arbitrary and capricious decisions by juries. Executions began again in 1977 and have continued since. In 2005 there were thirty-eight states which had statutes enabling capital punishment; sixty people were executed, one of them a woman, nineteen of them in Texas; forty-one were white, nineteen were black; there were 3,314 persons in state and federal prisons under sentence of death.

The United States remains one of the very few liberal democracies that operate the death penalty. However, there has been a gradual movement in the Supreme Court against the use of the death penalty in certain circumstances. In 1988 the Court decided that an offender who committed murder when under the age of sixteen should not be executed (*Thompson* v. *Oklahoma*), but in the following year the Court allowed the execution of a person who was under the age of eighteen when the crime was committed (*Stanford* v. *Kentucky*) and of a mentally retarded offender, because there was no 'national consensus' to the contrary (*Penry* v. *Lynaugh*). But in *Atkins* v. *Virginia*, in 2002, the Court invalidated the execution of a mentally retarded murderer and in 2005, in *Roper* v. *Simmons*, it decided that a person convicted of committing murder in Mississippi when under the age of eighteen should not be executed. A combination of the laws passed by state legislatures, the decisions of the courts and public opinion determines this important area of government policy, with no intervention by president or Congress.

The 'War on Terror' and civil rights

In the aftermath of the terrorist attacks of 11 September 2001 Congress hastily passed the USA Patriot Act, or, to give it its full title, the Uniting and Strengthening America by Providing Appropriate Tools Required to Intercept and Obstruct Terrorism Act of 2001. Largely aimed at aliens, the Act gave the government powers to set up military tribunals to try suspected terrorists, with no appeals from their verdicts; to arrest suspects and hold them indefinitely, although they had to be charged within seven days; to listen in on conversations between lawyers and clients in detention; to obtain the library and medical records of suspects; to intercept telephone and internet communications; to search premises without a warrant; and to use other measures not normally acceptable by the courts. The legislation was renewed in 2006, and a number of the measures it contained were made permanent.

The atrocities perpetrated in September 2001 had far-reaching consequences for almost every aspect of American life; not least for the rights of American citizens and foreigners held in American custody. The war in Afghanistan led to the taking of many prisoners suspected of links with al-Qaeda; similarly the war in Iraq resulted in the incarceration of 'insurgents'; at home the fear of further terrorist attacks provoked actions by the administration and by Congress to try to prevent them. The impact of these events, both on a society proud of its record on civil rights and upon international opinion, was profound. This story will not be over for a long time to come, but we can examine what happened in the first four years following '9/11'.

The taking of hundreds of prisoners in Afghanistan who were Taliban fighters or might be members of al-Qaeda and might have information which could lead to the capture of Osama bin Laden or other leaders of the organisation presented the United States authorities with a problem. If these men had information, how best to interrogate them, and once interrogated should they be set free, perhaps to commit further terrorist acts? Normally prisoners of war are interned in camps for the duration of hostilities where they should be treated in accordance with the Geneva Convention which prescribes the conditions under which prisoners may be kept and the way in which the 'Detaining Power' must treat them. In particular, the convention lays down the following rules concerning the treatment of prisoners of war:

> Every prisoner of war, when questioned on the subject, is bound to give only his surname, first names and rank, date of birth, and army, regimental, personal or serial number, or failing this, equivalent information.

No physical or mental torture, nor any other form of coercion, may be inflicted on prisoners of war to secure from them information of any kind whatever. Prisoners of war who refuse to answer may not be threatened, insulted, or exposed to any unpleasant or disadvantageous treatment of any kind.

Prisoners of war shall be quartered under conditions as favourable as those for the forces of the Detaining Power who are billeted in the same area. The said conditions shall make allowance for the habits and customs of the prisoners and shall in no case be prejudicial to their health.

However, the 'War on Terror' proclaimed by President George W. Bush was seen by his administration to be very different from a normal war, and the status of prisoners was therefore also different. Ari Fleischer, the White House Press Secretary, stated that the prisoners 'are not and will not be considered POWs'. He explained the administration's view as follows:

Under Article 4 of the Geneva Convention . . . Taliban detainees are not entitled to POW status. To qualify as POWs under Article 4, Al Qaeda and Taliban detainees would have to have satisfied four conditions: They would have to be part of a military hierarchy; they would have to have worn uniforms or other distinctive signs visible at a distance; they would have to have carried arms openly; and they would have to have conducted their military operations in accordance with the laws and customs of war.

The Taliban have not effectively distinguished themselves from the civilian population of Afghanistan. Moreover, they have not conducted their operations in accordance with the laws and customs of war. Instead, they have knowingly adopted and provided support to the unlawful terrorist objectives of the Al Qaeda.

Al Qaeda is an international terrorist group and cannot be considered a state party to the Geneva Convention. Its members, therefore, are not covered by the Geneva Convention, and are not entitled to POW status under the treaty.

The prisoners were therefore classified as 'enemy combatants', and a special camp was set up at the US naval base at Guantánamo Bay on the island of Cuba. The treatment of prisoners there did not fit the conditions normally accorded prisoners of war, and pictures and press reports of prisoners in orange uniforms, housed in individual cages, being transported on stretcher trolleys, being made to kneel by guards, shocked many people in the United States and around the world. The prisoners were of many nationalities, and efforts were made by the British and other governments to obtain the release of their nationals, with only partial success. Other individuals suspected of links to al-Qaeda were arrested, including some with American citizenship and held in military prisons on American soil. The legality of these detentions, without trial, for potentially unlimited periods, provoked many legal

challenges. Federal District Court Judges around the country gave conflicting rulings about the procedures that were constitutionally acceptable for
dealing with these cases. In 2002 one Federal Judge, Robert G. Doumar,
ruled that a prisoner being held incommunicado in a naval prison in Norfolk,
Virginia, should be given access to a lawyer with a view to entering a plea for
a writ of habeas corpus. Judge Doumar said that 'fair play and fundamental
justice require it', pointing out that the government 'could not cite one case
where a prisoner of any variety within the jurisdiction of a United States
District Court, was held incommunicado and indefinitely.' The prisoner concerned was Yaser Esam Hamdi, holding dual American and Saudi Arabian
citizenship, who had been captured in Afghanistan, allegedly a member of the
Taliban. He had been sent to Guantánamo Bay, but transferred to the naval
prison in Virginia when his American citizenship was established. However,
Judge Doumar's decision was overruled by the Federal Appeals Court for the
Fourth Circuit. The Chief Judge of the Appeals Court held that 'the federal
courts have many strengths, but the conduct of combat operations has been
left to others. The executive is best prepared to exercise the military judgment attending the capture of alleged combatants . . . it is the President who
has been charged to use force against those "nations, organization or persons
he determines" were responsible for the September 11 terrorist attacks.'

The *Hamdi Case* reached the Supreme Court in 2004 (*Hamdi* v. *Rumsfeld*).
The Court held that citizens detained by the government on the grounds of
being enemy combatants must receive an opportunity to 'rebut the government's factual assertions before a neutral decision-maker'. Justice Sandra
Day O'Connor stated:

> History and common sense teach us that an unchecked system of deten-
> tion carries the potential to become a means for oppression and abuse
> of others who do not present that sort of threat . . . We reaffirm today
> the fundamental nature of a citizen's right to be free from involuntary
> confinement by his own government without the due process of law.

Thus the Court rejected the argument that, in time of war, the executive
branch of government could be both prosecutor and judge, incarcerating
citizens without trial, incommunicado and indefinitely, without the intervention of the judiciary. As a result of this decision, after three years' detention
without having been charged with any offence, Hamdi reached an agreement
with the US government that he would be released, on condition that he returned to Saudi Arabia and renounced his American citizenship. Another US
citizen, José Padilla, was arrested in Chicago in 2002 suspected of intending
to carry out a terrorist attack in the United States. He was detained without
charge as an 'enemy combatant' in the same naval prison as Hamdi. After
the *Hamdi* decision of the Supreme Court he was charged with 'conspiracy to
murder, kidnap, and maim people overseas' and in May 2006 was still await-
ing trial.

A potentially more difficult problem arises in the case of the status of those prisoners, not American citizens, who are being held at Guantánamo Bay, which is not on American soil. In a treaty of 1903 Cuba gave the United States a perpetual lease over the base and 'full jurisdiction' over it, although the ultimate sovereignty of Cuba continued to be recognised. In 2004, in the case of *Rasul* v. *Bush* the Supreme Court handed down another significant decision. By a majority of six to three the Court held that the prisoners in the Guantánamo Bay camp came under the jurisdiction of the United States courts, irrespective of their nationality. (Shafiq Rasul, a British citizen, had been transferred to Britain and released before the Supreme Court decided the case.) The majority opinion, written by Justice Stevens, stated that 'The fact that petitioners are being held in military custody is immaterial.' Thus the Court opened the door to the possibilty of hundreds of habeas corpus petitions from the Guantánamo prisoners. Although there was no way of knowing what the consequences would be for individual prisoners, they were presumably entitled to be heard in open court to challenge the accusations made against them. However, the situation was immediately complicated by legislation passed by Congress shortly after the Court's decision in *Rasul* v. *Bush*. The Detainee Treatment Act, 2005, was a compromise between those Republicans who wish to outlaw torture in American prison camps, and those who want to prevent the courts from reviewing the right of the government to hold enemy combatants without trial. The Act provided that:

> No court, justice, or judge shall have jurisdiction to hear or consider an application for a writ of *habeas corpus* filed by or on behalf of an alien detained by the Department of Defense at Guantanamo Bay, Cuba; or any other action against the United States or its agents relating to any aspect of the detention by the Department of Defense of an alien at Guantanamo Bay, Cuba.

As a result, hundreds of habeus corpus applications that had been submitted by prisoners were held up. Nevertheless, the Supreme Court agreed to hear the case of *Hamdan* v. *Rumsfeld* involving the detention of an alleged aide to Osama bin Laden, and its decision was handed down in June 2006. When denying the application of the Geneva Convention to the detainees, President Bush had set up a system of military commissions to try them for alleged offences. He had done so on his authority as commander-in-chief, without consulting Congress. The procedures to be adopted by the commissions would be laid down by the president without adhering to the normal rules of procedure of civil or military courts. In its decision, by a five-to-three majority, the Court ruled that the military commissions were illegal because they violated both federal law and the Geneva Convention. 'The Executive must comply with the prevailing rule of law,' the Court stated. Justice Breyer in a concurring opinion said:

> The Court's conclusion ultimately rests upon a single ground: Congress has not issued the Executive a 'blank check.' Indeed, Congress has denied

the President the legislative authority to create military commissions of the kind at issue here. Nothing prevents the President from returning to Congress to seek the authority he believes necessary.

Within days the Bush Administration accepted the Court's opinion that members of al-Qaeda are protected by the Geneva Convention. However, this did not mean that the prisoners would be released, and the Administration immediately began to urge Congress to pass legislation that would narrowly define the rights granted to detainees under the Convention. The debate on this issue promised to be protracted, but the setback to the arbitrary exercise of power by the president was clear.

Hurricane Katrina

On Monday 29 August 2005 a Category 3 hurricane struck the coast of Louisiana. The city of New Orleans was in its path and because much of the city is below sea level, protected by 'levees', banks of earth and stone, when the levees were breached flood waters poured into the city. Hurricane Katrina caused 1,326 deaths, nearly all in Louisiana. More than 700,000 people were displaced and an estimated 300,000 homes were destroyed or damaged in Louisiana, Mississippi and Alabama. New Orleans lost its electricity supply, communications failed, roads and bridges were destroyed and law and order broke down. The disaster affected over 90,000 square miles of the Gulf Coast area. The effects of Hurricane Katrina are important, not just because of what happened to the people of the Gulf Coast, but because they illustrate important political and governmental problems that arise from the system of federalism, the divided responsibilities of the federal, state and local authorities and the inherent difficulties of coordinating them. In a country as rich and powerful as the United States, for a number of reasons, the political system failed to cope with a situation, certainly extremely difficult, but one which clearly should have been handled more competently than it was.

Hurricanes are not new to the Gulf Coast. Every year during the season hurricanes come up from the Caribbean, and sophisticated tracking systems have been evolved to give as much warning as possible to the threatened population and to the emergency services. Over many years over one hundred federal government agencies had been established to deal with various aspects of natural emergencies and state and local authorities created their own organisations. The development of nuclear power added further concerns about the need to cope with disaster situations. However, in the 1960s and 1970s a series of strong hurricanes and two earthquakes led President Carter in 1979 to bring these federal agencies together by creating an independent agency, the Federal Emergency Management Agency (FEMA). The terrorist attacks of 11 September 2001 brought new responsibilities to the Agency to prepare for, and respond to, disastrous events. In 2003 FEMA was incorporated into the newly established Department of Homeland Security (DHS). FEMA's Director was Michael D. Brown and shortly after the reorganisation, according to the *Washington Post*, he warned the then Secretary of Homeland Security, Tom Ridge, that the result would be 'an ineffective and uncoordinated response' to a terrorist attack or a natural disaster. The problems of creating a new department, incorporating existing organisations such as FEMA, which had been independent and had had its own budget, resulted in 'turf wars' and personality clashes that proved to be a disaster in themselves. Before being absorbed into the Department of Homeland Security the Director of FEMA had reported directly to the president on disaster situations; now it was up to the Secretary of DHS to determine the way in which situations were handled. Furthermore the new emphasis on the 'War on Terror' distracted attention and funds from planning for natural disasters. As well as the battles going on within the DHS there were interdepartmental fights between the Department and the Department of Health and Human Services concerning the location and control of the teams responsible for providing emergency medical services.

There were several days warning of the approach of Hurricane Katrina, although the exact path of a hurricane is never certain. The responsibility for the evacuation of the endangered population lay with state and local authorities who were required to activate their emergency plans as a prerequisite to requesting federal assistance. Mayor Nagin of New Orleans issued an evacuation order on Sunday when it was feared that the city might be struck by a Category 5 hurricane. A high proportion of the population of the city left, but many chose to stay and others were unable to leave, because they did not have cars or were disabled or elderly. When the flooding began many refugees went for shelter to the Superdome, a large football stadium, and later to a huge convention centre in the city on higher ground. However, the Superdome soon became overcrowded, without food supplies or air-conditioning. The *New York Times* reported:

> At the convention center, food and water grew scarce. Dead bodies sagged in wheelchairs. Residents reported hearing burst of sporadic gunfire. A number of city police officers walked off their jobs in despair ... 'The tourists are walking around there and as soon as these individuals see them, they're being preyed upon,' said P. Edwin Compass III, superintendent of police. 'They are beating, they are raping them in the streets.'

FEMA aid workers had to leave the Superdome because of the lawless conditions. The poor and the black suffered much more than the affluent, and it took a long while for effective relief to arrive.

The plan had been to set up command centres to deal with the emergency, combining federal, state and local resources; this was achieved in Mississippi and Alabama, but was never fully implemented in Louisiana. Relations between federal and state officials in Louisiana were bad. The Governor of Louisiana blamed FEMA; the Mayor of New Orleans blamed the state and federal authorities; FEMA officials blamed Louisiana for shortcomings. The lack of coordination between federal departments and with the National Guard exacerbated the problem. In 2006 a report by the Inspector General of the Department of Homeland Security stated that:

> Some FEMA officials expressed frustration at the requirement for approval by the Secretary of Defense before Department of Defense resources could be used in support of a domestic incident response. Officials indicated the Department of Defense approval process sometimes required 24 to 48 hours, creating delays for life saving and life sustaining missions. For example, on the evening of August 28, 2005, FEMA requested Department of Defense assistance to airlift eight California swift water rescue task forces to Louisiana. Because the Secretary of Defense must approve such requests, the order approving the airlift was not signed until August 30, 2005, and the task forces did not begin water rescue operations in Louisiana until August 31, 2005.

The *Washington Post* reported that the National Disaster Medical team 'was summoned late, then sent to Texas instead of Louisiana, then parked in Baton Rouge for a week while New Orleans suffered. When the team was finally sent to the disaster zone, it was immediately overwhelmed'. The National Guard and federal troops were eventually deployed to restore order and to make relief work possible, but only after a dispute between the Governor of Louisiana and President Bush about their use. The report of the DHS Inspector General issued in March 2006 stated: 'The federal government, in particular the Federal Emergency Management Agency, received widespread criticism for a slow and ineffective response to Hurricane Katrina. Much of the criticism is warranted.' The report continued: 'the magnitude of the storm and its catastrophic effects completely overwhelmed FEMA's disaster response system and resources, and those of state and local governments. In addition, differences in disaster response and emergency management capabilities across states resulted in varied levels of response success.'

Although the magnitude of the disaster that the government had to cope with should not be underestimated, it is clear that the complexity of the federal administrative structure, the rivalries between federal agencies and the difficulties of coordinating the actions of the differing levels of government contributed to what one Congressman, Bill Pascrell, called 'the chilling consequences of these deficiencies.'

Policy-making in America

Although a set of case studies such as those presented in this chapter can never be wholly representative of the way in which decisions are made in a political system, nevertheless they do illustrate a number of the distinctive characteristics of American political life. First, there is no single channel through which decisions are made. In many countries it is clear that for important decisions there is only one accepted route – a single person, a single group, a single party – and that attempts to get decisions taken by any other route will fail, sometimes with serious consequences for those who try. In the United States there are elite groups who play an important role in the way decisions are taken, but there is no single power elite. Important decisions can be made by the Congress, or by the president, or the judiciary; they can be made at the level of the federal government, or at state level. Nor is it the case that each of these institutions is internally coherent; there are warring groups within each branch of the government, and furthermore the branches of government battle against each other. Each branch has different constitutional powers and, most importantly, different procedures through which they must act.

Second, the processes of decision-making are almost always deeply pluralistic, involving a number of different groups, each pursuing their interests by whatever seems to them to be the most fruitful route. Groups choose to fight where they can hope to win, and if thwarted they will move the focus of their actions from one arena to another, from the Congress to the president, from the legislature to the judiciary, from the federal government to the states. Although the federal system can be a cause of deadlocks in the decision-making process, it has the advantage of allowing the states to pursue policies which the federal government rejects. An example is stem cell research using human embryos, which many scientists believe can lead to the cure or prevention of many diseases. This process is deeply controversial, particularly with Christian groups who see it as involving the murder of the embryo. Because of the opposition to this type of research President Bush has only allowed the use of federal funds for a very limited range of research; congressional leaders have promoted legislation to enable federal funds to be used more widely, but President Bush has threatened to veto any such legislation. However, a small number of states, including Connecticut, have passed their own legislation to provide state funding for stem cell research, and others are considering doing so. The federal structure therefore allows the states to follow their own policies and in so doing to put pressure on the federal government to follow suit. Another rather different example is policy on same-sex marriage. Marriage is a matter for state law, and federal legislation on the subject could be ruled unconstitutional. President Bush has therefore been urging Congress to pass a constitutional amendment banning same-sex marriage, but so far without success. However, a large number of states have amended their own constitutions or passed laws banning same-sex marriages, and a handful of states have made them, or civil unions, lawful.

The fragmentation of legal authority in the Constitution results in a political system with multiple points of access, making it possible for pressure groups to pursue their interests through numerous channels. The policy outcomes are inevitably compromises, sometimes the lowest common denominator, and often deadlock. America undoubtedly has the most democratic system of government in the world, but there is a price to be paid. The system is constructed in a way that makes for the fullest representation of the interests involved, but gives little room for the exercise of leadership in any sphere of policy, with the exception of military power. Yet the social, economic and diplomatic problems that face America demand continuing and effective leadership. The challenge for the American political system in the twenty-first century lies in the need to moderate the influence of pluralism, and to devise a means of addressing those problems.

Further reading

Epstein, L. and Kobylka, J.E. (1992) *The Supreme Court and Legal Change: Abortion and the Death Penalty*, Chapel Hill, NC: University of North Carolina Press.
McKay, D., Houghton, D. and Wroe, A. (2002) *Controversies in American Politics and Society*, Oxford: Blackwell.
Peele, G., Bailey, C.J., Cain, B. and Peters, B.G. (eds) (2002) *Developments in American Politics 4*, Basingstoke: Palgrave.

Websites

The American Immigration Law Foundation: www.alf.org
National Immigration Law Center: http://nilc.org
Department of Homeland Security, Office of the Inspector General: A Performance Review of FEMA's Disaster Management Activities in Response to Hurricane Katrina: http://www.npr.org/documents/2006/apr/katrina/dhsreport.pdf
Death Penalty Information Center: www.deathpenaltyinfo.org
Global Security.org: www.globalsecurity.org/military/facility/guantanamo-bay_x-ray.htm

12 The making of American foreign policy

The power of the president in foreign affairs, combining the roles of national leader, chief diplomat and commander-in-chief, is the major factor that distinguishes the making of foreign policy from the domestic policy process. But the president's power is by no means unrestrained. The Constitution provides for the ratification of treaties by the Senate and for the declaration of war by Congress, and these provisions retain significance, even though presidents since Franklin Roosevelt have found ways to circumvent them. Congress has the final say over finance, and can legislate to determine policies in the field of foreign affairs if it wishes. The president can, in certain circumstances, take decisive action in foreign policy but, though freer to act than in the domestic sphere, is not wholly free from pluralistic pressures in this field, particularly when, as in trade policy, it is necessary to get the approval of Congress. Thus, since the Second World War, there has been a long list of presidential initiatives in the use of American forces abroad, involving differing degrees of action independent of Congress. These situations provide a sharp contrast to the problems presidents have faced in the attempt to regulate America's trade relations with foreign nations.

During the nineteenth century the United States was hardly involved in world affairs outside the Western hemisphere. This was partly the result of a natural isolationism, a wish to remain aloof from the 'decadent' politics of Europe, but it was also because the United States was engaged in a great imperial adventure to acquire the entire American continent stretching from the Appalachians to the Pacific. However, the Americans were concerned from the beginning of the Union to prevent incursions into any part of the Americas, and President Monroe enunciated the Monroe Doctrine in 1823 stating that 'the American continents, by the free and independent condition which they have assumed and maintain, are henceforth not to be considered as subjects for future colonization by any European powers.' However, the ability of the United States to engage in territorial expansion and at the same time to 'guarantee' the integrity of the whole hemisphere was really dependent on the existence of the British Navy. The United States did not become a significant naval power until the beginning of the twentieth century. Nevertheless, the right of the United States itself to intervene in the internal politics of foreign states in the Western hemisphere was asserted by President Theodore Roosevelt in 1904. This was the *ex post facto* justification of the Spanish–American war of 1898, resulting in the acquisition of the Philippines, Puerto Rico and Guam, the bringing of Cuba under US protection and incidentally the annexation of Hawaii.

The determination to remain aloof from European political squabbles continued until 1917, when America reluctantly entered the First World War, largely as a result of German submarine warfare against American merchant shipping and Allied ships in which Americans were killed. However, isolationism remained a potent force in American politics and after the war the Senate refused to ratify the Treaty of Versailles, although President Woodrow Wilson had been its chief architect. As a result the United States did not become a member of the League of Nations, a considerable contribution to the ineffectual nature of that body. Isolationism remained strong in Congress and among influential pressure groups during the inter-war period; three Neutrality Acts were passed, the last of which, in 1937, forbad the export of arms or ammunition to foreign nations at war with each other, and prohibited the arming of American merchant ships. It was not until the Japanese bombed Pearl Harbour in December 1941 that the United States entered the Second World War.

Although isolationist voices were to be heard after the end of the Second World War and still are today, an isolationist foreign policy could no longer be sustained. President Franklin Roosevelt, along with Churchill and Stalin, inspired the establishment of the United Nations, whose Charter was drafted at the San Francisco conference and signed in June 1945, two months after the death of Roosevelt. But the American commitment to an internationalist foreign policy was also assured by the circumstances of the post-war period. The fear of communism, long a potent force in America, was reinforced by the Soviet takeover of Eastern Europe and the blockade of West Berlin in 1948. American troops were to remain in Europe and Japan and in bases around the world for the foreseeable future. The build-up of nuclear weapons became a top priority. Furthermore, the United States played a decisive role in the creation of Israel by the United Nations in 1948. The continuing American support of Israel, in the face of the hostility of Arab states and other Muslim countries, laid the foundation for the present-day involvement in the Middle East and became a central element in the neoconservative approach to foreign policy that would be so important in the presidency of George W. Bush.

One of the consequences of the relative decline of isolationism and the continued role of the armed forces of the United States around the world has been the increased significance of the Department of Defense in the administration. The Department of State, the American ministry of foreign affairs, was formerly the department which formulated foreign policy, but since the Second World War, and particularly during conflicts such as the Vietnam War and the wars in Iraq, the Department of Defense has challenged its position. Traditionally Americans were suspicious of a standing army and of the power of the military, as evidenced by President Eisenhower's warning about the dangers of the 'military-industrial complex'. In 2004, however, the defence budget of the federal government totalled $455.9 billion, representing 18.4 per cent of federal government expenditures and nearly 4 per cent of the American gross national income. In the lead-up to the Iraq conflict in 2002 Donald Rumsfeld, the Secretary of Defense, eclipsed the Secretary of State, Colin Powell, in the formulation of foreign policy, and the President's National Security Adviser in the White House, Condoleezza Rice, for whatever reason does not seem to have moderated Rumsfeld's influence on the President. Let us turn then to the history of the development of American power and the roles of the various actors in the making of foreign policy.

Korea and Vietnam

In 1950, President Harry S. Truman committed United States troops to the support of South Korea without consulting Congress. In 1945 Korea had been divided between the communist regime north of the 38th parallel of latitude and a regime supported by the United States south of that line. With the approval of Stalin, on 25 June 1950 in a surprise move the North Korean army moved across the 38th parallel in force, pushing back the much weaker South Korean forces. Truman, who was strongly committed to resisting Soviet expansion, chose to go to the United Nations for its consent to the use of military force, rather than to the United States Congress. Having won UN approval, he immediately despatched American troops to the Korean peninsula. The Chinese intervened to support North Korea; fifteen countries took some part in the UN action in support of the Americans. A cease fire was negotiated and hostilities ceased in July 1953, restoring the dividing line between North and South essentially where it had been before the war began. It has been estimated that more than 2 million people were killed, including more than 50,000 Americans. Truman's failure to obtain congressional approval for military action drew heavy criticism, and earned the sobriquet 'Truman's War' for the action.

Unlike the Korean War the war in Vietnam did not begin with a sudden surprise attack. Vietnam had been part of the French colonial regime in Indochina. After the defeat of the French by communist insurgents at Dien Bien Phu in 1954, the 'temporary' division of Vietnam into northern and southern zones was decided on at the Geneva Conference of that year. However, the intended unification of the country after free elections did not take place; in the North the communist government of Ho Chi Minh was established and in the South an American-backed regime resisted his attempts to take over. In November 1955 President Dwight D. Eisenhower sent a Military Assistance

Advisory Group to help train the army of South Vietnam. The presence of American 'advisers' marked the beginning of involvement in Vietnam which was to last until the withdrawal of American troops in 1973.

As the conflict between the North and the South intensified, in 1961 President John F. Kennedy increased the number of advisers by sending 400 'Green Berets' to Vietnam and, by the time of his assassination in 1963, he had despatched a total of 16,000 troops there, but still only under the pretence that they were 'advisers'. However, his successor, Lyndon B. Johnson, changed the whole nature of the conflict. In 1965 he ordered American combat units into South Vietnam and also ordered the bombing of targets in North Vietnam. Although no congressional declaration of war was sought, Johnson did ask Congress to pass the Gulf of Tonkin Resolution, which they duly did in 1964. This Resolution was based on the highly contentious assertion that a US warship had been attacked in the Gulf of Tonkin by North Korean forces. The resolution provided that Congress 'approves and supports the determination of the President, as Commander in Chief, to take all necessary measures to repel any armed attack against the forces of the United States and to prevent further aggression.' On the basis of this vague grant of authority Johnson gradually increased the number of American troops in Vietnam until in August 1966 there were 429,000 American servicemen there. The exercise of presidential power as commander-in-chief reached its peak when President Richard Nixon ordered the invasion of Cambodia in 1970 and of Laos in 1971, both neutral states. Arthur M. Schlesinger wrote:

> With Nixon as with Johnson, the central role for Congress in foreign affairs was to provide aid and comfort to the Commander in Chief. He never sought its advice before major initiatives, and acknowledged its existence afterwards mainly by inviting members of Congress to hear Henry Kissinger tell them in mass briefings what they had already read, if less stylishly expressed, in the newspapers.

Congress began to move against Nixon's conduct of the war in the way most open to a legislature – by the withholding of funds. The Resolution on the War in Cambodia prohibited the use of public funds 'to finance combat activities . . . over or from off the shores of North Vietnam, South Vietnam, Laos or Cambodia'. This was followed by the War Powers Resolution of 1973, which forbad the president to commit troops to hostilities, except after a declaration of war, under specific statutory authorisation from Congress or in a national emergency created by an attack on the United States or its possessions. Even in case of a national emergency the president is required to consult with Congress 'in every possible instance'. The practicability of this assertion of the power of the legislature was soon put in question by President Ford's action in retaking the *Mayaguez*. In 1975, Khmer Rouge soldiers seized the *Mayaguez*, a US merchant ship. President Ford responded by ordering air strikes on Cambodian oil installations and the landing of troops at Koh Tang Island. The ship was seized and the crew repatriated. As we shall see the War Powers Resolution has generally been ignored by American presidents when they considered military action to be necessary.

Police actions

The wars in Korea and Vietnam, even though characterised by presidential actions that were taken without congressional approval or prior knowledge, were protracted and necessarily conducted in a blaze of publicity. A number of military adventures, however, were planned and executed in secrecy. These were essentially attempts to control the course of events in an area, the Caribbean and Central America, that Americans consider to be their 'own back yard'.

The United States had intervened a number of times in the politics of the Dominican Republic, the eastern part of the island of Hispaniola, during the twentieth century. In 1965 political instability in the Republic led President Lyndon Johnson to fear that there was danger of a communist takeover and he despatched 22,000 troops there. Initially he claimed that he acted to protect the lives of American citizens, but it became clear that the real reason was to prevent a 'Cuban-style' revolution. A similar situation developed on the island of Grenada in 1983 when an avowedly communist leader seized power. President Ronald Reagan ordered an invasion of the island. Although Grenada was a member of the Commonwealth, with a British Governor-General, Reagan did not even consult his good friend Margaret Thatcher, prime minister of the United Kingdom, before the invasion. Because of the importance of the Panama Canal, strategically and to American trade, the United States has long had an interest in the internal politics of Panama and was instrumental in Panama gaining its independence from Colombia in 1903. The United States was in charge of the administration of the Canal Zone, but it had been agreed that this arrangement would come to an end in 1989. The rise of a dictator, General Manuel Noriega, thought to have been involved in drug-trafficking and possibly not going to cooperate with the United States, represented a threat to American interests in this vital strategic facility. President Bush ordered 25,000 American troops into Panama. Noriega sought asylum in the Vatican Embassy, but was arrested by the Americans and sentenced to a long term of imprisonment.

Haiti, the western part of Hispaniola, has also been an object of American attention over its tumultuous history; it was under American occupation from 1915 to 1934. In 1994 a repressive military regime incurred the wrath of the United Nations Security Council, which authorised member states to use all necessary means to facilitate the departure of Haiti's military leadership and to restore the constitutionally elected government to power. President Clinton sent American troops to Haiti to ensure the return of the democratically elected president, Jean-Bertrand Aristide. Whatever the rights and wrongs of each of these interventions they involved presidential actions to maintain American dominance in the area, without seeking the approval of Congress.

Secret operations

The policies described so far relate to events where the president may have acted without consulting Congress, or precipitated situations by unilateral action. There are, however, some foreign policy acts where it seems that it was assumed by the president, or at least by some of his advisers, that perhaps the truth would never come out. Such was the disastrous Bay of Pigs adventure in 1961 when a force of Cuban exiles, trained and supplied by the CIA, attempted an invasion of Cuba with the aim of overthrowing the Castro regime. The planning for the operation had begun secretly under President Eisenhower and it was launched under President Kennedy's administration. The invasion was a miserable failure and Kennedy initially denied any involvement. The Iran–Contra affair was a similarly ill-judged operation carried out in secrecy by members of President Reagan's staff. What exactly the president himself knew about the operation was never established. In 1985 the United States government began selling arms to Iran, with the intention of obtaining the release of American hostages taken by Hezbollah in the Lebanon. Although illegal under American law, the operation was approved and conducted by Reagan's closest advisers. To make things worse the proceeds of the arms sales, millions of dollars, were used to finance the activities of the Contra guerrillas in Nicaragua who were fighting against the democratically elected communist government. John Poindexter, the president's National Security Adviser, and Lieutenant-Colonel Oliver North, a member of his staff, conducted the affair in a series of extraordinary operations worthy of a James Bond film; both were convicted, although later the convictions were overturned.

Other secret operations about which presidents may, or may not, have known include attempted assassinations in which the CIA and US government officials were involved. In 1975 a Senate Select Committee chaired by Senator Frank Church (the Church Committee) investigated allegations that the CIA had been implicated in assassinations or attempted assassinations of the leaders of a number of Third World countries – Patrice Lumumba of the Congo, Fidel Castro of Cuba, Rafael Trujillo of the Dominican Republic, Hgo Dinh Diem of South Vietnam and General Rene Schneider of Chile. The Committee concluded that in 1960 two CIA officials were asked by their superiors to assassinate Lumumba and poison was sent to the Congo; Lumumba was later assassinated, but the Committee concluded that there was no evidence that the United States was involved in the killing. As for Castro the Committee reported that:

> United States Government personnel plotted to kill Castro from 1960 to 1965. American underworld figures and Cubans hostile to Castro were

used in these plots, and were provided encouragement and material support by the United States.

Trujillo was shot by Dominican dissidents in 1961, but although 'three pistols and three carbines were furnished by American officials' it was not known if these weapons were used in the killing. The killing of Diem in 1963, the Committee decided, was 'carried out without United States involvement or support'; and, although the United States had supplied financial aid and machine guns to groups plotting a military coup in Chile in 1970, the Committee concluded that there was no evidence of CIA involvement in the assassination of General Schneider. The Committee also reported that it had 'received evidence that ranking Government officials discussed and may have authorized, the establishment within the CIA of a generalized assassination capability.'

As is the case with so many of the secret operations we have discussed, it is impossible to determine how far up the chain of command these activities were known about or initiated. In particular the involvement of the presidents in office at the time remains in doubt. The Church Committee reported that 'the system of executive command and control was so ambiguous that it is difficult to be certain at what levels assassination activity was known and authorized ... Whether or not the respective presidents knew of or authorized the plots, as chief executive officer of the United States, each must bear the ultimate responsibility for the activities of his subordinates.' As a result of these investigations President Gerald Ford issued an Executive Order in 1976 proclaiming a ban on involvement in assassination plots, and both President Carter and President Reagan later issued similar orders. However, the terrorist attacks of 11 September 2001 led to demands that these Executive Orders should be revoked by President George W. Bush or overridden by Congress, so that those responsible for the attacks could be targeted wherever they might be. Indeed in September 2001 Congress passed a wide-ranging measure authorising the president to 'use all necessary and appropriate force against those nations, organizations, or persons he determines planned, authorized, committed, or aided' the terrorist attacks. A Congressional Research Service Report in 2002 expressed the view that this legislation 'might be viewed as sufficient, insofar as U.S. responses to the events of September 11, 2001 are concerned, to encompass actions that might otherwise be prohibited under the assassination ban.'

The Clinton years

The collapse of the Soviet Union in 1991 faced the United States with a completely new world. The Cold War was over; the US was now the sole superpower; there was no obvious threat to America. When President Clinton took office in 1993 there were no clear foreign policy guidelines to follow, so he responded with a series of ad hoc responses to problems as they arose. The Clinton years were a transitional period between the certainties of the Cold

War and the effects that the events of 11 September 2001, in the context of the neoconservative philosophy of a number of members of the administration, had on American foreign policy. One aspect of Clinton's policies that distinguished him from his successor, however, was his determination, as far as possible, to follow a multilateral approach to foreign policy issues, involving collaboration with other like-minded countries, and acting through international institutions, rather than the unilateralist tendencies of the administration under his successor, George W. Bush. However, during six of the eight years of his presidency Clinton was faced with a Republican-controlled Congress, which was more than usually partisan, largely as a result of the leadership in the House of Representatives exercised by the Speaker, Newt Gingrich.

The first foreign policy problem faced by Clinton was really inherited from his predecessor. George H.W. Bush had supported United Nations efforts to assure humanitarian supplies to the people of Somalia. The lawless character of that area meant that humanitarian workers came under attack from the 'warlords' who dominated Somalia. In October 1993 a US-led operation in the capital, Mogadishu, was ambushed and eighteen US soldiers were killed and another seventy-nine were injured. This led to the withdrawal of American troops and the 'Battle of Mogadishu' profoundly affected Clinton's foreign policy. No intervention was undertaken to try to halt the genocide in Rwanda in 1994 and, as we shall see, he was very reluctant to commit ground troops in the Balkans.

Clinton also had to deal with the early terrorist attacks on America and American targets. Only a month after his inauguration a huge truck bomb was exploded in the car park under one of the towers of the World Trade Center, later to be destroyed in the 2001 attack. The bomb killed six people and injured a thousand. A number of people were convicted of planning or carrying out this atrocity, including Sheikh Omar Abdel Rahman, an extremist Sunni Muslim cleric. Also in 1993, an attempted terrorist attack was directed at former President George H.W. Bush, who was to make a speech at Kuwait University; the atack was foiled by the Kuwaitis, who blamed Saddam Hussein, and in June the US launched a retaliatory missile attack on Baghdad. On 7 August 1998, the American embassies in Kenya and Tanzania were attacked, and Osama bin Laden was considered to be responsible. On 20 August, President Clinton ordered cruise missile strikes, code-named Operation Infinite Reach, against a terrorist training camp in Afghanistan and a suspected chemical weapons plant in the Sudan. Just before the end of his presidency, al-Qaeda suicide bombers attacked an American destroyer, the *USS Cole*, in Aden harbour, killing seventeen sailors. Clinton has been criticised for not having done enough to counter the growing threat of al-Qaeda during his presidency. A special unit was set up within the CIA to track bin Laden and plans were made to try to capture him, but never implemented. Neither the Clinton administration nor the new Bush administration before

9/11 was able to develop a coherent plan for reviewing intelligence about potential terrorist attacks or developing a counter-terrorist policy.

The most difficult foreign policy problems faced by President Clinton arose from the break-up of the former Yugoslavia, as successive provinces sought independence from the multi-ethnic federation dominated by Serbia. First Slovenia and Croatia declared independence from Yugoslavia in 1991, and then in the following year a referendum was held in Bosnia and Herzegovina. The Province of Bosnia and Herzegovina was composed of three major ethnic groupings, Serbs who wished to remain part of Yugoslavia, Croats and Bosnian Muslims. The Bosnian Serbs boycotted the referendum and independence was approved by a majority of 98 per cent of those who voted. The declaration of independence in April 1992 resulted in the outbreak of hostilities. A United Nations peace-keeping force was sent to the area, but was never strong enough to keep the peace; a number of atrocities were committed, particularly the massacre of approximately 8,000 Muslim males by the Bosnian Serb army under the command of General Mladić at Srebrenica in July 1995.

During the election campaign of 1992 Clinton said he would, if necessary, use military force to bring humanitarian aid to the citizens of Bosnia and Herzegovina. But when in office he faced considerable opposition, not least by the Pentagon, to military involvement in the Balkans, and he soon made clear that American troops would only be used to enforce a peace agreement when one was achieved, although France, Britain, Canada, Spain and other countries had already contributed troops to the UN peace-keeping force. However, he did authorise the dropping of food and supplies to embattled enclaves in Bosnia by the US Air Force, and US planes took part in enforcing a no-fly zone by the Serbians over Bosnia. Clinton did propose that the US should provide arms for Bosnian Muslims, but this plan was rejected by the European countries. In April 1994 the increasing violence in Bosnia, and the siege of Goräzde, led the British general in command of United Nations peace-keepers in Bosnia, Sir Michael Rose, to request limited air strikes by NATO planes, and Clinton quickly agreed. Frequent changes of policy by the Clinton administration and differences of opinion with the European powers about strategy bedevilled the whole operation. However, President Clinton undertook a vigorous diplomatic operation to achieve an accord between the warring groups, culminating in a meeting of the parties in Dayton, Ohio, in November 1995. Agreement was reached, even though during the process of the negotiations the House of Representatives voted by 243 to 171 to deny the use of funds to send US troops to join a peace-keeping force in Bosnia. Once the agreement was reached President Clinton ordered American troops to Bosnia, and both the Senate and the House gave their approval.

The situation that developed in Kosovo had many similarities to the Bosnian conflict. Kosovo, a province of Serbia, which was then part of the Federal Republic of Yugoslavia, has an overwhelming majority of ethnic Albanians, and a history of demands for independence, strongly resisted by the Serbian and Yugoslav governments. Separatist groups of Albanians agitated for independence, and inter-communal violence occurred during the 1990s. After the Dayton Accord of 1995 a Kosovo Liberation Army was formed and carried out attacks on Serbian security forces and others; the Yugoslav army entered the conflict and there was widespread violence and the movement of refugees on a large scale. NATO attempted to broker a settlement between the Kosovo Albanians and Slobodan Milošević, who became President of Yugoslavia in 1997. However, these attempts failed and NATO began a bombing campaign against Serbia in March 1999, using predominantly American aircraft together with cruise missiles.

The NATO action did not have the sanction of the United Nations, and President Clinton's decision to commit American forces to NATO met strong opposition in Congress. The Senate had voted to support air strikes, but in April the House of Representatives voted 249 to 180 to bar the President from sending ground troops to Yugoslavia without Congressional approval. In a further vote, which was tied, the House also refused to support the NATO air strikes which were taking place against Serbia. The air strikes continued and after some weeks and considerable destruction and loss of life Milošević accepted the entry of NATO troops, under UN control, into Kosovo; American and other troops arrived in June, and Kosovo became in effect a UN protectorate. The *New York Times* summarised the results of Clinton's foreign policy in the Balkans:

> On Bosnia in the early years and then on Kosovo in 1999, the president did shrink from military action while hostilities continued and innocent people died. But the war in Bosnia was settled at an administration-sponsored peace conference in Ohio in 1995, and a few weeks of American bombing persuaded Slobodan Milosevic to give up his assault on Kosovo in 1999. By the time Clinton left office, Bosnia was in the midst of a peaceful recovery, and Milosevic had been deposed from power and was awaiting trial as a war criminal.

The wars in Iraq

In August 1990 Saddam Hussein, President of Iraq, ordered his army to attack neighbouring Kuwait. This small but oil-rich country was quickly overrun and annexed by Iraq. The United Nations passed a number of resolutions condemning the Iraqi occupation, setting a deadline for Iraq to withdraw from Kuwait and authorising the use of force if it did not. The United States played a leading role in the diplomatic manoeuvres at the United Nations and, when Saddam Hussein ignored the demand to withdraw, President George H.W. Bush led a coalition of thirty nations to eject the Iraqis from Kuwait. The American Congress also passed a resolution authorising the use of force, so that, although differing views were held about the real motives for the United States engaging in the war, the legality of the action and the openness of the process were not in doubt. The military superiority of the American-led forces over those of Iraq was overwhelming; the Iraqi army was quickly defeated in Kuwait and in the neighbouring border regions of Iraq itself. It would have been easy for President Bush to order the US forces to continue their drive to Baghdad to depose Saddam Hussein, as a number of his advisers wished. However, Bush decided to adhere to what he considered to be the intention of the United Nations, to free Kuwait, and the troops were halted and withdrawn from the territory of Iraq.

Although the legality of the Gulf War, as it was called, was not in doubt, the political background to the conflict was complex. The politics of oil, the human rights record of Saddam Hussein's regime, a possible challenge to the role of America's ally, Saudi Arabia, and not least Saddam Hussein's hostility to Israel all played a part in the reaction of the Bush administration to the attack on Kuwait. The Gulf War eliminated none of these factors and indeed heightened some of them in the eyes of many interested groups in the United States. The accession of Bill Clinton to the presidency in 1993 masked somewhat the importance of these groups on the American political scene, but they remained very focused in their attitudes towards Iraq and the regime of Saddam Hussein.

An interesting example of the activities of a pressure group on this issue is the behaviour of a neoconservative group called 'The Project for the New American Century'. This group concerned itself with the assertion that Saddam Hussein was developing 'weapons of mass destruction' and if allowed to continue to do so would threaten the stability of the whole of the Middle East. In a letter to President Clinton in January 1998 the group called for a new strategy, arguing that 'That strategy should aim, above all, at the removal of Saddam Hussein's regime from power.' The authors of the letter argued that the process of using United Nations inspectors to determine whether Iraq was developing weapons of mass destruction was ineffective and causing great uncertainty. The letter continued:

> Such uncertainty will, by itself, have a seriously destabilizing effect on the entire Middle East. It hardly needs to be added that if Saddam does acquire the capability to deliver weapons of mass destruction, as he is almost certain to do if we continue along the present course, the safety of American troops in the region, of our friends and allies like Israel and the moderate Arab states, and a significant portion of the world's supply of oil will all be put at hazard. As you have rightly declared, Mr. President, the security of the world in the first part of the 21st century will be determined largely by how we handle this threat.

'Regime change' in Iraq was, therefore, the aim of this group, long before the decision was taken to invade Iraq in 2002, but this was no ordinary pressure group. The letter was signed by Donald Rumsfeld, later to become Secretary of Defense in George W. Bush's administration, and by Paul Wolfowitz, the future Deputy Secretary of Defense. Although he did not sign this letter, Richard B. Cheney, the future Vice-President, was a member of the group, as were John Bolton and Richard Perle. On 11 September 2001 four commercial airliners were hijacked by terrorists. Two were flown into the twin towers of the World Trade Center in New York, killing nearly three thousand people, one crashed into the Pentagon Building, housing the Department of Defense in Virginia, killing 184 people, and the fourth was heading for Washington, DC, when it crashed in Pennsylvania as a result of actions taken by passengers. The terrorists were linked to Osama bin Laden, the leader of al-Qaeda, a group dedicated to the establishment of a radical Islamic regime. Bin Laden was resident in Afghanistan and associated with the Taliban, the group then in power there. In the wake of the public outrage following this atrocity, on 14 September Congress passed a resolution authorising the use of force in Afghanistan. The reaction of the United States was rapid; in collaboration with British forces, attacks on Kabul, the capital of Afghanistan, began in October.

According to Bob Woodward in *Bush at War* both Donald Rumsfeld and Paul Wolfowitz began urging President Bush to include Iraq in the list of targets for military action in the days immediately after the 11 September attacks, although there was no evidence that Saddam Hussein had any connection with the terrorists. Very early it was assumed that the War on Terror would extend beyond Afghanistan. In October 2001 Secretary of Defense Donald Rumsfeld warned his department that action would need to be taken against states harbouring or supporting terrorism. In his speeches President Bush continually linked Iraq with al-Qaeda and terrorism, but above all his administration concentrated on the alleged existence of weapons of mass destruction in Iraq. The United Nations had been conducting inspections in Iraq, attempting to determine whether Saddam Hussein was developing weapons of mass destruction, and he had placed considerable obstacles in their way. However, Hans Blix, the UN's Chief Inspector, later stated that:

> In January 2003, we had performed quite a lot of inspections to sites which were given by intelligence and they had not shown any weapons of mass destruction, so we began to be doubtful . . . among the 700 inspections that we performed, none brought us any evidence of weapons of mass destruction. I warned the Security Council about that.

Attempts were made to gain authorisation from the United Nations to undertake military operations against Iraq, but they failed. Evidence that did not fit the picture the administration wanted to portray was swept aside, and in October 2002 Congress gave Bush full authority to attack Iraq. The assault, in collaboration with the United Kingdom and other nations, began in 2003. The initial military campaign was soon over, as was only to be expected in view of the overwhelming superiority of the United States' weaponry. But then began the process of attempting to pacify Iraq and to establish an effective democratic government. The difficulty of achieving these aims had apparently not been appreciated by those who, rather naively, had assumed that deposing Saddam Hussein was all that would be necessary. Three years after the invasion these aims had still not been achieved and, as the number of American military personnel killed passed 2,500 in June 2006 and continued to climb, George W. Bush's approval rating with the American public fell to 30 per cent, and a majority of Americans who were polled expressed the view that the invasion of Iraq had been a mistake.

How do we explain the whole series of events leading up to the invasion of Iraq? The attack on Afghanistan is understandable in the light of the support it had given to al-Qaeda, but Iraq had not given such support, nor had it weapons of mass destruction. A particularly well-placed pressure group was able to influence a president already disposed towards their point of view by emphasising those points which supported their well-publicised belief in the need to depose Saddam Hussein and rejecting the arguments which threw doubt on their analysis. But the invasion of Iraq was not like the Korean War when American troops were sent within days of the outbreak of hostilities between North Korea and South Korea. The build-up of armed forces in the Gulf took months, and it was necessary to have the support of public opinion. The president was able to carry the majority in Congress with him, and also to obtain popular support for his policy. The acceptance by the public of the alleged link between Saddam Hussein and al-Qaeda is easy to understand because the information they were being given pointed in that direction, and there was little being provided to the contrary. So many elements of the situation fitted in with the beliefs and interests of those at the centre of decision-taking. The importance of oil to America and to Americans is difficult to exaggerate, and both President Bush and Vice-President Cheney had close connections with the oil interests. The threat that Iraq posed to Israel, a country that the United States has strongly supported for nearly sixty years, was a theme that would draw a great deal of public approval. The sense that the Christian world might be under attack from those Muslim extremists wishing to destroy it could tap deep wells within the emotions of that large section of the American population that professes fundamental Christian beliefs. Saddam Hussein's autocratic regime and his undoubted cruelty to large numbers of his own people made the aspiration to establish democracy in Iraq an appealing one. All these elements were to be found in the neoconservative ideology that bound together a number of the members of President Bush's advisers, particularly those in the Department of Defense, which was inevitably central to the formation of policy in the wake of 11 September 2001, and they were shared to a greater or lesser degree by many members of Congress.

The 'Axis of Evil'

In January 2002, in the highly charged atmosphere following the terrorist attacks of the previous September, President George W. Bush delivered his

State of the Union speech to Congress. Having pointed with satisfaction to the rapid defeat of the Taliban in Afghanistan, the President continued:

> Our second goal is to prevent regimes that sponsor terror from threatening America or our friends and allies with weapons of mass destruction. Some of these regimes have been pretty quiet since September the 11th. But we know their true nature. North Korea is a regime arming with missiles and weapons of mass destruction, while starving its citizens.
>
> Iran aggressively pursues these weapons and exports terror, while an unelected few repress the Iranian people's hope for freedom.
>
> Iraq continues to flaunt its hostility toward America and to support terror. The Iraqi regime has plotted to develop anthrax, and nerve gas, and nuclear weapons for over a decade. This is a regime that has already used poison gas to murder thousands of its own citizens – leaving the bodies of mothers huddled over their dead children. This is a regime that agreed to international inspections – then kicked out the inspectors. This is a regime that has something to hide from the civilized world.
>
> States like these, and their terrorist allies, constitute an axis of evil, arming to threaten the peace of the world. By seeking weapons of mass destruction, these regimes pose a grave and growing danger. They could provide these arms to terrorists, giving them the means to match their hatred. They could attack our allies or attempt to blackmail the United States. In any of these cases, the price of indifference would be catastrophic.

Since this speech was made, the United States and its allies have tried to deal with the threat of Iraq, whatever the truth of Bush's statements about the intentions of its government, but the problems of Iran and North Korea remain. Nuclear proliferation lies at the heart of the dilemma facing the United States in dealing with the regimes in these countries to which it has been hostile for decades. North Korea already has nuclear weapons and it is feared that Iran is seeking to develop them. However, nuclear proliferation is not the sole concern, for Israel, India and Pakistan all possess a nuclear capability and these developments have been met with different reactions from American administrations. North Korea, the most hard-line communist regime still in existence, had to be handled very carefully, partly because of the possibility it might actually use its nuclear weapons against South Korea, a close ally of the United States, and partly because of its proximity to China. Iran, however, has been threatened with sanctions, and the Bush administration did not wholly rule out some kind of military strikes against nuclear installations, probably using cruise missiles. However, the experience of the war in Iraq has dented American confidence in this type of military action, and a Gallup poll taken in May 2006 found that only one in three Americans would support military action against Iran. The pressure on the United States to use diplomatic and economic measures to deal with the problem of North Korea and Iran, in collaboration with Europe and China, is considerable.

Cuba and Helms–Burton

The dominant role of the president in the formulation and implementation of foreign policy has always been recognised. We have seen that it has led to accusations of an 'Imperial Presidency', and that there are many examples of presidents committing the United States to armed combat with little or no involvement by the legislative branch. But these are the dramatic decisions to engage in military intervention, such as in Korea, Vietnam, and the Caribbean, or what are intended to be 'short-term' interventions, such as President Clinton's decision to attack terrorist bases with cruise missiles in Afghanistan and Sudan in 1998. Other foreign policy issues, though less dramatic, are more characteristic of the pluralistic nature of the American decision-making process. The history of American policy towards Cuba, situated just 90 miles from the southern tip of Florida, is just such an issue.

The close involvement of the United States with Cuba began in 1898 with the Spanish–American War. The United States was instrumental in obtaining the independence of Cuba from Spain, but effectively transformed the island into an American protectorate, subject to the so-called Platt Amendment of 1901, which gave the United States the right to intervene to preserve Cuban independence and to maintain law and order. The internal government of Cuba, however, was characterised by graft, corruption and social injustice under a succession of presidents and dictators, until Fidel Castro overthrew the dictator Fulgencio Batista in 1958 and established a communist regime. Many Cubans escaped to the United States, settling mainly in Florida, establishing there a community implacably opposed to the Castro regime. In 1961 a group of Cuban exiles, with the support of the CIA, mounted the ill-fated invasion of Cuba at the Bay of Pigs. The close collaboration established between Castro and the government of the Soviet Union led to the Cuban missile crisis of 1962, resulting from the attempt by the Soviet Union to install nuclear missiles on Cuba, a very real threat to the American mainland. The ensuing confrontation between the United States and the Soviet Union brought the world to the brink of nuclear war, averted only when the Soviet Union backed down and diverted the ships carrying the missiles away from Cuba.

As part of its implementation of the communist commitment to the abolition of private property the Castro regime confiscated, without compensation, American-owned sugar mills, petrol refineries and other assets, then valued at $2 billion. In retaliation Congress in 1961 passed the Foreign Assistance Act, which empowered the president to lay an embargo on all trade with Cuba, and President Kennedy duly complied the following year; the embargo has been in force ever since. For many years this had little effect on Cuba, because the Soviet Union heavily subsidised the Castro regime. Cuba traded extensively with the Soviet Union and with the communist countries of Eastern Europe. In 1991, however, the Soviet Union collapsed, and Cuba found itself isolated and facing severe economic difficulties. The American embargo had never attempted to prevent Cuba trading with other countries, and in the difficult situation now facing it, the Castro government decided to try to encourage foreign investment in Cuba, by authorising overseas companies to collaborate with state enterprises in the development of Cuban resources. The enterprises with which they collaborated, and in which they invested their capital, were often based on properties which had been confiscated over thirty years earlier from Americans or from Cubans then living in America. The fact that these foreign companies were profiting from confiscated assets brought together a formidable alliance whose aim was to deter foreign companies from investing in Cuba in this way.

In 1995 the House of Representatives passed a Bill sponsored by Republican Congressman Dan Burton from Indiana. The Bill set out a number of ways in which pressure would be put upon foreign firms trading with Cuba. American visas would be denied to the officers of foreign companies purchasing expropriated properties in Cuba, and Cuban-Americans could sue these foreign companies for damages in United States courts. Senator Jesse Helms, the Republican Chairman of the Foreign Relations Committee, introduced a similar Bill in the Senate. President Clinton made clear his opposition to the Bill, but there were powerful groups pressing for its passage. The Bill had become known as the 'Libertad' Bill, and Cuban exiles protested in Washington and Miami against Clinton's opposition to it. Cuban-Americans are important in the politics of Florida and of New Jersey, states that could influence the outcome of the election of November 1996 that was then looming on the horizon. Cuban pressure groups, such as the Cuban-American National Foundation, exercise considerable influence on Senators and Members of the House. The President's objections centred on the 'extra-territorial' sections of the Bill that would allow foreign corporations to be sued in US courts. This provision would anger nations friendly to the United States, such as Canada and the European countries, who would object to their nationals being subject to American law for activities carried on outside the United States, and with whom the administration had to deal on many other foreign policy issues. There was strong opposition also in the Senate to these extra-territorial provisions.

The potential deadlock over this legislative proposal was ended by an event that occurred in February 1996. Two civilian aircraft operated by 'Brothers to the Rescue', a group of Cuban exiles based in Miami, were shot down by a MiG fighter of the Cuban air force, and four people were killed. The Brothers frequently flew over the Florida Straits looking for refugees attempting to escape by boat to the United States. The Government of Cuba asserted that the planes had entered Cuban air space, but the United States maintained that they were shot down over international waters. In the wake of this incident the Senate quickly approved a radical version of the Helms–Burton Bill, and President Clinton signed the Cuban Liberty and Democratic Solidarity Act into law in March 1996.

The effect upon the international community was immediate. The European Union had been energetically developing trade links with Cuba; Canada and Mexico had companies operating in Cuba. The top executives of a Canadian company were declared ineligible to enter the United States, because it was mining nickel on property confiscated from an American company; a Mexican cement firm quickly agreed to suspend its activities in Cuba. Canada and the European Union protested against the Helms–Burton Act, and began intensive negotiations with the United States in order to get the Act amended. As part of the final negotiations for the passage of the Act, President Clinton had been able to get a clause inserted into the legislation authorising him to suspend that section of the Act which made it possible to sue foreign firms in American courts, if in his opinion to do so was in the national interest and would be likely to expedite a transition to democracy in Cuba. The suspension could be for a period of up to six months, and could be renewed. In January 1998 the President suspended this section for the fourth time in succession, drawing protests from Senator Helms about the failure of the Administration to implement the law.

There have been many attempts to repeal the Helms–Burton Act on the grounds that it has not brought down Castro's government and that more might be achieved by closer relationships with Cuba than by shunning it. Many business and agricultural groups oppose the policy because they lose the opportunity to trade with Cuba. In 2000 these groups had some success with the passage of the Trade Sanctions and Reform Export Enhancement Act which allowed the sale of agricultural products to Cuba on a cash basis. However, in general the prohibition on travel to, and trade with, Cuba remains in force, including the prohibition on the import of Cuban cigars, which some Americans find hard to bear. The 'extra-territorial' intent of Helms–Burton was illustrated in 2006 when the US Treasury ordered the Sheraton Hotel in Mexico City to evict a number of Cuban guests at the hotel who were participating in a conference on trade between the US and Cuba. The hotel complied.

International trade policy: CAFTA

The making of policy regarding trade with other nations is, perhaps, the most complex area of government action in American politics. It involves complicated negotiations with other governments and with international organisations. The foreign governments will themselves be very divided in their interests and in their attitudes towards the United States: Europe, China, Japan, the developing countries. Internally, the cross-cutting divisions between contending economic groups affected by trade policy are endless; producers versus consumers, workers versus employers, industry versus agriculture, one agricultural product versus another product, one industry versus another industry, large business versus small business. Overlaid on this complexity is a thick soup of ideological attitudes: free trade versus protectionism, internationalism versus isolationism, environmental concerns, anti-globalisation, and concern with human rights. Pluralism can go no further, yet the president and the administration must attempt to pick their way through this thicket, with the knowledge that in international trade policy, unlike the sphere of military action, every aspect of the outcome will be subject to the approval of Congress. In principle, successive administrations have been committed to a free trade policy, but in practice they come up against the deeply entrenched attitudes of those who consider that they will be adversely affected by this policy, or those who consider it to be morally indefensible.

The effects of this context of policy-making can be seen in the creation of the North American Free Trade Agreement (NAFTA), which was approved by Congress in 1993. This established a free trade area covering Mexico, the United States and Canada; in principle it provided for the abolition of tariffs and trade barriers between these three countries, but in practice President Clinton had to make so many concessions to different groups of American producers in order to get the necessary legislation through Congress that the actual result was far from the creation of a genuine free trade area. This issue created internal divisions within both political parties, and in order to win the votes in Congress President Clinton had to rely on the support of Republicans, as a majority of his own party were opposed to the Agreement. An extraordinary coalition formed in opposition to the passage of the legislation. The democratic leadership in the House of Representatives was joined by a most unusual alliance of pressure groups. David Houghton describes it thus:

> The labour unions were especially determined to defeat the agreement . . . The congressional black caucus and former Democratic Party candidate Jesse Jackson had similar misgivings . . . The conservative journalist and Reform Party candidate Pat Buchanan, the consumer advocate and Green Party candidate Ralf Nader and the Reform Party presidential candidate and Texan billionaire Ross Perot all weighed in against NAFTA.

The negotiations for NAFTA had started under President Bush and there was much more support for the agreement among industrial and commercial interests. Clinton had to rely therefore on the support of Republicans to pass the measure; in the event the vote in the Senate was thirty-four Republicans and twenty-seven Democrats for the agreement, and ten Republicans and twenty-eight Democrats against; in the House there was a similar pattern – 132 Republicans and 102 Democrats in favour, 43 Republicans and 156 Democrats against.

The federal government's involvement in the World Trade Organization (WTO) has been, if anything, more contentious. The WTO was the successor

to GATT, the General Agreement on Tariffs and Trade, devoted to furthering free trade throughout the world. Set up in 1995 WTO incorporates a
mechanism for settling trade disputes between members, and the United
States has been involved in many such disputes; with the European Union
over genetically modified organisms, with Venezuela over oil, with Pakistan
over cotton, with Japan over steel products, and so on. Each of these disputes involves considerable internal political controversy, provoking lobbying
activities by the producer or consumer groups affected, and when a WTO
decision goes against the United States it may be necessary for Congress to
change the offending legislation, raising protests from protectionists.

The most dramatic effect of membership of the WTO, however, has come
from the reaction of groups protesting about globalisation, who see the WTO
as an arm of economic imperialism, being used by the United States and
other developed countries to open up markets in underdeveloped countries
and to subject them to unfair competition whilst retaining farm subsidies
at home and protectionist policies when it suits them. Protests, which have
often turned violent, followed the annual meetings of the WTO around the
world; one of the worst took place in Seattle in 1999.

The United States is officially committed to the furtherance of free trade
throughout the world, but this policy is fraught with difficulties, because
there are so many interests hostile to it, both in the United States itself
and in the countries affected by the policy. The latest chapter in this saga is
the establishment of the Central America Free Trade Agreement initiated
by the administration of President George W. Bush. The agreement is intended to establish a free trade zone covering the United States, Costa Rica,
El Salvador, Guatemala, Honduras, Nicaragua and the Dominican Republic.
However, the fear of loss of jobs and of the commitment to an area often
hostile to American economic power led to considerable opposition to Bush's
proposals. There was particularly strong opposition from sugar producers in
the United States who feared an influx of cheap sugar from Central America.
When the legislation necessary to implement the Agreement was introduced
in Congress in 2005 it was by no means certain that it would pass. As with
NAFTA there was opposition both on the left and on the right, from the
trades unions to the John Birch Society. The Bush administration engaged in
an unprecedented operation to persuade Congressmen to their point of view.
President Bush and Vice-President Cheney met with members of Congress
to urge them to vote for the measure. The *Washington Post* reported that 'so
many top Bush administration officials were working the Capitol ... that
Democrats joked that the hallways looked like a Cabinet meeting.' In the
event the Bill was passed by the House of Representatives by a majority of
only two votes, and only because fifteen Democrats joined the Republican
majority to offset the twenty-seven Republicans who voted against.

The proposal to open the markets of Central American countries to United States producers caused as much controversy in those countries, if not
more, as opening up the United States to them had caused in that country.

The fear was that CAFTA would benefit United States multinational companies at the expense of Central American farmers and small businesses. Although by the beginning of April 2006, eight months after President Bush had signed the legislation, Costa Rica was the only country which had not ratified the agreement, only three of the six Central American countries – El Salvador, Honduras and Nicaragua – had fully implemented it. The US trade initiative in Central America reawakened opposition in South America to the Free Trade Area of the Americas (FTAA), the attempt to create a free trade area for the whole Western hemisphere. This had begun at the Summit of the Americas, held in 1994 in Miami. At that time thirty-four governments signed a declaration, urged on by President Clinton, agreeing that a free trade area would be established by 2005. Progress, however, was slow and the aim was not achieved. Despite President Bush's continued support, a number of the original thirty-four countries have expressed opposition, led by President Hugo Chavez of Venezuela. In November 2005 at a meeting of the Summit of the Americas, Chavez attacked US policy and supported anti-Bush demonstrations. For the time being, at least, the FTAA and American international trade policy in South America are stalled.

American exceptionalism

Every nation follows the path it considers best suits its interests and the United States cannot be blamed for doing the same. However, in recent years, the course of American policy in a number of areas has seemed to emphasise the determination of the administration of George W. Bush to act unilaterally and to reject the restraints that other nations have accepted – the decision to withdraw from both the Kyoto Protocol on global warming and the Antiballistic Missile Treaty, and the refusal to accept the Comprehensive Test Ban Treaty and the jurisdiction of the International Criminal Court.

Although American presidents have found ways around the Constitution's requirement that treaties with foreign nations should be subject to the advice and consent of the Senate, there are situations in which it cannot be avoided in practice. These are agreements which have significant *internal* consequences, and which would require congressional action for their implementation; such was the Kyoto Protocol of 1997. This agreement was intended to stabilise carbon emissions as a way of beginning to reduce the impact of global warming, which was perceived to be a serious threat to the future of the planet. It was signed by over 160 countries, including the United States, but it would not be binding on a member country until that country had ratified the Protocol. Even before the negotiation of the agreement the US Senate had passed a resolution, by ninety-five votes to nil, stating that the United States should not enter into any agreement which was not binding on developing as well as industrialised countries, or which 'would result in serious harm to the economy of the United States'. Although Vice-President Al Gore signed the agreement, President Clinton did not submit it to the

Senate for ratification. The objections to the agreement centred on the cost of implementing it and the possible consequences to the economy because of the need to adopt restrictions on industry which would affect its competitive position, a view shared by Democrats and Republicans alike. George W. Bush made it clear soon after his election that he did not intend to submit the treaty to the Senate. He stated:

> Kyoto is, in many ways, unrealistic. Many countries cannot meet their Kyoto targets. The targets themselves were arbitrary and not based upon science. For America, complying with those mandates would have a negative economic impact, with layoffs of workers and price increases for consumers. And when you evaluate all these flaws, most reasonable people will understand that it's not sound public policy.

Bush did not deny the reality of global warming, but he questioned the ways of achieving the stabilisation of greenhouse gases: 'I've asked my advisors to consider approaches to reduce greenhouse gas emissions, including those that tap the power of markets, help realize the promise of technology and ensure the widest-possible global participation.' However, his administration was criticised for throwing doubt on the extent to which carbon emissions are responsible for global warming, and was even accused of doctoring scientific reports on the subject. Although the Bush administration has come closer to acknowledging the need for action to limit global warming there is little likelihood that its position on Kyoto will change significantly, and even less that the Senate would ratify the treaty if asked to do so. However, a number of the states have declared that they will adopt Kyoto-like policies to limit carbon emissions. In 2003 California passed legislation requiring the state Air Resources Board to 'develop and adopt regulations that achieve the maximum feasible and cost-effective reduction of greenhouse gas emissions from motor vehicles.'

The Anti-Ballistic Missile Treaty was concluded in 1972 between the United States and the Soviet Union. It was intended to limit the systems used by the defences of both countries against nuclear attack. It remained in force for thirty years, until in 2002, after giving the appropriate notice, the United States withdrew from the treaty. The reason for taking this unusual step was, in the words of President Bush:

> Today, our security environment is profoundly different. The Cold War is over. The Soviet Union no longer exists. Russia is not an enemy, but in fact is increasingly allied with us on a growing number of critically important issues . . . Today, the United States and Russia face new threats to their security. Principal among these threats are weapons of mass destruction and their delivery means wielded by terrorists and rogue states. A number of such states are acquiring increasingly longer-range ballistic missiles as instruments of blackmail and coercion against the

United States and its friends and allies. The United States must defend its homeland, its forces and its friends and allies against these threats. We must develop and deploy the means to deter and protect against them, including through limited missile defense of our territory.

Although the abrogation of this treaty suggested that the United States wished to be less inhibited in its arrangements for nuclear defence, at least a more positive step was taken later the same year when the Treaty on Strategic Offensive Reductions was signed by President Bush and President Putin, limiting the number of nuclear warheads of the United States and Russia to 1,700–2,200 each. Welcome as this was, it of course left enough nuclear warheads in existence to destroy all life on the planet if they were to be used. The Treaty was approved by Senate in 2003 by ninety-five votes to nil.

Another initiative by President Clinton was his support for the negotiations in 1996 for the Comprehensive Test Ban Treaty, which banned all nuclear explosions for military or civilian purposes. The treaty could only come into force when signed by 44 countries including those who possessed nuclear weapons. However, when President Clinton submitted it for ratification by the Senate, then controlled by a Republican majority, it was rejected by 51 votes to 48. During the election of 2000 George W. Bush made it clear that he did not approve of the treaty, and no further action has been taken. In any event it is unlikely that the treaty would ever come into force because it was not signed by North Korea, India or Pakistan and it has not been ratified by, among others, China, Iran or Israel.

The International Criminal Court was established under the Rome Statute of 1998 as a permanent tribunal to prosecute individuals for genocide, crimes against humanity and war crimes. It came into operation in 2002 when more than sixty states had ratified it; however the United States has not ratified it, and refuses to be bound by it. President Clinton signed the agreement setting up the Court, but did not submit it to the Senate for ratification; in 2001 President Bush nullified the signature and made it clear that the United States did not intend to ratify the agreement. The main objection to adhering to the treaty, an objection which is widely supported in the United States, is that American soldiers or officials could be subject to politically motivated prosecutions, and that any wrongdoing by Americans should be dealt with by American courts. In 2002 Congress went further by passing the American Servicemembers' Protection Act, which was intended 'to protect United States military personnel and other elected and appointed officials of the United States government against criminal prosecution by an international criminal court to which the United States is not party'. The Act authorised the president to use military force to free US military personnel held by the Court. The Act also prohibits the provision of military assistance to countries that have not signed 'Article 98' agreements; an 'Article 98' agreement is a bilateral agreement whereby countries pledge not to seek the prosecution of US citizens in the International Criminal Court. However, in 2005, the Security Council of the United Nations decided to hand over to the

International Criminal Court details of crimes against humanity allegedly committed in Darfur in the Sudan, and the United States did not seek to prevent that from happening. Questioned about this the White House Press Secretary, Scott McClellan stated:

> Our view of the International Criminal Court has not changed, nor has our view that those who were responsible for atrocities in Darfur need to be held accountable. We strongly support holding individuals who are responsible for the atrocities that have taken place accountable for their actions. And the reason we didn't stand in the way of that resolution was for two reasons. One, we believe strongly that people need to be held accountable for the atrocities committed. Two, it provides protections for Americans in that resolution. And that's why we do not stand in the way of that resolution passing.

These four examples of the approach of the United States to foreign policy issues suggest that there is, under the Bush Administration, a sense that America has a special status, and should not be bound by the rules which apply to other countries. Equally they illustrate that in many foreign policy issues the pluralist character of American politics is very strong. The ability of the president to achieve policy objectives is subject to congressional approval, and the role of pressure groups in arriving at decisions is critical. The outcomes of the battles around many American foreign policy issues are subject to all the constitutional, legal and political complexities which characterise the American system of government.

Further reading

Houghton, D. (2002) 'America as a Global Economic Player: Free Trade versus Protectionism,' in D. McKay, D. Houghton and A. Wroe, *Controversies in American Politics*, Oxford: Blackwell.

Mayer, J. and McManus, D. (1988) *Landslide: The Unmaking of the President, 1984–1988*, London: Collins.

Sands, P. (2005) *Lawless World: America and the Making and Breaking of Global Rules*, London: Allen Lane.

Schlesinger, A.M. Jr (2005) *War and the American Presidency*, New York: Norton.

Woodward, B. (2003) *Bush at War*, London: Pocket Books.

Websites

Earlham College, Cuba and Helms–Burton: www.earlham.edu/~pols/ps17971/weissdo/index.html

National Commission on Terrorist Attacks Upon the United States: www.9-11commission.gov/report

The University of Michigan Documents Center, Iraq War Debate: www.lib.umich.edu/govsdocs/iraqwar.html

World Trade Organization: www.wto.org

Postscript

American politics in the twenty-first century

In the functioning of any political system there are two kinds of forces at work. There are those long-term historical and structural factors which form the basis of the system, and there are the recent developments, economic, political, social, which bring change to the day-to-day working of politics and modify its character. The problem for the observer is to try to judge the extent to which recent developments represent significant permanent change, or are merely transient. Significant changes have taken place in American politics in recent decades; we will attempt to summarise them here, and to comment on their likely effects.

We have seen that pluralism, a continual series of changing coalitions of innumerable groups operating to make policy compromises through a complex mechanism of institutions, has characterised the American political system. An essential prerequisite of this system has been the fluid character of the party system in the Congress, allowing groups to form and re-form according to the issue: issue-oriented politics. This enabled not only compromise within Congress between contending interests, but also compromises between president and Congress, so that coalitions could form in favour of, or against, presidential policies; a president could sometimes be defeated because sections of the president's party voted against the administration's policies, and could sometimes win because a significant number of Senators or Congressmen of the opposing party would vote for the administration's policies. This fluidity was particularly important in the second half of the twentieth century when 'divided government', a president of one party faced by a majority of the other party controlling one or both Houses of Congress, became so common; it could work only because many votes in Congress were taken by bipartisan majorities. A rigid system of party discipline along the lines of the British system would have resulted in total deadlock.

Since 1994 there has been a significant increase in partisanship in the Congress. Party discipline has not reached European heights, it is true, but in the House of Representatives in particular the atmosphere of party politics has been more confrontational, more passionate, in which deviations

from the party line, at any rate by Republicans, became more difficult to justify. There were three major reasons for this. First, the changing politics of
the South has meant that many conservative Southerners have moved from
the Democratic Party to the Republican Party. Thus a major divisive factor *within* both parties, that between conservatives and liberals, has become
less important and has been transferred to the division *between* the parties,
making them more partisan in character. Second, the emergence of the neoconservative philosophy, adopted by many Republicans, gave an ideological
tinge to the American political scene not experienced since the height of
Roosevelt's New Deal policies in the 1930s. Third, the terrorist attacks on
America in 2001, followed by the wars in Afghanistan and Iraq, inevitably
demanded an almost unquestioning support from a Republican Congress for
a Republican president exercising his powers as commander-in-chief. The
realignment of politics in the South is almost certainly going to persist, and
perhaps go even further than at present. This will undoubtedly give to the
party political debate a different quality from that in the 1970s and 1980s,
strengthening the sense of party unity in the Republican Party; however, it is
unlikely to result in the kind of persistently high party unity common in European states. Senators and congressmen are very sensitive to local interests
and local pressures. Where their perception of the views of their constituents
differs on individual policies from those of the president or of other members
of Congress, they will vote the way their constituents wish, not the way their
party leaders would hope.

It is more difficult to determine the continuing effect of the neoconservative philosophy. Undoubtedly it will continue to influence many people, but it
is already coming under considerable criticism. The credibility of the neoconservative approach to foreign policy is inextricably bound up with the success
or failure of the war in Iraq. The loss of American lives, the continued insur-
gency in Iraq, the revelations about the prison of Abu Ghraib, and other deficiencies in the aftermath of the invasion have had a considerable impact on
American public opinion, with over half of Americans considering that it was
a mistake to enter the war. The neoconservative approach to foreign policy
centred on the assertion of the right of the United States to take pre-emptive
action, to wage pre-emptive war, in furtherance of the American national
interest – the so-called 'Bush Doctrine'. One of the signatories of the 1998
letter to President Clinton from the neoconservative group, The Project for
a New American Century, demanding 'regime change' in Iraq, was Francis
Fukuyama. In 2006, however, Fukuyama published *After the Neocons: America at
the Crossroads*, in which he announced that he could no longer support neoconservatism as either a political symbol or a body of thought. He predicted that
'one of the consequences of a perceived failure in Iraq will be the discrediting
of the entire neoconservative agenda and a restoration of the authority of
foreign policy realists.' However, the volatility of the situation in the Middle
East, the way in which American policy impacts upon the Israeli–Palestinian

conflict, and American hostility towards Syria and Iran, all have the potential to provoke crises which inevitably increase the importance of presidential power and the influence of hawks in the administration.

Another long-standing characteristic of the American political system is the tension between president and Congress, and the determination of the latter to limit the power of the president. The structure of the separation of powers established by the Founding Fathers was intended to achieve this result and it has done so with considerable success over the past 215 years. However, the Founding Fathers' intention could have been frustrated by a strongly disciplined party system, binding members of the president's party in Congress to support the administration's policies; no such party system ever emerged. Indeed, had it done so the result could have been disastrous; the differing electoral systems for the presidency and the Congress can, and often do, result in 'divided government', a president of one party and one or both Houses of Congress dominated by the opposing party. In fact, in the mid-term elections of 2006 the Democrats won majorities in both the Senate and the House of Representatives. For the final two years of his presidency George W. Bush will, therefore, be faced by a Congress controlled by the opposing party. Divided government, which has characterised American politics during much of the period following the Second World War, has returned.

Apart from these structural considerations the degree of partisan support enjoyed by George W. Bush in the early years of his presidency had come under considerable strain by 2006. Not only the setbacks in Iraq, but a number of domestic policy considerations led to questions being raised by Republicans in Congress about the policies of his administration. The large-scale programme of secret interceptions of telephone calls, emails and bank transfers, on which the administration failed to consult Congress, caused disquiet among legislators. In July 2006 President Bush vetoed a bill which would have provided government funds for stem cell research using human embryos. The Bill had been passed by the Senate by a vote of sixty-three to thirty-seven; the majority was composed of forty-three Democrats, one Independent and nineteen Republican Senators, including the Republican Senate Majority Leader, Bill Frist. An attempt to overturn the President's veto in the House of Representatives failed to get the necessary two-thirds majority although fifty-one Republicans contributed to the vote of 253–193 against the President. The Supreme Court's decision, *Hamdan* v. *Rumsfeld* in 2006, placed directly on Congress the responsibility of determining the conditions under which prisoners would be held at Guantánamo Bay, and the way in which they would be tried. The need for Congress to act, rather than merely to acquiesce, disclosed deep divisions within the Republican Party.

The *Hamdan* decision made it clear that the Supreme Court will continue to act as the arbiter of constitutional rectitude, but the way in which the Court will perform this role in the future is less clear. In *Hamdan* there was a five-to-three majority in favour of putting limits to the power of the President; the new Chief Justice Roberts took no part in the case. President George W. Bush was able to nominate two Justices to the Court, both of whom are expected to take conservative stances on many issues: Chief Justice John Roberts and Justice Samuel Alito. There are already two other recognised conservatives on the Court, Justice Antonin Scalia (nominated by Ronald Reagan) and Justice Clarence Thomas (nominated by George H.W. Bush). There are four Justices currently on the Court who tend to take a more liberal stand: Justices John Paul Stevens (Ford), David Souter (Bush Sr), Ruth Bader Ginsburg (Clinton), and Stephen Breyer (Clinton). The ninth member of the Court, Justice Anthony Kennedy, appointed by President Reagan, has come to be seen as the 'swing vote' on the Court, throwing decisions either to the conservative wing or to the liberal wing. The Court is therefore nicely balanced, but new appointments could tip the balance one way or another. Justice Stevens is 86 years old. If President Bush has the opportunity to appoint another Justice before his term of office ends in January 2009, there could be a conservative majority on the Court; this might have implications for cases on abortion and on civil rights. As the Democrats won a majority in the Senate in the election of 2006, albeit a very slim one, the President's room for manoeuvre will be severely limited. If a Democrat were to be elected to the presidency in 2008, the opportunity for the nomination of new liberal members would open up. However, it should be emphasized that Supreme Court Justices do not simply toe the party line, and no president can be sure that the Justices he or she nominates will vote the way expected of them.

The basic characteristics of the American political system remain. Party realignments change its mode of working but not its fundamentals. Individual politicians come and go, political groupings rise and fall; under the pressure of events decisions are taken which otherwise would be unacceptable. In the early years of the twenty-first century it is likely that the decisive events will be those that occur in the Middle East, or in Asia; the reactions of American policy-makers to these events will shape both foreign and domestic policies. It is to be hoped that the traditional values of the American polity, sometimes lost sight of, will be reasserted.

Appendix 1

The Constitution of the United States of America

(The passages in italics have been replaced by subsequent Amendments.)

We the People of the United States, in Order to form a more perfect Union, establish Justice, insure domestic Tranquility, provide for the common defence, promote the general Welfare, and secure the Blessings of Liberty to ourselves and our Posterity, do ordain and establish this Constitution for the United States of America.

Article I

Section 1   All legislative Powers herein granted shall be vested in a Congress of the United States, which shall consist of a Senate and House of Representatives.

Section 2   The House of Representatives shall be composed of Members chosen every second Year by the People of the Several States, and the Electors in each State shall have the Qualifications requisite for Electors of the most numerous Branch of the State Legislature.

No person shall be a Representative who shall not have attained to the Age of twenty five Years, and been seven Years a Citizen of the United States, and who shall not, when elected, be an Inhabitant of that State in which he shall be chosen.

Representatives and direct Taxes shall be apportioned among the several States which may be included within this Union, according to their respective Numbers, *which shall be determined by adding to the whole Number of free Persons, including those bound to Service for a Term of Years, and excluding Indians not taxed, three fifths of all other persons.*[1] The actual Enumeration shall be made within three Years after the first Meeting of the Congress of the United States, and within every subsequent Term of ten Years, in such Manner as they shall by Law direct. The Number of Representatives shall not exceed one for every thirty Thousand, but each State shall have at Least one Representative; and until such enumeration shall be made, the State of New Hampshire shall be

1   See Fourteenth Amendment.

entitled to chuse three, Massachusetts eight, Rhode Island and Providence Plantations one, Connecticut five, New York six, New Jersey four, Pennsylvania eight, Delaware one, Maryland six, Virginia ten, North Carolina five, South Carolina five, and Georgia three.

When vacancies happen in the Representation from any State, the Executive Authority thereof shall issue Writs of Election to fill such Vacancies.

The House of Representatives shall chuse their Speaker and other Officers; and shall have the sole Power of Impeachment.

Section 3   The Senate of the United States shall be composed of two Senators from each State, *chosen by the Legislature thereof*[2] for six Years; and each Senator shall have one Vote.

Immediately after they shall be assembled in Consequence of the first Election, they shall be divided as equally as may be into three Classes. The Seats of the Senators of the first Class shall be vacated at the Expiration of the second Year, of the second Class at the Expiration of the fourth Year, and of the third Class at the Expiration of the sixth Year, so that one third may be chosen every second Year *and if Vacancies happen by Resignation or otherwise, during the Recess of the Legislature of any State, the Executive thereof may make temporary Appointments until the next Meeting of the Legislature, which shall then fill such Vacancies*.[3]

No Person shall be a Senator who shall not have attained to the Age of thirty Years, and been nine Years a Citizen of the United States, and who shall not, when elected, be an Inhabitant of the State for which he shall be chosen.

The Vice-President of the United States shall be President of the Senate, but shall have no Vote, unless they be equally divided.

The Senate shall chuse their other Officers, and also a President pro tempore in the Absence of the Vice-President, or when he shall exercise the Office of President of the United States.

The Senate shall have the sole Power to try all Impeachments. When sitting for that Purpose, there shall be an Oath or Affirmation. When the President of the United States is tried, the Chief Justice shall preside: And no Person shall be convicted without the Concurrence of two thirds of the Members present.

Judgment in Cases of Impeachment shall not extend further than to remove from Office, and disqualification to hold and enjoy any Office of honor, Trust or Profit under the United States: but the Party convicted shall nevertheless be liable and subject to Indictment, Trial, Judgment and Punishment, according to Law.

Section 4   The Times, Places and Manner of holding Elections for Senators and Representatives, shall be prescribed in each State by the Legislature thereof; but the Congress may at any time by Law make or alter such Regulations, except as to the Places of chusing Senators.

---

2   See Seventeenth Amendment.
3   See Seventeenth Amendment.

The Congress shall assemble at least once in every Year, and such Meeting shall be on the first Monday in December, unless they shall by Law appoint a different Day.[4]

Section 5   Each House shall be the Judge of the Elections, Returns and Qualifications of its own Members, and a Majority of each shall constitute a Quorum to do Business; but a smaller Number may adjourn from day to day, and may be authorized to compel the Attendance of absent Members, in such Manner, and under such Penalties as each House may provide.

Each House may determine the Rules of its Proceedings, punish its Members for disorderly Behaviour, and, with the Concurrence of two thirds, expel a Member.

Each House shall keep a Journal of its Proceedings, and from time to time publish the same, excepting such Parts as may in their Judgment require Secrecy; and the Yeas and Nays of the Members of either House on any question shall, at the Desire of one fifth of those Present, be entered on the Journal.

Neither House, during the Session of Congress, shall, without the Consent of the other, adjourn for more than three days, nor to any other Place than that in which the two Houses shall be sitting.

Section 6   The Senators and Representatives shall receive a Compensation for their Services, to be ascertained by Law, and paid out of the Treasury of the United States. They shall in all Cases, except Treason, Felony and Breach of the Peace, be privileged from Arrest during their Attendance at the Session of their respective Houses, and in going to and returning from the same; and for any Speech or Debate in either House, they shall not be questioned in any other Place.

No Senator or Representative shall, during the Time for which he was elected, be appointed to any civil Office under the Authority of the United States, which shall have been created, or the Emoluments whereof shall have been encreased during such time; and no Person holding any Office under the United States, shall be a Member of either House during his Continuance in Office.

Section 7   All Bills for raising Revenue shall originate in the House of Representatives; but the Senate may propose or concur with Amendments as on other Bills.

Every Bill which shall have passed the House of Representatives and the Senate, shall, before it become a Law, be presented to the President of the United States; If he approve he shall sign it, but if not he shall return it, with his Objections to that House in which it shall have originated, who shall enter the Objections at large on their Journal, and proceed to reconsider it. If after such Reconsideration two thirds of that House shall agree to pass the Bill, it shall be sent, together with the Objections, to the other House, by which it shall likewise be reconsidered, and if approved by two thirds of that House, it shall become a Law. But in all such Cases the Votes of both Houses shall be determined by Yeas and Nays, and the Names of the Persons voting for and against the Bill shall be entered on the Journal of each House

4   See Twentieth Amendment.

respectively. If any Bill shall not be returned by the President within ten Days (Sundays excepted) after it shall have been presented to him, the Same shall be a Law, in like Manner as if he had signed it, unless the Congress by their Adjournment prevent its Return, in which Case it shall not be a Law.

Every Order, Resolution, or Vote to which the Concurrence of the Senate and House of Representatives may be necessary (except on a question of Adjournment) shall be presented to the President of the United States; and before the Same shall take Effect, shall be approved by him, or being disapproved by him, shall be repassed by two thirds of the Senate and House of Representatives, according to the Rules and Limitations prescribed in the Case of a Bill.

Section 8   The Congress shall have Power to lay and collect Taxes, Duties, Imposts and Excises, to pay the Debts and provide for the common Defence and general Welfare of the United States; but all Duties, Imposts and Excises shall be uniform throughout the United States.

To borrow Money on the credit of the United States;

To regulate Commerce with foreign Nations and among the several States, and with the Indian Tribes;

To establish an uniform Rule of Naturalization, and uniform Laws on the subject of Bankruptcies throughout the United States;

To coin Money, regulate the Value thereof, and of foreign Coin, and fix the Standard of Weights and Measures;

To provide for the Punishment of counterfeiting the Securities and current Coin of the United States;

To establish Post Offices and post Roads;

To promote the Progress of Science and useful Arts, by securing for limited Times to Authors and Inventors the exclusive Right to their respective Writings and Discoveries;

To constitute Tribunals inferior to the Supreme Court;

To define and punish Piracies and Felonies committed on the high Seas, and Offences against the Law of Nations;

To declare War, grant Letters of Marque and Reprisal, and make Rules concerning Captures on Land and Water;

To raise and support Armies, but no Appropriation of Money to that Use shall be for a longer Term than two Years;

To provide and maintain a Navy;

To make Rules for the Government and Regulation of the land and naval Forces;

To provide for calling forth the Militia to execute the Laws of the Union, suppress Insurrections and repel Invasions;

To provide for organizing, arming, and disciplining, the Militia, and for governing such Part of them as may be employed in the Service of the United States, reserving to the States respectively, the Appointment of the Officers, and the Authority of training the Militia according to the discipline prescribed by Congress;

To Exercise exclusive Legislation in all Cases whatsoever, over such District (not exceeding ten Miles square) as may, by Cession of particular States, and the Acceptance of Congress, become the Seat of the Government of the United States, and to exercise like Authority over all Places purchased by the Consent of the Legislature of the State in which the Same shall be, for the Erection of Forts, Magazines, Arsenals, Dock-Yards, and other needful Buildings; And

To make all Laws which shall be necessary and proper for carrying into Execution the foregoing Powers, and all the Powers vested by this Constitution in the Government of the United States, or in any Department or Officer thereof.

Section 9   The Migration or Importation of such Persons as any of the States now existing shall think proper to admit, shall not be prohibited by the Congress prior to the Year one thousand eight hundred and eight, but a Tax or duty may be imposed on such Importation, not exceeding ten dollars for each Person.

The Privilege of the Writ of Habeas Corpus shall not be suspended, unless when in Case of Rebellion or Invasion the public Safety may require it.

No Bill of Attainder or ex post facto Law shall be passed.

No Capitation, or other direct, Tax shall be laid, unless in Proportion to the Census or Enumeration herein before directed to be taken.[5]

No Tax or Duty shall be laid on Articles exported from any State.

No Preference shall be given by any Regulation of Commerce or Revenue to the Ports of one State over those of another nor shall Vessels bound to, or from, one State, be obliged to enter, clear, or pay Duties in another.

No Money shall be drawn from the Treasury, but in Consequence of Appropriations made by Law; and a regular Statement and Account of the Receipts and Expenditures of all public Money shall be published from time to time.

No title of Nobility shall be granted by the United States: And no Person holding any Office of Profit or Trust under them, shall, without the Consent of the Congress, accept of any present, Emolument, Office, or Title of any kind whatever, from any King, Prince, or foreign State.

Section 10   No State shall enter into any Treaty, Alliance or Confederation; grant Letters of Marque and Reprisal; coin Money; emit Bills of Credit; make any Thing but gold and silver Coin a Tender in Payment of Debts; pass any Bill of Attainder, ex post facto Law, or Law impairing the Obligation of Contracts, or Grant any Title of Nobility.

No State shall, without the Consent of the Congress, lay any Imposts or Duties on Imports or Exports, except what may be absolutely necessary for executing its inspection Laws: and the net Produce of all Duties and Imposts, laid by any State on Imports or Exports, shall be for the Use of the Treasury of the United States; and all such Laws shall be subject to the Revision and Controul of the Congress.

No State shall, without the Consent of Congress, lay any Duty of Tonnage, keep Troops, or Ships of War in time of Peace, enter into any Agreement or

5   See Sixteenth Amendment.

Compact with another State, or with a foreign Power, or engage in War, unless actually invaded, or in such imminent Danger as will not admit of delay.

Article II

Section 1 The executive Power shall be vested in a President of the United States of America. He shall hold his Office during the Term of four Years, and, together with the Vice-President, chosen for the same Term be elected as follows:

Each State shall appoint, in such Manner as the Legislature thereof may direct, a Number of Electors, equal to the whole Number of Senators and Representatives to which the State may be entitled in the Congress but no Senator or Representative, or Person holding an Office of Trust or Profit under the United States, shall be appointed an Elector.

The Electors shall meet in their respective States; and vote by Ballot for two Persons, of whom one at least shall not be an Inhabitant of the same State with themselves. And they shall make a List of all the Persons voted for, and of the Number of Votes for each, which List they shall sign and certify, and transmit sealed to the Seat of the Government of the United States, directed to the President of the Senate. The President of the Senate shall, in the Prescence of the Senate and House of Representatives, open all the Certificates, and the Votes shall then be counted The Person having the greatest Number of Votes shall be the President, if such Number be a Majority of the whole Number of Electors appointed, and if there be more than one who have such a Majority, and have an equal Number of Votes, then the House of Representatives shall immediately chuse by Ballot one of them for President, and if no Person have a Majority, then from the five highest on the List the said House shall in like Manner chuse the President. But in chusing the President, the Votes shall be taken by States, the Representation from each State having one Vote; A quorum for this purpose shall consist of a Member or Members from two thirds of the States, and a Majority of all the States shall be necessary to a Choice. In every Case, after the Choice of the President, the Person having the greatest Number of Votes of the Electors shall be the Vice President. But if there should remain two or more who have equal Votes, the Senate shall chuse from them by Ballot the Vice President.[6]

The Congress may determine the Time of chusing the Electors, and the Day on which they shall give their Votes; which Day shall be the same throughout the United States.

No Person except a natural born Citizen, or a Citizen of the United States, at the time of the Adoption of this Constitution, shall be eligible to the Office of President; neither shall any Person be eligible to that Office who shall not have attained to the Age of thirty five Years, and been fourteen Years a Resident within the United States.

In Case of the Removal of the President from Office, or of his Death, Resignation, or Inability to discharge the Powers and Duties of the said Office, the Same shall devolve on the Vice President, and the Congress may by Law provide for the Case of Removal, Death, Resignation or Inability, both of the President and Vice President, declaring what Officer

6   Superseded by the Twelfth Amendment.

shall then act as President, and such Officer shall act accordingly, until the Disability be removed, or a President shall be elected.[7]

The President shall, at stated Times, receive for his Services, a Compensation which shall neither be encreased nor diminished during the Period for which he shall have been elected, and he shall not receive within that Period any other Emolument from the United States, or any of them.

Before he enter on the Execution of his Office, he shall take the following Oath or Affirmation: 'I do solemnly swear (or affirm) that I will faithfully execute the Office of President of the United States, and will to the best of my Ability, preserve, protect and defend the Constitution of the United States'.

Section 2   The President shall be Commander in Chief of the Army and Navy of the United States, and of the Militia of the several States, when called into the actual Service of the United States; he may require the Opinion, in writing, of the principal Officer in each of the executive Departments, upon any Subject relating to the Duties of their respective Offices, and he shall have Power to grant Reprieves and Pardons for Offences against the United States, except in Cases of Impeachment.

He shall have Power, by and with the Advice and Consent of the Senate, to make Treaties, provided two thirds of the Senators present concur; and he shall nominate, and by and with the Advice and Consent of the Senate shall appoint Ambassadors, and other public Ministers and Consuls, Judges of the supreme Court, and all other Officers of the United States, whose Appointments are not herein otherwise provided for, and which shall be established by Law: but the Congress may by Law vest the Appointment of such inferior Officers, as they think proper, in the President alone, in the Courts of Law, or in the Heads of Departments.

The President shall have Power to fill up all Vacancies that may happen during the Recess of the Senate, by granting Commissions which shall expire at the End of the next Session.

Section 3   He shall from time to time give to the Congress Information of the State of the Union, and recommend to their Consideration such Measures as he shall judge necessary and expedient; he may, on extraordinary Occasions, convene both Houses, or either of them, and in Case of Disagreement between them, with Respect to the Time of Adjournment, he may adjourn them to such Time as he shall think proper; he shall receive Ambassadors and other public Ministers, he shall take Care that the Laws be faithfully executed, and shall Commission all the Officers of the United States.

Section 4   The President, Vice President and all civil Officers of the United States, shall be removed from Office on Impeachment for, and Conviction of Treason, Bribery or other high Crimes and Misdemeanors.

Article III

Section 1   The judicial Power of the United States shall be vested in one supreme Court, and in such inferior Courts as the Congress may from time

7   See Twenty-fifth Amendment.

to time ordain and establish. The Judges, both of the supreme and inferior Courts, shall hold their Offices during good Behaviour, and shall, at stated Times, receive for their Services, a Compensation, which shall not be diminished during their Continuance in Office.

Section 2 The judicial Power shall extend to all Cases, in Law and Equity, arising under this Constitution, the Laws of the United States, and Treaties made, or which shall be made, under their Authority; – to all Cases affecting Ambassadors, other public Ministers and Consuls; – to all Cases of admiralty and maritime Jurisdiction; – to Controversies to which the United States shall be a Party; – to Controversies between two or more States; – *between a State and Citizens of another State*;[8] – between Citizens of different States; – between Citizens of the same State claiming Lands under Grants of different States, *and between a State or the Citizens thereof, and foreign States, Citizens or Subjects.*[9]

In all cases affecting Ambassadors, other public Ministers and Consuls, and those in which a State shall be Party, the supreme Court shall have original Jurisdiction. In all the other Cases before mentioned, the supreme Court shall have appellate Jurisdiction, both as to Law, and Fact, with such Exceptions, and under such Regulations as the Congress shall make.

The Trial of all Crimes, except in Cases of Impeachment, shall be by Jury; and such Trial shall be held in the State where the said Crimes shall have been committed; but when not committed within any State, the Trial shall be at such Place or Places as the Congress may by Law have directed.

Section 3 Treason against the United States, shall consist only in levying War against them, or in adhering to their Enemies, giving them Aid and Comfort. No Person shall be convicted of Treason unless on the Testimony of two Witnesses to the same overt Act, or on Confession in open Court.

The Congress shall have Power to declare the Punishment of Treason, but no Attainder of Treason shall work Corruption of Blood, or Forfeiture except during the Life of the Person attainted.

Article IV

Section 1 Full Faith and Credit shall be given in each State to the public Acts, Records, and judicial Proceedings of every other State. And the Congress may by general Laws prescribe the Manner in which such Acts, Records, and Proceedings shall be proved, and the Effect thereof.

Section 2 The Citizens of each State shall be entitled to all Privileges and Immunities of Citizens in the several States.

A Person charged in any State with Treason, Felony, or other Crime, who shall flee from Justice, and be found in another State, shall on Demand of the executive Authority of the State from which he fled, be delivered up, to be removed to the State having Jurisdiction of the Crime.

8   See Eleventh Amendment.
9   See Eleventh Amendment.

No Person held to Service or Labour in one State, under the Laws thereof escaping into another, shall, in Consequence of any Law or Regulation therein, be discharged from such Service or Labour, but shall be delivered up on Claim of the Party to whom such Service or Labour may be due.[10]

Section 3   New States may be admitted by the Congress into this Union; but no new State shall be formed or erected within the Jurisdiction of any other State; nor any State be formed by the Junction of two or more States, or Parts of States, without the Consent of the Legislatures of the States concerned as well as of the Congress.

The Congress shall have Power to dispose of and make all needful Rules and Regulations respecting the Territory or other Property belonging to the United States; and nothing in this Constitution shall be so construed as to Prejudice any Claims of the United States, or of any particular State.

Section 4   The United States shall guarantee to every State in this Union a Republican Form of Government and shall protect each of them against Invasion; and on Application of the Legislature, or of the Executive (when the Legislature cannot be convened) against domestic Violence.

Article V

The Congress, whenever two thirds of both Houses shall deem it necessary, shall propose Amendments to this Constitution, or, on the Application of the Legislatures of two thirds of the several States, shall call a Convention for proposing Amendments, which, in either Case, shall be valid to all Intents and Purposes, as Part of this Constitution, when ratified by the Legislatures of three fourths of the several States, or by Conventions in three fourths thereof, as the one or the other Mode of Ratification may be proposed by the Congress; Provided that no Amendment which may be made prior to the Year One thousand eight hundred and eight shall in any Manner affect the first and fourth Clauses in the Ninth Section of the first Article; and that no State, without its Consent, shall be deprived of its equal Suffrage in the Senate.

Article VI

All Debts contracted and Engagements entered into, before the Adoption of this Constitution, shall be as valid against the United States under this Constitution, as under the Confederation.

This Constitution, and the Laws of the United States which shall be made in Pursuance thereof; and all Treaties made, or which shall be made, under the Authority of the United States, shall be the supreme Law of the Land; and the Judges in every State shall be bound thereby, any Thing in the Constitution or Laws of any State to the Contrary notwithstanding.

The Senators and Representatives before mentioned, and the Members of the several State Legislatures, and all executive and judicial Officers, both

10   See Thirteenth Amendment.

of the United States and of the several States, shall be bound by Oath or Affirmation, to support this Constitution; but no religious Test shall ever be required as a Qualification to any Office or public Trust under the United States.

Article VII

The Ratification of the Conventions of nine States, shall be sufficient for the Establishment of this Constitution between the States so ratifying the Same.

Done in Convention by the Unanimous Consent of the States present the Seventeenth Day of September in the Year of our Lord one thousand seven hundred and eighty seven and of the Independence of the United States of America the twelfth. In witness whereof We have hereunto subscribed our Names.

Amendments

(Ratification of the first ten amendments was completed 15 December 1791.)

Amendment I

Congress shall make no law respecting an establishment of religion, or prohibiting the free exercise thereof; or abridging the freedom of speech, or of the press; or the right of the people peaceably to assemble, and to petition the Government for a redress of grievances.

Amendment II

A well regulated Militia, being necessary to the security of a free State, the right of the people to keep and bear Arms, shall not be infringed.

Amendment III

No Soldier shall, in time of peace be quartered in any house, without the consent of the Owner, nor in time of war, but in a manner to be prescribed by law.

Amendment IV

The right of the people to be secure in their persons, houses, papers, and effects, against unreasonable searches and seizures, shall not be violated, and no Warrants shall issue, but upon probable cause, supported by Oath or Affirmation, and particularly describing the place to be searched, and the persons or things to be seized.

Amendment V

No person shall be held to answer for a capital, or other infamous crime, unless on a presentment or indictment of a Grand Jury, except in cases arising in the land or naval forces, or in the Militia, when in actual service in time of War or public danger, nor shall any person be subject for the same offence to be twice put in jeopardy of life or limb; nor shall be compelled in any criminal case to be a witness against himself, nor be deprived of life, liberty, or property, without due process of law; nor shall private property be taken for public use, without just compensation.

Amendment VI

In all criminal prosecutions, the accused shall enjoy the right to a speedy and public trial, by an impartial jury of the State and district wherein the crime shall have been committed, which district shall have been previously ascertained by law, and to be informed of the nature and cause of the accusation; to be confronted with the witnesses against him; to have compulsory process for obtaining witnesses in his favor, and to have the Assistance of Counsel for his defence.

Amendment VII

In Suits at common law, where the value in controversy shall exceed twenty dollars, the right of trial by jury shall be preserved, and no fact tried by a jury, shall be otherwise re-examined in any Court of the United States, than according to the rules of the common law.

Amendment VIII

Excessive bail shall not be required, nor excessive fines imposed, nor cruel and unusual punishments inflicted.

Amendment IX

The enumeration in the Constitution, of certain rights, shall not be construed to deny or disparage others retained by the people.

Amendment X

The powers not delegated to the United States by the Constitution, nor prohibited by it to the States, are reserved to the States respectively, or to the people.

Amendment XI (ratified 8 January 1798)

The Judicial power of the United States shall not be construed to extend to any suit in law or equity, commenced or prosecuted against one of the United States by Citizens or Subjects of any Foreign State.

Amendment XII (ratified 25 September 1804)

The Electors shall meet in their respective states and vote by ballot for President and Vice-President, one of whom, at least, shall not be an inhabitant of the same state with themselves; they shall name in their ballots the person voted for as President, and in distinct ballots the person voted for as Vice-President, and they shall make distinct lists of all persons voted for as President and of all persons voted for as Vice-President, and of the number of votes for each, which lists they shall sign and certify, and transmit sealed to the seat of the government of the United States, directed to the President of the Senate; – The President of the Senate shall, in the presence of Senate and House of Representatives, open all the certificates and the votes shall then be counted; – The person having the greatest number of votes for President, shall be the President, if such number be a majority of the whole number of Electors appointed; and if no person have such majority, then from the persons having the highest numbers not exceeding three on the list of those voted for as President, the House of Representatives shall choose immediately, by ballot, the President. But in choosing the President, the votes shall be taken by states, the representation from each state having one vote; a quorum for this purpose shall consist of a member or members from two thirds of the states, and a majority of all the states shall be necessary to a choice. And if the House of Representatives shall not choose a President whenever the right of choice shall devolve upon them, *before the fourth day of March next following*,[11] then the Vice-President shall act as President, as in the case of the death or other constitutional disability of the President. – The person having the greatest number of votes as Vice-President, shall be the Vice-President, if such number be a majority of the whole number of Electors appointed, and if no person shall have a majority, then from the two highest numbers on the list, the Senate shall choose the Vice-President; a quorum for the purpose shall consist of two-thirds of the whole number of Senators, and a majority of the whole number shall be necessary to a choice. But no person constitutionally ineligible to the office of President shall be eligible to that of Vice-President of the United States.

Amendment XIII (ratified 18 December 1865)

Section 1   Neither slavery nor involuntary servitude, except as a punishment for crime whereof the party shall have been duly convicted, shall exist within the United States, or any place subject to their jurisdiction.

11   Altered by the Twentieth Amendment.

Section 2   Congress shall have power to enforce this article by appropriate legislation.

Amendment XIV (ratified 28 July 1868)

Section 1   All persons born or naturalized in the United States, and subject to the jurisdiction thereof, are citizens of the United States and of the State wherein they reside. No State shall make or enforce any law which shall abridge the privileges or immunities of citizens of the United States; nor shall any State deprive any person of life, liberty, or property, without due process of law; nor deny to any person within its jurisdiction the equal protection of the laws.

Section 2   Representatives shall be apportioned among the several States according to their respective numbers, counting the whole number of persons in each State, excluding Indians not taxed. But when the right to vote at any election for the choice of electors for President and Vice President of the United States, Representatives in Congress, the Executive and Judicial officers of a State, or the members of the Legislature thereof, is denied to any of the male inhabitants of such State, being twenty-one years of age, and citizens of the United States, or in any way abridged, except for participation in rebellion, or other crime, the basis of representation therein shall be reduced in the proportion which the number of such male citizens shall bear to the whole number of male citizens twenty-one years of age in such State.

Section 3   No person shall be a Senator or Representative in Congress, or elector of President and Vice President, or hold any office, civil or military, under the United States, or under any State, who, having previously taken an oath, as a member of Congress, or as an officer of the United States, or as a member of any State legislature, or as an executive or judicial officer of any State, to support the Constitution of the United States, shall have engaged in insurrection or rebellion against the same, or given aid or comfort to the enemies thereof. But Congress may by a vote of two thirds of each House, remove such disability.

Section 4   The validity of the public debt of the United States, authorized by law, including debts incurred for payment of pensions and bounties for services in suppressing insurrection or rebellion, shall not be questioned. But neither the United States nor any State shall assume or pay any debt or obligation incurred in aid of insurrection or rebellion against the United States, or any claim for the loss or emancipation of any slave; but all such debts, obligations, and claims shall be held illegal and void.

Section 5   The Congress shall have power to enforce, by appropriate legislation, the provisions of this article.

Amendment XV (ratified 30 March 1870)

Section 1   The right of citizens of the United States to vote shall not be denied or abridged by the United States or by any State on account of race, color, or previous condition of servitude.
Section 2   The Congress shall have power to enforce this article by appropriate legislation.

Amendment XVI (ratified 25 February 1913)

The Congress shall have power to lay and collect taxes on incomes, from whatever source derived, without apportionment among the several States, and without regard to any census or enumeration.

Amendment XVII (ratified 31 May 1913)

The Senate of the United States shall be composed of two Senators from each State, elected by the people thereof, for six years; and each Senator shall have one vote. The electors in each State shall have the qualifications requisite for electors of the most numerous branch of the State legislatures.

When vacancies happen in the representation of any State in the Senate, the executive authority of such State shall issue writs of election to fill such vacancies: *Provided*, That the legislature of any State may empower the executive thereof to make temporary appointments until the people fill the vacancies by election as the legislature may direct.

This amendment shall not be so construed as to affect the election or term of any Senator chosen before it becomes valid as part of the Constitution.

Amendment XVIII (ratified 29 January 1919)

Section 1   After one year from the ratification of this article the manufacture, sale, or transportation of intoxicating liquors within, the importation thereof into, or the exportation thereof from the United States and all territory subject to the jurisdiction thereof for beverage purposes is hereby prohibited.
Section 2   The Congress and the several States shall have concurrent power to enforce this article by appropriate legislation.
Section 3   This article shall be inoperative unless it shall have been ratified as an amendment to the Constitution by the legislatures of the several States, as provided in the Constitution, within seven years from the date of the submission hereof to the States by the Congress.[12]

Amendment XIX (ratified 26 August 1920)

The right of citizens of the United States to vote shall not be denied or abridged by the United States or by any State on account of sex.

12   Repealed by the Twenty-first Amendment.

Congress shall have power to enforce this article by appropriate legislation.

Amendment XX (ratified 6 February 1933)

Section 1   The terms of the President and Vice President shall end at noon on the 20th day of January, and the terms of Senators and Representatives at noon on the 3rd day of January, of the years in which such terms would have ended if this article had not been ratified; and the terms of their successors shall then begin.

Section 2   The Congress shall assemble at least once in every year, and such meeting shall begin at noon on the 3rd day of January, unless they shall by law appoint a different day.

Section 3   If, at the time fixed for the beginning of the term of the President, the President elect shall have died, the Vice President elect shall become President. If a President shall not have been chosen before the time fixed for the beginning of his term, or if the President elect shall have failed to qualify, then the Vice President elect shall act as President until a President shall have qualified; and the Congress may by law provide for the case wherein neither a President elect nor a Vice President elect shall have qualified, declaring who shall then act as President, or the manner in which one who is to act shall be selected and such person shall act accordingly until a President or Vice President shall have qualified.

Section 4   The Congress may by law provide for the case of the death of any of the persons from whom the House of Representatives may choose a President whenever the right of choice shall have devolved upon them, and for the case of the death of any of the persons from whom the Senate may choose a Vice President whenever the right of choice shall have devolved upon them.

Section 5   Sections 1 and 2 shall take effect on the 15th day of October following the ratification of this article.

Section 6   This article shall be inoperative unless it shall have been ratified as an amendment to the Constitution by the legislatures of three-fourths of the several States within seven years from the date of its submission.

Amendment XXI (ratified 5 December 1933)

Section 1   The eighteenth article of amendment to the Constitution of the United States is hereby repealed.

Section 2   The transportation or importation into any State, Territory, or possession of the United States for delivery or use therein of intoxicating liquors, in violation of the laws thereof, is hereby prohibited.

Section 3   This article shall be inoperative unless it shall have been ratified as an amendment to the Constitution by conventions in the several States, as provided in the Constitution, within seven years from the date of the submission hereof to the States by the Congress.

Amendment XXII (ratified 1 March 1951)

Section 1   No person shall be elected to the office of the President more than twice, and no person who has held the office of President, or acted as President, for more than two years of a term to which some other person was elected President more than once. But this Article shall not apply to any person holding the office of President when this Article was proposed by the Congress, and shall not prevent any person who may be holding the office of President, or acting as President, during the term within which this Article becomes operative from holding the office of President or acting as President during the remainder of such term.

Section 2   This article shall be inoperative unless it shall have been ratified as an amendment to the Constitution by the legislatures of three-fourths of the several States within seven years from the date of its submission to the States by the Congress.

Amendment XXIII (ratified 29 March 1961)

Section 1   The District constituting the seat of Government of the United States shall appoint in such manner as the Congress may direct:

A number of electors of President and Vice President equal to the whole number of Senators and Representatives in Congress to which the District would be entitled if it were a State, but in no event more than the least populous State; they shall be in addition to those appointed by the States, but they shall be considered, for the purposes of the election of President and Vice President, to be electors appointed by a State; and they shall meet in the District and perform such duties as provided by the twelfth article of amendment.

Section 2   The Congress shall have power to enforce this article by appropriate legislation.

Amendment XXIV (ratified 23 January 1964)

Section 1   The right of citizens of the United States to vote in any primary or other election for President or Vice President, for electors for President or Vice President, or for Senator or Representative in Congress, shall not be denied or abridged by the United States or any state by reason of failure to pay any poll tax or other tax.

Section 2   The Congress shall have power to enforce this article by appropriate legislation.

Amendment XXV (ratified 10 February 1967)

Section 1   In case of the removal of the President from office or of his death or resignation, the Vice President shall become President.

Section 2   Whenever there is a vacancy in the office of the Vice President the President shall nominate a Vice President who shall take office upon confirmation by a majority vote of both Houses of Congress.

Section 3   Whenever the President transmits to the President pro tempore of the Senate and the Speaker of the House of Representatives his written declaration that he is unable to discharge the powers and duties of his office, and until he transmits to them a written declaration to the contrary, such powers and duties shall be discharged by the Vice President as Acting President.

Section 4   Whenever the Vice President and the majority of either the principal officers of the executive departments or of such other body as Congress may by law provide, transmit to the President pro tempore of the Senate and the Speaker of the House of Representatives their written declaration that the President is unable to discharge the powers and duties of his office, the Vice President shall immediately assume the powers and duties of the office as Acting President.

Thereafter, when the President transmits to the President pro tempore of the Senate and the Speaker of the House of Representatives his written declaration that no inability exists, he shall resume the powers and duties of his office unless the Vice President and a majority of either the principal officers of the executive departments or of such other body as Congress may by law provide, transmit within four days to the President pro tempore of the Senate and the Speaker of the House of Representatives their written declaration that the President is unable to discharge the powers and duties of his office. Thereupon Congress shall decide the issue, assembling within forty-eight hours for that purpose if not in session. If the Congress, within twenty-one days after receipt of the latter written declaration, or, if Congress is not in session, within twenty-one days after Congress is required to assemble, determines by two thirds vote of both Houses that the President is unable to discharge the powers and duties of his office, the Vice President shall continue to discharge the same as Acting President; otherwise, the President shall resume the powers and duties of his office.

Amendment XXVI (ratified 30 June 1971)

Section 1   The right of citizens of the United States, who are 18 years of age or older, to vote shall not be abridged by the United States or by any state on account of age.

Section 2   The Congress shall have the power to enforce this article by appropriate legislation.

Amendment XXVII (ratified 7 May 1992)

No law varying the compensation for the services of the Senators and Representatives shall take effect, until an election of Representatives shall have intervened.

Appendix 2
Factual tables

Table A1 Presidents and Vice-Presidents of the United States

	Presidents	*Vice-Presidents*
1789–97	George Washington	John Adams
1797–1801	John Adams	Thomas Jefferson
1801–9	Thomas Jefferson	Aaron Burr
		George Clinton (from 1805)
1809–17	James Madison	George Clinton
		Elbridge Gerry (from 1813)
1817–25	James Monroe	D.D. Tompkins
1825–9	John Q. Adams	John C. Calhoun
1829–37	Andrew Jackson	John C. Calhoun
		Martin Van Buren (from 1833)
1837–41	Martin Van Buren	R.M. Johnson
1841	William H. Harrison (1)	John Tyler
1841–5	John Tyler	–
1845–9	James K. Polk	George M. Dallas
1849–50	Zachary Taylor (1)	Millard Fillmore
1850–3	Millard Fillmore	–
1853–7	Franklin Pierce	William R King
1857–61	James Buchanan	J.C. Breckinridge
1861–5	Abraham Lincoln (2)	H. Hamlin
		Andrew Johnson (1865)
1865–9	Andrew Johnson	–
1869–77	U.S. Grant	S. Colfax
		H. Wilson (from 1873)
1877–81	Rutherford B. Hayes	W.A. Wheeler
1881	James A. Garfield (2)	Chester A. Arthur
1881–5	Chester A. Arthur	–
1885–9	Grover Cleveland	A. Hendricks

Table A1 Continued

	Presidents	Vice-Presidents
1889–93	Benjamin Harrison	Levi P. Morton
1893–7	Grover Cleveland	Adlai E. Stevenson
1897–1901	William McKinley (2)	G.A. Hobart
		Theodore Roosevelt (1901)
1901–9	Theodore Roosevelt	C.W. Fairbanks (from 1905)
1909–13	William H. Taft	J.S. Sherman
1913–21	Woodrow Wilson	T.R. Marshall
1921–3	Warren G. Harding (1)	Calvin Coolidge
1923–9	Calvin Coolidge	–
		Charles G. Dawes (from 1925)
1929–33	Herbert C. Hoover	Charles Curtis
1933–45	Franklin D. Roosevelt (1)	John N. Garner
		Henry A. Wallace (from 1941)
		Harry S. Truman (1945)
1945–53	Harry S. Truman	–
		Alben W. Barkley (from 1949)
1953–61	Dwight D. Eisenhower	Richard M. Nixon
1961–3	John F. Kennedy (2)	Lyndon B. Johnson
1963–9	Lyndon B. Johnson	–
		Hubert H. Humphrey (from 1965)
1969–74	Richard M. Nixon (3)	Spiro Agnew (3)
		Gerald R. Ford (from 1973)
1974–77	Gerald R. Ford	Nelson A. Rockefeller
1977–81	Jimmy Carter	Walter F. Mondale
1981–9	Ronald Reagan	George Bush
1989–93	George Bush	Dan Quayle
1993–2001	William J. Clinton	Al Gore
2001–	George W. Bush	Richard B. Cheney

Notes
Until the passage of the Twentieth Amendment in 1933 the inauguration of the President took place in the March following his election. The inauguration of the President now takes place on 20th January.
(1) Died in office. (2) Assassinated. (3) Resigned.

Table A2 Chief Justices of the United States Supreme Court

1789–95	John Jay
1795	John Rutledge
1796–9	Oliver Ellsworth
1801–35	John Marshall
1836–64	Roger B. Taney
1864–73	Salmon P. Chase
1874–88	Morrison R Waite
1888–1910	Melville W. Fuller
1910–21	Edward D. White
1921–30	William H. Taft
1930–41	Charles E. Hughes
1941–6	Harlan F. Stone
1946–53	Fred M. Vinson
1953–69	Earl Warren
1969–86	Warren E. Burger
1986–2005	William Rehnquist
2005–	John G. Roberts

Table A3 Presidential elections: the Popular Vote and Electoral College votes, 1932–2004

	Democrat			Republican			Others	
		Popular vote 000s	Electoral College vote		Popular vote 000s	Electoral College vote	Popular vote 000s	Electoral College vote
1932	F.D. Roosevelt	22,829	472	H. Hoover	15,760	59	1,163	
1936	F.D. Roosevelt	27,758	523	A.M. Landon	16,684	8	1,215	
1940	F.D. Roosevelt	27,313	449	W. Willkie	22,348	82	262	
1944	F.D. Roosevelt	25,612	432	T.E. Dewey	22,017	99	347	
1948	H.S. Truman	24,179	303	T.E. Dewey	21,991	189	2,616	39
1952	A. Stevenson	27,315	89	D.D. Eisenhower	33,936	442	149	
1956	A. Stevenson	26,023	73	D.D. Eisenhower	35,590	457	402	1
1960	J.F. Kennedy	34,227	303	R.M. Nixon	34,108	219	502	15
1964	L.B. Johnson	43,129	486	B. Goldwater	27,178	52	337	
1968	H.H. Humphrey	31,275	191	R.M. Nixon	31,785	301	10,145	46
1972	G. McGovern	29,170	17	R.M. Nixon	47,170	520	1,345	1
1976	J. Carter	40,831	297	G.R. Ford	39,148	240	1,527	1
1980	J. Carter	35,484	49	R. Reagan	43,904	489	7,128	
1984	W. Mondale	37,577	13	R. Reagan	54,455	525	621	
1988	M.S. Dukakis	41,809	111	G. Bush	48,886	426	899	
1992	W.J. Clinton	44,909	370	G. Bush	39,104	168	20,412	
1996	W.J. Clinton	47,402	379	W. Dole	39,199	159	9,677	
2000	A. Gore	51,004	266	G.W. Bush	50,459	271	3,949	1
2004	J. Kerry	59,028	251	G.W. Bush	62,041	286	1,166	1

Table A4 Composition of Congress, 1933–2005

	President			House Major party	House Minor party	House Others	Senate Major party	Senate Minor party	Senate Others
1933–4	Roosevelt	D	73rd	D-313	R-117	5	D-59	R-36	1
1935–6	"	D	74th	D-322	R-103	10	D-69	R-25	2
1937–8	"	D	75th	D-333	R-89	13	D-75	R-17	4
1939–40	"	D	76th	D-262	R-169	4	D-69	R-23	4
1941–2	"	D	77th	D-267	R-162	6	D-66	R-28	2
1943–4	"	D	78th	D-222	R-209	4	D-57	R-38	1
1945–6	Truman	D	79th	D-243	R-190	2	D-57	R-38	1
1947–8	"	D	80th	R-246	D-188	1	R-51	D-45	–
1949–50	"	D	81st	D-263	R-171	1	D-54	R-42	–
1951–2	"	D	82nd	D-234	R-199	2	D-48	R-47	1
1953–4	Eisenhower	R	83rd	R-221	D-213	1	R-48	D-47	1
1955–6	"	R	84th	D-232	R-203	1	D-48	R-47	1
1957–8	"	R	85th	D-234	R-201	–	D-49	R-47	–
1959–60	"	R	86th	D-283	R-154	–	D-66	R-34	–
1961–2	Kennedy	D	87th	D-263	R-174	–	D-64	R-36	–
1963–4	Johnson	D	88th	D-258	R-176	–	D-68	R-32	–
1965–6	"	D	89th	D-295	R-140	–	D-67	R-33	–
1967–8	"	D	90th	D-248	R-187	–	D-64	R-36	–

Table A4 Continued

	President		House			Senate		
			Major party	Minor party	Others	Major party	Minor party	Others
1969–70	Nixon	91st	D-243	R-192	–	D-58	R-42	–
1971–2	”	92nd	D-255	R-180	–	D-54	R-44	2
1973–4	Ford	93rd	D-243	R-192	–	D-56	R-42	2
1975–6	”	94th	D-291	R-144	–	D-61	R-37	2
1977–8	Carter	95th	D-292	R-143	–	D-61	R-38	1
1979–80	”	96th	D-276	R-157	–	D-58	R-41	1
1981–2	Reagan	97th	D-243	R-192	–	R-53	D-47	–
1983–4	”	98th	D-269	R-166	–	R-55	D-45	–
1985–6	”	99th	D-252	R-182	–	R-53	D-47	–
1987–8	”	100th	D-258	R-177	–	D-55	R-45	–
1989–90	Bush	101st	D-259	R-174	–	D-55	R-45	–
1991–2	”	102nd	D-267	R-167	1	D-56	R-43	–
1993–4	Clinton	103rd	D-259	R-175	1	D-57	R-43	–
1995–6	”	104th	R-231	D-203	1	R-53	D-47	–
1997–8	”	105th	R-227	D-207	1	R-55	D-45	–
1999–2000	”	106th	R-223	D-211	1	R-55	D-45	–
2001–2	G.W. Bush	107th	R-221	D-212	2	D-50	R-49	1
2003–4	”	108th	R-229	D-205	1	R-51	D-48	1
2005–6	”	109th	R-231	D-202	1	R-55	D-44	1

Note
D = Democrat, R = Republican

Index